January 2005

To Yoke.

with many thanks
for assistance with
burdensome tasks

Patrick,

Minorities, Peoples and Self-Determination

Essays in Honour of Patrick Thornberry

Minorities, Peoples and Self-Determination

Essays in Honour of Patrick Thornberry

Edited by

Nazila Ghanea and Alexandra Xanthaki

Martinus Nijhoff Publishers
Leiden • Boston

A C.I.P. Catalogue record for this book is available from the Library of Congress.

Printed on acid-free paper.

ISBN 90 04 14301 7
© Copyright 2005 by Koninklijke Brill NV, Leiden, The Netherlands.
Koninklijke Brill NV incorporates the imprints Brill Academic Publishers, Martinus Nijhoff
Publishers and VSP.

http://www.brill.nl

Typeset by jules guldenmund layout & text, The Hague – jules.guldenmund@planet.nl

Printed and bound in The Netherlands.

Table of Contents

Contributors

Sia Spiliopoulou Åkermark
Sia Åkermark, Juris doctor, is Associate Professor at the Faculty of Law, Uppsala University, Sweden where she teaches international law, international organisations, European law and human rights. In 2002-03 she was a fellow at the Swedish Collegium for the Study of the Social Sciences and in 2003-04 she was a fellow at the Center for Advanced Study in the Behavioral Sciences in Stanford, California, United States. Since the mid-1990s she has been working with development issues and was member of the Board of Directors of the Swedish NGO Foundation for Human Rights (1999-2003). She has published several books including *Justifications of Minority Protection in International Law* (1997) and *Human Rights of Minority Women – a manual of international law* (2000).

Gudmundur Alfredsson
Gudmundur Alfredsson is an Icelandic lawyer with an MCJ-degree from New York University School of Law (1976) and an SJD-degree from Harvard Law School (1982). He was a staff member with the UN Secretariat for 12 years, with the Office of Legal Affairs in New York (1983-85) and the Centre for Human Rights in Geneva (1985-95). He is now Professor of Law and Director of the Raoul Wallenberg Institute of Human Rights and Humanitarian Law at the University of Lund in Sweden. He is since 2004 member of the UN Sub-Commission on the Promotion and Protection of Human Rights. He is the author of dozens of articles and official reports on the rights of minorities and indigenous peoples.

Michael Banton
Michael Banton, born 1926, United Kingdom; Justice of the Peace, 1966-96; Professor of Sociology in the University of Bristol, 1965-92; President, Royal Anthropological Institute of Great Britain and Ireland, 1987-89. Member of the UN Committee on the Elimination of Racial Discrimination 1986-2001; chairman 1996-98. Author of Racial and Ethnic Competition, Cambridge: Cambridge University Press, 1983; Discrimination, Buckingham: Open University Press, 1994; International Action Against Racial Discrimination, Oxford: Oxford University Press, 1996; Racial Theories, 2nd ed., Cambridge: Cambridge University Press, 1998; Ethnic and Racial Consciousness, Addison-Wesley-Longman, 1997; The International Politics of Race, Oxford: Polity, 2002.

Joshua Castellino
Joshua Castellino completed his PhD in International Law at the University of Hull, UK in 1998. He worked as a journalist in India before being awarded the Chevening Scholar-

ship in 1995. He is the author of two books: *International Law and Self-determination* (The Hague: Kluwer, 2000) and *International Law and the Acquisition of Territory* (Dartmouth: Ashgate, 2002 with Steve Allen), and has co-edited a collection of essays entitled *International law and Indigenous Peoples* (Raoul Wallenberg Institute: Kluwer, 2004). He currently lectures at the Irish Centre for Human Rights, in Galway and participates on funded projects hosted by governmental and intergovernmental organisations.

Erica-Irene A. Daes
Visiting Professor of International Law; Phd, Doctor honoris causa of the Universities of Saskatswan, Canada; and Tromsoe, Norway; Special Rapporteur of the United Nations Sub-Commission for the Promotion and Protection of Human Rights; Honorary member for life of the United Nations Working Group on Indigenous Populations; former Vice-Chairperson and Chairperson of the Sub-Commission for the Promotion and Protection of Human Rights; former Chairperson and Rapporteur of the Working Group of Indigenous Populations for 12 years; former Vice-Chairperson and Chairperson of the Joint Inspection Unit of the United Nations System; editor of many books, United Nations studies, reports and articles on international law, human rights and international humanitarian law, on the protection of the rights of indigenous peoples and minorities; Principal drafter of the United Nations draft declaration of Indigenous Peoples; winner of the United Nations Human Rights prize in 1993.

María Amor Martín Estébanez
María Amor Martín Estébanez is a Spanish lawyer, ASIR, M. Phil in International Relations (University of Amsterdam). She is a doctoral candidate at the Law Faculty of the University of Oxford, based at its Centre for Socio-Legal Studies. She has been lecturing International Law for the Foreign Service Programme of the University of Oxford and is a researcher, project manager and lecturer at the IHR/Department of Law of the Åbo Akademi. She has been a consultant for MRG, ECMI, IDEA, the Council of Europe and the OSCE HCNM, visiting fellow at the BIM and external adviser on human dimension issues to the Spanish Delegation to the OSCE.

Nazila Ghanea
Nazila Ghanea is Senior Lecturer in International Law and Human Rights at the University of London, Institute of Commonwealth Studies. She studied at the Universities of Leeds and Keele, and completed her doctorate at Keele University in 1999 under the supervision of Professor Thornberry. Her recent publications include the monograph *Human Rights, the UN and the Bahá'ís in Iran* (The Hague: Kluwer Law, 2003); the edited collection *The Challenge of Religious Discrimination at the Dawn of the New Millennium* (Leiden: Martinus Nijhoff, 2003); a UN publication on ethnic and religious minorities in Iran *UN Doc. E/CN.4/Sub.2/AC.5/2003/WP.8* and the journal article *Human Rights of Religious Minorities and of Women in the Middle East* 26.3 Human Rights Quarterly (2004). Her areas of interest include minority rights, freedom of religion or belief and the UN human rights machinery.

Geoff Gilbert
Department of Law/Human Rights Centre, University of Essex.
Professor Geoff Gilbert's main areas of interest are human rights, minority rights, refugee law and international criminal law. He has published widely in the field and he is the Editor-in-Chief of the International Journal of Refugee Law. He was Director of the Human Rights Centre's OSCE Project which received funding from the Foreign and Commonwealth Office. The Council of Europe has used him as a consultant expert working with governments on minority rights legislation. He has been an academic member of the UN Working Group on Minorities and prepared reports for it. He has lectured on human rights and minority rights in Central and Eastern Europe, the Balkans, the former Soviet Union and North America.

Bülent Gökay
Bülent Gökay is a Senior Lecturer in International Relations at Keele University. He is the Editor of the Eurasian Studies Network. He has authored many books on global politics, the Middle East, the Balkans and Central Asia. These include: *A Clash of Empires: Turkey between Russian Bolshevism and British Imperialism* (1997), *The Politics of Caspian Oil* (2001) and *Eastern Europe Since 1970* (2002). He is the co-editor of *11 September 2001: War, Terror and Judgement* (2003). His latest book, *Soviet Eastern Policy and Turkey, 1920-1991*, is going to be published in 2005.

Tom Hadden
Tom Hadden is a part-time Professor of Law at the School of Law, Queen's University, Belfast. He was for a long period actively involved with his colleague Professor Kevin Boyle in the search for a political settlement in Northern Ireland and in 1996 they were both commissioned by the Irish Government to write a study on The Protection of Human Rights in the Context of Peace and Reconciliation in Ireland. He is currently a part-time Commissioner of the Northern Ireland Human Rights Commission. He has written extensively in the human rights field on issues of emergency law and minority rights and is currently working on the inter-relationship of human rights law, the law of armed conflict and refugee law and their relevance to issues of conflict resolution.

Dominic McGoldrick
Dominic McGoldrick is Professor of Public International Law and Director of the International and European Law Unit, Liverpool Law School, University of Liverpool. He is a specialist in Human Rights Law. In 1999-2000 he was a Fulbright Distinguished Scholar and a Human Rights Fellow at the Harvard Law School. He is the author of books on the *Human Rights Committee*, *International Relations Law of the European Union* and *From '9-11' to the Iraq War 2003 – International Law in an Age of Complexity*. Among his recent works are articles on the European Union Charter of Fundamental rights, the United Kingdom's Human Rights Act 1998, war crimes trials, the Milosevic trial, jurisdiction over reservations, State Responsibility, and Emergency Powers in

International Law. He is the co-editor of *The Permanent International Criminal Court – Legal and Policy Issues* (Oxford: Hart, 2004).

Timothy Murithi

Timothy Murithi, Ph.D, is a Programme Officer in the programme in Peacemaking and Preventive Diplomacy at the United Nations Institute for Training and Research (UNITAR) in Geneva. He is responsible for coordinating the Regional Training Programme to Enhance Conflict Prevention and Peacebuilding in Africa. He has worked as a consultant to the UNDP and the UN University for Peace. In 2003 he was a Visiting Research Fellow at the Africa Centre for Peace and Conflict Studies, in Department of Peace Studies, University of Bradford, United Kingdom. He has contributed journal articles to the *Africa World Review, International Journal for World Peace, and Peace Review*. He is currently working on the publication of a manuscript on the African Union. His most recent publication was 'The Myth of Violent Human Nature' which appeared in *Peace and Policy: Violence in a Nonviolent World*.

John Packer

John Packer is currently a Fellow at the Carr Center for Human Rights Policy at the John F. Kennedy School of Government at Harvard University, and a Visiting Assistant Professor of International Law at the Fletcher School of Law and Diplomacy at Tufts University. Until February 2004, he was Director in the Office of the High Commissioner on National Minorities (HCNM) of the Organization for Security and Co-operation in Europe (OSCE), located in The Hague. Between September 1995 and March 2000, Mr. Packer was Senior Legal Advisor to the HCNM. He was previously a Human Rights Officer at the Office of the United Nations High Commissioner for Human Rights in Geneva where he held responsibilities for the Commission on Human Rights investigative mandates on, *inter alia*, Iraq, Myanmar (Burma) and the Independence of the Judiciary. Prior to his employment with the UN, Mr. Packer was a consultant for the International Labour Organisation and the UN High Commissioner for Refugees. He holds degrees in Political Studies and Law and has lectured at a number of universities and professional institutions around the world.

Chandra K. Roy

Chandra K. Roy is an indigenous lawyer from the Chittagong Hill Tracts, Bangladesh. She received her LL.B degree from the Punjab University, Lahore and holds an LL.M in international law from The American University, Washington DC. She has been actively engaged in human rights, indigenous peoples and development issues for many years. Chandra has a diverse and varied career and has worked at law firms in Washington DC and Buenos Aires and non-governmental organizations e.g. the Unrepresented Nations and Peoples Organization and the Minority Rights Group. Chandra also worked at the Standards Department of the International Labour Office (ILO), Geneva for some years, with a special focus on Conventions Nos. 107 and 169 relating to indigenous peoples. She was instrumental in establishing the ILO Project to Promote ILO Policy on Indigenous and Tribal Peoples, which is ongoing. Chandra is currently engaged in human rights training, and in providing law and policy advice to indigenous peoples, UN agencies and NGOs. Her publications include *Land Rights of the Indigenous Peoples of the CHT* (Copenhagen: JUPNET-IWGIA, 2000) and *The International Labour Organization: A Handbook for Minorities and Indigenous Peoples* (co-author, London: Anti-Slavery International-Minority Rights Group, 2002) in addition to various reports and articles on a wide range of issues.

Martin Scheinin

Martin Scheinin is, since 1998, Armfelt Professor of Constitutional and International Law and the director of the Institute for Human Rights at Åbo Akademi University, Finland. In that capacity he also leads a national and a Nordic Graduate School in Human Rights Research. Before joining Åbo Akademi University he graduated from the Law Faculty of University of the Turku (1982), took a doctorate in law at the Law Faculty of the University of Helsinki (1991) and served as associate professor of constitutional law at the latter university (1993-1997), before spending a year as a visiting scholar at the University of Toronto (1997-1998). He is a member of the Human Rights Committee acting under the International Covenant on Civil and Political Rights (1997-2004) and a member of a group of experts established for the purpose of drafting a treaty on the rights of the indigenous Saami people in relation to Finland, Norway and Sweden (2003-2005). Previously he has been involved as an expert in various constitutional amendments in Finland, including the total reform of the chapter on constitutional rights (1989-1995). He teaches indigenous peoples' rights at the University of Tromsø (Norway).

Malcolm Shaw

Professor Malcolm N. Shaw QC is the Sir Robert Jennings Professor of International Law, University of Leicester and a practising barrister. He is a Member of the Advisory Board (Public International Law) of the British Institute of International and Comparative Law. He is a Member of a number of editorial boards including the *British Yearbook of International Law*; and Co-Rapporteur of the International Law Association Committee on International Organisations. He was a Member of the Law Panel for the 1996 and 2001 Research Assessment Exercises. He is the author of *International Law*, 5th ed. 2003, Cambridge University Press, and *Title to Territory in Africa: International Legal Issues*, 1986, Oxford University Press and of a number of articles.

Alexandra Xanthaki

Alexandra Xanthaki is a lecturer in law at Brunel University, U.K. After graduating from Athens Law Faculty, Alexandra completed an LLM in Human Rights at Queens University, Belfast and a PhD at Keele University under the supervision of Professor Patrick Thornberry. Her focus is indigenous and minority rights. Recently she has published pieces on the rights of indigenous peoples in the Russian Federation; land rights of indigenous peoples in Southeast Asia; Roma rights; and European criminal records and human rights. She is currently completing a monograph on indigenous issues in the United Nations context to be published by Cambridge University Press. She has participated in several projects and studies funded by the European Commission, DfID and international NGOs. In 2001 and 2003 she acted as a consultant to the UN Special Rapporteur on Indigenous Issues, professor Rodolfo Stavenhagen. She has previously taught in Keele University and Liverpool University.

Introduction and Acknowledgements

The past two decades have evidenced an intense interest in minority and indigenous rights. The international instruments on minority rights adopted in the 1990s, most notably the 1992 United Nations Declaration on the Rights of Persons Belonging to National or Ethnic, Religious and Linguistic Minorities and the 1995 Council of Europe Framework Convention for the Protection of National Minorities, have served as important confirmations of state obligations towards minorities, but also as solid bases for valuable discussions on standards. The monitoring mechanisms, including the United Nations Treaty bodies and the Advisory Committee on the Framework Convention for the Protection of National Minorities, and the various fora on minorities, such as the UN Working Group on Minorities and the OSCE, have continue to be alerted to problematic situations around the world. This enables these bodies to highlight weaknesses in the existing system and to suggest possible solutions in the furtherance of the protection of minority and indigenous rights.

Although minority rights were the first to capture the international community's attention, indigenous rights quickly caught up, largely because of the tireless work of indigenous representatives and their supporters. The belief of indigenous peoples in international law as a central vehicle in their quest for justice has lead to the creation of no less than three United Nations fora, several regional bodies, one international convention and three draft declarations on their rights. Challenging well-established concepts, indigenous claims have gradually become an integral component of debates on wider topics such as multiculturalism and cultural identity. Apart from being a dominant theme in international decision-making bodies, indigenous issues have also become a recurring and challenging subject of debate in academic circles and literature.

The decision to examine issues related to minorities and indigenous peoples in the same volume derives from an understanding that both groups, although different, face similar challenges and have some similar claims. Even though indigenous peoples were originally reluctant to be linked to minority groups – understandably so, since states tried to avoid the recognition of their additional rights by equating them to minorities – years of debate have largely untangled the relationship between the two groups. It is now widely accepted that both groups can use the protection of general human rights as well as minority rights; further, indigenous peoples have the protection of instruments specifically dedicated to cover their particular characteristics. This volume addresses issues falling within all the above categories.

Years of intense focus on minority and indigenous rights have largely settled some basic, generic questions. Even the most impatient observer would agree that some long-term positive results have been achieved, as more groups have received protection, state policies are scrutinised more than ever and minority and indigenous rights are continuously being re-evaluated and expanded. Still, a lot of work remains to be done.

Long-standing issues continue to preoccupy the international community, whereas new challenges have come to the surface. Based on their deep knowledge and long experience, the contributors to this volume aim to advance the debate on minorities and indigenous peoples further. Controversial issues, such as definitions, collective rights and self-determination have long been used as a rhetorical device to avoid the evolution of the existing international standards in this field. Several contributors have defied that stagnation by taking a fresh approach to such issues. They make interesting suggestions that move the debate forward with regard to, for example, natural resources of indigenous peoples. Other chapters unravel challenges that have not attracted much attention thus far, such as colour as a ground for discrimination, and the economic and social rights of minority groups. Some contributions also explore concepts such as multiculturalism and integration, that have been used in the past without sufficient critical analysis and rarely from a human rights perspective. These contributions serve as excellent starting points for debates that could contribute to the protection of the human rights of minorities and indigenous peoples. The volume also looks at the recent work of international organisations on minorities and indigenous peoples. Refreshingly, these chapters set aside rhetoric and focus on a genuine evaluation of policies and practice. The volume also includes two case studies, of the Kurds and Jumma peoples, that highlight the regrettable similarities in the suffering of groups in different parts of the world as well as the stark contrast between state claims and actual practice.

This volume is the result of our academic interest on minorities and indigenous rights, which benefited from the excellent guidance of Professor Patrick Thornberry during our doctoral studies. Indeed, even more than its academic *raison d'être*, this volume has been published in honour of Patrick Thornberry and in order to celebrate his long-standing contributions to human rights and international law. Patrick's focus on non-discrimination, minority and indigenous rights; his prolific publications which combine the legal with the philosophical; and his input to both the theory and the practice of international law have all brought him wide recognition as one of the most prominent legal experts in minority and indigenous rights in the world.

Patrick's longstanding contribution to human rights thinking, in particular in the field of minorities and indigenous peoples, has seen a series of influential publications. His book on minorities, *International Law and the Rights of Minorities* (Oxford: Clarendon Press, 1993) has gained repute as an enduring, often-cited and highly authoritative study of minority rights. His second substantial monograph *Indigenous Peoples and Human Rights* (Manchester: Manchester University Press, 2002) has already been received warmly by academics, practitioners and indigenous peoples, as it considerably evolves the debate. His most recent addition, *Minority Rights in Europe* (with M. A. Martín Estébanez – Council of Europe, 2004) combines legal analysis with a refreshingly genuine critique of the work of the Council of Europe on minorities. He has widely published on the issue of self-determination and has examined it as a minority claim, an indigenous claim and a justification for the use of force, topics which are also addressed in the current volume. His publications demonstrate a rare ability to adopt with ease a multi-disciplinary approach, dealing with difficult political, critical, and other theoretical concepts in an accessible way and combining laborious legal analysis with literature and even poetry on occasions. Patrick is passionate in his quest for justice, but manages at the same time to give a serious, comprehensive and balanced treatment of minority and indigenous rights. The number of citations and references reveal his meticulous research, but also indicate his real desire to share his sources and views with others.

Indeed, colleagues – especially young academics and students – are sometimes surprised by his willingness to share his sources with them. In an academic world where careers are based on findings and research, Patrick has always been eager to give opportunities, to share his vision and is a real team-player. Currently, he is Professor of International Law at the University of Keele, and a Visiting Fellow of Kellogg College, University of Oxford. He was also a Visiting Professor from 1993 to 1995 at the East-West Forum at the Academy of European Law, European University Institute, Florence. He has inspired many students with his passion for human rights and has supervised tens of academic studies on various aspects of international law. Many of his students have since become academics, practitioners and international civil servants and often cite and thank their supervisor for his time and genuine interest.

His passion for human rights is also evident in his work for various international organisations. A deep believer that theory must lead to policy changes, Patrick Thornberry has liberally given his expertise and time to several non-governmental organisations concerned with the rights of minorities and indigenous peoples. He served from November 1994 to 2002 as a member of the International Council of Minority Rights Group International, and as Chairman of that Council from 1999-2002. Since 1997, he has also served as a member of the Advisory Council of the European Centre for Minority Issues. Through his experience of many United Nations fora on minorities and indigenous peoples and due to his expertise and his eye for detail, he has participated in the drafting committees of several instruments on minorities and indigenous rights, where he has initiated changes with positive repercussions for these groups. At the same time, Patrick has always insisted that the groups in question must themselves decide on their priorities and strategies and has therefore respectfully chosen to be absent from minority and indigenous fora focussed on deciding strategies.

His work has made him known to many international bodies that implement international legal standards. His expertise combined with his balanced view on difficult questions, his diplomatic – but also sincere – manner and willingness to work tirelessly have lead to his membership to a Team of Experts to Hungary and Slovakia on behalf of the OSCE High Commissioner on National Minorities between 1994 and 1996. In 1994, he was appointed by the Foreign and Commonwealth Office to the list of six UK Experts for the CSCE Human Dimension Mechanism. He is currently a member of the UN Committee on the Elimination of Racial Discrimination (CERD), and within this context has served as Country Rapporteur for many countries including Cyprus, Croatia, New Zealand, Russian Federation, and Argentina.

All contributors in this volume share one thing: they have all worked with Patrick Thornberry. They are not the only people who have worked with Patrick, neither are they necessarily his closest colleagues. Patrick has worked with so many people that colleagues could easily fill three volumes in his honour! All of them have been affected by his passion for justice and human rights.

We are sincerely grateful to the contributors who joined us with enthusiasm towards this project. They have all contributed their chapters in honour of Patrick and made this a priority in their heavy workloads. David Duffy, Lynda Warrington and Christopher Tinker kindly allowed us to benefit from the editorial expertise, Charlene Yates assisted with the proofreading and Jules Guldenmund did an excellent job with the typesetting. Any remaining shortcomings are clearly our own. We also thank Lindy Melman of Martinus Nijhoff/Brill Publishers for enthusiastically supporting this collection. As for the editors, the time during which this collection has been compiled has been a very happy time of celebrating a birth, promotion and a wedding. It has been a pleasure to have had 'Patrick's surprise project' as a constant presence with us in this happy time.

Finally, we are grateful to Patrick Thornberry for his inspiration, his mentoring, his support and, above all, his friendship.

Alexandra Xanthaki and Nazila Ghanea, with Francesca Thornberry

Section I

Self-Determination and Indigenous Peoples

Chapter 1

What Are Indigenous Peoples?

Martin Scheinin[1]

It was in June 1999 that Professor Patrick Thornberry participated in a Midnight Sun Conference on Indigenous Peoples' Right to Self-Determination, organised jointly by the Sami Parliament in Finland and the Institute for Human Rights at Åbo Akademi University. His paper, as included in a book published one year later by the Institute, starts with the question 'What is self-determination?'.[2]

As he has already answered this, this chapter will be about a different theme, namely: 'What are indigenous peoples?' The question is far from new, and many have exerted great effort in finding an answer to this, either for pragmatic reasons or as a matter of principle.

For instance, the Draft United Nations Declaration on the Rights of Indigenous Peoples includes neither a definition of indigenous peoples nor even a provision that would specify the scope of application of the instrument.[3] This does not mean that one, merely for that reason, needs to give up striving at a conceptual understanding of the legal meaning of the term indigenous peoples. In fact, at least three characteristics of the groups that appear to fall within the scope of application of the Draft Declaration can be inferred from its preamble:

Characteristics

1. '*Distinctiveness,* in the sense of being different and wanting to be different.[4] This aspect of being indigenous is closely related to the importance given to the group's self-identification as indigenous.'[5]

---

1   Armfelt Professor of Constitutional and International Law and Director of the Institute for Human Rights at Åbo Akademi University, Finland.
2   P. Thornberry, 'Self-Determination and Indigenous Peoples: Objections and Responses', in P. Aikio and M. Scheinin (eds.) *Operationalizing the Right of Indigenous Peoples to Self-Determination* (Turlen: Institute for Human Rights, Åbo Akademi University, 2000) pp. 39-64.
3   UN Doc. E/CN.4/Sub.2/1994/2/Add.1, United Nations Draft Declaration on the Rights of Indigenous Peoples (1994).
4   Ibid. First recital of the preamble of the Draft Declaration.
5   Ibid. Article 8 of the Draft Declaration and article 1 (2) of ILO Convention No. 169 concerning Indigenous and Tribal Peoples in Independent Countries, 72 ILO Official Bull. 59 (1989).

Nazila Ghanea & Alexandra Xanthaki (eds.), Minorities, Peoples and Self-Determination, *pp. 3-13.*
© *2005 Koninklijke Brill NV. Printed in The Netherlands. ISBN 90 04 14301 7.*

2.   '*Dispossession* of lands, territories and resources, through colonisation or other comparable events in the past, causing today a denial of human rights or other forms of injustice.'[6]

3.   '*Lands* (located in a specific geographic area) as a central element in the history, identity and culture of the group, usually giving rise to traditional economic activities that depend on the natural resources specific to the area in question.'[7]

There are two important characteristics that do not appear to be reflected in the preamble to the (Draft) Declaration but that must also be understood to form a part of the overall context of the Declaration and the notion of indigenousness within the instrument. These are:

4.   *Being first* in the geographic area referred to as 'lands' above under item 3, at least in relation to the present dominant population.[8]

5.   *Lack of political control* in respect of the internationally recognized state that today exercises sovereignty in the area where the 'lands' are located.[9] This dimension points to the situational or relational nature of indigenousness.[10] In short, indigenous peoples can be said to be in a minority situation in relation to the dominant population, even in the rare instance they happen to be in the numerical majority.

Biological Notions

It is above all the last-mentioned criterion that results in a marked difference in the biology-based notion of indigenousness and the use of the same term in international law and human rights law. A standard dictionary entry for the adjective 'indigenous' would read:

'1.   Originating and living or occurring naturally in an area or environment. See Synonyms at 'native'.

2.   Intrinsic; innate.'[11]

Such biological usage of the notion of indigenous does not include the dimension of a relationship of dispossession or subordination in relation to another group that arrived later. Nevertheless this criterion is essential in the legal usage of the term.

---

6   Ibid. Fifth recital of the preamble of the Draft Declaration.
7   Ibid. Fifth, sixth and eighth recital of the preamble. See also article 25.
8   Ibid. Article 27.
9   Ibid. Articles 37 and 39.
10   See T. Makkonen *Identity, Difference and Otherness: The Concepts of 'People', 'Indigenous People' and 'Minority' in International Law* (Helsinki: Helsinki University Press, 2000).
11   Lexico Publishing Group, LLC 2004 at www.dictionary.com.

Although the Draft Declaration does not include a definition for the concept of indigenous peoples, there have been efforts towards a definition within the United Nations framework. The most commonly used is the 'working definition' formulated by the Special Rapporteur of the Sub-Commission, José R. Martinez Cobo in his study of the problem of discrimination against indigenous populations:

> Indigenous communities, peoples and nations are those which, having a historical continuity [4] with pre-invasion and pre-colonial societies [2] that developed on their territories [3], consider themselves distinct [1] from other sectors of the societies now prevailing [5] in those territories, or parts of them. They form at present non-dominant sectors of society and are determined to preserve, develop and transmit to future generations their ancestral territories, and their ethnic identity, as the basis of their continued existence as peoples, in accordance with their own cultural patterns, social institutions and legal systems.[12]

ILO Convention 169

A third starting-point in the quest for a definition is ILO Convention No. 169 which includes in article 1 a complex provision on the scope of application of the convention:

1. This Convention applies to:
(a) Tribal peoples in independent countries whose social, cultural and economic conditions distinguish them from other sections of the national community, and whose status is regulated wholly or partially by their own customs or traditions or by special laws or regulations;
(b) Peoples in independent countries who are regarded as indigenous on account of their descent from the populations which inhabited the country, or a geographical region to which the country belongs, at the time of conquest or colonisation or the establishment of present State boundaries and who, irrespective of their legal status, retain some or all of their own social, economic, cultural and political institutions.
2. Self-identification as indigenous or tribal shall be regarded as a fundamental criterion for determining the groups to which the provisions of this Convention apply.
3. The use of the term 'peoples' in this Convention shall not be construed as having any implications as regards the rights which may attach to the term under international law.[13]

---

12   UN Doc. E/CN.4/Sub.2/1986/7/Add.4, para. 379. The numbers in brackets have been inserted by the present author and they refer to the five characteristics presented above in the discussion on the Draft Declaration.

13   International Labour Organisation 169 (note 5).

Some parts of this provision will be commented upon later on in this chapter. At this point it suffices to state that the above-mentioned characteristics Nos. 2, 3 and 4 are clearly visible in paragraph 1 (b), and characteristic No. 1 in paragraph 2. The relational dimension of characteristic No. 5 is implied in paragraph 1 (b), but is also apparent in most of the substantive provisions of the Convention which address the relationship between an indigenous people and the state, the latter being presumably in the hands of a group other than the indiginous people in question.

The International Covenants

Two further international human rights instruments need to be brought into the discussion, namely the International Covenants of 1966 (the International Covenant on Economic, Social and Cultural Rights 'ICESCR' and the International Covenant on Civil and Political Rights 'ICCPR').[14] This might seem odd to the reader as neither instrument includes any reference to the notion of indigenousness. However, article 27 of the ICCPR includes a provision on the rights of persons belonging to ethnic, linguistic or religious minorities, and both Covenants proclaim in their common article 1 that the right of self-determination belongs to 'all peoples'. On the basis of the practice of the Human Rights Committee, the body entrusted with the task of interpreting the ICCPR, it can be asserted that the groups qualifying as indigenous peoples under the Draft Declaration, under the Martinez Cobo definition or under ILO Convention No. 169, generally fall under the protection of ICCPR article 27 as 'minorities' and that at least some of them also constitute 'peoples' for the purposes of article 1 and are beneficiaries of the right of self-determination.

Hence, the ICCPR and the ICESCR do *not* give support to a position according to which indigenous peoples are a specific category located between minorities and peoples, not entitled to the right of self-determination. Indigenous groups that are in a minority situation, i.e. subject to a greater or lesser degree of dispossession or subordination by another now dominant group, are entitled to protection as minorities under ICCPR article 27. At the same time, those who within these groups are ethnically, linguistically, geographically, historically and politically sufficiently distinct from the dominant population to qualify as 'peoples' under public international law, are entitled to the right of self-determination under common article 1. In the same breath, it must however be emphasised that in most cases the ultimate form of exercising the right of self-determination, unilateral secession, is not available to indigenous peoples. Instead, they usually have to satisfy themselves with other arrangements that allow for their exercise of the right of self-determination, including autonomy and land management regimes based on the role of freely chosen political structures of the indigenous people itself.

Although ICCPR article 27 does not employ the notion of 'indigenous peoples', much of the law developed under the provision has been related to claims by such

---

14   International Covenant on Economic, Social and Cultural Rights, 999 UNTS 3 (1966), and International Covenant on Civil and Political Rights, 999 UNTS 171 (1966).

groups. In General Comment No. 23 the Committee emphasised the applicability of article 27 in respect of indigenous peoples.[15] In particular, the notion of 'culture' has been interpreted as affording protection to the nature-based way of life, land rights and economy of indigenous peoples. In the terms of paragraph 7 of the general comment:

> With regard to the exercise of the cultural rights protected under article 27, the Committee observes that culture manifests itself in many forms, including a particular way of life associated with the use of land resources, especially in the case of indigenous peoples. That right may include such traditional activities as fishing or hunting and the right to live in reserves protected by law.

Let us now move to the question of the right of self-determination. Having earlier referred to ILO Convention No. 169, it needs to be clarified that the fact that this convention does not include a clause on the right of self-determination does not mean that indigenous peoples would never qualify as beneficiaries of that right. Article 1, paragraph 3, of ILO Convention No. 169 should be taken as meaning what it says, namely that the use of the term 'peoples' in that Convention does not have 'any implications' as regards the rights which may attach to the term 'peoples' under public international law. Just as the reference to 'peoples' in the ILO Convention does not have positive implications in respect of turning into peoples groups that otherwise would fall short of the distinctiveness required under international law, the same reference does not have the negative implication of denying the status of a people to a group that irrespective of the ILO Convention qualifies as a people under public international law. The reason for article 1 paragraph 3 in the ILO Convention is the broad and inclusive criteria for indigenous and tribal peoples in the preceding parts of article 1. This broad remit results in the Convention being applicable to a number of minorities and groups that would *not* qualify as peoples under public international law. Nevertheless, within that broad scope of application of the ILO Convention, there is a smaller group of indigenous peoples that also qualify as 'peoples' under international law.

As previously stated, a people's right to self-determination does not automatically entail a right of unilateral secession (statehood) for every group that qualifies as a distinct people. The right of secession is recognized only under specific conditions, for instance as was maintained by the Supreme Court of Canada in the *Quebec Secession Case*:

> In summary, the international law right to self-determination only generates, at best, a right to external self-determination in situations of former colonies; where a people is oppressed, as for example under foreign military occupation; or where a definable group is denied meaningful access to government to pursue their political, economic, social and cultural development. In all three situations, the people in question are

---

15   General Comment No. 23 (50) by the Human Rights Committee, UN Doc. HRI/GEN/1/
      rev.5 (1994) pp. 147-150, paras. 3.2 and 7.

entitled to a right to external self-determination because they have been denied the ability to exert internally their right to self-determination.[16]

In the context of the case, it is clear that by 'external self-determination' the Supreme Court of Canada was referring to the possible unilateral secession by the province of Quebec from the union of Canada. It should, however, be emphasized that there might be other 'external' forms of self-determination that are not subject to the very demanding conditions international law attaches to secession, for instance the right to represent internationally an indigenous people in relevant international negotiations or conferences.[17]

Paragraph 2 of common article 1 in the International Covenants elaborates further the resource dimension of self-determination, through proclaiming the right of all peoples to dispose of their natural wealth and resources. This clause, and especially its last sentence, according to which a people may not be deprived of its own means of subsistence, has been relied upon in support of land rights by many groups that proclaim themselves as distinctive indigenous peoples in countries where other ethnic groups, typically of European descent, are in a dominant position.

The term 'peoples' is not defined in article 1 or elsewhere in the International Covenants. Hence, the Covenants leave room for different interpretations as to whether the whole population of a State Party constitutes 'a people' in the meaning of common article 1, or whether several distinct peoples exist in at least some of the States Parties to the two Covenants. The Human Rights Committee's pronouncements in relatively recent Concluding Observations on reports by countries with indigenous peoples reflect an understanding that at least certain indigenous groups qualify as 'peoples' under article 1. This approach was first made explicit in the Committee's concluding observations on Canada:

> The Committee notes that, as the State party acknowledged, the situation of the aboriginal peoples remains 'the most pressing human rights issue facing Canadians'. In this connection, the Committee is particularly concerned that the State party has not yet implemented the recommendations of the Royal Commission on Aboriginal Peoples (RCAP). With reference to the conclusion by RCAP that without a greater share of lands and resources institutions of aboriginal self-government will fail, the Committee emphasizes that the right to self-determination requires, *inter alia*, that all peoples must be able to freely dispose of their natural wealth and resources and that they may not be deprived of their own means of subsistence (art. 1, para. 2). The Committee recommends that decisive and urgent action be taken towards the full

---

16   *Reference re Secession of Quebec*, [1998] 2 S.C.R. 217, paragraph 128.
17   For instance, section 6 of the Saami Parliament Act of Finland (Act No. 974 of 1995) recognizes this external form of self-determination to the Saami, to be exercised by the elected Saami Parliament.

implementation of the RCAP recommendations on land and resource allocation. The Committee also recommends that the practice of extinguishing inherent aboriginal rights be abandoned as incompatible with article 1 of the Covenant.[18]

It is to be noted that the recognition of the existence of more than one 'people' within the territory of the country and the enjoyment by them of the right of self-determination (albeit not of its extreme manifestation, secession), had been expressed by the highest judicial authority of the country concerned in the *Quebec Secession Case*, which was decided in 1998. The Supreme Court of Canada stated, *inter alia*:

> It is clear that 'a people' may include only a portion of the population of an existing state. The right to self-determination has developed largely as a human right, and is generally used in documents that simultaneously contain references to 'nation' and 'state'. The juxtaposition of these terms is indicative that the reference to 'people' does not necessarily mean the entirety of a state's population. To restrict the definition of the term to the population of existing states would render the granting of a right to self-determination largely duplicative, given the parallel emphasis within the majority of the source documents on the need to protect the territorial integrity of existing states, and would frustrate its remedial purpose.[19]

Meanings of 'Indigenous Peoples'

After this excursion into the realm of self-determination, it is time to return to the issue of defining the notion of indigenous peoples. The illustration below is aimed at clarifying the different meanings of the term 'indigenous peoples' when used as a legal term in relation to such existing treaties as the International Covenant on Civil and Political Rights and ILO Convention No. 169.

---

18 Concluding Observations on Canada, UN Doc. CCPR/C/79/Add.105 (1999) paragraph 8.

19 *Reference re Secession of Quebec*, (note 16) para. 124. In para. 139 of the opinion the Court refers to the importance of the rights and concerns of aboriginal peoples in the event of a unilateral secession by the province of Quebec, with an explicit reference to the issue of 'defining the boundaries of a seceding Quebec with particular regard to the northern lands occupied largely by aboriginal peoples'. However, as the Court came to the conclusion that the hypothetical right of self-determination of Quebec could not carry as far as to unilateral secession, it was 'unnecessary to explore further the concerns of the aboriginal peoples'.

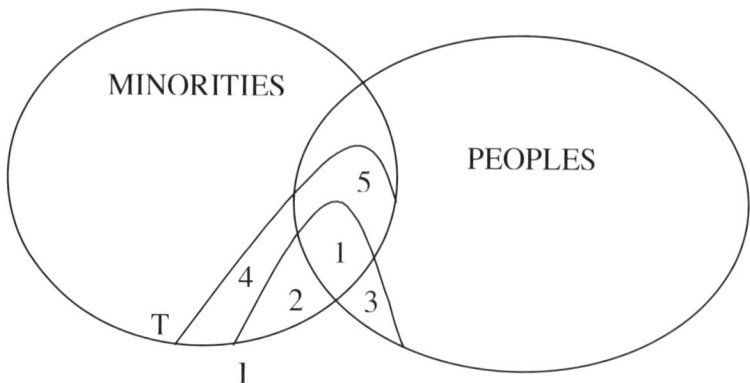

Different meanings of the term indigenous peoples.
I = indigenous.
T = tribal.

The starting-point for the illustration above is that the categories of 'minorities' and 'indigenous peoples' are not mutually exclusive. As the jurisprudence of the Human Rights Committee shows, one and the same group can simultaneously constitute a minority under ICCPR article 27 and a people under article 1 of the same treaty. Hence, in the illustration there is considerable overlap between the notions of minorities and peoples. At the same time, the illustration indicates that there are numerous minorities that do not qualify as peoples under common article 1; and that there are many peoples, primarily nation-building ones, that do not constitute a minority. The overlap of the two ovals represents groups that qualify simultaneously as minorities for the purposes of ICCPR article 27 and as peoples in relation to common article 1.

The lines marked with 'I' and 'T' relate to article 1 of ILO Convention No. 169, so that 'I' refers to indigenous peoples as described in article 1 (1) (b) and 'T' refers to tribal peoples in the meaning of article 1 (1) (a). Several observations need to be made as to how the two lines have been drawn.

Firstly, ILO Convention No. 169, or at least article 1 of it, represents a broad understanding on which groups should be entitled to the protection of the Convention as indigenous peoples. Hence, line I extends into the oval representing minorities beyond the point where that notion overlaps with the other oval referring to peoples. This means that under ILO Convention No. 169, many groups that would not qualify as peoples under general international law or common article 1 of the Covenants are referred to as indigenous peoples. In line with this approach, article 1 of the Convention also includes paragraph 3 according to which the use of the term 'peoples' in the Convention shall not be construed as having any implications as regards the rights which may attach to the term under international law. The fact that a group qualifies as an indigenous people under ILO Convention 169 does not, therefore, lead to the conclusion that the group in question would enjoy the right of self-determination.

Secondly, textually, article 1 (1) (b) may be understood to also cover such groups that meet the criterion of being first in a territory but which today are not in a subordinated position in relation to another, dominant population group. Therefore, line 'I' has been drawn to extend into the oval representing peoples beyond the point of overlap with the oval representing minorities. However, in the view of this author such a textual reading would be a misunderstanding of the notion of indigenousness in human rights law. A reading of ILO Convention 169 as a whole makes it clear that this instrument also relies on the relational criterion for its scope of application: the material provisions in the Convention regulate the relationship between a state and an indigenous group residing in that state, systematically presuming that the state in question is in the hands of someone else, i.e. the dominant population.

Thirdly, the notion of tribal peoples in article 1 (1) (a) is a further extension of the notion of indigenous peoples. As there are in various parts of the world groups that were not first, or at least cannot prove to have been first, in a specific geographic area but that nevertheless are in a situation that in the context of human rights is analogous to indigenous peoples proper, the scope of application of the Convention has been deliberately extended to tribal peoples, i.e. groups that due to their situation deserve the same protection as indigenous peoples. As the logic of this extension is based on a relationship of subordination to a dominant population group, there is no need to extend line 'T' to the right beyond the bordering line of the notion of minorities. Nevertheless, as there might be cases where a tribal people would qualify as a people under general international law or common article 1 of the 1966 Covenants, line 'T' has been drawn into the area representing the overlap between 'minorities' and 'peoples'.

After these explanations, it is time to reflect on the characteristics of the different groups referred to in the illustration by the numbers 1 to 5. Together all these groups constitute 'indigenous peoples' in the broadest possible sense, including the extension of the term to groups that strictly speaking do not meet the criterion of 'being first' (tribal minorities and tribal peoples) but that are in relevant respects in a position analogous to that of indigenous peoples in the strict sense. At the other end of the spectrum, this broad notion of indigenousness extends to groups that were historically first in a given geographic area and are today in control of their own nation state.

No. 1 refers to indigenous peoples in the narrowest sense, i.e. groups that are peoples for the purposes of general international law and common article 1 of the 1966 International Covenants but that nevertheless remain in a situation of dispossession in respect of another, now dominant population that controls the nation state. These groups are entitled to the right of self-determination under common article 1 but also to protection as minorities in the meaning of ICCPR article 27. The Saami of the Nordic countries and the Maori of New Zealand would fall into this category. It goes without saying that ILO Convention No. 169 is applicable in respect of these groups.

No. 2 refers to indigenous groups that meet the criteria of article 1 (1) (b) in ILO Convention No. 169 and that, because of their minority situation within a nation state, enjoy the protection of ICCPR article 27. These groups meet the criterion of being first in a geographic area but do not, at least for the time being, qualify as 'peoples' under general international law – perhaps merely because of their small number or because they have not articulated a claim for peoplehood and for the right to self-determination that would follow it. Many aboriginal bands in Canada would on their own belong to this category, possibly at the same time constituting together with related bands a people in the meaning of category No. 1.

No. 3 comprises groups that technically meet the criteria of article 1 (1) (b) in ILO Convention 169 but that do not fit into the relational dimension of the concept of indigenousness, because they have obtained power in the nation state. Fiji or Greenland may in the future constitute cases of such circumstances. When an indigenous people comes into power it retains its status as a people but loses the minority protection attached to being in a situation of dispossession in relation to the dominant population. ICCPR article 27 and ILO Convention No. 169 cease to apply.

No. 4 refers to most tribal groups in the world, in the sense of being in a situation of dispossession analogous to indigenous peoples but not qualifying as indigenous under the strict application of the criterion of 'being first'. They are entitled to protection under article 1 (1) (a) of ILO Convention 169 and under ICCPR article 27 but do not qualify as peoples under common article 1. Similarly to groups in category No. 2, they are not 'peoples' in the strict sense but it is nevertheless practical to include them in a unifying notion of 'indigenous and tribal peoples' due to the similarities of the situations. Many of the distinct communities of persons of African origin in Central America, being the offspring of former slaves, would belong to this category.

Finally, category No. 5 comprises tribal groups that due to their size, history, social and cultural distinctiveness and articulated self-identification as 'peoples' meet the criteria of peoples under general international law but not the criterion of 'being first' in a specific geographic area. Hence, they are 'tribal peoples' in the meaning of article 1 (1) (b) of ILO Convention No. 169, 'peoples' in the meaning of common article 1, and at the same time entitled to minority protection under ICCPR article 27. As a consequence of historical population movements in Africa, there are in several groups in African countries that live side by side with other more strictly indigenous groups but have less long-lasting ties to the territory. When they nevertheless are in a minority situation in relation to a dominant population group, they fall into category No. 5.

Conclusion

What is the sense of all this? Is it not divisive and destructive to construct lines of separation within the united world movement of indigenous peoples? Is there not much wisdom in the approach represented by the Draft Declaration of not 'defining' indigenous peoples but of taking, instead, a pragmatic approach of accepting on the bandwagon all groups that are similarly situated in terms of being dispossessed through colonisation or other historical events? Are not all peoples equal, for instance in relation to the right of self-determination?

In my view it makes sense to strive for analytical clarity. The rest of the questions posed must, however, be answered in the negative. The perceived unity of all indigenous peoples in the world is a fallacy if one tries to be serious about how specific rights flow from the fact of being an indigenous people. The pragmatic approach of not including a definition, as in the Draft Declaration, is tempting but the victories resulting from this pragmatism may be Pyrrhic in nature: the international community – which still today is primarily constituted of states – will not grant far reaching rights to indigenous peoples unless the scope of application of the legal concept of indigenous peoples is at least reasonably precise. In the ILO tradition of primarily focusing on workers' rights, it was probably wise to include a broad notion of indigenousness, extended to tribal groups and giving emphasis to the group's self-identification as indigenous or tribal.[20] But the price tag attached to that extensive solution is visible in the product: article 1 (3) of ILO Convention No. 169 makes it clear that *no* group, even if it meets all criteria of general international law for being a people, may invoke that Convention as an argument for its recognition as 'a people' under international law.

As to the equality of all peoples, my answer is that yes, indeed all *peoples* are equal and entitled to the right of self-determination. But this equality only strengthens the case for a need to make a distinction between *peoples* and 'people', as only the former enjoy the right of self-determination. Allowing all self-proclaimed indigenous minorities and groups to jump on the bandwagon of the Draft Declaration damages the credibility of article 3 of the Draft, according to which 'indigenous peoples have the right of self-determination'. In order to have their right of self-determination recognized, indigenous peoples will have to accept that being indigenous does not *automatically* bring with it being 'a people'.

---

20   See, article 1(2) (note 13).

Chapter 2

THE RIGHT TO SELF-DETERMINATION: MEANING AND SCOPE

Alexandra Xanthaki[1]

Introduction

Self-determination is a thorny topic in international law with remarkable contradictions in its usage. While the concept has been liberally used as a slogan of universal application, its application always seems to be a rather complex matter with several obstacles. Its importance is well-accepted and recorded, yet its precise meaning has not yet been agreed. States accept and proclaim that 'peoples' should decide on their future; nevertheless, who is a 'people' is still to a large degree decided by states themselves. Self-determination has been the basis for numerous successful movements for secession, but it has also been the reason for the rise of many ethnic conflicts.

Although proclaimed previously,[2] self-determination did not emerge as a principle of international law until the Second World War. Its potential implications for the stability of the international community has meant that there is no consensus about its meaning. In this chapter, I will explore the different interpretations that have been given to self-determination. An overview of the evolution of self-determination highlights the fact that its meaning has been expanding in order to accommodate the changing needs of the international community at different periods. Currently, there are two prevailing understandings of the right: the minimalist one, which results in restricting the meaning of self-determination; and the maximalist, which allows for a wide scope. I will expose the problems that both approaches present and make some suggestions that recognise and allow for the evolution of the right, but avoid over-expanding it.

---

1   Lecturer in Law, Brunel University.
2   Proclaimed by Lenin and Wilson and used by the Allies as the main justification for the First World War. The concept was not included in the League Covenant, although the winners applied self-determination to a certain degree in the inter-war period, and the Atlantic Charter referred to self-determination. For the concept before the formation of the United Nations, see E. Kamenka, 'Human Rights, Peoples' Rights' in J. Crawford (ed.) *The Rights of Peoples* (Oxford: Clarendon Press, 1988) pp. 127-139; I. Brownlie 'The Rights of Peoples in Modern International Law' in Crawford, ibid., pp. 1-16; H. Hannum 'Rethinking self-determination' 34 *Virginia Journal of International Law* (1993) pp. 82-151; and A. Cassese *International Law in a Divided World* (Oxford: Clarendon Press, 1994) p. 131.

Nazila Ghanea & Alexandra Xanthaki (eds.), Minorities, Peoples and Self-Determination, *pp. 15-33.*
© *2005 Koninklijke Brill NV. Printed in The Netherlands. ISBN 90 04 14301 7.*

Evolution of the Meaning of Self-determination

The inclusion of the principle of self-determination in the United Nations Charter[3] was a major advance; unfortunately, no clarifications were given about its content or its beneficiaries. However, the *travaux préparatoires* indicate that discussions focused on the right of peoples to determine their internal political status.[4] The first instrument that tried to clarify the content of self-determination was the Declaration against Colonialism.[5] Previously self-determination was recognised as a principle; this declaration recognised it for the first time as the *right* of peoples to 'freely determine their political status and freely pursue their economic, social and political development'.[6] Even though the declaration implied both an external and an internal aspect of self-determination, the right was equated with decolonisation, a bigger and more accepted need than any other application of the right at that time. This understanding was evident from the title of the declaration, but also from the recommendation in paragraph 5 for immediate steps for 'independence', the inclusion of the principle of territorial integrity and the description of the beneficiaries, which limited it to peoples under 'alien subjugation, domination and exploitation'.[7] Resolution 1541,[8] adopted the very next day, was in the same spirit: the right of self-determination was recognised only for non-self-governing territories, defined as territories which are 'geographically separate and distinct ethnically and/or culturally from the country administering them' and arbitrarily placed 'in a position or status of subordination' to the administering state.[9] From the description of the beneficiaries, as well as the explicit reference to territorial integrity, it was once again clear that self-determination was equated with decolonisation. The 1970 Declaration on Principles of International Law concerning Friendly Relations and Co-operation among States[10]

---

3   Articles 1.2, 55 and 73.

4   See C. Iorns, 'Indigenous Peoples and Self-Determination: Challenging State Sovereignty', 24 *Case Western Reserve Journal of International Law* (1992) p. 246.

5   UN Doc. A/L.323 and Add.1-6 (1960), *Declaration on the Granting of Independence to Colonial Countries and Peoples*, GA Res. 1514, UN GAOR, 15th Session, Supp. No. 16, p. 67.

6   Ibid. para. 2.

7   Ibid. para. 5.

8   Three years earlier, in 1967, the General Assembly had established a Special Committee on the Situation with regards to the Implementation of the Declaration on the Granting of Independence to Colonial Countries and Peoples, charged mainly with reporting and making recommendations but also with visiting areas of concern. GA Resolution 1541, UN GAOR, 15th Session, Supplement no 16, UN Doc. A/4651 GA Resolution 1541, UN GAOR, 15th session, Supplement No. 16 (1960), para 29.

9   Resolution 1541 also defined self-government, as including independence, 'free association with another state' or integration in the basis of equality with an independent state. Ibid. Principle XI.

10   *GA Res. 2526*, UN GAOR, 25th Sess., Supp. 28 (1971), 9 ILM 1292. Also see the 1965 *Declaration on the Inadmissibility of Intervention in the Domestic Affairs of States and the Protection of Their Independence and Sovereignty*, which was in the same spirit.

expanded the beneficiaries to peoples under colonial or racist regimes or other forms of alien domination, and implied the extension of the right to peoples whose government does not represent 'the whole people without distinction as to race, creed or colour'.[11] The apartheid of South Africa had become the focus of the international community at that time and again the meaning of self-determination tried to accommodate this pre-occupation of the international community. The declaration also listed the ways in which the right could be implemented, as follows: a) establishment of a sovereign and independent state; b) free association; c) integration with an independent state; or d) emergence into any other political status freely determined by a people.[12] These applications referred clearly to the external aspect of self-determination.

This was the prevailing understanding of the right of self-determination in 1976, when the International Covenants[13] were finally adopted. Common article 1 of the Covenants included a general description of the right as the right of peoples to 'freely determine their political status and freely pursue their economic, social and cultural development' and more specific references to the free disposal by peoples of natural wealth and resources (paragraph 2) and to external self-determination (paragraph 3). It is noteworthy that the provision does not include any reference to the principle of territorial integrity.[14] It is also clear that article 1 does not refer to minorities, as the Covenants create two sets of rights, one for 'peoples' in Article 1 and another for 'minorities' in Article 27.[15]

Gradually, after the adoption of the International Covenants, there was a shift in international documents and legal literature towards the internal aspect of self-determination. One of the first instruments that recorded this shift was the 1975 Final Act of the Conference on Security and Co-operation in Europe[16] (Helsinki Declaration). Principle VII reads:

> By virtue of the principle of equal rights and self-determination of peoples, all peoples always have the right, in full freedom to determine, when and as they wish, their

---

11   Ibid. para. 7.

12   Ibid. para. 4.

13   UN Doc. A/6316 (1966), *International Covenant on Civil and Political Rights*, UNGA Res.2200 A (XXI), 16 December 1996 and *International Covenant on Economic, Social and Cultural Rights*, UNGA Res.2200 A (XXI), 16 December 1966

14   However, article 5.1. of the *International Covenant on Civil and Political Rights*, ibid, reads:

> Nothing in the present Covenant may be interpreted as implying for any State, group or person any right to engage in any activity or perform any act aimed at the destruction of any of the rights or freedoms recognised herein or at their limitation to a greater extent than is provided for in the present Covenant.

15   For national minorities and the right of secession, see J. Castellino 'Order and Justice: National Minorities and the right to secession' 6 *International Journal on Minorities and Group Rights* (1999) pp. 389-415.

16   *Final Act*, Conference on Security and Co-operation, August 1, 1975, 14 ILM 1292.

internal and external status, without external interference, and to pursue as they wish their political, economic, social and cultural development.[17]

The Helsinki Declaration projected self-determination as an ongoing process that urges peoples to adapt to new structures, demands and needs, as the right of peoples to decide a certain form of governance and/or re-evaluate their decisions. This focus corresponded to the international reality of the Cold War and Western states' interest in emphasising the principles of democracy, free elections and participation and their fears about secession. As the 35 states participating in the Helsinki Declaration were independent states, the mere adoption of the Declaration also expanded the beneficiaries of the right to populations of independent states. Nevertheless, the principle of territorial integrity was once again present. In the early 1990s, several documents urged states to rethink participatory structures within the state,[18] to ensure democracy by monitoring elections,[19] to consider the possibility of autonomous regimes[20] and stressed the link between the on-going process of self-determination and human rights guarantees.[21]

During the same period, the collapse of the former Soviet Union and Yugoslavia and the new states that emerged in Eastern Europe brought claims for independence to the surface. This time it was different from decolonisation: claimants were not in territories far away from Europe, but on Europe's doorstep. European states wanted to ensure

---

17   Principle VIII of the Principles Guiding Relations between Participating States.

18   For example, UN Doc.A/47/49 (1993), *Declaration on the Rights of Persons Belonging to National or Ethnic, Religious or Linguistic Minorities*, 1992, United Nations General Assembly Res.47/135, Annex, 47 UNGAOR Supp.(No.49) p. 210; U.N. Doc. E/CN.4/1995/60 (1995), *Resolution 1995/60 on 'ways and means of overcoming obstacles to the establishment of a democratic society and requirements for the maintenance of democracy'*, UN Commission on Human Rights ESCOR Supp. (No. 4) p. 183, preamble; section VI of the (1990) *Document of the Copenhagen Meeting of the Conference on the Human Dimension of the CSCE*, 11 HRLJ 232 (1990).

19   For example, the (1990) CSCE *Document of the Copenhagen Meeting of the Conference on the Human Dimension*, paras 6- I.8; the (1991) *Geneva CSCE Meeting of Experts on National Minorities*, http://www.osce.org/docs/english/1973-1990/other_experts/gene91e.htm (accessed 2 August 2004), section III; CSCE *Paris Summit*, the *Charter of Paris for a New Europe* (1990), http://www.osce.org/docs/english/1990-1999/summits/paris90e.htm (accessed 2 August 2004). Also, the 1991 General Assembly *OAS Resolution* stated that the principles of the OAS Charter 'require the political representation of [member] States to be based on effective exercise of representative democracy'. Resolution 1080 AG/RES, 21-0/91 adopted on 5 June 1991.

20   For example, *Recommendation 1201 on 'an additional protocol on the rights of national minorities to the European Convention on Human Rights'*, Council of Europe Parliamentary Assembly Text adopted on 1 February 1993 (22nd Sitting), article 11; the (1990) CSCE *Document of the Copenhagen Meeting of the Conference on the Human Dimension of the CSCE*, para. 35; the (1991) *Geneva CSCE Meeting of Experts on National Minorities*, section 4.

21   For example, UN Doc. CCPR/C/21/Add.3, *General Comment 12(21)*, Human Rights Committee, GAOR, 39th Sess., Supp.40, Annex VI; also, A/CONF.157/23 (1993), *Vienna Declaration and Program of Action*.

that although they appeared to defend the right to self-determination, they clearly discouraged secession. The (1993) Vienna Declaration and Program of Action[22] affirmed the right of peoples to take legitimate action in accordance with the UN Charter to realise their right of self-determination,[23] but included the usual restrictions of territorial integrity and political unity. Although the formula used was that of the 1970 Declaration on Friendly Relations,[24] the Vienna Declaration expanded the right to self-determination to peoples whose government does not represent the whole people 'without distinction of *any kind*'.[25] In addition, the language implied exceptions to the principle of territorial integrity. The Committee on the Elimination of Racial Discrimination (CERD) General Recommendation XXI (48) was clearer on the issue of secession.[26] After recognising the right to internal self-determination for minorities, the Committee concluded that:

> ...international law has not recognised a general right to peoples unilaterally to declare secession from a State. In this respect, the Committee follows the views expressed in An Agenda for Peace (paras. 17 and following), namely that a fragmentation of States may be detrimental to the protection of human rights, as well as the preservation of peace and security. This does not however, exclude the possibility of arrangements reached by free agreements of all parties concerned.[27]

---

22   The *Vienna Declaration and Program of Action* was the outcome of the (1993) Second World Conference on Human Rights, where 180 States participated and hundreds of non-governmental organisations attended.

23   The Declaration recognised in para. 2.2:

> the right of peoples to take any legitimate action, in accordance with the Charter of the United Nations, to realise their alienable right of self-determination. The World Conference on Human Rights considers the denial of self-determination as a violation of human rights and underlines the importance of the effective realisation of this right.

24   UN Doc. A/8028 (1971), *Declaration on Principles of International Law Concerning Friendly Relations and Co-operation among States in Accordance with the Charter of the United Nations*, UNGA Res. 2625 (XXV), UN GAOR, 25th Sess., Supp. No. 28, p. 121, adopted by consensus on October 24, 1970.

25   Author's emphasis. Article 2.3 of the Declaration reads:

> In accordance with the 1970 Declaration on principles of International Law Concerning Friendly Relations and Co-operation Among States in Accordance with the Charter of the United Nations, this [the right to self-determination] shall not be construed as authorising or encouraging any action which could dismember or impair, totally or in part, the territorial integrity or political unity of sovereign and independent states conducting themselves in compliance with the principle of equal rights and self-determination of peoples and thus, possessed of a government representing the whole peoples belonging to the territory without distinction of any kind.

26   CERD/C/49/CRP.2/Add.7, *General Recommendation*, adopted by the Committee at the 1147th meeting, on March 1996.

27   Ibid.

In conclusion, since the formation of the United Nations, self-determination has undergone a dynamic transformation. The description of the right as 'the right of the peoples to freely determine their political status and freely pursue their economic, social and cultural development' leaves space for various interpretations. It is for the international community to tune the meaning and use of the right according to contemporary needs. This should be interpreted as allowing political concerns to determine the scope of every human right. Allowing the international community – rather than states unilaterally – to interpret each right in accordance with the current realities, albeit always within the contours set by the standards of international law, is consistent with the dynamic character of international law. This, in my understanding, has been one of the greatest teachings of Thornberry's writings.[28]

Prevailing Current Understandings of Self-determination

There is currently an obvious contradiction between the different understandings of self-determination,[29] which leads to substantially different outcomes as to the use and the beneficiaries of the right. These understandings can be grouped into two approaches: the minimalist approach, which is adopted by most states and limits the scope and consequently the beneficiaries of the right; and the maximalist approach, which is adopted by many claimants and advocates a wide understanding of the right to self-determination.

1.   The Minimalist Approach

Minimalists either refuse to accept that self-determination is a right in international law; or equate it to secession; or divide the right into two, namely independence and democratic government and apply the former to whole populations of the state and the latter to minorities.[30] The minimalist approach has clear and precise answers and provides certainty about the use of the right, based on state practice.[31] It is considered by many as

---

28   For example, P. Thornberry *Indigenous peoples and human rights* (Manchester: Manchester University Press, 2002) p. 133.

29   R. Stavenhagen, 'Self-determination: Right or Demon?' in D. Clark and R. Williamson (eds.) *Self-determination: International Perspectives* (London: Macmillan Press, 1996), p. 2.

30   For examples of states' views on self-determination, see the following: UN Doc. E/CN.4/ 1996/84 (1995) *Report of the Working Group established in accordance with Commission on Human Rights resolution 1995/32 of 3 March 1995*, UNHCR paras. 42-46; UN Doc. E/CN.4/ 1997/102 (1996), *Report of the Working Group established in accordance with Commission on Human Rights resolution 1995/32 of 3 March 1995*, UNHCR, paras. 311-346; UN Doc. E/ CN.4/1998/106 (1997) *Report of the Working Group established in accordance with Commission on Human Rights resolution 1995/32 of 3 March 1995*, UNHCR, para. 44; UN Doc. E/CN.4/ 1998/WG.15/CRP.1 (1998) *draft Report of the Working Group established in accordance with Commission on Human Rights resolution 1995/32 of 3 March 1995*, UNHCR, paras. 60-63.

31   H. Hannum, 'Self-Determination in the Post-Colonial Era' in Clark and Williamson (note 29) pp. 12-44; also H. Hannum, 'A principled response to ethnic self-determination claims'

'the safe option' that protects the legal status of the right. As it protects the *status quo* and discourages separatist attempts, arguably it also protects world peace. Yet, despite the certainty it gives, it has several shortcomings. These are explored below.

a.   Non-recognition as a legal right

In its most extreme form, the minimalist approach does not recognise self-determination as a legal right, because of its vague nature and inconsistent application.[32] Yet, the International Covenants, the main universal human rights treaties, clearly bind the participating states to respecting the right to self-determination. The right of self-determination has also been recognised in several United Nations resolutions adopted by many states, by the International Court of Justice,[33] in formal statements by governments, and in international practice. It would be erroneous to use its vague nature and political component to diminish its legal status. As Thornberry has emphasised,[34] legal rules are made to be general to allow for a wide spectrum of application. International legal instruments set basic, general, even vague rules that are interpreted and applied *ad hoc* in any case. Notions like sovereignty, freedom, participation, and the right to expression all have a certain degree of generality which can be interpreted as vagueness. However, this generality allows them to evolve according to the international realities and needs. In essence, the evolution of the meaning of self-determination, the gradual expansion of its beneficiaries and the continuous violation of the right in many areas of the world does not take away its legal status but reaffirms the need for self-determination.

The validity of self-determination as a *human right* does not abolish its validity as a *principle* of international law. Notions such as the respect for human life and dignity or equality have been treated as both general principles and human rights. The same applies to self-determination. Stavenhagen maintains:

> Self-determination is an idée force of powerful magnitude, a philosophical stance, a moral value, a social movement, a potent ideology, that also may be expressed, in one of its many guises, as a legal right in international law.[35]

---

in G. Alfredsson and M. Stavropoulou (eds.) *Justice Pending: Indigenous peoples and other good causes* (The Hague: Martinus Nijhoff Publishers, 2002) pp. 263-266.

32   D. McGoldrick *The Human Rights Committee, its Role in the Development of the ICCPR* (Oxford: Clarendon Press, 1991) p. 257.

33   In its *Advisory Opinion on the Legal Consequences for states of the continued presence in South Africa in Namibia (South-west Africa) notwithstanding Security Council Res. 276 (1970)*, Advisory Opinion of 21 June 1971; also in its *Advisory Opinion on Western Sahara*, Advisory Opinion of 16 October 1975 http://www.icj-cij.org/icjwww/idecisions.htm (accessed 2 August 2004).

34   For example, see P. Thornberry 'Self-determination and indigenous peoples: objections and responses' in P. Aikio and M. Scheinin (eds.) *Operationalizing the right of indigenous peoples to self-determination* (Turku/Abo:, Abo Akademi University, 2000) p. 49.

35   Stavenhagen (note 29) p. 12.

The dual application of self-determination as a principle and as a right is supported by positive law. It is recognised as a principle in the UN Charter and is included as a right in the International Covenants. It is explicitly recognised as both a principle and a right in the Helsinki Declaration.[36] As a principle, self-determination needs to be taken into account when decisions are made, alongside other principles of international law such as territorial integrity, national sovereignty, and equality of persons. As a human right, self-determination provides its beneficiaries with a specific claim for the exercise of the right.

b.   Equating it with secession

Several states insist on equating self-determination with secession and reach the conclusion that a very limited number of peoples have the right to self-determination. For example, the representative of Japan has stated in the Working Group on a draft Declarration on Indigenous Rights:

> The concept of self-determination was set forth in the context of decolonisation, mainly for colonised people who requested independence from states.[37]

Secession is the real thorn in the evolution of self-determination. States focus so much on this application of self-determination that they avoid even discussing the right and certainly resist in allowing new beneficiaries. As Falk explains, the successful creation of new states as a result of struggles for self-determination has 'both strained conceptual boundaries and created an increasingly awkward gap between doctrinal and experiential accounts of self-determination, resulting, as might be expected, in controversy and confusion'.[38]

This understanding of self-determination gives the state the central role on the international stage and ignores the dramatic changes that have occurred in perceptions, values and loyalties in a world referred to by many as 'post-national'. Events such as the emergence of several new states that used to be constituent parts of the former Soviet Union (USSR), the peaceful division of Czechoslovakia and the bloody division of Yugoslavia have seriously challenged the doctrinal purity of territorial integrity and state sovereignty as principles that secure the existing status quo.[39] The decline of the state is also reflected in international legal norms: it is widely accepted today that international law is

---

36   Section VIII of the Declaration.

37   UN Doc. E/CN.4/1997/102, *Report of the working group on the elaboration of a draft "United Nations Declaration on the Rights of Indigenous Peoples"*, UNCHR, para. 336.

38   R. Falk *Human Rights Horizons, The pursuit of justice in a Globalising World* (New York: Routledge 2000) p. 98. Also see B. Kingsbury, 'Reconstructing self-determination: A relational approach' in P. Aikio and M. Scheinin (eds.) *Operationalizing the right of indigenous peoples to self-determination* (Turku/Abo:, Abo Akademi University, 2000) pp. 19-37.

39   See M. Koskenniemi, 'National Self-Determination today: Problems of Legal Theory and Practice', 43 *International and Comparative Law Quarterly* (1994) pp. 243-244.

not only made by states, that states are not the sole subjects of international law, and that human rights do not merely constitute part of the internal affairs of states. Accordingly, the meaning of self-determination is not centred around the state and the creation of a state.

Equating self-determination with secession also disregards the *reason d'etre* for human rights: human rights are established to protect human beings, rather than states. It is important to affirm that self-determination is a *peoples'* right and not a *government's* right.[40] As Falk suggests, 'it is the underlying legitimacy of peoples, not the transient legitimacy of governments that constitute the purpose and rationale for the instruments protecting human rights...'[41] Self-determination cannot be recognised – directly or indirectly – as belonging to states; otherwise, as Crawford notes, it could become a pretence for governments to dispose of the 'peoples' in questioning the ways that conflict with their rights of self-determination.[42]

In addition, the fear of states that the beneficiaries of self-determination will try to secede is not justified, as the recognition of the right of self-determination does not automatically mean the recognition of the right to secede. International law does not give a precise answer as to whether a right to secede exists; and even if its existence is agreed, its exercise is subject to several conditions. According to many commentators, resolution 1541, in conjunction with the Declaration on Principles of International Law concerning Friendly Relations and Co-operation among States and the Vienna Declaration, implies that there may be a right to secession for populations of well-defined territories only when the government is not representative and severely discriminates against particular segments of the population.[43] An argument could be put forward that

---

40   Of course, as Crawford notes, to the extent that it applies, self-determination qualifies the right of governments to dispose of the 'peoples' in question in ways that conflict with their rights of self-determination. See J. Crawford, 'The Rights of Peoples: 'Peoples' or 'Governments'?' in Crawford (note 2) p. 59.

41   R. Falk, 'The Rights of Peoples (In particular Indigenous Peoples)' in Crawford (note 2) p. 25.

42   Crawford (note 40) p. 59. (Note 9)

43   See *Resolution 1541* (note 21); the *Declaration on Principles of International Law concerning Friendly Relations and Co-operation among States*; and the *Vienna Declaration*. See for example T.D. Musgrave *Self-determination and National Minorities* (Oxford: Clarendon Press, 1997) pp. 188-192; N. Shaw 'Re: Order in Council P.C. 1996-1997 of September 1996' in A. Bayefsky (ed.) *Self-determination in International Law: Quebec and Lessons Learned* (Dorderecht: Kluwer Law International, 2000); T.M. Franck 'Postmodern Tribalism and the Right to Secede' in C. Brolmann, R. Lefeber and M. Zieck (eds.) *Peoples and Minorities in International Law* (Dordrecht: Martinus Nijhoff, 1993) pp. 3-27; O. Schlachter 'Sovereignty – Then and Now' in R. St Macdonald (ed.) *Essays in Honour of Wane Tieya* (Dordrecht: Martinus Nijhoff, 1993) p. 684; A. Heraclides 'Secession, Self-determination and Non-intervention: In Quest of a Normative Symbiosis' 45 *Journal of International Affairs* (1992) pp. 400-411; J. Crawford *The Creation of States* (Oxford: Clarendon Press, 1979) pp. 100-101; B. Kingsbury 'Claims by Non-state Groups' 25 *Cornell International Law Journal* (1992) p. 487. Also see case law: judgement of Judge Wildhaber in *Loizidou v. Turkey* (Merits), European Court on Human Rights, 18 December 1996, reproduced in 18 *H.R.L.J.* (1997) p. 59;

the above instruments are not legally binding and that state practice contradicts such a possibility.[44] Kirgis has responded that the above declarations reflect an *opinio juris* and that in the human rights system, strong evidence of *opinio juris* may overcome a weak demonstration of state practice in order to establish a customary law.[45] Even authors who recognise that a right to secession may exist insist on the level of human rights violations that would activate secession: a 'people' must be persistently and egregiously denied political and social equality as well as the opportunity to retain their cultural identity;[46] exploitation or discrimination must be systematic[47] and must constitute in real terms colonial or alien domination.[48] Other conditions that must be fulfilled include: that the claimants must inhabit a well-defined territory which overwhelmingly supports separatism;[49] that secession is a realistic prospect of conflict resolution and peace; and that all other political and diplomatic avenues have been seriously examined.[50] Thornberry supports a theoretical recognition of a right to secession if the government is not representative. He warns though that 'even this cautious and careful account of criteria appears as possibility rather than a probability in terms of a normative development of general international law'.[51]

If secession can only be a possibility if the government consistently discriminates against the members of a people and fails to protect them, and only after all avenues have been exhausted, the minimalists' fear that self-determination will bring secession is to a large degree unjustified. Secession occupies a very limited part of the scope of the right to self-determination.

Katangese Peoples Congress v. Zaire, African Commission on Human and Peoples Rights, Communication 75/92, reproduced in 3 *IHRR* (1996) p. 136; and Supreme Court of Canada, Reference re Secession of Quebec, judgement published 20 August 1998, reproduced in Bayefsky (this note) p. 504.

44   Hannum argues that recognition of new states in the 90s was based either on the agreement of the component parts of the state concerned (USSR, Ethiopia, Czechoslovakia) or on a factual determination that the state no longer existed (Yugoslavia). See Hannum in Clark and Williamson (note 31).

45   Kirgis (note 43).

46   Franck (note 43) pp. 13-14.

47   Heraclides (note 43).

48   UN Doc. E/CN.4/Sub.2/ 405/Rev.1 (1980), H.G. Espiel *The Right to Self-Determination, Implementation of United Nations Resolutions* paras. 85, 87 and 95.

49   Franck (note 43) and Heraclides (note 43).

50   Heraclides (note 47).

51   P. Thornberry 'The United Nations and principle of self-determination' in V. Lowe and C. Warbrick (eds.) *The United Nations and the Principles of International Law, Essays in memory of Michael Akehurst* (London: Routledge, 1995) p. 183. Hannum seems to tentatively agree with him, see Hannum 'Justice Pending: Indigenous Peoples and Other Good Causes' (note 31) p. 266. For a critique of this view, see G. Pentassuglia 'State sovereignty, minorities and self-determination: A comprehensive legal view' 9 *International Journal on Minorities and Group Rights* (2001) pp. 310-312.

c.   Definition by its applications

Another expression of the minimalist approach defines self-determination by the applications of the right. Indeed, the right to self-determination can be exercised in various ways. Applications of the external aspect of the right include independence, association, or integration with another state. Applications of the internal aspect of self-determination include democratic governance, participation and autonomy. Many minimalists exhaust the meaning of self-determination to the above options. It is argued that this approach limits the scope of the right. Alfredsson has noted:

> The tentative listing of suggested forms and expressions of self-determination is undoubtedly not exhaustive and definitely not final. After all, self-determination has not been and should not be a stagnant phenomenon. Further evolution is likely and it must be admitted that, not surprisingly, the outcome is uncertain.[52]

It must be accepted that in international history we have become familiar with *some* applications of the right. To identify the whole right just as the applications of self-determination that we have already experienced limits its scope and makes the future inclusion of new applications impermissible. The meaning of self-determination must remain open to new aspects being incorporated into the concept. Anaya explains:

> Under a human rights approach, the concept of self-determination is capable of embracing much more nuanced interpretations and applications, particularly in an increasingly interdependent world in which the formal attributes of statehood mean less and less.[53]

Any claim based on the right of self-determination must be considered in relation to the meaning of the right itself, rather than in relation to the applications of the rights already in existence. Although a claim falling within these applications will be more easily accommodated because of the plethora of instruments empowering its application, other claims must also be seriously considered.

An example that highlights the argument is peoples' claims for autonomous representation in international fora, especially in matters that affect them, as part of their exercise of self-determination. This is an application of the external aspect of self-determination that has not yet been widely accepted as part of the right. If the right is understood by its applications, this claim will be rejected on the basis that it does not correspond to any of the existing applications of self-determination and thus, goes

---

52   G. Alfredsson 'Different Forms of and Claims to the Right of Self-Determination' in D. Clark and R. Williamson (eds.) *Self-determination: International Perspectives* (London: Macmillan Press, 1996) p. 79.

53   See S.J. Anaya 'The Capacity of International Law to Advance Ethnic or Nationality Rights Claims' 75 *Iowa Law Review* (1990) p. 842.

beyond its current meaning. If however self-determination is understood in more general terms, this claim makes sense and could be accommodated.[54]

Because of its inability to deal with the challenges of our era, the minimalist understanding of self-determination has already been declining in the last few years. One can see the seeds of a shift of emphasis away from an absolute, unconditional right to political sovereignty and territorial integrity towards a more flexible, less statist understanding of self-determination. Even states that are traditionally in favour of the minimalist approach have recognised this shift: the US representative stated in the 1995 Working Group on the draft Declaration of Indigenous Peoples stated that '…while current views among scholars and governments may be changing on the meaning of self-determination, there is not yet an international consensus…'[55]

2. *The Maximalist Approach*

Maximalists give the right of self-determination a wide meaning; usually it includes an economic[56] and/or cultural aspect.[57] The preamble of the 1992 Indigenous Peoples Earth Charter illustrates this maximalist approach:

> We indigenous peoples maintain our inherent right to self-determination. We have always had the right to decide our own forms of government, to use our own ways to raise and educate our children, to our own identity without interference.[58]

The (1993) Mataatua Declaration on Cultural and Intellectual Property Rights of Indigenous Peoples also expresses this approach:

---

54   The draft Declaration on the Rights of Indigenous Peoples includes other similar claims such as the right of indigenous peoples to maintain and develop contacts, relations and co-operation across borders for political reasons (article 35); to 'determine their relationships with States'; and to have the agreements and arrangements made with States enforced (article 36). Also see M. Scheinin this volume, especially his footnote 17.

55   1996 United Nations Working Group on the elaboration of a draft 'United Nations Declaration on the Rights of Indigenous Peoples', on file with author. For a summary of the U.S. statement, see http://www.cwis.org/fwdp/International/wgrpt-2.txt (accessed 3 August 2004).

56   For example, S. Trifunovska, 'One theme in two variations- Self-determination for minorities and indigenous peoples', 5 *International Journal on Minority and Group Rights* (1997) pp. 182-183.

57   For example, T. Moses in Aikio and Scheinin (note 34) pp. 155-177.

58   The *Kari-oca Declaration* is the Preamble of the *Indigenous Peoples Earth Charter*, which was adopted by indigenous representatives in the World Conference of Indigenous Peoples on Territory, Environment and Development, held at Kari-Oca, Brazil on May 25-30 1992, just before the Sustainable Development at the United Nations Conference on Environment and Development (UNCED) in Rio de Janeiro. The text of the declaration is at the http://www.dialoguebetweennations.com/IR/english/KariOcaKimberley/intro.html (accessed 2 August 2004) para. 4.

We declare that indigenous peoples of the world have the right to self-determination, and in exercising that right must be recognised as the exclusive owners of their cultural and intellectual property...[59]

In general, as Alfredsson notes,

...an ever increasing number of peoples, groups and even states and advocates on their behalf are claiming, demanding and fighting for their enjoyment of self-determination, with claims to a wide range of external and internal applications in the political, economic and cultural fields.[60]

The maximalist approach appears to be supported by the language of common article 1 of both the International Covenants (International Covenant on Civil and Political Rights and International Covenant on Economic, Social and Cultural Rights), which defines self-determination as the right of peoples to pursue their *economic, cultural and social* development; many other instruments call for attention to the connection between self-determination and human rights.[61] Of all the meanings maximalists integrate into the right, economic self-determination seems the most accepted. The right of peoples to economic growth and to their natural resources is included in paragraph 2 of article 1 of the International Covenants; surely, this implies that the right of self-determination has an economic aspect. In its General Comment 12, the Human Rights Committee maintained that paragraph 2 of article 1 'affirms a particular aspect of the economic content of the right to self-determination'.[62] Several commentators agree with this understanding of self-determination.[63] Less accepted is the cultural aspect of self-determination, which refers to the right of peoples to determine, preserve and develop their own cultural fate. Other claims made on the basis of self-determination include claims for democracy and political rights; for distinct political and judicial systems; for respect of treaties between indigenous nations and states; for territorial integrity, political independence and non-intervention;

---

59   The *Mataatua Declaration* was adopted in 1993 at the end of the First International Conference on the Cultural and Intellectual Property Rights of Indigenous Peoples (12–18 June 1993, Whakatane) attended by 150 indigenous representatives from 14 states. See http://aotearoa.wellington.net.nz/imp/mata.htm (accessed 2 August 2004) preamble, para. 5.

60   Alfredsson (note 52) p. 58.

61   (note 21).

62   UN Doc. HRI/GEN/1 (1992), *Compilation of General Comments and General Recommendations adopted by Human Rights Treaty Bodies*, para. 5.

63   Including Rosas and Spiry; A. Rosas, 'The right to self-determination' in A. Eide, C. Krause and A. Rosas (eds) *Economic, Social and Cultural Rights, A Textbook* (Dordrecht, Boston, London: Martinus Nijhoff, 1995) p. 83; also E. Spiry, 'From 'Self-Determination to a Right to 'Self-Development' for Indigenous Groups', 38 *German Yearbook of International Law* (1995) p. 144, where he notes that 'the label "internal self-determination" is biased, and should be abandoned in favour of more "neutral" and objective expressions, such as "self-government" or, if we include economic rights..."self-development" or "self-preservation"'.

claims concerning the name of a country as well as border adjustments; religious freedom; and educational provision. In its distorted form, nationalism, fundamentalism, racism and even ethnic cleansing have all been justified in the name of self-determination.

The maximalist approach has important qualities: it views self-determination as an evolving concept and attempts to adjust its meaning according to the current international needs. It also aims to restore global justice, the ultimate goal of human rights, by accommodating the claims of vulnerable groups. However, treating self-determination as an 'umbrella-right'[64] for all has several downsides.

First, such a wide interpretation of the right to self-determination is not doing any favours to the claims in question. Using self-determination as the basis for claims vaguely linked to the right hinders their realisation. Distant links with existing standards, and especially with a right as controversial as self-determination, does not normally lead to the satisfaction of the claims. Very often, other human rights can serve as a legitimate basis for the claims, but the use of self-determination conceals them.

This is the case with the cultural aspect of self-determination: the right to language, education, religion and the generic right to a culture are usually more appropriate to use for claims related to cultural freedom and its various expressions, educational issues and religious practices. Other separate issues, for example cultural co-operation and assistance through international and bilateral channels, are also established in the United Nations Scientific, Educational and Cultural Organization (UNESCO) instruments and other relevant international texts. Adding a cultural aspect to the right of self-determination fails to provide culture-related claims with a solid basis, adds nothing to the human rights canon and practically disempowers a series of cultural rights, by drawing attention away from them and thus hindering their further interpretation and evolution.[65]

Other claims made in the name of self-determination, such as the right to a state's name[66] and border adjustments are not even related to human rights, but to state rights. Irrespective of the validity of these claims, using self-determination as their basis is an unfortunate choice. As mentioned above, mixing state rights with human rights is erroneous and waters down the meaning and use of self-determination.[67]

Indeed, the maximalist approach can result in opposite results to those its supporters expect. Using self-determination as an umbrella right is a poor legislative method which runs the danger of distorting its meaning and scope. Stavenhagen maintains that this approach:

…may not only lead to chaos and anarchy…More than this, a 'maximalistic' position will end up demeaning and devaluing the idea of self-determination itself, and will thereby only harm those collectivities who require it the most.[68]

64   As used by Alfredsson (note 52).
65   Ibid. pp. 75-76.
66   The government of the Former Yugoslav Republic of Macedonia based its right to call the newly established state Macedonia on the right to self-determination.
67   Alfredsson (note 52) pp. 75-76; also see Falk (note 41) p. 25.
68   Stavenhagen (note 29) p. 7.

Peru's statement on indigenous self-determination highlights this argument:

> ...self-determination would not be national in character, rather it would have a cultural and social identity within a national formation. Government delegations would find this approach much more fruitful.[69]

By seemingly accepting the right, Peru clearly avoided any recognition of the politically sensitive scope of self-determination. Peru thereby disregards the real meaning of the right and this statement works to the detriment of indigenous self-determination.

An Alternative Approach

Both the minimalist and the maximalist approaches offer important advantages that cannot be overlooked. The minimalist approach offers certainty and clarity to the right of self-determination, whereas the maximalist approach offers space for evolution and adjustment of the right to contemporary and future international realities. A balance needs to be found that would use the advantages of both approaches and try to dispose of their weaknesses.

The flexible understanding of the right to self-determination is important. Apart from forms that have been previously implemented, such as independence, democratic governance and autonomy, new forms of the right must be allowed to be developed and applied. For example, indigenous groups' claims for contacts, their relations and co-operation across borders for political reasons, and recognition of their international legal personality do not fit into the traditional applications of the right, but are certainly within its contours. In September 2004, during the tenth session of the working group on the draft Declaration of the rights of indigenous peoples, the US government actually acknowledged that the meaning of the right of self-determination includes the preservation of their distinct law enforcement systems; local taxation; the ability of peoples to establish a Freeport and to participate in international fora.

On the other hand, most authors, including Thornberry,[70] refer mainly to aspects related to the political status of the collectivity and do not address other possible aspects of self-determination. Indeed, the right of self-determination has essentially been linked to political power. Dinstein maintains:

> Whereas it is explicitly enunciated in this text [article 1 of the International Covenants] that the right of self-determination has certain economic, social and cultural

---

69   Statement made on 8 December 1998 by the Peruvian representative to the fourth session of the United Nations working group on the draft declaration on the rights of indigenous peoples (on file with the author).

70   P. Thornberry 'The Democratic or Internal Aspect of Self-Determination' in C. Tomuschat (ed.) *Modern Law of Self-Determination* (London: Martinus Nijhoff, 1993) pp. 101-138.

ramifications, it is uncontrovertible that the core of the right is political in nature. The gist of self-determination is political control of the people's destiny (accompanied by other forms of control).[71]

It is true that the concept of self-determination is related to freedoms 'a people' can have; it is about giving peoples the freedom to determine their lives and destinies. In this way, it incorporates political, economic, cultural and social claims of all kinds. Yet, this generic understanding is better left to the *principle*, rather than the *right*. The *principle* of self-determination runs through several human rights in their collective capacity. It would make more sense if any claim based on the *right* of self-determination is closely related to its concept and cannot be accommodated by any more relevant right. Subsidiarity can be a great help in deciding whether this right is the best basis for a group claim. If claims based on self-determination can be accommodated by other rights and concepts, they should be transferred under their aegis. In the previous section, it has been explained that cultural claims, for example, would better be accommodated by cultural rights, rather than the right to self-determination. Furthermore, claims for fairer representation of 'a people' in elections fall more appropriately within article 21 of International Covenant on Civil and Political Rights (ICCPR) as relating to political power rather than the right of self-determination.

Although this transfer of claims is certainly beneficial for political and cultural claims, more difficult is the issue of economic self-determination. An economic meaning of the right is particularly important to indigenous peoples. They often assert that the right of self-determination is strongly linked to their right to decide their own development and to have control over their lands and resources.[72] Indigenous claims for permanent sovereignty over their lands, for their right to exercise their traditional activities, to apply indigenous practices for sustainable development, to enjoy the natural resources of the lands they live in, and to share the benefits of using such resources all closely relate to the idea of participation and autonomy; and ultimately self-determination.

Can the right to development better accommodate these claims that are currently based on the right to self-determination? Indeed, indigenous representatives have used the right to self-determination and the right to development interchangeably as a basis for claims concerning ownership of their lands or resources.[73] General Assembly Resolution 1803 (XVII) of 14 December 1962 on Permanent Sovereignty over Natural Resources referred to 'the right of peoples and nations to permanent sovereignty over their natural resources',[74] but did not clarify the beneficiaries of the right. Later, the 1986

---

71   Y. Dinstein 'Self-Determination revisited' in *International World in an Evolving World, In Tribute to Professor Eduardo Jimenez de Arechaga* (Montevideo: Fondacion de cultura Universitaria, 1994) p. 245.

72   *Report of the United Nations Working Group on Indigenous Populations*, E/CN.4/Sub.2/2001/17 (2001) para. 38.

73   Ibid.

74   Cited in Alfredsson (note 53) pp. 74-75.

Declaration on the Right to Development[75] was the first instrument that recognised the right to development, even though at the time not all states recognised such a right. A consensus on the right of development as a human right was reached in 1993 at the UN World Conference on Human Rights, which was attended by almost all Member States. The resulting Vienna Declaration and Programme of Action reaffirmed the right as a 'universal and inalienable right and an integral part of fundamental human rights'.[76] According to article 1, paragraph 1 of the Declaration on the Right to Development, the right of self-determination relates to a particular process of 'economic, social, cultural and political development' through which 'all human rights and fundamental freedoms can be fully realized'. Further, the declaration explicitly mentions that the right to self-determination includes the exercise of the peoples' right to full sovereignty over their natural wealth and resources.[77]

Indeed, the right to development is included in article 47 of the ICCPR and article 25 of the ICESCR which read:

> Nothing in the present Covenant shall be interpreted as impairing the inherent right of all peoples to enjoy and utilise freely their natural wealth and resources.

The above articles could serve as the basis for economic claims. Paragraph 2 of common article 1 could also serve in this respect. Again, though, the right included in this paragraph is not necessarily related to the *economic aspect of the right of self-determination*, but to the separate *right of peoples to development*.

There are two strong counter-arguments to the position argued above, i.e. that economic claims of peoples could be served by the right to development rather than the right to self-determination. Firstly, the language of several international instruments implies the acknowledgment of an economic aspect to the right to self-determination. Common article 1 of the International Covenants (ICCPR and ICESCR) proclaims that self-determination means the right of peoples 'to pursue their political, economic, social and cultural development'. Yet, if the language is taken literally, then self-determination means development, in which case the right to development becomes void, at least for 'peoples'. The second paragraph of the same article is more convincing. It reads:

> All peoples may, for their own ends, freely dispose of their natural wealth and resources without prejudice to any obligations arising out of the international economic co-operation, based upon the principle of mutual benefit, and international law. In no case may a people be deprived of its own means of substance.

---

75 The *Declaration on the Right to Development* was adopted by the General Assembly in its resolution 41/128 of 4 December 1986.

76 A/CONF.157/23 (1993), *Vienna Declaration and Programme of Action*, World Conference on Human Rights, Vienna, 14-25 June 1993, para. 10.

77 Article 1.1 and 1.2 of the Declaration.

It can be argued that this paragraph refers to the right to development, rather than to an added aspect of self-determination. Still, the position of the paragraph in the middle of an article on self-determination implies more. Also, the inclusion of an economic aspect to the right of self-determination has been endorsed by UN bodies. For example, in its General Comment 12, the Human Rights Committee maintained that paragraph 2 of article 1 'affirms a particular aspect of the economic content of the right to self-determination'.[78] Again, it can be argued that the opinions of the Human Rights Committee are not binding; nevertheless, they do have weight as interpretations of the authorised monitoring bodies to particular treaties.

Secondly, the right to development presents the same weaknesses that we have tried to address regarding the right to self-determination. Its meaning is still contestable, with the minimalist approach focussing on its economic aspect and the maximalist approach giving it an economic, social, political and cultural dimension. Its beneficiaries are vague, and even more vague are its duty holders.[79] Abi-Saab has pointed out the great resemblance between the two rights.[80] Consequently, by transferring economic claims from the scope of self-determination to the scope of development are we just transferring the problem instead of solving it? I think not. Contrary to self-determination, claims for economic development and benefit sharing are at the heart of the right to development. Essentially, the validity of the claims remains the same, or is even strengthened; it is their basis that changes. In other words, the right to development provides a solid basis for such claims, and such claims present the perfect opportunity for the advancement of the right to development.

Conclusions

In this chapter, I have explored the meaning and scope of self-determination. Although the legal character of the right is widely accepted, the reading of self-determination as secession continues. Yet, this echoes an earlier period of the right in the midst of decolonisation. Since then, the meaning of self-determination has evolved considerably to include, apart from independence, integration or association with another state, democratic governance, participation and autonomy. These applications indicate the ways the right can be exercised, rather than define the scope of the right. The definition of the right solely by the above applications would limit its meaning and hinder any further evolution of the right to match the needs of the time. Having said this, the right cannot be used as an umbrella sheltering every claim crying out for justice. This would hinder the right as well as the claims.

---

78   (Note 62) para. 5.

79   J. Donnelly 'In Search of a Unicorn: The Jurisprudence of the Right to Development' 12 *California International Law Review* (1985) pp. 473-509.

80   G. Abi-Saab 'Technological Development and the Right to Development' in L-A. Sicilianos and M. Gavouneli (eds.) *Scientific and Technological Developments and Human Rights* (Athens: Ant. N. Sakoulas Publishers, 1990) p. 266.

When reflecting on its meaning, it is important to remember that self-determination is both a principle and a right in international law. As a principle, it runs through various rights; as a right, it revolves essentially around political power, participation and control. Limiting the scope of the right to political power does not address the validity of claims made in the name of self-determination. It just transfers them to other rights, which can better serve the claims in question. Participation and control at some levels should be addressed by other rights, such as the right to culture. Greater difficulty exists in relation to economic control and to participation in decision-making with regards to natural resources. The alternative to economic self-determination, namely the right to development, faces many of the same criticisms as self-determination. Nevertheless, it is suggested that it is better suited to accommodate claims related to natural resources.

Chapter 3

SELF-DETERMINATION AND THE USE OF FORCE

Malcolm N. Shaw[1]

> *It is an honour and a pleasure to contribute to this book of essays for Patrick Thornberry, a friend since we first met at Liverpool Polytechnic in October 1972. I have chosen this topic in the light of his many influential works in the area of self-determination.*

Self-determination is one of the most compelling and creative principles in modern international relations. Derived from the potent nineteenth century mix of nationalism and nascent democracy, it has driven forward a number of key concepts in international law. But it has at the same time manifested its own often schizophrenic nature. Nationalism and democracy are both notoriously difficult to define precisely, and they often do not coincide. Practice has shown universal agreement as to the application of the right to self-determination in the true and full sense of free choice of political status only with regard to the decolonisation of the overseas territories of the European empires. But even this is subject to the key proviso that such free choice takes place within the spatial framework of the colonially defined territories, unless all relevant parties have otherwise consented. Further, it is critical to differentiate the principle of self-determination within international relations generally and the right of self-determination as it exists as a binding norm in international law. The two are not identical and the fecundity of the former is not matched by that of the latter.

The constraints on the resort to the use of force by states in international relations have grown during the centuries of the evolution of international law, particularly since the conclusion of the First World War. It is now universally accepted that there is a presumption in law against the use of force by states. This presumption may be rebutted in two clear instances, where such force is used by a state in self-defence and where the use of force is mandated by a binding decision of the Security Council of the United Nations. There are, of course, legitimate differences and difficulties in interpretation with regard to certain actions taken in self-defence, for example, where action is taken before the attack has actually taken place, and where there are uncertainties as to the pre-

---

[1]   Sir Robert Jennings Professor of International Law, University of Leicester.

Nazila Ghanea & Alexandra Xanthaki (eds.), Minorities, Peoples and Self-Determination, pp. 35-54.
© *2005 Koninklijke Brill NV. Printed in The Netherlands. ISBN 90 04 14301 7.*

cise meaning of a Security Council decision. Beyond these areas, it has been suggested that force may be used in cases of extreme humanitarian need. But recent decades have brought forward other challenges, ranging from international terrorism, to the use of force against non-state entities and groups, to the uncertain legal condition of imploded states.

The principles of self-determination and the prohibition of the use of force by states, save in carefully defined circumstances, intersect at certain points. In some situations the relevant norms have become clear and accepted, in other situations all that is clear is that the law is evolving.

The final point to be made in this introductory section is that the very complex of international law is changing. Just as international relations is not immutable and shifts every so often to reflect basic structural changes arising out of changing power relationships, so international legal principles evolve to take account of new political conditions. To put it another way, the understanding of international norms and how they are created, modified and terminated is contingent upon a clear comprehension of the changing patterns of international political relationships.

It is proposed first to trace the status and definition of the principle of self-determination and then to examine briefly the relationship between this principle and the norms relating to the use of force.

Self-Determination in International Law[2]

Self-determination in the general sense evolved primarily in Europe as a marriage between nationalism and democracy in the sense of positing the choice of political status

---

2   See in general e.g. A. Cassese *Self-Determination of Peoples* (Cambridge: Cambridge University Press, 1995); K. Knop *Diversity and Self-Determination in International Law* (Cambridge: Cambridge University Press, 2002); U. O. Umozurike *Self-Determination in International Law* (Hamden CT: Archon Books, 1972); A. Rigo-Sureda *The Evolution of the Right of Self-Determination* (Leiden: A.W. Sijthoff, 1973); M. Shukri *The Concept of Self-Determination in the United Nations* (Leiden: A.W. Sijthoff, 1967); M. Pomerance *Self-Determination in Law and Practice* (Leiden: Martinus Nijhoff, 1982); M.N. Shaw *Title to Territory in Africa: International Legal Issues* (Oxford: Oxford University Press, 1986) pp.59-144; J. Crawford *Creation of States in International Law* (Oxford: Oxford University Press, 1979) pp. 84-105; 'The General Assembly, the International Court and Self-Determination' in A.V. Lowe and M. Fitzmaurice (eds.) *Fifty Years of the International Court of Justice* (Cambridge: Cambridge University Press, 1996) p. 585 and 'State Practice and International Law in Relation to Secession', *BYIL*, (1998) p. 85; C. Tomuschat (ed) *Modern Law of Self-Determination* (Dordrecht: M. Nijhoff, 1993); M. Koskenniemi 'National Self-Determination Today, Problems of Legal Theory and Practice' 43 *ICLQ* (1994) p. 241; H. Quane, 'The UN and the Evolving Right to Self-Determination', 47 *ICLQ* (1998) p. 537 and W. Ofuatey-Kodjoe 'Self Determination' in O. Schachter and C. Joyner (eds.) *United Nations Legal Order* (Cambridge: Cambridge University Press, 1995) vol. 1, p. 349. See also M.N. Shaw *International Law* (Cambridge: Cambridge University Press, 5th edition, 2003) from which material in this article draws.

by clear national groups. It thus created both a challenge and an alternative to the large continental multinational empires of Russia, Austria-Hungary and the Ottomans, and provided an ideological justification for the unifications of Italy and of Germany and the independence of the various Balkan states from Greece onwards. The principle first appeared in major international form after the First World War, driven by the liberal political philosophy of US President Wilson and by the refusal of the United States to enter the conflict simply in order to protect and enlarge European empires.

However, despite President Wilson's efforts, self-determination was not included in the League of Nations Covenant and it was clearly not regarded at that time as a legal principle.[3] However, its influence can be seen in a very modified form in the various provisions for minority protection in Central and Eastern Europe[4] and in the establishment of the mandates system by which the colonies of the defeated powers were not simply transferred over to the victorious states, but given a special international status based upon the notion of the 'sacred trust'.[5] In the ten years before the Second World War, there was relatively little practice regarding self-determination in international law, although the USSR concluded a number of treaties in this period referring to the principle.[6] In the *Aaland Islands* case it was clearly accepted by both the International Commission of Jurists and the Committee of Rapporteurs dealing with the situation in question that the principle of self-determination was not a legal rule of international law, but purely a political concept.[7]

The nature of the principle shifted as a consequence of the Second World War and became allied to the growing concern with human rights, such that the balance between nationalism and democracy in this context changed. In fact, the post-war period marked a clear change in orientation in that the principle of self-determination was understood to focus on the twin concerns of human rights and decolonisation and less on more general notions of group rights to political independence.

Self-determination was included in the United Nations Charter. Article 1(2) noted as one of the organisation's purposes the development of friendly relations among nations based upon respect for the principle of equal rights and self-determination, and Article 55 reiterated the phraseology. While it is doubtful that the reference to the principle in these very general terms was sufficient to entail its recognition as a binding right, its inclusion

---

3   See A. Cobban *The Nation-State and National Self-Determination* (London: Apollo Editions, 1969); D.H. Miller, *The Drafting of the Covenant* (vol. II, 1928) pp. 12-13 and S. Wambaugh *Plebiscites since the World War* (vol. I, 1933) p. 42.

4   See P. Thornberry *International Law and Minorities* (Oxford: Oxford University Press, 1991); I. Claude *National Minorities* (Cambridge: Cambridge University Press, 1955) and J. Lador-Lederer *International Group Protection* (Leiden: A.W. Sijthoff, 1968).

5   See Q. Wright *Mandates under the League of Nations* (New York: Greenwood Press, 1930) and H. Duncan Hall *Mandates, Dependencies and Trusteeships* (Washington: Carnegie Endowment, 1948).

6   See the Baltic States treaties, Martens *Recueil Général de Traités* 3rd Series, XI, pp. 864, 877 and 888 and Cobban (note 3) pp. 187-218.

7   LNOJ Supp. no.3, 1920, pp. 5-6 and Doc. B7/21/68/106[VII] pp. 22-23. See also J. Barros *The Aaland Islands Question* (New Haven: Yale University Press, 1968).

in the Charter, particularly within the context of the statement of purposes of the UN, provided the opportunity for the subsequent interpretation of the principle both in terms of its legal effect and consequences and with regard to its definition. It is also to be noted that Chapters XI and XII of the Charter deal with non-self-governing and trust territories respectively and may be seen as relevant within the context of the development and definition of the right to self-determination, although the term is not expressly used.[8]

Practice since 1945 within the UN, both generally as regards the elucidation and standing of the principle and more particularly as regards its perceived application in specific instances, can be seen as having ultimately established the legal standing of the right in international law. This was accomplished by the traditional methods of international law creation, that is by treaty, custom and, arguably, by virtue of constituting a general principle of law. The UN Charter is a multilateral treaty which can be interpreted by subsequent practice, while the range of state and organisation practice evident within the UN system can lead to the formation of customary law. The amount of material dealing with self-determination in the UN testifies to the importance of the concept. It is included in: resolution 1514 (XV), termed the Colonial Declaration, adopted in 1960; the two International Covenants on Human Rights, 1966, which contain an identical first article, declaring that: '[a]ll peoples have the right to self-determination. By virtue of that right they freely determine their political status'; and the 1970 Declaration on Principles of International Law Concerning Friendly Relations which can be regarded as constituting an authoritative interpretation of the seven Charter provisions it expounds. This Declaration states that 'by virtue of the principle of equal rights and self-determination of peoples enshrined in the Charter of the United Nations, all people have the right freely to determine...their political status' while all states are under the duty to respect this right in accordance with the Charter.

In addition, UN organs have dealt with self-determination in a series of specific resolutions with regard to particular situations and this practice may be adduced as reinforcing the conclusions that the principle has become a right in international law by virtue of a process of Charter interpretation. Numerous resolutions have been adopted in the General Assembly and also in the Security Council.[9] In addition to the Charter interpretation route, self-determination has also become binding as a principle of customary law in the light of the relevant international practice.[10]

---

8   See e.g. N. Bentwich and A. Martin *Commentary on the Charter of the UN* (London: Routledge and Paul, 1950) p. 7; D. Nincic *The Problem of Sovereignty in the Charter and the Practice of States* (The Hague: Martinus Nijhoff, 1970) p. 221; H. Kelsen *Law of the United Nations* (New York: F.A. Praeger, 1951) pp. 51-53 and H. Lauterpacht *International Law and Human Rights* (London: Stevens and Sons, 1950) pp. 147-49. See also Judge Tanaka, *South West Africa* cases, ICJ Reports, 1966, pp. 288-89.

9   See e.g. General Assembly resolutions 1755 (XVII); 2138 (XXI); 2151 (XXI); 2379 (XXIII); 2383 (XXIII) and Security Council Resolutions 183 (1963); 301 (1971); 377 (1975) and 384 (1975).

10   Outside of UN practice, see also Article 20 of the African Charter of Human and Peoples Rights (1981) and the Helsinki Final Act (1975).

The International Court of Justice has also affirmed the existence of the principle of self-determination, although without taking this very much further. In the *Namibia* case, it was emphasised that 'the subsequent development of international law in regard to non-self-governing territories as enshrined in the Charter of the United Nations made the principle of self-determination applicable to all of them'.[11] This approach was underlined in the *Western Sahara* case where the Court was asked for an opinion with regard to the legal ties between that territory at the time of colonisation and Morocco and the Mauritanian entity. The Court stressed that the request for an opinion arose out of the consideration by the General Assembly of the decolonisation of Western Sahara and that the right of the people of the territory to self-determination constituted a basic assumption of the questions put to the Court.[12] After analysing the Charter provisions and various General Assembly resolutions, the Court concluded that the ties which had existed between the claimants and the territory during the relevant period of the 1880s were not such as to affect the application of resolution 1514 (XV), the Colonial Declaration, in the decolonisation of the territory and in particular the right to self-determination. Thus, the Court regarded the principle of self-determination as a legal one in the context of such territories.

The Court moved one step further in the *East Timor (Portugal v Australia)* case,[13] noting that 'Portugal's assertion that the right of peoples to self-determination, as it evolved from the Charter and from United Nations practice, has an erga omnes character, is irreproachable'. The Court emphasised that the right of peoples to self-determination was 'one of the essential principles of contemporary international law'.[14] However, in that case, the Court, while noting that for both Portugal and Australia, East Timor (under Indonesian military occupation at that time) constituted a non-self-governing territory, and pointing out that the people of East Timor had the right to self-determination, held that the absence of Indonesia from the litigation meant that the Court was unable to exercise its jurisdiction.[15] The Court also referred to the principle of self-determination in passing in its Advisory Opinion on the *Legal Consequences of the Construction of a Wall in the Occupied Palestinian Territory*,[16] leaving open a number of critical and controversial questions.

There is thus in law a right to self-determination. This was reaffirmed relatively recently by the Supreme Court of Canada, which, in 1998, faced with the question as

---

11   ICJ Reports, 1971, p. 16 and p. 31.

12   Ibid. p. 68. See in particular the views of Judge Dillard that 'a norm of international law has emerged applicable to the decolonisation of those non-self-governing territories which are under the aegis of the United Nations', Ibid. pp. 121-22. See also Judge Petren, Ibid. p. 110.

13   ICJ Reports, 1995, p. 90 and p. 102.

14   Ibid.

15   Ibid. pp. 105-6. The reason related to the principle that the Court is unable to exercise jurisdiction over a state without the consent of that state. The Court took the view that Portugal's claims against Australia could not be decided upon without an examination of the position of Indonesia, which had not consented to the jurisdiction of the Court.

16   ICJ Reports, 2004, paras. 88, 149, 156 and 159.

to whether there existed in international law a right to self-determination which would give the province of Quebec the right unilaterally to secede, declared that the principle of self-determination 'has acquired a status beyond "convention" and is considered a general principle of international law'.[17]

The question therefore arises as to the definition of this principle. UN formulations of the principle from the 1960 Colonial Declaration to the 1966 International Covenants on Human Rights and the 1970 Declaration on Principles of International Law, stress that it is the right of 'all peoples'. If this is so, then all peoples would become thereby to some extent subjects of international law as the direct repositories of international rights, and if the definition of 'people' used was the normal political-sociological one,[18] a major re-arrangement of international law perceptions would have been created. In fact, that has not occurred and a particular concept in international law of what constitutes a people for the purposes of the full application of the norm in the sense of free political choice up to and including independence has evolved so that it is in effect and with rare exceptions limited to the accepted colonial territorial framework.

Attempts to broaden this have not been successful and the UN has always strenuously opposed any attempt at the partial or total disruption of the national unity and territorial integrity of a country.[19] The UN has based its policy on the proposition that 'the territory of a colony or other non-self-governing territory has under the Charter a status separate and distinct from the territory of the state administering it' and that such status was to exist until the people of that territory had exercised the right to self-determination.[20] Self-determination has also been used in conjunction with the principle of territorial integrity so as to protect the territorial framework of the colonial period in the decolonisation process and to prevent a rule permitting secession from independent states from arising.[21] The Canadian Supreme Court noted in the *Quebec* case that 'international law expects that the right to self-determination will be exercised by peoples within the framework of existing sovereign states and consistently with the maintenance of the territorial integrity of those states'.[22]

The principle of territorial integrity protects the territorial framework of independent states and is part of the overall concept of the sovereignty of states. In terms of the freezing of territorial boundaries as at the moment of independence (save by mutual consent), the norm is referred to as *uti possidetis juris*. This aspect of the principle is

---

17   (1998) 161 DLR (4th) 385 pp. 434-5.

18   See e.g. Cobban (note 3) p.107, and the *Greco-Bulgarian Communities* case, PCIJ, Series B, no. 17.

19   See e.g. the Colonial Declaration (1960); the Declaration on Principles of International Law (1970) and Article III [3] of the OAU Charter.

20   The Declaration on Principles of International Law (note 19).

21   See e.g. T. M. Franck *The Power of Legitimacy Among Nations* (Oxford: Oxford University Press, 1990), p. 153 *et seq.* and Shaw *Title to Territory* (note 2) Chapters 3 and 4.

22   (1998) 161 DLR (4th) paras. 385 and 436.

widely supported by international instruments[23] and by judicial pronouncement. In the *Burkina Faso/Mali* case,[24] for example, the Chamber of the International Court of Justice linked the principle to the protection of the independence and stability of new states by seeking to prevent self-determination from precipitating conflict through challenges to boundaries. As the Arbitration Commission of the European Conference on Yugoslavia emphasised in Opinion No. 2: 'it is well established that, whatever the circumstances, the right to self-determination must not involve changes to existing frontiers at the time of independence (*uti possidetis juris*) except where the states concerned agree otherwise'.[25]

Outside of the accepted definition of self-determination in its full sense to mean the right of European colonial territories to sovereignty presumptively within the existing colonial boundaries, there has also developed a principle of self-determination in international law that does not engage issues as to independence and thus territorial title, but operates within the recognised territory of a sovereign state.[26] This approach develops the human rights focus that made an appearance in the UN Charter and has been the subject of analysis particularly by the UN Human Rights Committee established by the International Covenant on Civil and Political Rights. This approach builds upon a distinction drawn between 'external' self-determination, that is the principle in its fullest extent, and 'internal' self-determination. The latter concept of self-determination marks the intersection of individual and group rights.

In its General Comment on Self-Determination adopted in 1984,[27] the Committee emphasised that the realisation of the right was 'an essential condition for the effective guarantee and observance of individual human rights'. Nevertheless, the principle is seen as a collective one and not one that individuals could seek to enforce through the individual petition procedures provided in the First Optional Protocol to the Covenant.[28] The Committee took the view that 'external self-determination requires a state to take action in its foreign policy consistent with the attainment of self-determination

---

23 See e.g. General Assembly resolutions 1514 (XV) and 1541 (XV) and Organisation of African Unity resolution 16(I)(1964).

24 ICJ Reports, 1986, pp. 554 and 566-7.

25 92 *ILR*, p. 167 and p. 168.

26 See e.g. Crawford (ed.) *The Rights of Peoples* (Oxford: Oxford University Press, 1988); C. Brölmann, R. Lefeber and M. Zieck (eds.) *Peoples and Minorities in International Law* (Dordrecht: Kluwer, 1993); P. Thornberry 'Self-Determination, Minorities, Human Rights: A Review of International Instruments', 38 *ICLQ* (1989) p. 867; M. Koskenniemi 'National Self-Determination Today' 43 *ICLQ* (1994) p. 241; G. Simpson 'The Diffusion of Sovereignty: Self-Determination in the Post-Colonial Age' 32 *Stanford Journal of International Law* (1996) p. 255 and R. McCorquodale 'Self-Determination: A Human Rights Approach', 43 *ICLQ* (1994) p. 857.

27 General Comment 12, see HRI/GEN/1/Rev.1, p. 12, 1994.

28 See e.g. the *Kitok* case, Report of the Human Rights Committee, A/43/40, para. 221 and para. 228;; the *Lubicon Lake Band* case, A/45/40, vol. II, pp. 1, 27; 96 *ILR*, para. 667 and para. 702; *EP v Colombia*, A/45/40, vol. II, para. 184 and para. 187 and *RL v Canada* A/47/40, para. 358 and para. 365. See also *Diergaardt et al. v. Namibia,* A/55/40, vol. II, annex IX, sect. M, para 10.3.

in the remaining areas of colonial or racist occupation. But internal self-determination is directed to their own peoples'.[29] In the context of the significance of the principle of self-determination within independent states, the Committee has, for example, encouraged states parties to provide in their reports details about participation in social and political structures,[30] and in engaging in dialogue with representatives of states parties, questions are regularly posed as to how political institutions operate and how the people of the state concerned participate in the governance of their state.[31] This necessarily links in with consideration of other articles of the Covenant concerning, for example, freedom of expression (article 19), freedom of assembly (article 21), freedom of association (article 22) and the right to take part in the conduct of public affairs and to vote (article 25). The right of self-determination, therefore, can be seen as providing the overall framework for the consideration of the principles relating to democratic governance.[32]

The Committee on the Elimination of Racial Discrimination adopted General Recommendation 21 in 1996 in which it similarly divided self-determination into an external and internal aspect and noted that the latter referred to the 'right of every citizen to take part in the conduct of public affairs at any level'. [33] The Canadian Supreme Court in the *Quebec* case emphasised that self-determination: 'is normally fulfilled through *internal* self-determination – a people's pursuit of its political, economic, social and cultural development within the framework of an existing state'.[34]

There is an argument, however, that seeks to build upon a savings clause in the 1970 Declaration on Principles of International Law Concerning Friendly Relations in order to justify an exception to the principle of territorial integrity and self-determination in this context. The clause in question states that nothing in the section on self-determination shall be construed as authorising or encouraging the dismembering or impairing of the territorial integrity of states conducting themselves in compliance with the principle of self-determination 'and thus possessed of a government representing the whole people belonging to the territory without distinction as to race, creed or colour'.[35]

However, this may be seen first, as establishing the primacy of the principle of territorial integrity and secondly, as indicating the content of self-determination within the territory (or internal self-determination). Whether it can also be seen as offering legitimacy to secession from an independent state in exceptional circumstances is the

---

29   See R. Higgins 'Postmodern Tribalism and the Right to Secession' in C. Brölmann, R. Lefeber and M. Zieck (eds.) *Peoples and Minorities in International Law* (note 26) p. 31.

30   See e.g. the Report of Colombia, CCPR/C/64/Add.3, p. 9 *et seq.*, 1991.

31   See e.g. with regard to Canada, A/46/40, p. 12. See also A/45/40, pp. 120-1, with regard to Zaire.

32   See P. Thornberry, 'The Democratic or Internal Aspect of Self-Determination' in *Modern Law of Self-Determination* (note 2) p. 101 and T. Franck 'The Emerging Right to Democratic Governance', 86 *AJIL* (1992) p. 46.

33   A/51/18.

34   (1998) 161 DLR (4ᵗʰ) para. 385 and paras. 437-8. Emphasis in original.

35   Tomuschat (ed.) *Modern Law of Self-Determination* (note 2) p. 118 *et seq.*

subject of much debate. Cassese, for example, concludes that 'a racial or religious group may attempt secession, a form of external self-determination, when it is apparent that internal self-determination is absolutely beyond reach. Extreme and unremitting persecution and the lack of any reasonable prospect for peaceful challenge may make secession legitimate'.[36]

The issue was discussed by the Canadian Supreme Court in the *Quebec* case. The Court noted that: '[A] right to *external* self-determination (which in this case potentially takes the form of the assertion of a right to unilateral secession) arises in only the most extreme of cases and, even then, under carefully defined circumstances', while '[T]he various international documents that support the existence of a peoples right to self-determination also contain parallel statements supportive of the conclusion that the exercise of such a right must be sufficiently limited to prevent threats to an existing states territorial integrity or the stability of relations between sovereign states'.[37] The exceptional circumstances which might ground a right to external self-determination outside of the colonial context is, in the words of the Court, in the 'exceptional circumstances' where: 'a definable group is denied meaningful access to government to pursue their political, economic, social and cultural development'.[38] Since Quebec clearly did not fall within this category, the Court pursued the matter no further and left its rather loose statement as it was. Nevertheless, considerable work remains to be done, firstly, to prevent such 'exceptional circumstances' from being regarded as normal thus raising the risk of precipitating a round of bloody secessions and secondly, to establish clearly and realistically the necessary criteria where such an exception might perhaps operate. In so doing, consideration of UN and other practice concerning intervention would be instructive.

The Intersection of the Norms Relating to the Use of Force and Self-Determination

Questions as to self-determination and the use of force are raised whichever form of the principle is under consideration in the particular situation. The basic norms governing the use of force since 1945 are essentially clear, but what is currently happening in practice, in the face of modifications of the international political system and through a revised approach to self-determination, is a rather more nuanced view as to the application of the rules as to resort to force.

Article 2(4) of the UN Charter calls upon states to refrain in their international relations from the threat or use of force against another state. It does not cover as such the resort to force by a people seeking self-determination against the colonial power. Until comparatively recently such situations were regarded as purely internal matters.

---

36   Ibid. p. 120. See also R. Rosenstock 'The Declaration on Principles of International Law' 65 *AJIL* (1971) p. 713 and p. 732.

37   (1998) DLR (4th) 385 at pp. 437-8.

38   Ibid. p. 442.

The colonial authority could use such force as it deemed necessary to suppress a riot or a rising without the issue impinging upon article 2(4). With the growing acceptance of self-determination as a legal right, the question as to the legitimacy of the use of force was raised. It was discussed at length in the debates of the Special Committee leading to the adoption of the Declaration on Principles of International Law in 1970.[39] In the event, the Declaration emphasised that all states were under a duty to refrain from any forcible action which deprives people of their right to self-determination.[40] This can now be regarded as accepted by the international community.

The Declaration also noted that 'in their actions against, and resistance to, such forcible action' such peoples could receive support in accordance with the purpose and principles of the UN Charter. This modest and ambiguous formulation could not be taken as recognition of a right to resort to force in claimed self-defence as inherent in the right of peoples entitled to self-determination. The UN Charter neither confirms nor denies a right of rebellion. It is neutral. International law does not forbid rebellion, it leaves it within the purview of domestic law. The General Assembly, however, began adopting resolutions in the 1970s reaffirming the legitimacy of the struggle of peoples for liberation from colonial domination and alien subjugation, 'by all available means including armed struggle'.[41] This approach was intensively debated in the process leading to the adoption by the Assembly of the Consensus Definition of Aggression in 1974.[42] In particular the issue centred upon whether the use of force by peoples entitled to self-determination was legitimate as self-defence against the very existence of colonialism itself, or as a response to force utilised to suppress the right of self-determination. The former view was taken by most Third World states and the latter by many Western states. In the event, a rather cumbersome formulation was presented in article 7 of the Definition which referred *inter alia* and in ambiguous vein to the right of peoples entitled to but forcibly deprived of the right of self-determination, 'to struggle to that end and to seek and receive support, in accordance with the principles of the Charter and in conformity' with the 1970 Declaration.[43]

---

39   See e.g. A/5746, para. 20 and 23 and paras. 42-45 and A/7326, paras. 103, 105, 109, 175 and 177. See also A/7619, paras. 167 and 168. The matter was argued indecisively with regard to India's invasion of Goa, see SCOR, 16th Year, 897th meeting, pp.9-11. See also S/5032 and S/5033 and Q. Wright, 'The Goa Incident', 56 *AJIL* (1962) p. 617.

40   See also para. 4 of the 1960 Colonial Declaration (note 19) and S. Schwebel, 'Wars of Liberation as Fought in UN Organs' in J.N. Moore (ed.) *Law and Civil War in the Modern World* (Baltimore: Johns Hopkins University Press, 1974) p. 446.

41   See e.g. resolutions 3070 (XXVIII), 3103 (XXVIII), 3246 (XXIX), 3328 (XXIX), 3481 (XXX), 31/91, 31/92, 32/42 and 32/154.

42   See e.g. A/7185/Rev.1, para. 60 and A/7402, paras. 16 and 61. See also A/8019, para. 47 and A/8929, paras. 34, 73, 74, 142 and 143.

43   Comments made following the adoption of the Definition clearly revealed the varying interpretations made by states of this provision, see e.g. A/C.6/SR.1472, paras. 5, 27 and 48 and A/C.6/SR.1480, paras. 8, 17, 25 and 73.

The argument as to whether self-determination (or national liberation) wars could be regarded as international, as distinct from internal, armed conflicts was also raised in the Diplomatic Conference on International Humanitarian Law,[44] which led to the adoption in 1977 of two Additional Protocols to the Geneva 'Red Cross' Conventions of 1949. Ultimately, article 1(4) of Protocol I was approved. It provides that international armed conflict situations 'include armed conflicts in which peoples are fighting against colonial domination and alien occupation and against racist regimes in the exercise of their right to self-determination' as enshrined in the Charter of the UN and the 1970 Declaration. The effect of this (within the clear self-determination context as defined in the Charter and the 1970 Declaration) is that the argument that valid self-determination conflicts are now to be accepted as within the international sphere of the activity of states has been greatly strengthened. The view that articles 2(4) and 51 of the Charter now apply to self-determination conflicts so that the peoples in question have a valid right to use force in self-defence is controversial and difficult to maintain. It is more likely that the principle of self-determination itself provides that where forcible action has been taken to suppress the right, force may be used in order to counter this and achieve self-determination. The use of force to suppress self-determination is now clearly unacceptable.

The question of third party assistance whether to suppress or support peoples seeking to manifest a right to self-determination leads logically to a consideration of the concept of intervention in international law as it has evolved to date.[45]

The principle of non-intervention is part of customary international law and founded upon the concept of respect for the territorial sovereignty of states.[46] Intervention is prohibited where it bears upon matters in which each state is permitted to decide freely by virtue of the principle of state sovereignty. This includes, as the International Court of Justice noted in the *Nicaragua* case,[47] the choice of political, economic, social and cultural systems and the formulation of foreign policy. Intervention becomes wrongful when it uses methods of coercion in regard to such choices, which must be free ones. There was 'no general right of intervention in support of an opposition within another state' in international law. In addition, acts constituting a breach of the customary principle of non-intervention will also, if they directly or indirectly involve the use of force, constitute a breach of the principle of the non-use of force in international rela-

44   See e.g. CDDH/SR.2 paras. 8-11 and 44-45.
45   See e.g. C. Gray *International Law and the Use of Force* (Oxford: Oxford University Press, 2000), Chapter 3; T. M. Franck *Recourse to Force* (Cambridge: Cambridge University Press, 2002); T. Farer 'The Regulation of Foreign Armed Intervention in Civil Armed Conflict' 142 II *HR* (1974) p. 291 and J. E. S. Fawcett, 'Intervention in International Law', 103 II *HR*, (1961) p. 347.
46   See the *Corfu Channel* case, ICJ Reports, 1949, p. 4 and p. 35 and the *Nicaragua* case, ICJ Reports, 1986, p. 14 and p. 106. See also the Declaration on the Inadmissibility of Intervention in the Domestic Affairs of States (1965) and the Declaration on the Principles of International Law (note 19).
47   ICJ Reports, 1986, p. 14 and pp. 108-11.

tions. The principle of respect for the sovereignty of states was another principle closely allied to the principles of the prohibition of the use of force and of non-intervention.

Classical international law treats civil wars[48] as purely internal matters. Article 2(4) of the UN Charter prohibits the threat or use of force in international relations, not in domestic situations. There is no rule against rebellion in international law. It is within the domestic jurisdiction of states and is left to be dealt with by internal law. Should the rebellion succeed, the resulting situation would be dealt with primarily in the context of recognition. As far as third parties are concerned, traditional international law developed the categories of rebellion, insurgency and belligerency.

Once a state has defined its attitude and characterised the situation, different international legal provisions would apply. If the rebels are regarded as criminals, the matter is purely within the hands of the authorities of the country concerned and no other state may legitimately interfere. If the rebels are treated as insurgents, then other states may or may not agree to grant them certain rights. It is at the discretion of the other states concerned, since an intermediate status is involved. The rebels are not mere criminals, but they are not recognised belligerents. Accordingly, the other states are at liberty to define their legal relationship with them. Insurgency is a purely provisional classification and would arise for example where a state needed to protect nationals or property in an area under the *de facto* control of the rebels.[49] On the other hand, belligerency is a formal status involving rights and duties. In the eyes of classical international law, other states may accord recognition of belligerency to rebels when certain conditions have been fulfilled. These were defined as the existence of an armed conflict of a general nature within a state, the occupation by the rebels of a substantial portion of the national territory, the conduct of hostilities in accordance with the rules of war and by organised groups operating under a responsible authority and the existence of circumstances rendering it necessary for the states contemplating recognition to define their attitude to the situation.[50] This would arise, for example, where the parties to the conflict are exercising belligerent rights on the high seas. Other maritime countries would feel compelled to decide upon the respective status of the warring sides, since the recognition of belligerency entails certain international legal consequences.

---

48   See e.g. *Law and Civil War in the Modern World* (note 40); E. Luard (ed.) *The International Regulation of Civil Wars* (Oxford: Oxford University Press, 1972); R. A. Falk (ed.) *The International Law of Civil Wars* (Baltimore: Johns Hopkins Press, 1971); R. Higgins, 'Intervention and International Law' in H. Bull (ed.) *Intervention in World Politics* (Oxford: Oxford University Press, 1984), p. 29; and C. C. Joyner and B. Grimaldi, 'The United States and Nicaragua: Reflections on the Lawfulness of Contemporary Intervention', 25 *Virginia JIL* (1985) p. 621.

49   See e.g. H. Lauterpacht *Recognition in International Law* (Cambridge: Cambridge University Press, 1947) p. 275 *et seq.*

50   See e.g. N. Mugerwa, 'Subjects of International Law' in M. Sørensen (ed.) *Manual of Public International Law* (London: Macmillan, 1968), p. 247 and pp. 286-88. See also R. Higgins, 'International Law and Civil Conflict' in *The International Regulation of Civil Wars* (note 48) p. 169 and pp. 170-71.

Once the rebels have been accepted by other states as belligerents they become subjects of international law and responsible in international law for all their acts. In addition the rules governing the conduct of hostilities become applicable to both sides, so that, for example, the recognising states must then adopt a position of neutrality.

However, these concepts of insurgency and belligerency are lacking in clarity and are extremely subjective. The absence of clear criteria, particularly with regard to the concept of insurgency, has led to a great deal of confusion. The issue is of importance since the majority of conflicts in the years since the conclusion of the Second World War have been in essence civil wars. The reasons for this are many and complex and ideological rivalry and decolonisation within colonially imposed boundaries are amongst them.

The international law rules dealing with civil wars have historically depended upon the categorisation by third states of the relative status of the two sides to the conflict. In traditional terms, an insurgency means that the recognising state may, if it wishes, create legal rights and duties as between itself and the insurgents, while recognition of belligerency involves an acceptance of a position of neutrality (although there are some exceptions to this rule) by the recognising states. But in practice, states very rarely make an express acknowledgement as to the status of the parties to the conflict, precisely in order to retain as wide a room for manoeuvre as possible. This means that the relevant legal rules cannot really operate as intended in classical law and that it becomes extremely difficult to decide whether a particular intervention is justified or not.

It would appear that in general outside aid to the government authorities in traditional international law[51] to repress a revolt is perfectly legitimate, provided, of course, it was requested by the legitimate government.[52] The general proposition, however, that aid to recognised governmental authorities is legitimate would be further reinforced where it could be shown that other states were encouraging or directing the subversive operations of the rebels. In such cases, it appears that the doctrine of collective self-defence would allow other states to intervene openly and lawfully on the side of the government authorities.[53] Practice further suggests that many forms of aid, such as economic, technical and arms provision arrangements, to existing governments faced with civil strife, may be acceptable.[54]

---

51   See e.g. L. Doswald-Beck, 'The Legal Validity of Military Intervention by Invitation of the Government', 56 *BYIL* (1985) p. 189 and Gray (note 45) p. 60 *et seq.*

52   As to difficulties in defining what a legitimate government may be in controversial situations such as the Grenada and Panama interventions, see Shaw, *International Law* (note 2) pp. 1042-43. See also J.N. Moore *Law and the Grenada Mission* (Charlottesville: Virginia University Press, 1984).

53   But in the light of the principles propounded in the *Nicaragua* case, ICJ Reports, 1986, p. 104 and pp. 120-3.

54   With regard to the UK continuance of arms sales to Nigeria during its civil war, see: Higgins 'International Law and Civil Conflict' (note 48) p.173. Note also the US policy of distinguishing between traditional supplier of arms and non-traditional supplier of arms in such circumstances. It would support aid provided by the former (as the UK in Nigeria), but not the latter, see *DUSPIL* (1976) p. 7.

However, an exception to these traditional rules would seem to exist with regard to self-determination, so that where foreign armed assistance is given to a government actively suppressing the legitimate right of a people to self-determination, such assistance would constitute an act in pursuance of an unlawful policy and thus itself contrary to international law. This, of course, is predicated upon the right to self-determination being relevant in the situation in question. The obvious example would be armed support to repress a colonial people seeking sovereignty, but such instances barely exist today. Other examples of claimed self-determination are more controversial and may be unlikely to accumulate the necessary international approval.

However, the question may be posed as to whether armed assistance may be provided to a government which is forcibly repressing the right to internal self-determination of its people. Here the matter is rather more complex. First, the definition of internal self-determination is to a meaningful extent ambiguous and amorphous. A group may indeed have the right to participate in the governance of the state in question, but it is at this stage unclear as to what forcible repression of this right may amount to, nor more critically at what stage the international community may legitimately conclude that the 'internal right of self-determination' was being 'forcibly suppressed.[55] On the other hand, it is also true that a full-scale armed assault by a state upon the human rights of its inhabitants may lead to UN intervention undertaken under current interpretations of Chapter VII of the Charter. It may also be the case that a right of humanitarian intervention exists where the level of that assault reaches critical levels enabling states outside of the UN framework to take forcible remedial action. An example where such an issue arose was in Kosovo in 1999.[56]

The justification for the NATO bombing campaign, acting out of area and without UN authorisation, in support of the repressed ethnic Albanian population of that province of Yugoslavia, was that of humanitarian necessity.[57] The Security Council by twelve votes to three rejected a resolution condemning NATO's use of force.[58] After the

---

55   Ibid. p. 9.

56   See as to the intervention by NATO states in Kosovo in 1999, Gray, *Use of Force,* p. 31; B. Simma, 'NATO, the UN and the Use of Force: Legal Aspects', 10 *EJIL* (1999) p. 1; Kofi A. Annan *The Question of Intervention: Statements by the Secretary-General* (New York, 1999); 'NATOs Kosovo Intervention', various writers, 93 *AJIL* (1999) pp. 824-62; D. Kritsiotis, 'The Kosovo Crisis and NATOs Application of Armed Force Against the Federal Republic of Yugoslavia', 49 *ICLQ* (2000) p. 330; P. Hilpod 'Humanitarian Intervention: Is There a Need for a Legal Reappraisal?', 12 *EJIL* (2001) p. 437 and 'Kosovo: House of Commons Foreign Affairs Committee 4th Report, June 2000', various memoranda, 49 *ICLQ* (2000) pp. 876-943.

57   See UKMIL, 70 *BYIL* (1999) p. 586. A British Foreign Office Minister wrote that, 'a limited use of force was justifiable in support of the purposes laid down by the Security Council but without the Councils express authorisation when that was the only means to avert an immediate and overwhelming humanitarian catastrophe', Ibid. p. 587 and see also Ibid. p. 598.

58   SCOR, 3989th meeting, 26 March 1999.

conflict, and after an agreement had been reached between NATO and Yugoslavia,[59] the Council adopted resolution 1244 (1999) which welcomed the withdrawal of Yugoslav forces from the territory and decided upon the deployment under UN auspices of international civil and military presences. There was no formal endorsement of the NATO action, but no condemnation, which could arguably be interpreted as acquiescence.[60] However, what is of particular interest for present purposes is that resolution 1244 reaffirmed the territorial integrity of the Federal Republic of Yugoslavia (now Serbia and Montenegro), so that it is difficult to extract from this case recognition of the right of the Kosovan population to self-determination in the sense of secession, although the violation of the human rights of the majority population by government forces was both condemned and acted against.[61]

Linked with this issue is the changing practice of the UN with regard to the meaning of 'international peace and security'. Initially predicated upon a clear differentiation between 'international' and 'internal' matters, with the latter falling within the domestic jurisdiction of states and thus outwith community action, current approaches have seen a blurring of such a distinction. Many issues that would prior to 1990 and the conclusion of the Cold War, and consequential almost automatic application of the Security Council veto by one of the two superpowers where its interests were seen as challenged, have been seen as purely internal and thus beyond the competence of UN interference or intervention, are now recognised as falling within the jurisdiction of international community action. One may instance the case of Haiti as a relevant example.

UN observers monitored an election in that country in 1990, but on 30 September 1991 the elected President Aristide was ousted. The UN Secretary-General appointed a Special Representative for Haiti on 11 December 1991, the General Assembly authorised a joint UN-Organisation of American States civilian mission on human rights (MICIVIH) on 20 April 1993[62] and on 16 June 1993, the Security Council imposed an arms and oil embargo on Haiti with sanctions to enter into force on 23 June 1993 unless the Secretary-General and the OAS reported that such measures were no longer warranted.[63] The Security Council referred to the fact that 'the legitimate Government of President Jean-Bernard Aristide' had not been reinstated and noted: 'the incidence of humanitarian crises, including mass displacements of population, becoming or aggravating threats to international peace and security'. The Council determined therefore that 'in these unique and exceptional circumstances', the continuation of the situation constituted a threat to international peace and security.

---

59   See 38 *ILM* (1999) p. 1217.
60   See e.g. J. Charney 'Anticipatory Humanitarian Intervention in Kosovo' 32 *Journal of Transnational Law*, (1999) p. 1231.
61   Note, however, the relative lack of concern of the international community with Chechnya, see e.g. J. Charney, 'Self-Determination: Chechnya, Kosovo and East Timor' 34 *Vanderbilt Journal of Transnational Law* (2001) p. 455.
62   See General Assembly resolution 47/20 B.
63   Security Council resolution 841 (1993).

Thus although the Security Council did not go so far as to declare that the removal of a legitimate Government constituted of itself a threat to peace, it was clearly the precipitating factor that taken together with other matters could enable a determination to be made under article 39 thus permitting the adoption of binding sanctions. The sanctions were suspended following the Governors Island Agreement of 3 July 1993.[64] However, in resolution 873 (1993), the Council determined that the failure by the military authorities in Haiti to fulfil obligations under that agreement constituted a threat to international peace and security, and sanctions were reimposed.[65] As the Appeal Chamber declared in the *Tadić* case: 'Indeed, the practice of the Security Council is rich with cases of civil war or internal strife which is classified as a 'threat to the peace' and dealt with under Chapter VII...It can thus be said that there is a common understanding, manifested by the 'subsequent practice' of the membership of the United Nations at large, that the 'threat to the peace' of article 39 may include, as one of its species, internal armed conflicts.[66]

Resolutions concerning Sierra Leone[67] affirmed that the civil war in that country constituted a threat to international peace, while resolutions concerning the mixed civil war/foreign intervention conflicts in the Democratic Republic of the Congo affirmed that there existed a 'threat to international peace and security in the region.'[68] The Security Council has also determined that 'widespread violations of international humanitarian law' constitutes a threat to peace.[69]

It thus logically follows that 'internal armed conflicts' constituting threats to international peace and security thus permitting outside intervention, at least by the UN and possibly also by regional organisations, would include such conflicts precipitated by the forcible suppression of the bundle of human rights known as 'internal self-determination'.

But if this situation is controversial and difficult, much more so is the question of aid to the people in question. Under traditional rules of international law, aid to rebels is unlawful. The 1970 Declaration on Principles of International Law emphasised that: '[n]o state shall organise, assist, foment, finance, incite or tolerate subversive, terrorist or armed activities directed towards the violent overthrow of the regime of another state, or interfere in civil strife in another state'.[70] The Declaration also provided that: '[e]very

---

64   Security Council resolution 861 (1993).
65   Security Council resolution 873 (1993). Further sanctions were imposed in resolution 917 (1994). Sanctions were finally lifted by resolution 944 (1994),
66   105 *ILR* pp. 419, 466.
67   See e.g. Security Council resolutions 1132 (1997); 1156 (1995); 1181 (1998); 1220 (1999); 1231 (1999); 1260 (1999); 1299 (2000) and 1436 (2002).
68   See e.g. Security Council resolutions 1291 (2000); 1376 (2001); 1399 (2002) and 1468 (2003).
69   See Security Council resolutions 808 (1993), with regard to former Yugoslavia and 955 (1994) with regard to Rwanda.
70   See also in similar terms the Declaration on the Inadmissibility of Intervention in the Domestic Affairs of States, 1965. Article 3(g) of the General Assembly's Consensus Defini-

state shall refrain from any action aimed at the partial or total disruption of the national unity and territorial integrity of any other state or country'.

This would seem fairly conclusive, but in fact state practice is far from unanimous on this point. Where a prior, illegal intervention on the government side has occurred, it may be argued that aid to the rebels is acceptable. This was argued by a number of states with regard to the Afghanistan situation, where it was felt that the Soviet move into that state amounted to an invasion.[71]

The case of the Democratic Republic of the Congo is instructive. Intervention took place by Uganda and Rwanda initially against rebel movements acting against them from Congolese territory and then to assist rebels against the Congolese government, and by a number of states including Zimbabwe, Angola and Namibia on behalf of the government. In resolution 1234 (1999), the Security Council reaffirmed the need for all states to refrain from interfering in the internal affairs of other states and called upon states to bring to an end the presence of uninvited forces of foreign states.[72] The Council called for the orderly withdrawal of all foreign forces from the Congo in accordance with the Lusaka Ceasefire Agreement[73] in 1999.[74] Security Council resolution 1304 (2000) went further and acting under Chapter VII demanded that 'Uganda and Rwanda, which have violated the sovereignty and territorial integrity of the Democratic Republic of the Congo withdraw all their forces from the territory of the Democratic Republic of the Congo without delay'. An end to all other foreign military presence and activity was also called for in conformity with the provisions of the Lusaka agreement.[75] The UN also established a mission in the Congo (MONUC) in 1999, whose mandate was subsequently extended. It can thus be seen that the UN clearly distinguished between aid to the government and aid to rebels and was less sympathetic to the latter.

The question of third party assistance to peoples struggling to attain self-determination is highly controversial, and has been the subject of disagreement between western and some Third World states. A number of UN General Assembly resolutions have called on states to provide all forms of moral and material assistance to such peoples,[76]

---

tion of Aggression, 1974, characterises as an act of aggression 'the sending by or on behalf of a state of armed bands, groups, irregulars or mercenaries, which carry out acts of armed force against another state'. See also the *Nicaragua* case, ICJ Reports, 1986, p. 14.

71   See e.g. *Keesings Contemporary Archives,* pp. 30339, 30364 and 30385. See also General Assembly resolutions ES-62; 35/37; 36/34; 37/37 and 38/29 condemning the USSR for its armed intervention in Afghanistan. See also Doswald-Beck, 'Legal Validity', p. 230 *et seq.*

72   See Gray (note 45) p. 53.

73   See S/1999/815.

74   Security Council resolution 1291 (2000).

75   See also Security Council resolutions 1341 (2001) and 1355 (2001). Security Council resolution 1376 (2001) welcomed the withdrawal of some forces, including the full Namibian contingent, from the Congo. See also resolutions 1417 (2002), 1457 (2003) and 1468 (2003).

76   See e.g. resolutions 2105 (XX), 2160 (XX), 2465 (XXIII), 2649 (XXV), 2734 (XXV), 2787 (XXVI), 3070 (XXVIII), 3163 (XXVIII), 2328 (XXIX), 3421 (XXX), 31/29, 31/33, 32/10 and 32/154.

but the legal situation is still far from clear and the provision of armed help would appear to be unlawful.[77]

A further point, of particular resonance today, is that any use of force as between a government and a people recognised as being entitled to self-determination which was being forcibly repressed, would be constrained by the evolution of rules both of international humanitarian law and of those concerning the prohibition of terrorism.

Insofar as the former is concerned, the basic rule formulated in article 48 of Protocol I to the Geneva Conventions 1977 is that the parties to the conflict must at all times distinguish between such population and combatants and between civilian and military objectives and must direct their operations only against military objectives. Article 51 provides that the civilian population as such, as well as individual civilians, 'shall not be the object of attack. Acts or threats of violence the primary purpose of which is to spread terror among the civilian population are prohibited.' Additionally, indiscriminate attacks[78] are prohibited. Article 57 provides that in the conduct of military operations 'constant care shall be taken to spare the civilian population, civilians and civilian objects'. The International Court in its Advisory Opinion on the *Legality of the Threat or Use of Nuclear Weapons*[79] summarised the situation in the following authoritative way:

> 'The cardinal principles contained in the texts constituting the fabric of humanitarian law are the following. The first is aimed at the protection of the civilian population and civilian objects and establishes the distinction between combatants and non-combatants; states must never make civilians the object of attack and must consequently never use weapons that are incapable of distinguishing between civilian and military targets. According to the second principle, it is prohibited to cause unnecessary suffering to combatants; it is accordingly prohibited to use weapons causing them such harm or uselessly aggravating their suffering. In application of that second principle, states do not have unlimited freedom of choice of means in the weapons they use'.

The Court emphasised that the fundamental rules flowing from these principles bound all states since they constituted 'intransgressible principles of international customary law'.[80]

---

77   See e.g. 17/8018, paras. 234 and 235, and J. Stone *Conflict Through Consensus* (Baltimore: John Hopkins University Press, 1977) pp. 66-86 and B. Ferencz *Defining International Aggression* (Dobbs Ferry: Oceana, vol.2, 1975) p. 48, with regard to the ambiguous formulation in the 1974 Definition of Aggression.

78   These are defined in article 51(4) as: (a) those which are not directed at a specific military objective; (b) those which employ a method or means of combat which cannot be at a specific military objective; or (c) those which employ a method or means of combat the effects of which cannot be limited as required by Protocol I; and consequently in each such case are of a nature to strike military objectives and civilians or civilian objects without distinction.

79   ICJ Reports, 1996, p. 226 and p. 257.

80   Ibid.

At the heart of such rules and principles, lies the 'overriding consideration of humanity'.[81]

In so far as international terrorism is concerned, the UN has adopted twelve international conventions concerning terrorism, dealing with issues ranging from hi-jacking, hostages and terrorist bombings. Many of these conventions operate on a common model, establishing the basis of quasi-universal jurisdiction with an interlocking network of international obligations. The General Assembly adopted in 1994 a Declaration on Measures to Eliminate International Terrorism,[82] condemning 'all acts, methods and practices of terrorism, as criminal and unjustifiable, wherever and by whomever committed', and noting that 'criminal acts intended or calculated to provoke a state of terror in the general public, a group or person or persons or particular persons for political purposes are in any circumstance unjustifiable, whatever the considerations of a political, philosophical, ideological, racial, ethnic, religious or any other nature that may be invoked to justify them'. Further, the Security Council has characterised international terrorism as a threat to international peace and security.[83]

The Council took this a stage further in resolution 1373 (2001) which demanded *inter alia* the prevention and suppression of the financing of terrorist acts, the criminalisation of wilful provision or collection of funds for such purposes and the freezing of financial assets and economic resources of persons and entities involved in terrorism. Further, states were called upon to refrain from any support to those involved in terrorism and take action against such persons, and to cooperate with other states in preventing and suppressing terrorist acts and acting against the perpetrators. The Council also established a Counter-Terrorism Committee to monitor implementation of the resolution.[84]

In addition to UN activities,[85] a number of regional instruments condemning terrorism have been adopted. These include the European Convention on the Suppression of Terrorism 1977; the South Asian Association for Regional Cooperation Regional Convention on Suppression of Terrorism 1987, the Arab Convention for the Suppression of Terrorism 1998, the Convention of the Organisation of the Islamic Conference on Combating International Terrorism 1999 and the Organisation of American States Inter-American Convention against Terrorism 2002. In addition, the Organisation on Security and Cooperation in Europe adopted a Ministerial Declaration and Plan of Action on Combating Terrorism in 2001.

---

81   Ibid. and pp. 262-63. See also the *Corfu Channel* case, ICJ Reports, 1949, p. 4 and p. 22. Note also the critical point made by Judge Higgins in her Separate Opinion in the *Legal Consequences of the Construction of a Wall* case that: 'the protection of civilians remains an intransgressible obligation of humanitarian law, not only for the occupier but equally for those seeking to liberate themselves from occupation', ICJ Reports, 2004, para. 19.

82   General Assembly resolution 49/60.

83   See e.g. resolutions 731 (1992); 1070 (1996) and 1368 (2001).

84   See also resolution 1377 (2001).

85   See also e.g. the statement by the UN Committee on the Elimination of Racial Discrimination of 8 March 2002 condemning the September 11th 2001 attacks in the US and affirming that all acts of terrorism were contrary to the UN Charter and human rights instruments, A/57/18, pp. 106-7.

Conclusion

The old certainties as to the use of force are fading under the impact of the changed international situation with regard to failing states and consequential pressures for secession, international terrorism and more active international community behaviour through the UN and regional organisations. To this one may add increased activity by the US in the light of its changed perception as to its interests in the world and challenges thereto. In so far as self-determination is concerned, increasing uncertainties arise due to the consequences now becoming apparent of a broader approach to definition concerning what has been called internal self-determination. In particular, questions will need to be addressed as to the extent to which the rules governing the resort to and use of force apply to repression of this version of self-determination. As domestic pressures increase and as the international competence and will to act in what only a decade and a half ago were regarded as purely internal matters, the frailties of the existing norms and principles concerning self-determination and force will become ever more apparent.

Chapter 4

Conceptual Difficulties and the Right to Indigenous Self-Determination

Joshua Castellino [1]

Introduction

The discussion of the issue of self-determination and indigenous peoples always seems extremely unsatisfying for the reason that while self-determination is the ultimate goal that reifies statehood, this goal seems particularly impossible to reconcile with many of the specific instances in which indigenous peoples live. [2] Difficulties arise at every turn in seeking to accommodate indigenous claims. For a start, the language of self-determination itself is extremely problematic and has undergone several different manifestations at various points in history. As a result it has a multitude of meanings that are tedious to unpack, and whose true content varies significantly from situation to situation and from era to era. [3] The confusion in discourse has not been helped by constant references to self-determination at various points in time by leaders such as Woodrow Wilson who have raised its emotive banner without being fully aware of its consequences, or the hopes that these could nourish. [4] As a result the discourse of self-determination has always come across as international double-speak with uncertain meaning. Indigenous

---

[1]   Lecturer, Irish Centre for Human Rights, National University of Ireland, Galway, Republic of Ireland.

[2]   For a general reading on self-determination and indigenous peoples see L. Maivan-Clech *At the Edge of the State: Indigenous Peoples and Self-Determination* (Ardsley, NY: Transnational, 2000) and B. Kingsbury 'Self-determination and "Indigenous Peoples"' 86 *Proceedings of the American Society of International Law* (1992) pp. 383-394.

[3]   For a general reading on self-determination see G. Binder 'The Case for Self-determination' 29 *Stanford Journal of International Law* (1993) pp. 223-270; L. C. Buchheit *Secession: The Legitimacy of Self-determination* (New Haven: Yale University Press, 1978); A. Cassese *Self-Determination of Peoples, A Legal Reappraisal* (Cambridge: Cambridge University Press, 1995); H. Hannum *Autonomy, Sovereignty and Self-determination: The Accommodation of Conflicting Rights* (Philadelphia, University of Pennsylvania Press, 1990).

[4]   See A. Whelan 'Wilsonian Self-Determination and the Versailles Settlement' 43 *International and Comparative Law Quarterly* (1994) pp. 99-115, and especially I. Jennings *The Approach to Self-Governance* (Cambridge: Cambridge University Press, 1956) pp. 55-56.

Nazila Ghanea & Alexandra Xanthaki (eds.), Minorities, Peoples and Self-Determination, *pp. 55-74.*
© *2005 Koninklijke Brill NV. Printed in The Netherlands. ISBN 90 04 14301 7.*

peoples' first real brush with international society at large involved this very idea and occurred precisely for the reason of the aspirations such a banner raised.

The incident in question took place in 1924 when General Levi, chief of the Younger Bear Clan – one of the six nations of the Iriquos Confederacy in North America – sought to petition the League of Nations. Spurred by the stirring statements of Woodrow Wilson to the effect that the new organisation would recognise all nations great and small,[5] the Chief arrived with his grievance in Geneva in 1923 and spent a year preparing his petition. His plea was straight-forward: to challenge the basis of the *Indian Act* passed by the Canadian government at the end of World War I. It was clear that the provisions of this new act would see a fundamental revocation of the provisions in the *Jay Treaty of 1794* and the *Treaty of Ghent 1814* signed between Great Britain and the United States,[6] which sought to guarantee Iriquois sovereignty. Instead it would bring the affairs of the Six Nations Confederacy directly under the rule of Ottawa.

The statements of Wilson appealed to General Levi who saw this as a clear violation of sovereignty, and decided to appeal to the international community for support. He had already been unsuccessful in his petition to the Governor General of Canada, and subsequently in 1921 with a petition to King George V of Great Britain. But in approaching the League of Nations he believed he would be heard since the organisation was meant to be a guarantee to 'great and small states alike.' In Switzerland he managed to invoke some support for his cause notably from states such as Estonia, Ireland, Panama and Persia but Great Britain, representing Canada, effectively ensured that the plea was never presented to the League of Nations. Disappointed, General Levi was interviewed on Swiss radio and had the following to say:

> We appealed to Ottawa in the name of our right as a separate people and by right of our treaties, and the door was closed in our faces. We then went to London with our treaty and asked for the protection it promised and got no attention. Then we went to the League of Nations at Geneva with its covenant to protect little peoples and to enforce respect for treaties by its members and we spent a whole year patiently waiting but got no hearing.[7]

---

5   Wilson famously said: 'A general association of nations must be formed under specific covenants for the purpose of affording mutual guarantees of political independence and territorial integrity to great and small states alike. In regard to these essential rectifications of wrong and assertions of right we feel ourselves to be intimate partners of all the governments and peoples associated together against the Imperialists.' See W. Wilson, 'Speech on the Fourteen Points' (1918), Congressional Record, 65th Congress 2nd Session, pp. 680-81. See also R. S. Baker and W. E. Dodds *The Public Papers of Woodrow Wilson* (New York: Harper, 1925-1927).

6   See especially, Article 9, *Treaty of Ghent (1814)*, signed after the War of 1812 between Great Britain and the United States of America.

7   Radio speech on 10 March 1925, Rochester Radio, from *DESKAHEH – Iroquois Statesman And Patriot* (Akwesasne Notes – Mohawk Nation).

In tracing the history of the indigenous movement Malezer narrates this, and other incidents that were taking place at the same time as indigenous peoples sought recognition of their claims.[8] None of these claims was entertained as the international community still considered indigenous peoples as 'backward', and in need of 'civilisation'.[9] In a famous speech as late as 1937 Winston Churchill, British leader and recognised statesman had the following to say on the subject of subjugation:

> I do not agree that the dog in a manger has the final right to the manger even though he may have lain there for a very long time. I do not admit that right. I do not admit for instance, that a great wrong has been done to the Red Indians of America or the black people of Australia. I do not admit that a wrong has been done to these people by the fact that a stronger race, a higher-grade race, a more worldly wise race to put it that way, has come in and taken their place.[10]

Although speaking on that occasion in the context of the Palestinian claim to its homeland in the Middle East, Churchill's statement succinctly captures the sentiment that underlies the treatment of native populations in the wake of conquering powers.

It has been a significantly long road from the attitude met by General Levi in 1924, to the events of the 24th of May 2002. On this latter occasion Kofi Anan, UN Secretary General, ended a two week session discussing indigenous issues in New York with the words: 'You have a home at the United Nations … you will make an immense contribution to the Organization's mission of peace and governance'.[11] The occasion was the opening session of the Permanent Forum on Indigenous Peoples,[12] a high-level body consisting 8 indigenous representatives and 8 state representatives who meet annually to discuss issues relevant to indigenous peoples. The potential significance of this particular forum, is that unlike the Working Group on Indigenous Populations,[13] this body is directly responsible to the Economic and Social Council and the General Assembly.[14] In

---

8   Notably a Maori effort led by Mr. T.W. Ratana who came with a complaint that the *Treaty of Waitangi* had been violated. See L. Malezer 'Permanent Forum on Indigenous Issues: Welcome to the Family of the UN' in Castellino and Walsh (eds.) *Indigenous Peoples in International Law* (The Hague: Kluwer and the Raoul Wallenberg Institute, 2004) forthcoming.

9   For language that reflects this ideology see the text of ILO Convention No. 107 *Convention Concerning Indigenous and Tribal Populations* (1957).

10 As quoted by Arundhati Roy in 'Come September', a speech organised by the Lannon Foundation. See www.lannan.org (accessed 6 April 2004).

11 Statement available on www.un.org/esa/socdev/pfii/PFII1/pfii1.htm (accessed 6 April 2004).

12 Created by ECOSOC Res. 2000/22. Details of the organisation are available on www. un.org/esa/socdev/unpfii/index.html (accessed 6 June 2004).

13 Established pursuant to ECOSOC Res. 1982/34 as a subsidiary organ of the Sub-Commission on the Promotion and Protection of Human Rights.

14 For more information on the Permanent Forum see http://www.unhchr.ch/indigenous/mandate.htm (accessed 6 April 2004).

this sense it supersedes the entire human rights mechanism and reports directly to the United Nations.

Conceptual Difficulties Locating Indigenous Peoples in Human Rights Law

Despite the significant alleviation in the treatment of indigenous peoples in international human rights law, one of the biggest conceptual difficulties remains the indigenous claim to the right to self-determination. This particular problem is underpinned by a deep confusion as to how to locate indigenous peoples within the current system of burgeoning human rights law.[15] Kingsbury has sought to unravel this particular question by suggesting that there are at least five competing conceptual claims that can be advanced in advocating for indigenous rights, namely:

(1)   Human rights and non-discrimination claims
(2)   Minority Claims
(3)   Self-determination Claims
(4)   Historic sovereignty claims
(5)   *Sui generis* claims as Indigenous Peoples[16]

Accepting the interlocking nature of these five conceptual grounds Kingsbury admits:

> In political negotiations about normative matters, the question of which concept is applicable often is set up as a key threshold issue: its resolution is seen as a key to channelising arguments, determining which structure of analysis and legitimation will then prevail, and thus influencing outcomes.[17]

For a better understanding of the concept of indigenous peoples' rights and self-determination it is worth dwelling a little on some of the arguments within competing conceptual bases. These arguments are central to understanding why self-determination

---

15   This discussion has been captured in academic writing and is best summarised in P. Thornberry *Indigenous Peoples and International Law* (Manchester: Manchester University Press, 2002). For other notable works on the subject see R. L. Barsh 'Indigenous Peoples and the UN Commission on Human Rights: A Case of Immovable Object and Irresistible Force' 18 Human Rights Quarterly (1996) pp. 782-813; S. Wiessner 'Rights and Status of Indigenous Peoples: A Global Comparative and International Legal Analysis' 12 *Harvard Human Rights Law Journal* (1999) pp. 57-128; S. J. Anaya 'A Contemporary Definition of the International Norm of Self-Determination' 3 *Transnational Law and Contemporary Problems* (1993) pp. 131-147 (1993).

16   B. Kingsbury 'Reconciling Five Competing Conceptual Structures of Indigenous Peoples' Claims in International and Comparative Law' 34 *New York University Journal of International Law* (2002) pp. 189 – 245. For a different approach see W. Kymlicka 'Theorizing Indigenous Rights' 49 *University of Toronto Law Journal* (1999) pp. 281-292.

17   Ibid. p. 191.

remains fundamental to indigenous rights to the extent that it is currently stalling significant declarations before the United Nations[18] and the Inter-American Commission.[19]

It is worth considering first and foremost whether the claim of indigenous peoples rights has any merit as a *sui generis* category. There has been significant movement in this regard, as seen in the creation of the Permanent Forum on Indigenous Peoples. The ILO and the World Bank have also both attempted to create a *sui generis* category of rights for indigenous peoples and while the effect of the former has been less significant, owing to the small number of states that are party to ILO Convention 169, the latter is seriously altering the manner in which the World Bank operates in areas where indigenous peoples are present.[20] Arguably the high level of activity within the Inter-American system of Human Rights[21] on issues of indigenous rights also suggests that the day will not be far when indigenous rights come to occupy a more central position within human rights law in that region.

However the 'crafting [of] substantive legal rules on the basis of their applicability in cases involving a distinct category of indigenous peoples can be a subtle and perilous task if high priority is given to reconciling them with the [other] four existing frameworks'.[22] A less risky approach and one to be more commended is the approach adopted

---

18   The *Draft Declaration on the Rights of Indigenous Peoples* was passed in 1993 by the United Nations Working Group on Indigenous Populations – a body that reports to the Sub-Commission on Promotion and Protection of Human Rights. See *Draft United Nations Declaration on the Rights of Indigenous Peoples*, UN Doc. E/CN.4/Sub.2/1994/56, Sub-Commission on Prevention of Discrimination and Protection of Minorities, Report of the Sub-Commission on Prevention of Discrimination and Protection of Minorities on its 46th session, Resolution 45/1994. Annex. Despite the passage of the declaration into law being one of the main aims of the Decade of Indigenous Peoples, the Commission on Human Rights terminated the decade in 2004 without its passage. One of the key stumbling blocks has been identified as the right to self-determination. See E-I.Daes 'Equality of Indigenous Peoples under the Auspices of the United Nations Draft Declaration on the Rights of Indigenous Peoples' 7 *St. Thomas Law Review* (1995) pp. 493-519.

19   The *Proposed American Declaration on Indigenous Peoples* has been more successful than its international counterpart and has resulted in a significant spurt in the activities related to indigenous peoples in the Inter-American Commission on Human Rights. However due to the recalcitrance of some states this declaration too is awaiting passage. OEA/Ser./L/V/II. 110 Doc. 22 (2001), available at:
      http://www.cidh.oas.org/Indigenas/Indigenas.en.01/index.htm (accessed 24 May 2004).

20   F. MacKay 'Universal Rights or a Universe unto Itself? Indigenous Peoples' Human Rights and the World Bank's Draft Operational Policy 4.10 on Indigenous Peoples' 17 *American University International Law Review* (2002) pp. 527-624.

21   Evidenced by the preponderance of indigenous issues raised in every country report, and by the high number of individual complaints that raise indigenous issues to a certain extent. See R. J. Wilson and J. Perlin 'The Inter-American Human Rights System: Activities from Late 2000 Through October 2002' 18 *American University International Law Review* (2002) pp. 651-752.

22   B. Kingsbury (note 16) p. 238.

by the Human Rights Committee (HRC) which is willing to recognise indigenous peoples' claims in a separate category, but subject to the same human rights as every other human being.[23] This is particularly apparent in *Hopu v France*[24] where the HRC was prepared to interpret the general human rights provisions under their mandate, in a manner in which the particular belief of an indigenous group could be accommodated. According to Kingsbury, evidence suggests that a category of claims by indigenous peoples is emerging as a distinct conceptual structure though it certainly is not the case that every claim by an indigenous group or person falls into that category.[25]

The conceptual bases of minority rights and human rights identified by Kingsbury are closely interlinked.[26] The protection of the rights of minorities is arguably one of the axes along which international law itself evolved, with treaties as far back as 1250 seeking to guarantee the rights of linguistic and religious groups.[27] In tracing the early history of minority rights protection, Thornberry has revealed the wide proliferation of these standards all across Europe.[28] Yet though significant in terms of pedigree, minority rights law was relegated to a lesser status with the passage of the International Bill of Rights in the United Nations era. Article 27 of the International Covenant on Civil and Political Rights (ICCPR), the sole article that explicitly refers to minorities, is couched in cautious terms, leaving the onus on states 'in which national minorities exist'.[29] Instead discussion has centred around the extent to which the minority rights article interlinks with that of the self-determination provision in article 1.[30] In this particular context it is also worth remembering the discussion referred to as the 'Belgian Thesis' with regards

---

23   For a general reading on rights, including those of indigenous peoples before the Human Rights Committee see T. S. Orlin, A. Rosas and M. Scheinin *The Jurisprudence of Human Rights Law: A Comparative Interpretive Approach* (Institute for Human Rights: Åbo Akademi University, 2000) and S. Joseph, J. Schultz and M. Castan *The International Covenant on Civil and Political Rights: Cases, Materials, and Commentary* (Oxford: Oxford University Press, 2000).

24   *Hopu and Bessert v France*, (Communication No 549/1993), Views of the United Nations Human Rights Committee, adopted 29 July 1997 [1997] IIHRL 85 (29 July 1997).

25   B. Kingsbury (note 16) p. 244.

26   For an earlier work that looked at similar issues in the broader context of minority rights see P. Ramaga 'The Bases of Minority Identity' 14 *Human Rights Quarterly* (1992) pp. 409-428.

27   The *Promise of St. Louis of France* of 1250 to protect the Maronites. For this and a concise history of the evolution of minority rights law see P. Thornberry *International Law and the Rights of Minorities* (Oxford: Oxford University Press, 1994) p. 27.

28   Notably the *Treaty of Olivia of 1660*, the *Convention for the Settlement of the Frontier between Greece and Turkey, 1881*, the *Convention of Constantinople of 1879* and the *Treaties of Koutchouk-Kainardji of 1774*, and *Adrianople 1829*. Ibid. pp. 25-28

29   Article 27 states that '*In those States in which ethnic, religious or linguistic minorities exist, persons belonging to such minorities shall be not denied the right, in community with the other members of the group, to enjoy their own culture, to profess and practice their own religion, or to use their own language*'. [Emphasis added]

30   T.D. Musgrave *Self-determination and National Minorities* (Oxford: Oxford University Press, 2000).

to the twinning of the agenda of minority rights with that of self-determination and the right to the creation of a separate state.[31]

The interlinking of minority rights and general human rights law is also equally significant. While human rights law based on the principles of non-discrimination and equality seeks to guarantee the 'rights basket' to every individual, irrespective of identifying or distinguishing features, minority rights seek to add an extra layer of protection to those groups which are particularly vulnerable and whose rights have historically been trampled on due to their difference in ethnicity, language or religion amongst other criteria. Thus it could be argued that minority rights law seeks to provide an avenue, through the application of affirmative action measures, by which particular groups can seek to close the gap between themselves and the majority population of the state.[32]

The idea of using human rights law to further the cause of indigenous peoples has resulted in a plethora of cases before the HRC. While some of these have directly raised issues pertaining to article 27 of the ICCPR, other articles too have been highlighted.[33] One of the more controversial aspects in terms of the HRC and indigenous peoples has been its acceptance in more recent years of the validity of claims made by indigenous peoples in claiming violations of article 1(2) of the ICCPR, hitherto considered beyond the scope of the Committee.[34]

In rulings in the context of article 27, the definitive case is arguably *Ominayak v Canada* (also known as the Lubicon Lake Band Case).[35] In this case the HRC concluded that the historical inequity of the failure to assure the Band a reservation to which it had a strong claim, and the effect of this failure on the Band itself (in terms of mining concessions and oil exploring licences), constituted a violation of article 27. The *ratio* for the decision was that the failure ultimately 'threatened the way of life and culture of the Lubicon Lake Band…as long as they continue'.[36] The spirit of this finding was also

---

31   Thornberry (note 27) pp. 16-18. Also see UN Doc. A/AC.67/2, pp. 3-31. Also see 89 Rec. des Cours 321, *The Question of Aborigines Before the United Nations: The Belgian Thesis* (1954).

32   For more on the fight against racial discrimination see M. Banton *International Action Against Racial Discrimination* (Oxford: Oxford University Press, 1993).

33   For a list of cases concerning minority rights before the Human Rights Committee see http://www.minority-rights.org/docs.php#cases (accessed 6 April 2004).

34   Article 1(2) states that: 'All peoples may, for their own ends, freely dispose of their natural wealth and resources without prejudice to any obligations arising out of international economic co-operation, based upon the principle of mutual benefit, and international law. In no case may a people be deprived of its own means of subsistence'. For a general discussion of the HRC cases on this issue see M. Scheinin, in P. Aikio and M. Scheinin (eds) *Operationalizing the Right of Indigenous Peoples to Self-Determination,* (Tuku/Åbo: Institute for Human Rights, Åbo Akademi University, 2000).

35   *Bernard Ominayak, Chief of the Lubicon Lake Band* v. *Canada* (Communication 167/1984), Views adopted 26 March 1990, Report of the Human Rights Committee, GAOR, Thirty-eighth session, Suppl. No. 40 (A/38/40), pp. 1-30.

36   Ibid. p. 29.

reflected in concluding comments regarding the dam projects on the Biobio river in Chile and their effect on the Mapuche and other indigenous communities.[37]

The raising of issues under article 27 has also been relatively successful in the context of the violation of the rights (including land rights) of the Ainu in Japan.[38] The discussion surrounding the submission of the Japanese report spurred national debate which challenged for the first time the belief that the state was homogenous.[39]

Of course as far as indigenous peoples are concerned, the minorities clause is a double-edged sword, as was revealed in *Sandra Lovelace v Canada*.[40] Here it was established that when a group member uses article 27 to challenge the minority group itself, the special measures afforded to that group are defeated relatively easily. Showing great caution as to the potential ramifications of this defeat, the HRC carefully trod the line and rather than making general findings, restricted its scope to the specific circumstances of Sandra Lovelace and her divorce from the non-Indian she married, and her subsequent right to live on the Indian Reservation.

While the case law on article 27 is relatively well developed, Article 1, the self-determination article, was hitherto considered off bounds.[41] Several reasons can be attributed for this reluctance including: the political doctrine exception;[42] the fact that this was a collective right and thus could not be raised in an individual petition; that the substantive rights were contained in Part Two of the document and that article 1 was merely pre-ambular in nature. Thus when early complainants such as *Mikmaq* sought to raise this question the Committee dispelled it categorically.[43] Yet by the time of the two *Länsmann* cases[44] and *Äärelä and Näkkäläjärvi v. Finland*[45] a new approach could

---

37   See *Concluding Observations of the Human Rights Committee: Chile*, passed on 30th March 1999 UN Doc. CCPR/C/79/add.104, para. 22.

38   See *Concluding Observations of the Human Rights Committee: Japan*, passed on 19th November 1998 UN Doc. CCPR/C/79/Add.102, para. 14.

39   This also had an impact on work that Patrick Thornberry did later with regards to caste based discrimination and the Bukaku in this state. For the state reports of other states on article 27, as well as committee responses see http://www.minority-rights.org/docs.php#cases (accessed 6 April 2004).

40   *Sandra Lovelace* v. *Canada* (Communication No. 24/1977), Views adopted 30 July 1981, Report of the Human Rights Committee, GAOR, Thirty-sixth session, Suppl. No. 40 (A/36/40) pp. 166-175.

41   For a general reading on the attitude of the Committee to self-determination see P. Thornberry (note 15) pp. 124-129.

42   For more on the political doctrine exception see D. Kretzmer *The Occupation of Justice* (Albany, NY: State University of New York Press, 2002) pp. 22-25.

43   *Grand Council of the Mikmaq Tribal Society v Canada* (Communication No.205/1986), Views adopted 3 December 1991, Report of the Human Rights Committee. GAOR, Forty-Third session, UN Doc. CCPR/C/43/D/205/1986.

44   *Ilmari Länsman et al.* v. *Finland* ('*Länsman No. 1*') (Communication 511/1992), Views adopted 26 October 1994, Report of the Human Rights Committee, Vol. II, GAOR, Fiftieth Session, Suppl. No. 40 (A/50/40), pp. 66–76; and *Jouni E. Länsman et al.* v. *Finland*

be seen to the notion of an indigenous way of life and the right to subsistence, albeit raised through article 27.[46]

No matter how sophisticated a reading of article 1 by the HRC,[47] and no matter how willing a state might be to subject itself to the individual complaints mechanism of the Committee, this avenue remains extremely limited for winning rights for indigenous peoples, especially the right to self-determination. Rather, results are more likely to flow through national debate and discussion at the domestic rather than at the international level, a discussion which ought to be imperative in the face of increasingly divided and segregated societies.

It can be argued that the best way in which human rights law can protect the rights of indigenous peoples is through insistence on the creation of effective national institutions committed to these rights. For indigenous representatives, this approach remains limited since it still couches the discussion in terms of grants of rights by a state that is itself responsible for the original violation. There are also other important questions to be addressed such as the importance of the recognition of culpability by the state for the original violation and the precise extent to which the state has already set about fulfilling the equality agenda. It seems that one of the key problems underlying the conception of indigenous protection is a failure to focus on equality in facilitating the rebuilding of societies in the aftermath of persistent violation. Instead, the human rights agenda has focussed primarily on non-discrimination, but in the context of the unequal starting points of indigenous and non-indigenous populations this has been strikingly inadequate.

Internal Self-determination: Panacea or Starting Point?

Identified as one of the competing conceptual bases for the elaboration of indigenous peoples rights by Kingsbury, the notion of self-determination remains central to the furtherance of indigenous rights. At the discussions pursuant to the framing of the *UN Draft Declaration on the Indigenous Peoples*[48] a *démarche* was submitted by representatives of indigenous peoples with regards to self-determination, identifying it as 'the heart and

---

('*Länsman No. 2*') (Communication No. 671/1995), Views adopted 30 October 1996, Report of the Human Rights Committee, Vol. II, UN doc. A/52/40 (Vol. II) pp. 191-204.

45   *Anni Äärelä and Jouni Näkkäläjärvi* v. *Finland* (Communication No. 779/1997), Views adopted 24 October 2001, Report of the Human Rights Committee, Vol. II, UN doc. A/57/40 (Vol. II), pp. 117-130.

46   For a more detailed analysis see M. Scheinin 'The Right to Enjoy a Distinct Culture: Indigenous and Competing Uses of Land' in T.S. Orlin, A. Rosas and M. Scheinin *(note 23)* pp.159-222.

47   Article 1 has also been relevant in the interpretation of other rights protected by the Covenant, particularly 25, 26 and 27, as in *J.G.A. Diergaardt et al.* v. *Namibia* (Communication No. 760/1997), Views adopted 25 July 2000, Report of the Human Rights Committee, Vol. II, GAOR, Fifty-fifth Session, Suppl. No. 40 (A/55/40), pp. 140–160, paragraph 10.3.

48   For more on this document see Thornberry (note 15) pp. 370-396.

soul of the declaration'.[49] The terms bluntly state: 'We will not consent to any language which limits or curtails the right of self-determination.'[50] Resistance is also rife from states who remain unwilling to accommodate this central role for self-determination because of the potential it provides for fragmentation of the state.[51] The compromise language of the Draft Declaration suggests that:

> Indigenous peoples have the right of self-determination. By virtue of that right they freely determine their political status and freely pursue their economic, social and cultural development.

This position, a reflection of joint article 1 of the International Covenant on Economic, Social and Cultural Rights (ICESCR) and of the ICCPR, has ultimately stalled the process of further norm creation for indigenous peoples rights. It seems that states and indigenous representatives are locked in a game from which will have no real winner.

Self-determination has long been a 'conceptual morass'[52] in international law, partly because its application and meaning have not been formulated fully in agreed texts,[53] partly because it conflicts with other important principles such as territorial integrity[54] and specific rules concerning the non-violability of frontiers,[55] and partly because in practice, self-determination does not measure up well to some of the established textual formulations.[56] The crucial issue therefore remains whether this avenue can provide a panacea for the ordered co-existence of groups with different histories within the same boundary, and if so, which of the groups would be considered entitled to pursue the right. Kingsbury has suggested five categories where exercise of self-determination could be considered acceptable:

49   B. Kingsbury (note 16) p. 216.
50   S. Pritchard 'Working Group on Indigenous Populations: Mandate, Standard-Setting and Future Perspectives' in S. Pritchard (ed.) *Indigenous Peoples, the United Nations and Human Rights* (Annandale, Australia: Federation Press, 1998).
51   See Thornberry (note 15) pp. 419-421.
52   B. Kingsbury (note 16) p. 216.
53   Consider the use of the phrase 'peoples' in ILO Convention 169 and the caveat attached to it.
54   See L. Brilmayer 'Secession and Self-Determination: A Territorial Interpretation' 16 *Yale Journal of International Law* (1991) pp. 177-202.
55   For a discussion of territoriality in international law see J. Castellino and S. Allen *Title to Territory in International Law: A Temporal Analysis* (Dartmouth: Ashgate, 2003).
56   B. Kingsbury (note 16) p. 217. Consider for instance the process through which 'minorities' such as Eritreans and East Timorese gained self-determination by achieving 'peoplehood'. For Eritrea see E. Gayim *The Principle of Self-Determination: A Study of its Historical and Contemporary Legal Evolution* (Oslo: Norwegian Institute of Human Rights, 1990).

a.   Mandated/Trust territories
b.   Distinct political geographic entities subject to gross failure of the duties of the
     state
c.   Other territories where self-determination is applied by the parties
d.   Highest level constituent units of a federal state in the face of dissolution
e.   Formerly independent entities reasserting their independence with the tacit con-
     sent of the state, where their incorporation into the state was illegal or of dubious
     legality

In theory the expression of self-determination in international law involves free choice
for the self-determining unit, between integration with an existing state, free association
with an existing state or secession from the existing state.[57] In practice though, the latter
is seen, in all cases other than in pure decolonisation, as an exceptional measure that
cannot be accessed as a matter of course.[58] Any other view of self-determination would
place it in direct conflict with the principle of territorial sovereignty which is central to
the maintenance of the international system of sovereign states.[59] Self-determination
cannot ultimately overcome legitimate concerns about a process that potentially affords
continuous fragmentation and irredentism. Thus while the notion of self-determination
as a remedial measure in the face of human rights violations may be attractive for some
reasons, it is most unlikely to become normal.[60]

     Yet representatives of indigenous peoples have been extremely reluctant to yield
ground on the end-state model, including possible independence, due to the emotive
content of the notion of 'peoples' and 'nations'.[61] This can partly be attributed to the
explicit failure on the part of states to accept the original violations that underpin the
subjugation of indigenous rights. In this context, suggesting that those who suffered
through colonisation had a category of rights higher than that of indigenous peoples
– with links to the territory from time immemorial – is continuing the violation of treating indigenous peoples as having no international personality, while giving credence to
lines drawn on a map through a process of colonisation.

     One of the compromises struck in the 1993 Draft Declaration incorporates ideas
relevant to the reconstruction of self-determination, and is explicit in article 31:[62]

>   Indigenous peoples, as a specific form of exercising their right to self-determination,
>   have the right to autonomy or self-government in matters relating to their internal and

---

57   General Assembly Resolution 1541 (XV), 15th session, 1960.
58   See V.O. Bartkus *The Dynamic of Secession* (Cambridge, UK: Cambridge University Press,
     1999).
59   See L.C. Buchheit *Secession: The Legitimacy of Self-Determination*. (New Haven, CT: Yale
     University Press, 1978).
60   B. Kingsbury (note 16) p. 220.
61   See P. Thornberry (note 15) p. 418.
62   For a commentary from Patrick Thornberry on the issue see Ibid. pp. 382-385.

local affairs, including culture, religions, education, information, media, health, housing, employment, social welfare, economic activities, land and resources management, environment and entry by non-members, as well as ways and means for financing these autonomous functions.[63]

Although implying a great deal of freedom, article 31 does not link the question of autonomy to a land base, and is thus not a compromise in terms of external self-determination claims. Rather, it seems a clear expression of self-determination that excluded the external element, and can therefore be seen as 'internal self-determination'.[64] This is also consistent with the two general comments passed by the HRC and the Committee for the Elimination of Racial Discrimination (henceforth 'CERD').

The HRC's General Comment 12, passed at its twenty-first session in 1984, locates the discussion of self-determination very much within the UN's rhetoric of decolonisation. It stresses the essence of the right for 'the effective guarantee and observance of individual human rights and for the promotion and strengthening of those rights'.[65] However paragraphs 7 and 8 seem to give it a categorical interpretation with the former making reference to General Assembly Resolution 2625, passed in 1970, which clearly stresses territorial integrity; while paragraph 8, states that 'history has proved that the realization of and respect for the right of self-determination of peoples contributes to the establishment of friendly relations and cooperation between States and to strengthening international peace and understanding'.[66]

CERD is more categorical in its approach. It passed General Recommendation XXI in 1996 dealing with the right of self-determination, and the frequent references to it by ethnic, or religious groups or minorities.[67] While categorically recognising self-determination as a fundamental right, it seeks to distinguish this right as a right of peoples as distinct from minorities.[68] It then goes on to elaborate:

> In respect of the self-determination of peoples two aspects have to be distinguished. The right to self-determination of peoples has an internal aspect, that is to say, the rights of all peoples to pursue freely their economic, social and cultural development without outside interference. In that respect there exists a link with the right of every citizen to take part in the conduct of public affairs at any level…In consequence, Governments are to represent the whole population without distinction as to race, colour, descent or national or ethnic origin. The external aspect of self-determination implies that all peoples have the right to determine freely their political status and their place

---

63   Article 31, UN Draft Declaration.
64   See P. Thornberry 'Self-Determination, Minorities, Human Rights: A Review of International Instruments' 38 *International and Comparative Law Quarterly*, (1989) p. 867.
65   HRC General Comment 12 (1984), para. 1.
66   Ibid. para. 8.
67   CERD General Recommendation XXI, (1996), para. 1.
68   Ibid. para. 2.

in the international community based upon the principle of equal rights and exemplified by the liberation of peoples from colonialism and by the prohibition to subject peoples to alien subjugation, domination and exploitation.[69]

And to further emphasise the nature of state sovereignty the final paragraph of the Recommendation states:

> The Committee emphasizes that, in accordance with the Declaration on Friendly Relations, none of the Committee's actions shall be construed as authorizing or encouraging any action which would dismember or impair, totally or in part, the territorial integrity or political unity of sovereign and independent States conducting themselves in compliance with the principle of equal rights and self-determination of peoples and possessing a Government representing the whole people belonging to the territory, without distinction as to race, creed or colour. In the view of the Committee, international law has not recognized a general right of peoples unilaterally to declare secession from a State. In this respect, the Committee follows the views expressed in An Agenda for Peace (paras. 17 and following), namely, that a fragmentation of States may be detrimental to the protection of human rights, as well as to the preservation of peace and security.[70]

This categorical exposition of the doctrine of internal self-determination seems to close the door on self-determination expressed in a secessionist sense, though of course such action may be possible with the 'free agreements of all parties concerned'.[71] The key to understanding self-determination as a right then seems to flow from an ability to identify whether it guarantees a fundamental right to freedom or whether it seeks to assert a right to a particular type of relationship with the existing state.[72] While in classical terms the appeal to self-determination rose the romantic notion of independence and freedom whereby a subjugated people emerged from and threw off the yoke of colonialism,[73] in more recent times human rights law has seen self-determination as a process through which the group exercising the right and the state enter into a mutually beneficial relationship. Thus it seems that while in self-determination expressed through decolonisation the entity seeking to exercise the right did so by breaking away from the existing colony, in modern times the only option available is one whereby the entity exercising the right enters into a special relationship with the state under whose aegis it is seeking to exercise the right. This form of 'autonomy' or 'internal self-determination' seems the only way in which human rights law can accept the expression of the right

---

69   Ibid. para. 4.

70   Ibid. para. 6.

71   Ibid. para. 6.

72   B. Kingsbury (note 16) discusses the notion of the relationship aspect of self-determination on p. 225.

73   M. Koskenniemi 'National Self-determination Today: Problems of Legal Theory and Practice' 43 *International and Comparative Law Quarterly* (1994) pp. 241-269.

of self-determination.[74] The evidence for this is present in the Draft Declaration, which sees the right of self-determination for indigenous peoples as a right to maintain and strengthen their distinct characteristics and legal systems while retaining the right to participate fully in the affairs of the state.[75] Under this guise there has been some willingness from certain states to accept guidelines for relationships with indigenous peoples that incorporate elements of self-determination.[76]

CERD does make reference to land rights[77] in a later recommendation but does not link this to the right of self-determination, stating instead in paragraph 5 of General Recommendation XXIII on Indigenous Peoples:

> The Committee especially calls upon States parties to recognize and protect the rights of indigenous peoples to own, develop, control and use their communal lands, territories and resources and, where they have been deprived of their lands and territories traditionally owned or otherwise inhabited or used without their free and informed consent, to take steps to return those lands and territories. Only when this is for factual reasons not possible, the right to restitution should be substituted by the right to just, fair and prompt compensation. Such compensation should as far as possible take the form of lands and territories.[78]

While this may seem a happy compromise it still leaves open the key issue that underpins the indigenous claim to self-determination: namely the historical and continued suppression of sovereignty and dispossession of lands.[79] It is clear that the indigenous peoples' rights to property and territory were violated illegally by settlers on their lands. While in some instances treaties were signed between in-groups and existing populations,[80] in most situations land was merely commandeered by settlers despite the existence of laws preventing such acquisition of territory.[81] Thus self-determination expressed

---

74   For a detailed discussion of autonomy in this context see G. Gilbert 'Autonomy and Minority Groups: A Right in International Law?' 35 *Cornell International Law Journal* (2002) pp. 307-354.

75   B. Kingsbury (note 16) p. 227.

76   Among the states that now purport to accept this approach are: Canada, New Zealand, Australia, Denmark, Guatemala, Mexico, Philippines see Ibid. p. 230.

77   Also see P. Thornberry (note 15) pp. 214-223 for a narrative on land rights, self-determination and non-discrimination, and a comment on how the issues collided in the context of the Australian report before the Committee.

78   Paragraph 5, CERD, General Recommendation XXIII, (1997), 51st session.

79   For a discussion of native American sovereignty see H. Hannum 'Sovereignty and its Relevance to Native Americans in the 21st Century' in 23 *American Indian Law Review* (1999) pp. 487-496.

80   See generally S. Wiessner (note 15).

81   As examined by M. Chapman 'Indigenous Peoples and International Human Rights: Towards a Guarantee for the Territorial Connection' 26 *The Anglo-American Law Review* (1997) pp. 357-396.

in the current manner can only be a useful starting point if it also includes a mechanism which can deal with this fundamental question. It is towards this that we shall now turn.

Reconciliation and Remedies: Strengthening the Starting Point

It has to be stated categorically that indigenous sovereignty was stolen by arriving settlers, using and exploiting the law as a means to justify annexation of lands.[82] While UN decolonisation resulted in a rolling back of colonial acquisitions[83] it has been more difficult for indigenous nations to regain control over their political, civil, economic, social and cultural destinies since the settlers on these lands justified their ownership over resources through law and, rather than merely seeking to govern the area, chose to stay.

Decolonisation has had, amongst others, at least two specific manifestations in history. In Spanish decolonisation between 1810-1825 in Latin America it signified the process through which the Creoles laid claim to their independence from Madrid and Lisbon.[84] In this case indigenous peoples were not consulted at all. Thus the Creoles claimed self-determination and independence based on Enlightenment values that were not however, extended to the indigenous populations or the populations that had been transferred to the continent through slavery. Rather, this expression of self-determination merely transferred the violation of indigenous sovereignty from the colonisers onto their offspring. In UN-inspired decolonisation, sovereignty reverted back to sovereigns who ostensibly predated colonisation, though the process was undertaken through political means. Thus as Jackson points out, very often the control of the state was handed over to the most powerful aspirant and the juridical state was often larger in dimension (pertaining to colonial boundaries) than the *de facto* state.[85] However with emphasis laid on state sovereignty, other claimants to representation and independence were effectively quelled. It still remains extremely difficult to advance 'indigenous' claims in many of the states that emerged from this process, yet it can be argued that, unlike in Spanish decolonisation, there was a change of *status quo* in that, in many cases, pre-colonial rulers wrested control of the territory.

---

82   For a general reading of the phenomenon of dispossession in North America see W. Bradford 'With a Very Great Blame on Our Hearts: Reparations, Reconciliation, and an American Indian Plea for Peace with Justice' 27 *American Indian Law Review* (2003) pp.1-175. Also see S. H. Cleveland 'Powers Inherent in Sovereignty: Indians, Aliens, Territories and the Nineteenth Century Origins of Plenary Power over Foreign Affairs' 81 *Texas Law Review* (2002) pp. 1-284.

83   For an analysis of UN decolonisation see F. L. Kirgis 'The Degrees of Self-determination in the UN Era' 88 *American Journal of International Law* (1994) pp. 304-310.

84   For a general reading of the events surrounding Spanish decolonisation see A. Alvarez 'Latin America and International Law' 3(2) *American Journal of International Law* (1909) pp. 269-353.

85   R. Jackson 'Juridical Statehood in Sub-Saharan Africa' 46 *Journal of International Affairs* (1992) pp. 1-16.

When faced with the notion of self-determination and indigenous peoples' rights, the question that has arisen is the extent to which violations that occurred in the past can be remedied. While the straightforward revival of historic indigenous sovereignty may be attractive, since it potentially carries the hope of reversing the root-cause of the violation and the consequences that flowed from it, it has proved to be a step too far for most states to concede. As Kingsbury puts it:

> It takes little account of how things have changed, and its radical implications pro-voke damaging resistance from states. In practice, most indigenous peoples seeking to revive autonomous power utilise more nuanced structures that incorporate some of the same justifications: self-determination or the emerging conceptual structure of indigenous peoples' claims.[86]

The position in international law is confused by the *intertemporal rule* which suggests that actions of a party can only be judged against laws that existed at the time when those particular actions were committed, rather than by contemporary standards.[87] This means that if an act was committed when there was no law against that particular act, it is inappropriate to question that act later, if and when a law prohibiting that act has come into force. The prime purpose of this rule is that persecution based on retrospective laws will result in the perpetration of injustice and could potentially leave law open to being used as a tool of vengeance in the future. So strong is this stricture within international law that even within specific international human rights legal regimes, the right against retrospective laws[88] is considered to be non-derogable i.e. a right that cannot be suspended by the state even in times of extreme national emergency.[89] In this context it sits within these jurisdictions alongside other non-derogable rights such as the right to life and liberty and the enshrined guarantee from torture and slavery.

In support of the *intertemporal rule* it needs to be stressed that persecution under retrospective laws would clearly constitute a violation of fundamental human rights norms. The danger of allowing such a revisionist approach to culpability would be to render law open to malevolence. In addition the *intertemporal rule* does allow some flexibility as can be seen in war crimes tribunals undertaking to allocate responsibility for actions committed during armed conflict. The initial arguments made by opponents of the Nüremberg and Tokyo Trials that such trials were retrospective were easily countered by the presentation of evidence revealing that the atrocities perpetrated by the Nazi war criminals were illegal under domestic as well as customary international law at the

---

86   B. Kingsbury (note 16) p. 237.

87   For a general reading of the doctrine see T. O. Elias 'The Doctrine of Intertemporal Law' in 74.2 *American Journal of International Law* (1980) pp. 285-307.

88   Framed as article 9 The Right from Ex Post Facto Laws, *The American Convention on Human Rights*, O.A.S. Treaty Series No. 36, 1144 U.N.T.S. 123 entered into force July 18, 1978.

89   See article 27 *American Convention on Human Rights*, O.A.S. Treaty Series No. 36, 1144 U.N.T.S. 123 entered into force July 18, 1978.

time.[90] Thus the mere fact that such laws were not codified at the international level does not bring war criminals within the protection of the *intertemporal rule* since the activities were illegal at the time of their perpetration.

Thus the *intertemporal rule* is usually appropriate since unfettered application of modern law to ancient situations is patently unfair under the legal doctrine of protection from retrospective laws. Nonetheless it is arguable that the doctrine has often been used as a handmaiden for political interests. Clear demonstration of this can be seen in the response to criticisms of colonialism. Colonialism was clearly illegal, especially in its interpretation of the rules *vis-à-vis* the acquisition of territory.[91] To the extent that decolonisation has seen a return of territory to more local rulers, a process of forgiveness and reconciliation has been possible. While antagonisms still exist between post-colonial states and their former colonisers, they have been tempered by the perpetration of favourable trade terms which have aided the development of the post-colonial state. However, significant issues remain with respect to land rights that continue to come within the mandated protection of the *intertemporal rule*.

The situation of indigenous peoples in this regard is particularly instructive. As original inhabitants of large tracts of land from time immemorial, indigenous peoples failed to see the need to demarcate or lay claim to segments of it individually. This way of life came into sharp conflict with European expansion into territories such as the Americas, Northern Europe and Australia. While it also affected Asia and Africa the notion of 'indigenous peoples' in these continents was viewed as being concurrent with the idea of the post-colonial state. In recent years this vision of post-colonial African and Asian polities has been successfully unravelled; nonetheless the process is still too new to merit clear analysis.[92] In contrast, the Americas, Northern Europe and Australia have seen the expression of indigenous issues for longer and provide an ideal arena for the analysis of processes of forgiveness and reconciliation.

Conclusion

Since indigenous lands were commandeered through territorial expansion, an ideal starting point for mechanisms of forgiveness and reconciliation should be the return of these lands.[93] Modern norms on this issue, as enshrined in human rights legal docu-

---

90   See generally W. Schabas *Genocide in International Law: The Crime of Crimes* (Cambridge: Cambridge University Press, 2000).

91   For an analysis on the manner of interpretation of the principle of *terra nullius* see Castellino and Allen (note 55).

92   B. Kingsbury '"Indigenous Peoples" in International Law: A Constructivist Approach to the Asian Controversy' 92 *American Journal of International Law* (1998) pp. 414-457.

93   This discussion is already reflected in academic literature focussing on different parts of the world see e.g. G. Osherenko 'Indigenous Rights in Russia: Is Title to Land Essential for Cultural Survival?' 13 *Georgetown International Environmental Law Review* (2001) pp. 695-734; J. E. Brady 'The Huaorani Tribe of Ecuador: A Study in Self-determination for Indigenous

ments,[94] express the view that peoples should not be dispossessed of their lands, and that if such dispossession does take place it should be in extreme circumstances and even then adequate compensation must be paid.[95] This law is directed against the sedentary state that seeks to appropriate the territories of its indigenous peoples in the name of 'development' activities such as mining.[96] It is clear that contemporary human rights principles seek to place clear restrictions on the ability of a state to expropriate land for any purpose. The question that remains is the extent to which these contemporary developments reinforce the notion that ancient acquisition of territory by expansionist colonisers is beyond the realm of critique since it is covered by the protection of the *intertemporal rule*.

The argument for revisiting the rule is not to question its validity, but rather to examine the merits of the rule *vis-à-vis* the rights of indigenous peoples to their land. Some governments are making concerted efforts to remedy the situation by providing specific mechanisms by which indigenous peoples can reclaim possessions. However these mechanisms are usually only successful to the extent that they do not challenge the sedentariness of the modern state. Thus if remote areas of Northern Territory in Australia are being claimed the government is usually more willing to accede to the request than when the site of Sydney Harbour Bridge is being claimed as an ancient site of aboriginal heritage. This leaves open the extent to which such a process of re-examination can achieve forgiveness and reconciliation. Also significant is the fact that in many other circumstances a questioning of the past is occurring away from the realms of the *intertemporal rule* of law. Thus to be able to address the question of land rights that remains central to indigenous claims to self-determination, the following questions ought to be addressed: to what extent is the *intertemporal rule* of law necessary and desirable for the maintenance of human rights standards against retrospection in this context? If validity can be ascertained, what are the limitations that ought to be placed on its exercise? And finally, to what extent does the *intertemporal rule* harm the process of forgiveness and reconciliation?

Peoples' 10 Harvard *Human Rights Journal* (1997) pp. 291-313; in Canada, see J. Borrows 'Domesticating Doctrines: Aboriginal Peoples after the Royal Commission' in 46 *McGill Law Journal* (2001) pp. 615-662; in Australia see A. Lokan 'From Recognition to Reconciliation: The Functions of Aboriginal Rights Law' 23 *Melbourne University Law Review* (1999) pp. 65-120; L. Sargent 'The Indigenous Peoples of Bolivia's Amazon Basin Region and ILO Convention 169: Real Rights or Rhetoric?' 29 *University of Miami Inter-American Law Review* (1998) pp. 451-524 and L. Valenta 'Disconnect: the 1988 Brazilian Constitution, Customary International Law and Indigenous Land Rights in Northern Brazil' 38 *Texas International Law Journal* (2003) pp. 643-662.

94   E.g. article 31 of the Draft Declaration.

95   As captured in paragraph 5, CERD, General Recommendation XXIII, (1997), 51st session, discussed in Gilbert (note 74).

96   For a discussion of these developments in Australia including the *Mabo* case and its aftermath see G. Triggs 'Australia's Indigenous Peoples and International Law: Validity of the Native Title Amendment Act 1998 (Cth)' 23 *Melbourne University Law Review* (1999) pp. 372-415.

It could be argued that the *intertemporal rule* is being challenged as a result of dialogue between parties as part of global political processes. These processes seek financial damages for past actions of mass ill-treatment.[97] Rather than processes aimed at forgiveness and reconciliation these are based on admissions of culpability and subsequent ascription of monetary value in damages for that culpability.[98] At first sight this might seem similar to processes discussed above: in the case of the Nüremberg Trials and the Ad Hoc Tribunals for Former Yugoslavia and Rwanda to rectify past wrongs by punishment of perpetrators, in the case of decolonisation to return territory to local rulers, and in terms of contemporary standards for indigenous land rights to first ensure that lands will henceforth not be expropriated and then to provide adequate compensation to those dispossessed in the past. However the processes that challenge the *intertemporal rule* are in fact negotiations such as the civil class actions against German and Austrian perpetrators of World War II atrocities,[99] monetary compensation being sought by relatives of Korean comfort women for their treatment at the hands of Imperial Japanese forces[100] and efforts that led to the claim for damages for victims of slavery to be inserted into the agenda for the World Conference Against Racism held in South Africa in September 2001.

Unlike the Truth and Reconciliation type processes that have taken place in states as diverse as South Africa[101] and Guatemala,[102] and the criminal investigations taking place concomitant to conflict during World War II, in Former Yugoslavia and Rwanda, these new processes seek to gain financial recompense for the commitment of past wrongs. In this sense they require that the admission of culpability for past injustices and wrongs is quantified in monetary terms and damages are paid to either the survivors or the relatives of victims of past wrongs. The motivation for this is the need of victims'

---

97   For an analysis of the possibility of class actions in international law see W. J. Aceves 'Actio Popularis: The Class Action in International Law' *University of Chicago Legal Forum* (2003) pp. 353-402.

98   See for instance, the attempt to harness this in terms of children's rights as described in L. Graham 'Indigenous Peoples: Reparations and the Indian Child Welfare Act' 25 *Legal Studies Forum* (2001) pp. 619-640.

99   For a discussion of this particular situation and other similar claims see E. Barkan *The Guilt of Nations: Restitution and Negotiating Historical Injustices* (Baltimore: John Hopkins University Press, 2001).

100   For an analysis of the possibility of raising this before American courts' See B. Park 'Comfort Women During World War II: Are US Courts a Final Resort for Justice?' 17 *American University International Law Review* (2002) pp. 403-458.

101   For a general reading of the South African TRC process see A. Boraine *A Country Unmasked: Inside South Africa's Truth and Reconciliation Commission* (Cape Town: Oxford University Press, 2000).

102   For a general reading about indigenous issues in the Guatemalan genocide see M. Holley 'Recognizing the Rights of Indigenous People to their Traditional Lands: A Case Study of an Internally-Displaced Community in Guatemala' 15 *Berkeley Journal of International Law* (1997) pp. 119-157 especially in terms of remedies in that context.

families for closure to the atrocities perpetrated against them by powerful forces seemingly intent on their destruction.

Arguably the key to being able to unravel the tangle of indigenous rights to land is to, first and foremost, officially assert and recognise that the dispossession of land and subjugation of indigenous sovereignty, when it occurred, constituted a violation of existing customary law (analogous to the reasoning of the War Crimes Tribunals at the end of World War II). Thus these actions were illegal at the time they were committed even if international standards had not been universally accepted. The three examples enunciated above, namely, the treatment by the Nazis of Jews and other groups that did not meet their specific policies, the treatment of Korean comfort women and the acts concomitant to colonisation, have all been established as being illegal acts that could have been challenged at the time of their commission by relevant domestic laws existing at that time. However due to the specific nature of these actions and the manner in which they occurred, no legal challenge at the time was possible.

Therefore these processes, though challenging, do not violate the *intertemporal rule*. However the seizure of the territories of indigenous peoples, has not yet been accepted as coming within this category. The law that casts light on this issue is the law governing the occupation of territory. In international law, any territories that were deemed *terra nullius* were considered to be open to occupation. To be able to acquire a territory, an occupying power had to ensure that there were no organised communities that lived in it. Implicit in this statement of the law was a racist and biased perspective namely that to be considered a community capable of rendering a territory occupied, the occupants of a given territory would need to meet certain criteria defined by the occupying powers. The issue that facilitated the legality of colonialism and expropriation of territories was thus not the lack of existing law, but the manner in which it was interpreted. Once again while no universal legal standard existed with regards to the acquisition of territory, legal systems clearly existed within the domestic realm of the occupying powers that prevented wanton seizure of property by citizens or the state. What prevented this regime from being extended to other parts of the globe in the face of advancing armies was the inherently racist ideology that peoples who occupied those territories were not sufficiently organised to prevent their territory from being deemed *terra nullius*. And once states could establish that the territory was indeed *nullius* or unoccupied, they could legally lay claim to it.

Thus the key to determining how much room there is for indigenous expression of self-determination has to be the acceptance on the part of states of their culpability in the dispossession and subjugation of indigenous sovereignty. This process, in tandem with a re-invigoration of self-determination of the kind discussed above, and in discussion with the wider domestic society, is perhaps the only way in which these issues can move beyond rhetoric into the realisation of real rights for indigenous peoples.

Chapter 5

INDIGENOUS PEOPLES' RIGHTS TO LAND AND NATURAL RESOURCES

Erica-Irene A. Daes[1]

> *In deep appreciation of the valuable contribution made by Professor Patrick Thornberry to the protection of the rights of the world's indigenous peoples.*

I.   Introductory remarks

One of the most acute and complex situations facing indigenous peoples and governments of the states in which they live is the recognition, promotion and protection of the indigenous peoples' rights to land and natural resources. Reports submitted and statements delivered by indigenous peoples from all parts of the world during sessions of the United Nations Working Group on Indigenous Populations (WGIP) have made it clear that land and resource issues, particularly the non-recognition of indigenous rights and the dispossession of indigenous peoples from their lands, are problems of the most urgent and fundamental nature. At the same time, there has been great concern on the part of certain states, intergovernmental organisations, academic institutions, nongovernmental organisations (NGOs) and individuals that the recognition of these rights of indigenous peoples would supposedly require that all the lands and resources ever taken from indigenous peoples be returned. Because of the diversity of their history and of the political relationships and developments relating to the many indigenous peoples worldwide, and the complexity of past and present political and legal issues, such matters will have to be reviewed, if possible by both indigenous peoples and states, in order to resolve basic problems related to the rights to land and natural resources of indigenous peoples.

   In this respect, the course adopted in this chapter is to organise the multitude of issues into a framework and to attempt to identify which problems are of the most severe or most deserving nature, in a search for ways of alleviating the suffering and injustices endured by indigenous peoples.

---

[1]   Special Rapporteur of the United Nations Sub-Commission for the Promotion and Protection of Human Rights.

Nazila Ghanea & Alexandra Xanthaki (eds.), Minorities, Peoples and Self-Determination, *pp. 75-91.*
© *2005 Koninklijke Brill NV. Printed in The Netherlands. ISBN 90 04 14301 7.*

What core values should guide this work? First, the human rights principles embodied in the Universal Declaration of Human Rights (Universal Declaration), the International Human Rights Covenants (Covenants), the International Labour Organization (ILO) Convention 169, and other relevant international and regional instruments, specifically the principles of self-determination, equality and non-discrimination. In addition, the following fundamental values included in the draft United Nations Declaration on the Rights of Indigenous Peoples (Draft UN declaration) should be taken into consideration. These include among others, the preservation and well-being of indigenous cultures and communities, the elimination of poverty and the great goals of justice, the rule of law and equality before the law.

II.   Relationship of indigenous peoples to their lands, territories and natural resources

The first issue which should be discussed and examined is the relationship of indigenous peoples to their lands, territories and natural resources.

Indigenous peoples have repeatedly emphasised the urgent need for understanding by non-indigenous societies of the spiritual, cultural, social, political and economic significance to indigenous societies of their lands, territories and resources for their continued survival and vitality. In order to understand the profound relationship that indigenous peoples have with their lands, territories and resources, there is a need for recognition of the cultural differences that exist between them and non-indigenous people, particularly in the countries in which they live. Indigenous peoples have urged the world community to attach positive value to this distinct relationship. It is difficult to separate the concept of indigenous peoples' relationship with their lands, territories and resources from that of their cultural values and differences.

The relationship with the land and all living things is at the core of indigenous societies. In the context of the discussion about the territorial rights of indigenous peoples in the WGIP, Professor Williams stated that 'indigenous peoples have emphasised that the spiritual and material foundations of their cultural identities are sustained by their unique relationship to the traditional territories.'[2] Professor James Sakej Henderson attempts to illustrate this distinct relationship and conceptual framework by stating that

> the Aboriginal vision of property was ecological space that creates our consciousness, not an ideological construct or fungible resource...Their vision is of different realms enfolded into a sacred space...it is fundamental to their identity, personality and

---

2   R.A. Williams 'Encounters on the frontiers of international human rights law: redefining the terms of indigenous peoples' survival in the world', 39 *Duke Law Journal* (1990), p. 681.

humanity....[the] notion of self does not end with their flesh, but continues with the reach of their senses into the land.[3]

Such a relationship manifests itself in elements of indigenous peoples' cultures, such as language. For a number of different reasons, the international community has begun to respond to indigenous peoples in the context of a new philosophy and world perspective with respect to land, territory and resources. New standards are being devised, based in part upon the values that have been expressed by indigenous peoples and which are consistent with indigenous peoples' perspectives and philosophies about their lands, territories and resources.

Policy and guidance within the Sub-Commission for the Promotion and Protection of Human Rights (Sub-Commission) and other organs and bodies of the United Nations system, on the relationship of indigenous peoples with their lands, territories and resources, have been shaped by the conclusions, proposals and recommendations of the Special Rapporteur of the Sub-Commission, J. R. Martinez Cobo, the *Study of the Problem of Discrimination against Indigenous Populations*.[4] The Special Rapporteur states:

> It is essential to know and understand the deep special relationship between indigenous peoples and their land as basic to their existence as such and to all their beliefs, customs, traditions and culture. For such peoples the land is not merely a possession and a means of production. The entire relationship between the spiritual life of indigenous peoples and Mother Earth, and their land, has a great many deep-seated implications. Their land is not a commodity which can be acquired , but a material element to be enjoyed freely.[5]

Article 13 of the ILO Convention 1989/169 concerning Indigenous and Tribal Peoples in Independent Countries provides a further example of the recognition of this special relationship. The article makes a specific reference to 'the special importance for the cultures and spiritual values of the peoples concerned of their relationship with the lands or territories, or both as applicable, which they occupy or otherwise use, and in particular the collective aspects of this relationship.'[6]

The distinctive nature of indigenous peoples' relationship to lands and natural resources is also referred to in the Draft UN Declaration in both preambular and operative paragraphs. In particular, Article 25 states:

---

3   J. S. Henderson 'Mikmaq tenure in Atlantic Canada', 18.2 *Dalhousie Law Journal* (1995) p. 196.

4   J. Martinez Cobo *Study of the Problem of Discrimination against Indigenous Populations*, UN Document E/CN.4/Sub.2/1986/7.

5   Ibid. paras. 196 and 197.

6   International Labour Organisation, Convention concerning Indigenous and Tribal Peoples in Independent Countries, Convention 169 (1989).

Indigenous peoples have the right to maintain and strengthen their distinctive spiritual and material relationship with the lands, territories, waters and coastal seas and other resources which they have traditionally owned or otherwise occupied or used, and to uphold their responsibilities to future generations in this regard.[7]

Furthermore, the proposed American Declaration on the Rights of Indigenous Peoples (proposed American Declaration), elaborated by the American Commission on Human Rights and at present under consideration by the Permanent Council of Organization of American States, contains the following preambular language:

[The States] recognizing the respect for the environment accorded by the cultures of indigenous peoples of the Americas, and considering the special relationship between the indigenous peoples and the environment, lands, resources and territories on which they live... Recognizing that in many indigenous cultures, traditional collective systems for control and use of land and territory and resources, including bodies of water and coastal areas, are a necessary condition for their survival, social organization, development and their individual and collective well-being.[8]

Subsequently, each reference mentioned above underscores a number of elements that are unique to indigenous peoples:
(i)   a profound relationship exists between indigenous peoples and their lands, territories and resources;
(ii)   this relationship has various social, cultural, spiritual economic and political dimensions and responsibilities;
(iii) the collective dimension of this relationship is significant; and
(iv)   the intergenerational aspect of such a relationship is also crucial to indigenous peoples' identity, survival and cultural viability.

There may however be additional elements relating to indigenous peoples and their relationship to their lands, territories and resources which have not been detailed above.

The gradual deterioration of indigenous societies can mainly be traced to the lack of recognition of the profound relationship that indigenous peoples have to their lands, territories and resources, as well as the lack of recognition of other basic human rights.

The colonisation of indigenous territories has affected indigenous peoples in a number of ways. Demographic deterioration occurred through maltreatment, enslavement, suicide, punishment for resistance, warfare, malnutrition due to destruction of

---

7   *Draft United Nations Declaration on the Rights of Indigenous Peoples*, UN Doc. E/CN.4/
     Sub.2/1994/56, Sub-Commission on Prevention of Discrimination and Protection of
     Minorities, Report of the Sub-Commission on Prevention of Discrimination and Protection of Minorities on its 46th session, Resolution 45/1994. Annex.
8   Proposed Inter-American Declaration on the Rights of Indigenous Peoples, approved by the Inter-American Commission on Human Rights on 26th February 1997.

the natural environment or over-exploitation of natural resources, as well as disease and outright extermination.

With population decline came the destruction of the traditional social order. This resulted from a number of forces, including the efforts of missionaries and Western attitudes towards the divisions of labour and gender. The introduction of the practice of attaching a monetary value to things and of buying and selling things previously not considered merchantable, including land, introduced the stresses of an economic environment to their societies which was quite contrary to the traditional economic order of most indigenous communities.

It is of critical importance to underscore the cultural biases that contributed both to the conceptual framework constructed to legitimate colonisation and to the various methods used to dispossess indigenous peoples and illegally expropriate their lands, territories and natural resources. The attitudes, doctrines and policies developed to justify the taking of lands from indigenous peoples were and continue to be largely driven by the economic agendas of certain states.[9]

In certain situations, it was only through rationalisation and military domination that colonisers secured ownership of the lands, territories and resources of indigenous peoples. The territories of indigenous peoples in the Americas and elsewhere were taken mainly by military force. Where 'just war' could not be waged, treaties were sometimes concluded.

Many indigenous communities in North America were forced on to reservations. The severing of indigenous peoples from their lands and territories and the failure by states to recognise the social, cultural, spiritual and economic significance of land to indigenous peoples had both short- and long-term impacts on indigenous communities and peoples.

The doctrines of dispossession which emerged in the subsequent development of modern international law, particularly *terra nullius* and 'discovery' have had well-known adverse effects on indigenous peoples. The doctrine of *terra nullius*, as it is applied to indigenous peoples, holds that indigenous lands are legally unoccupied until the arrival of a colonial presence and can therefore become the property of the colonising power through effective occupation.[10] In the seventeenth, eighteenth and nineteenth centuries, the doctrine of 'discovery' gave to a 'discovering' state lands previously unknown to it, an inchoate title that could be perfected through effective occupation within a reasonable time.[11] The doctrine, as it has come to be applied by states with little or no support in international law, gives to the 'discovering' colonial power free title to indigenous lands subject only to indigenous use and occupancy in certain cases referred to as 'aboriginal

---

9   The views of early international legal theorists are discussed in R. Williams *The American Indian in Western Thought: The Discourses of Conquest* (Oxford: Oxford University Press, 1990). See also S. J. Anaya *Indigenous Peoples in International Law* (Oxford: Oxford University Press, 1966), p. 22.

10   Ibid.

11   J. L. Brierly *The Law of Nations* (Oxford: Oxford University Press, 1960) p. 154.

title'.[12] Only recently has the international community began to understand that such doctrines are illegitimate and racist. In this connection it should be noted that while the Permanent Court of International Justice based its decision in the Eastern Greenland case of 1933[13] upon the same framework and attitudes, in 1976 the International Court of Justice ruled that the doctrine of *terra nullius* had been erroneously and invalidly applied against the tribal peoples of the Western Sahara.[14]

The High Court of Australia in its 1992 decision in the case *Mabo v. Queensland*[15] discussed the legal and other effects of the doctrine of *terra nullius*. The Court denounced the doctrine by concluding that this 'unjust and discriminatory doctrine can no longer be accepted'. This decision of great importance gave rise to the Native Title Act[16] adopted by the Government of Australia in 1993, which was amended in 1998.[17] This established a framework and mechanisms by which Aboriginal peoples in Australia could secure land rights. Nevertheless, Australian Aboriginal peoples have reported to the WGIP that they have great difficulties with the Act, and regard as unjust and ill-founded the State's asserted authority, recognised in the Mabo decision, to extinguish indigenous land rights.[18]

On 18 March 1999 the Committee on the Elimination of Racial Discrimination (CERD) issued a decision finding that provisions in the 1998 Native Title Act Amendments extinguish or impair the exercise of indigenous title rights and interests and discriminate against native title holders.[19] This case demonstrates that Eurocentric and discriminatory ideas continue to be evident in legal theory and action and that such attitudes in national legislation and court decisions may trap indigenous peoples in a legal discourse that does not embrace their distinct cultural values, beliefs, institutions or perspectives.[20]

---

12   For example the case *Delgamuukw v. The Queen*, [1997] 3 S.C.R 1010, 153 D.L.R. (4ᵗʰ) 193, decided December 11, 1997, para. 38.

13   *Eastern Greenland (Denmark v. Norway)*, 1933 P.C. I. J (ser. AIR) No 53.

14   *Western Sahara*, Advisory Opinion, 1975 I.C.I. 12, See D. Sanders and others, 'Common Law Rulings on the Customary Land Rights of Aboriginal or Indigenous People', unpublished paper on author's file, 6 August 1999.

15   *Mabo v. Queensland (No2)* (1992) 175 CLR 1; 107 ALR 1.

16   *Native Title Act* (1993), Act No. 110 of 1993. For the text of the Act see http://www.austlii.edu.au/au/legis/cth/consol_act/nta1993147/ (accessed 21 July 2004).

17   *Native Title Amendment Act* (1998), Act No. 97 of 1998. For the text of the Act see http://www.scaleplus.law.gov.au/html/comact/10/5874/rtf/Act97of1998.rtf (accessed 21 July 2004).

18   UN Docs. E/CN.4/Sub.2/1993/29 (1993), E/CN.4/Sub.2/1994/30 and Corr. 1 (1994), *Reports of the Working Group on Indigenous Populations*.

19   CERD A/54/18., *Decision 2 (54)*, para 21.

20   See also UN Doc. HR/PUB/89/5 (1989), *Conclusions and Recommendations contained in the Report of the Seminar on the Effects of Racism and Racial Discrimination on the Social and Economic Relations between Indigenous Peoples and States*, Geneva, 16-20 January 1989.

III. Critical analysis of certain principal problems regarding indigenous land and natural resources

The principal problems related to indigenous land and natural resources are numerous and diverse. In this regard, reference should be made to the following:

a)   *Failure of the State to acknowledge indigenous rights to lands, territories and resources.*

This principal problem can be divided into two parts:
i)   failure of states to recognise the existence of indigenous use, occupancy and ownership, and
ii)   failure of state to accord appropriate legal status, judicial capacity and other legal rights in connection with indigenous peoples' ownership of land.

i)   Countries in many parts of the world are unaware of or ignore the fact that nations or communities of indigenous peoples inhabit and use areas of land and sea and have done so, in many cases, since time immemorial. These areas are typically far from the capitals and other urban areas of the country and certain countries regard these lands and resources as public or governmental lands. Although the indigenous people concerned regard themselves, with good reason, as owning the land and resources they occupy and use, the State itself, typically, disposes of the land and resources as if the indigenous peoples were not there. These governmental tendencies are further exacerbated in federal States such as Canada and the United States of America, where state, provincial and even municipal governments sometimes pursue such actions, either in co-ordination with the central or national government or independently and in pursuit of their own policy.[21] For example, two organisations have reported that the Saami of Norway are contending with a number of governmental actions which threaten their remaining lands and resources, including the conveyance of a large portion of land in Finnmark to a state-owned company, and the 'planned expansion and connection of two existing military training fields'.[22]

ii)   The problem regarding the failure of states to accord appropriate legal, judicial capacity and other legal rights is mainly based on the fact that although some states know that indigenous nations, communities or groups exist and have exclusive use and occupancy of an area, they do not acknowledge that the indigenous peoples concerned have legal entitlement or rights to the land or resources. In some situations the indig-

---

21   Quaker Aboriginal Affairs Committee (Canada) response to preliminary working paper on indigenous people and their relationship to land, by the Special Rapporteur E.-I. A. Daes, May 1999.

22   Communication from Heidi Salmi, Assistant Director, Samediggi Ministry of Foreign Affairs, 30 March 2000; Communication from Mikkel Oskal, Chairman, Mauken Reindeer Herding District, 3 April 2000.

enous peoples are regarded as using these lands, which they call 'public' or 'national' at the sufferance of the Government.

The legal concept of 'aboriginal title' and its relationship to the human rights of indigenous peoples is centrally important.

b)   *Discriminatory laws and policies affecting indigenous peoples in relation to their lands, territories and resources*

In those states that have developed a body of positive law and a body of jurisprudence with regard to indigenous peoples (and their number is increasing), the most acute and complex problems appear to arise because of persistent discriminatory laws and legal doctrines that are applied to indigenous peoples and their lands and resources.

The concept of aboriginal title is itself discriminatory in that it provides only defective, vulnerable and inferior legal status for indigenous land and resource ownership.

Specific reference should be made to the laws regarding the extinguishment of indigenous peoples' land and resource rights. Practically all countries where indigenous peoples live assert the power to 'extinguish' the land titles and rights of the indigenous peoples within their borders, without the consent of the indigenous peoples. The concept of 'extinguishment' includes voluntary purchase and sale of title, but more commonly the term is used to mean outright taking or expropriation, most often without just compensation. The problem of extinguishment is related to the concept of aboriginal title. The central defect of aboriginal title is that it is by definition a title that can be taken at will by the Sovereign – that is, by the colonial government or nowadays by the state. Like aboriginal title, the practice of involuntary extinguishment of indigenous land rights is a relic of the colonial period.

Another discriminatory legal doctrine that appears to be widespread is the doctrine that states have practically unlimited power to control or regulate the use of indigenous lands, without regard for constitutional limits on governmental power that would otherwise be applicable.

A further example of discriminatory legal doctrines is the law concerning treaties made with indigenous peoples. Treaties have been used, among other purposes, as mechanisms for gaining cessions of indigenous lands and for ostensibly guaranteeing rights to the remaining lands held by indigenous nations. The problem of discrimination arises when the state later abrogates or violates the treaty. Usually the injured indigenous nation or tribe has no legal remedy against the state either in domestic law or under international law. The denial of any remedy under international law is inconsistent with the use of treaties as a legal mechanism and with the status of indigenous peoples as subjects of international law.

In terms of frequency and scope of complaints, one of the most serious problems nowadays for indigenous peoples is the failure of states to demarcate indigenous lands.[23]

---

23   R.R. Ortega, 'Notes on the legal status and recognition of indigenous land rights in the Amazonian countries' in UN Doc. E/CN.4/Sub.2/AC.4/1996/6/Add. 1, *Report of the Expert*

Demarcation of lands is the formal process of identifying the actual locations and boundaries of indigenous lands or territories and physically marking those boundaries on the ground. Purely abstract or legal recognition of indigenous lands, territories or resources can be practically meaningless, unless the physical identity of the property is determined and marked.

An important case before the Inter-American Court of Human Rights has raised the issue of states' obligations to recognise and respect the lands, resources and territories of indigenous peoples, and states' obligations to demarcate those lands and territories. The case is that of the *Mayagna* indigenous community of Awas Tingni against Nicaragua: the Court unanimously dismissed Nicaragua's preliminary objections on 1 February 2000 and is proceeding with the case.[24]

c) *Failure of states to enforce or implement laws protecting indigenous lands and resources*

Some of the most grave situations, such as the massive invasion of Yanomami lands in Brazil and the resulting deaths of thousands of Yanomami Indians, came about in large part because of the state's failure to enforce existing laws.[25] Even after the demarcation of the Yanomami territory, the government of Brazil has not devoted the necessary resources and has not taken the appropriate measures to prevent the illegal invasion of thousands of goldminers. These goldminers have been responsible in part of the unprecedented fires that have burned extensively within the Yanomami territory, destroying vast areas of forest and food crops. The fires caused widespread outbreaks of diseases that resulted in the deaths of hundreds of Yanomami.[26]

d) *Expropriation of indigenous lands for national interest including development*

The legacy of colonialism is probably most acute in the area of expropriation of indigenous lands, territories and resources for the national economic interest including development, social and cultural interests. In every part of the globe, indigenous peoples are being impeded from proceeding with forms of development consistent with their own values, perspectives and interests. In Indonesia, it is reported that the Government purports to respect and adopt indigenous customary rights unless the national interest is at stake; unfortunately, economic development is equated with national interest and indig-

---

Seminar on Practical Experiences Regarding Indigenous Land Rights and Claims, Whitehorse, Canada, 24-28 March 1996 (1996).

24   Corte Interamericana de Depechos Humanos, Caso De La Comunidad Mayagna (Surno) Awas Tingni, Sentencia De Febrero De 2000, para. 60.

25   See E.-I. A. Daes *Report on her mission to Brazil* (1991) in the files of the OHCHR.

26   Inter-American Commission on Human Rights, *Report on the Situation of Human Rights in Brazil* (1997).

enous land rights are thus avoided.[27] The notion of development can be linked directly to the affirmation of 'permanent sovereignty over natural resources'[28] and the rights of States to 'freely utilize and exploit' their natural resources.[29] Of particular relevance in this context is the state's assertion that it has complete rights to sub-surface resources. This view has had numerous unfortunate social, economic, environmental and cultural consequences.

Oil and gas exploration, geothermal energy development, mining, dam construction, logging, agriculture, ranching and other forms of economic activity ostensibly in the national interest have had an adverse impact both on indigenous peoples who have already suffered from contact with colonialism and on indigenous peoples in areas long isolated. Often, development takes place without indigenous peoples' consent, consultation, participation or benefit.

e)   Removal and relocation

Removal of indigenous peoples from their lands and territories is considered by some states as an appropriate solution or a suitable means for 'removing' a problem, whether it is done purportedly to protect indigenous peoples or to promote State interests in their land, territories and resources. Removal and relocation are so widespread that the international community has responded in the context of human rights standard-setting, including article 16 of ILO Convention 169; Article 10 of the Draft UN Declaration; and Article XVIII.6 of the proposed Inter-American Declaration.

In connection with the elaboration of this specific standard, the term 'forced removal' has been used to describe the coercive and abusive actions taken by governments without prior consent of indigenous peoples to remove them from their land.

A joint statement to the WGIP at its eight session by indigenous organisations highlighted the negative impact of population-transfer on indigenous cultures. Govern-

---

27   See UN Doc. E/CN.4/Sub2/1989/36, *Report of the Working Group on Indigenous Populations of the Sub-Commission on Prevention of Discrimination and Protection of Minorities* (1989) *on its seventh session*.

28   N.J. Newton 'Indian claims in the courts of the conqueror' 41 *American University Law Review* (1992), pp. 753-854; also see R.L. Barsh, 'Indian claims policy in the United States', 58 *North Dakota Law Review* (1982) pp. 7-82; L. Orlando, 'Aboriginal title claims in the Indian Claims Commission: United States v Dann and its due process implications' 13 *Boston College Environmental Affairs Law Review* (1986) pp. 241-280.

29   See for example S. Tullberg, R. Coulter and C. Berkey, 'Violations of human rights of the Sioux Nation, the Six Nations Iroquois Confederacy, the Western Shoshone Nation and the Hopi Nation by the United States of America', a complaint of the Indian Law Resource Center communicated to the Commission of Human Rights under the confidential '1503 procedure' on 12 March 1980; Petition of Mary and Carrie Dann and the Dann Band of the Western Shoshone Nation to the Inter-American Commission on Human Rights, 3 April 1993, para. 30; and T.R. Berger *Long and Terrible Shadow, White Values, Native Rights in the Americas 1492-1992* (Vancouver: Douglas & Mcintyre, 1991) p. 99.

ments have used population transfer as a means of countering claims to self-determination, to impose non-indigenous national cultures and to facilitate the disposal of natural resources. Justifications given for relocations have included overpopulation, the need for resettlement, transmigration, resource exploitation and security.

f)   Other governmental programmes and policies adversely affecting indigenous peoples' relationship to their lands, territories and resources

These programmes and policies include:

i)   Allotment of land to individuals

Programmes of allotment of land to individuals invariably weaken the indigenous nation, community or people and usually result in their eventual loss of most or all of their land. The supposed advantages of permitting individuals to use their land as collateral for loans are in fact far outweighed by the almost inevitable loss of the land and the resulting overall decline in resources available to indigenous peoples. The experience of the Mapuche peoples in Chile during the 1970s and 1980s is a sorrowful example.[30]

ii)   Settlement programmes

States often view indigenous peoples' territories as areas suitable for settlement by non-indigenous peoples, even though resources in the area provide only a modest economy for the indigenous owners. The result of such programmes appears to be even greater poverty and social unrest. The encouragement of settlement in the Chittagong Hill Tracts in Bangladesh is an example; the problem has also been reported in South America. The Government of Bangladesh reports that a 'Peace Accord' reached in 1997 included specific provisions on tribal peoples' relationship to land. According to the Government, this accord with the indigenous representatives of the region has improved the situation substantially and the Government has stated its commitment to fully implementing the Peace Accord as soon as possible.[31] However, it has been reported by others that implementation of this peace agreement has been slow, that the region remains militarised and that the mechanisms for adjudication of land claims under the agreement have yet to be established.[32]

iii)   State assumption of trust title

In certain countries, particularly in the Americas, states have created the legal notion that the state itself holds title to all or most indigenous lands and holds that title in trust

---

31   UN Doc. E/CN.4/Sub.2/12000/SR.18, *Remarks of the observer of Bangladesh to the Sub-Commission* (2000).

32   IWGIA *The Indigenous World, 1999-2000* (Copenhagen: IWGIA, 2000) p. 288.

for the various indigenous nations, tribes or peoples. The legal status of this for Indian land has been given scholarly attention in the United States.[33] These systems are usually imposed without the indigenous peoples' consent. They often give to the state extensive power to control the use of the land and its resources.

iv)   Loan programmes

Programmes that encourage using indigenous lands as collateral for loans are likely to result in the eventual loss of indigenous lands and resources. This does not mean that indigenous peoples should not participate in market economies, but they should do so on terms of fairness, good faith and equality.

v)   Failure to protect the integrity of the environment of indigenous lands and territories

The problems regarding environmental degradation and development illustrate the specific matter of State failure to protect the integrity of indigenous peoples' lands, territories and resources from both direct and indirect adverse impacts. This question relates to global environmental problems as well as national development initiatives. Indigenous peoples whose territories transcend State boundaries are facing many environmental problems of vital importance. Thus, the diversity of interests, laws, policies, practices and in particular national development schemes in different jurisdictions can have direct adverse impacts upon the integrity of indigenous lands, territories and resources.

Other failures to protect the integrity of indigenous lands, territories and resources include trans-boundary pollution, dumping of hazardous or toxic waste, ocean dumping, ozone layer depletion, militarization and diminishing supplies of fresh water

vi)   Land and resource use and management and internal self-determination regarding indigenous lands, territories and resources

An important dimension of affirming indigenous land rights is the exercise of a measure of control over lands, territories and resources by indigenous peoples through their own institutions. Though rights to lands, territories and resources may be affirmed, the exercise of internal self-determination, in the form of control over, and decision-making concerning, development, use of natural resources, management and conservation measures, is often absent.

---

33   See for example, M.S. Ball 'Constitution, Courts, Indian tribes' *American Bar-Foundation Research Journal* (1987) pp. 1-63 ; N.J. Newton 'Enforcing the Federal-Indian Trust relationship after Michel' 31 *Catholic University Law Review* (1982) pp. 635-683.

IV. The principle of permanent sovereignty over natural resources and the scope of the right of indigenous peoples to own, develop, use, control and manage their lands, territories and natural resources.

Since the proclamation of the Universal Declaration of Human Rights and other relevant international and regional human rights instruments, there have been substantial developments in international law and State practice with respect to the rights of indigenous peoples to own, develop, use, control and manage their lands, territories and natural resources.

Moreover, every year new norms, jurisprudence and policies are being considered and articulated at both the international and domestic level. In most instances, these developments reflect greater recognition of indigenous peoples' rights to authority over their lands, territories and resources and to their own decision-making power regarding their use and development.[34] Logically arising from these property rights, as well as the right to self-determination and the right to development, there is also an increased recognition of indigenous peoples' right to give or withhold their prior and informed consent to activities within their lands and territories and to activities that may affect their lands, territories and natural resources.[35]

Indigenous peoples' permanent sovereignty over natural resources might properly be described as a collective right by virtue of which the state is obliged to respect, promote and protect the governmental and property interests of indigenous peoples as collectivities in their natural resources.

These interests are ownership interests, including all the normal incidents of ownership. The interests involved may vary depending on the particular circumstances, but in general these would be interests normally associated with ownership: the right to use or conserve resources, the right to manage and to control access to resources, the right to

---

34   Case of Maya Indigenous Community 'finding violation of the right to property when State granted logging and oil concessions to third parties within indigenous lands without effective consultation with and the informed consent of the Maya people'. See UN Doc, E/CN/4/Sub2/2003/38/Rev.2, *Commentary on the Norms on the Responsibilities of Transnational Corporations and Other Business Enterprises with Regard to Human Rights*, Sec.10(c) (2003) providing that [Transnational corporations and other business enterprises] shall respect the rights of local communities affected by their activities… respect the rights of indigenous peoples and similar communities to own, occupy, develop, control, protect and use their lands, other natural resources [and] respect the principle of free, prior and informed consent of the indigenous peoples and communities to be affected by their development projects'.

35   An expert-member of the Sub-Commission, Professor Yozo Yokota, at the 55th session, 12 August 2003, pointed out, among other things, the need for the free, prior and informed consent of indigenous peoples for development projects affecting their lives, environment and other interests. In her final report regarding the 'Protection of the Heritage of Indigenous Peoples' this author called for the free, prior and informed consent of indigenous peoples in the context of a number of 'principles and guidelines' concerning indigenous heritage. E/CN.4/Sub.2/1995/26, Annex paras. 9,26,28,35,46 (21 June 1995).

freely dispose of or sell resources and related interests. It may be that in some situations, indigenous peoples' interest may be something less than full ownership, such as the right of use, a right of hunting and fishing, or a shared right to use a resource.

What are indigenous peoples' natural resources? In general, these are the natural resources belonging to indigenous peoples in the sense that they have historically held or enjoyed the incidents of ownership; namely, use, possession, control, right of disposition and so forth. These resources can include air, coastal seas, and sea ice as well as timber, minerals, oil and gas, genetic resources and all other material resources pertaining to indigenous lands and territories. There appears to be a widespread understanding that natural resources located on indigenous lands or terrritories, resources such as timber, water, flora and fauna, belong to the indigenous peoples who own the land or territory. ILO Convention 169, Article 15 provides for indigenous rights to surface resources, although to a more limited extent. The area where the resources are located may be land or territory, owned by an indigenous people by reason of a historic right pre-dating the State, or it may be an area acquired in more recent times by purchase, grant or otherwise. The international law and jurisprudence as has developed through the *Awas Tingni case*, the *Maya Indigenous Communities v. Belize case* and ILO Convention 169, is the law that must be applied by States to determine what land and territories, and therefore what resources, belong to indigenous peoples.

There is no such agreement concerning sub-surface resources despite the fact that several international and domestic cases have recognised such a right.[36]

The system of state ownership of sub-surface resources is distinctly discriminatory towards indigenous peoples in its operation. It should be also noted that as a general matter it is clear that indigenous peoples were not participants in the process of adopting State constitutions and cannot be said to have consented to the transfer of their sub-surface resources to the State. In this connection, the consequences of the exclusion of indigenous peoples from constitution-making has been noted by this author in a previous work.[37]

What is meant by 'permanent sovereignty'? This concept was created in the context of decolonisation and referred to the rights and powers of former colonies that were becoming independent states. Of course, all states have this authority. When this term is used in reference to indigenous peoples within the state, it does not of course imply that the indigenous peoples have the status of independent states. The principle of ter-

---

36   The case *Maya Indigenous Communities v. Belize* involved a challenge, among other things, to oil and logging concessions granted by the government within Maya ancestral lands. In its preliminary report of December 2003, the Inter-American Commission further affirmed the rights and principles articulated by the Court in the *Awas Tingni* case and found that the 'Maya People of southern Belize have a communal property right to the lands that they have traditionally used and occupied', and that the character of these rights is a function of Maya customary land use patterns and tenure.

37   E.-I. A. Daes, 'Some Considerations on the Right of Indigenous Peoples to Self-determination' 3 *Transnational Law and Contemporary Problems* (1993) pp. 1-12.

ritorial integrity is to be respected. The term sovereignty is not limited to independent states and is widely used in reference to various governing authorities within states, without in any way diminishing the sovereign status of the state. The term refers to the right to manage, govern and regulate the use of the resources by the indigenous people itself, by individuals or by others. It is in this sense that the term 'sovereignty' is used in this chapter.

This authority or 'sovereignty ' is said to be 'permanent' because it refers to an inalienable human right of indigenous peoples. This right arises out of the right to self-determination, the right to own property, the right to exist as a people, and the right to be free from discrimination, among other rights, all of which are inalienable. The word 'permanent' is also intended to emphasise particularly that indigenous peoples are not to be deprived of their resources as a consequence of unequal or oppressive arrangements, contracts or concessions, especially those that are characterised by fraud, duress, unfair bargaining conditions and lack of mutual understanding. This does not mean that the indigenous peoples that own the resources can never sell or dispose of them. Rather, it means that the indigenous peoples have the permanent right to own and control their resources so long as they wish, free from economic, legal and political oppression or unfairness of any kind, including the often unequal and unjust conditions of the private marketplace.

Limitations, if any, on the right of indigenous peoples to their natural resources must flow only from the most urgent and compelling interest of the state. Few, if any, limitations on indigenous resource rights are appropriate, because the indigenous ownership of the resources is associated with the most important and fundamental human rights, including the rights to life, food, the right to self-determination to shelter and the right to exist as a people. The principal question is whether under any circumstances a state should exercise the state's powers of 'eminent domain' to take natural resources from an indigenous people for public use or national interest while providing fair and just compensation. Indigenous people's representative have argued in the *ad hoc* Working Group of the Commission on Human Rights during the further discussion of the Draft UN Declaration that states should never compulsory take indigenous lands or resources even with compensation.[38] All state authority over resources, even resources the state clearly owns, must be exercised in a manner consistent with the human rights of indigenous peoples.

V. Fundamental guiding principles for the recognition, promotion and protection of the rights to land and natural resources of indigenous peoples

a)   The rule of law must be rigorously established and maintained in every country with respect to indigenous peoples and their lands, territories and resources. The rule of

---

38   UN Doc.E/CN.4/2004/81, *Report of the Working Group established in accordance with Commission on Human Rights resolution 1995/32* (2004).

law is the establishment and consistent application by the state and its citizens of just and democratically adopted laws, including international human rights and humanitarian law;

b)   remedies for indigenous peoples and individuals must be available and legally enforceable;

c)   all international actions and State actions, legal and administrative measures in regard to indigenous lands, territories and resources must meet the standards of fundamental fairness to all indigenous and non-indigenous parties, and all such actions must be characterised by justice in political, legal, social and economic terms;

d)   all international actions and state actions, and legal and administrative measures in regard to indigenous lands, territories and resources must be non-discriminatory in their application and effect and must not subject indigenous peoples or individuals to any disadvantage or adverse consequence in comparison with non-indigenous persons in the state;

e)   all international actions and state actions, and legal and administrative measures in regard to indigenous lands, territories and resources must ensure that all indigenous peoples have lands, territories and resources sufficient to ensure their well-being and equitable development as peoples;

f)   all international actions and state actions, and legal measures with regard to indigenous lands, territories and resources must recognise the right of self-determination of indigenous peoples and conform with the obligation to deal with the appropriate indigenous institutions of government and the obligation to respect the right of indigenous peoples to promote, develop, control and protect their own lands, territories and resources;

g)   international and state measures that may affect indigenous lands, territories and resources, even indirectly, must provide for the full and direct participation of all affected indigenous peoples in the decision-making processes;

h)   international actions, state actions and legal measures in regard to indigenous lands, territories and resources must as a practical matter be fully accessible to indigenous peoples, and adequate technical and financial resources must be available to ensure that such measures, decisions and processes can be used effectively by them;

i)   international actions, state actions and legal measures in regard to indigenous lands, territories and natural resources must be carried out in the context of full respect for all the human rights and fundamental freedoms of indigenous peoples, particularly the minimum standards set forth in the Draft UN Declaration, ILO Convention 169 and the proposed American declaration;

j)   states where such specific legislation does not exist should enact legislation, including special measures to recognise, promote, protect and demarcate the lands, territories and resources of indigenous peoples in a manner that accords legal protection, rights and status equal to those accorded to other lands, territories and natural resources in the country;

k)   states must respect and protect the special relationship that indigenous peoples have to lands, territories and resources, particularly sacred sites, culturally significant areas, and uses of resources that are tied to indigenous cultures and religious practices;

l)   legislation must recognise indigenous peoples' traditional practices and law of land, tenure, and it must be developed only with the participation and free consent of the indigenous peoples concerned;

m)   within the legal context of each country, consideration must be given to the need to reform the relevant part of the constitution in order to ensure the necessary level of legal protection of indigenous lands and resources and particularly to ensure that indigenous rights to lands and resources are not subject to invasion or diminution by the government;

n)   governments should formally renounce discriminatory legal doctrines and policies, which deny human rights or limit indigenous land and rights to natural resources. Such doctrines include: 'discovery' and *terra nullius;* the doctrine that indigenous communities do not have the capacity to own land collectively; the doctrine that indigenous land, title or ownership or exploitation of natural resources may be taken or impaired by the state or third parties without due process and adequate, fair and just compensation;

o)   governments, in consultation with indigenous peoples, should establish fair procedures for reviewing, and taking corrective action if necessary in situations in which indigenous lands or resources have been taken or rights to them extinguished through past processes, which are claimed or are found to be basically unfair or discriminatory;

p)   effective legislative, economic and administrative measures should be adopted and provided by states for the implementation, amendment and enforcement of land or natural resource's settlements and agreements as well as for the resolution of disputes.

Chapter 6

THE WORLD BANK AND INDIGENOUS PEOPLES

Sia Spiliopoulou Åkermark[1]

Introduction

Patrick Thornberry's most recent book is dedicated to 'Indigenous Peoples and Human Rights'.[2] His lasting experience in the indigenous discourse inspires him in the introduction to the book to remind us of 'the profoundly ambiguous and often tragic relationship between indigenous peoples and the law of nations'. In evaluating international law in general and human rights law in particular with regard to indigenous issues, Thornberry offers two possible accounts: on one hand there is a pessimistic picture full of legal *lacunae,* while on the other there is a view of present international law as an opening up of 'dialogic spaces' in which a discourse on indigenous concerns can take place, including subjects such as the characteristics and membership of *indigeousness.* As Thornberry argues, indigenous discourse has its starting point either in a self-determination or in a human rights rhetoric.

However, there are two other frameworks in which indigenous issues have been an important element: environmental protection and development.[3] Both have been crucial parts of World Bank activities since the late 1970s and early 1980s. This article offers an overview of the indigenous discourse within the World Bank. It argues that the World Bank needs to be studied as an actor involved in the law-making process of international law and that it is not possible to maintain the conceptualisation of World Bank policies solely as internal staff regulations. It also shows that the World Bank can offer us many insights with regard to the modalities of participation of indigenous peoples in decision-making.

The World Bank and its sister organisation the International Monetary Fund (IMF) have been under heavy criticism from many different angles in recent years. According to one view, the funds made available to countries with an incompetent, corrupt and

---

1   Jur. Dr., Associate Professor, Faculty of Law, Uppsala University, Sweden.

2   P. Thornberry *Indigenous peoples and human rights* (Manchester: Manchester University Press, 2002).

3   Thornberry identifies a number of international fora, including the World Bank, where work on indigenous affairs takes place. Ibid. p. 28.

Nazila Ghanea & Alexandra Xanthaki (eds.), Minorities, Peoples and Self-Determination, *pp. 93-112.*
© *2005 Koninklijke Brill NV. Printed in The Netherlands. ISBN 90 04 14301 7.*

undemocratic government exacerbate moral hazard. This view looks at the World Bank and IMF as black holes where the contributions of the tax payers in developed countries constantly disappear. According to another view, the funds available through these two international organisations are completely insufficient to meet the needs of developing countries and of vulnerable groups in such countries, and have instead created a relation of dependency through the immense debt accumulated by the developing countries. In the present text I will focus on indigenous affairs in the World Bank only, since the IMF considers that indigenous matters and human rights fall outside its mandate. The issue of dependency is highly relevant with regard to indigenous peoples. To what extent do World Bank projects and programmes empower indigenous peoples? Or, conversely, to what extent do such projects and programmes create a further dependency upon state institutions and international funding?

A different angle of criticism against the international financial institutions has its starting point in the perceived lack of interest of the World Bank and IMF in the social implications of their activities. Linked to this latter point, is the critique concerning the participatory deficit in international organisations in general and in the World Bank and the IMF in particular. The argument is twofold. First, at a country and government level, it touches upon the weak position of developing countries in negotiations and decision-making. Second, it concerns claims for widened participation in international organisations not only by governments but also by all those affected by the activities of the organisation, including, in the case of the World Bank, indigenous peoples. In this last mentioned formulation, claims of participation challenge the prerogative of governments as sole representatives of their whole population.

An analysis of the development of the indigenous discourse in the World Bank illustrates still another phenomenon, namely the nexus of environmental and indigenous issues and, in that sense, the nexus of environmental protection and protection of human rights. In recent years, the discourse has been broadened to cover also some of the tensions involved, such as the difficult balance between protecting environmentally sensitive areas and allowing for continued use of natural resources by indigenous peoples. It will be amply evident from the information below that, institutionally, indigenous concerns entered the realm of the World Bank through the environmentalists employed by the Bank in the 1970s. More recently, the World Bank has also created a post of a coordinator of indigenous affairs.

Background: Amazon deforestation and the Indians

The Stockholm Declaration of the United Nations Conference on the Human Environment (1972)[4] emphasised the link between environmental protection and development. The World Bank was heavily involved in the preparation of the Conference and the

---

4   Stockholm Declaration of the United Nations Conference on the Human Environment, 16 June 1972, available at the website of the UN Environment Program: www.unep.org/Documents.

drafting of the Declaration and Robert McNamara, the then president of the Bank, in his address to the Conference committed the Bank to work for the environmental soundness of development operations.[5] With the Stockholm Conference in prospect, he had already in 1970 appointed the Bank's first environmental adviser, James Lee, and established a centralised Office of Environmental Affairs within the Bank. Robert Goodland, tropical ecologist, joined the Office in 1978 at the time when the World Bank was preparing the Amazon Program called Polonoroeste.

The Polonoroeste ('the northwest pole') project had as its main objective the building of a highway from Brazil's economic centre in the south-central region to the northwest part of the Amazon (in the states of Rondônia and Mato Grosso). Between 1981 and 1983 the Bank approved five loans to Brazil in support of Polonoroeste totalling 457 million US dollars. Robert Goodland sought to include the creation of Indian reserves in the project design and drafted a set of policies on tribal peoples in order to overcome internal resistance among officials in the Bank. In February 1982 the Bank adopted Operational Manual Statement 2.34 on 'Tribal People in Bank-Financed Projects'.[6] Robert Goodland wrote during the same period a study on the effects of economic development on the lands and cultures of tribal peoples.[7] Goodland's main thesis was based on his experience in development work in the Amazon and argued that it is possible to observe a 'continuum of acculturation', i.e. integration, of tribal groups in the wider societies in the country where they live. Isolated tribes became semi-isolated, and were later in permanent contact with national societies. Finally, they were fully integrated with their respective national societies and formed part of the 'indigenous peasant populations'.

The Office of Environmental Affairs became the institutional platform of the indigenous discourse in the Bank. James Lee explained his views on projects of the Bank at the time:

---

5   R. Wade 'Greening the Bank: The Struggle over the Environment, 1970-1995' in D. Kapur *et al.* (eds.) *The World Bank: Its First Half Century* (Washington: The Brookings Institution, 1997) Vol. II, pp. 611-734.

6   World Bank *Tribal People in Bank-Financed Projects* Operational Manual Statement No. 2.34 (2001).

7   R. Goodland *Tribal Peoples and Economic Development: Human Ecologic Considerations* (Washington: World Bank, May 1982). By that time the Bank had already adopted an Operational Manual Statement 2.33 on *Social Issues Associated with Involuntary Resettlement in Bank-Financed Projects* (1980). There has always been considerable overlap between issues of resettlement and indigenous peoples in the operations and policies of the World Bank. In 1986 Bank sociologist Michael Cernea wrote a report on *Involuntary Resettlement in Bank-Assisted Projects: A Review of the Application of Bank Policies and Procedures in FY 79-85* (Washington: The World Bank, Agriculture and Rural Development Department, February 1986) in which he concluded that resettlement very often involved tribal peoples, as in the case of the dam and irrigation projects along the Narmada river in India.

People were sort of looked upon as objects or economic entities....We began finding that the development that we were promoting ...had some very traumatic effects on these peoples. It introduced new diseases. The acculturation process which goes on when mainstream society comes up against these people was very unsavoury, was very traumatic. There clearly was a need for the Bank to get out in front of this and to adopt a policy...that said that the Bank was concerned about the future of these people and was going to do something about it.[8]

Lee admitted that these ideas were the result not only of internal reassessments but also of pressure from outside actors such as Amnesty International and the Harvard Group of Cultural Survival, while many borrowers resisted strongly any interference with their sovereign rights over their own people.[9] The biggest borrowers that were heavily affected by tribal and indigenous concerns, Brazil and India, have over the years been among the main opponents of the Bank's policies on indigenous peoples and resettlement.

The 'acculturation' era: Operational Manual Statement 2.34 on 'Tribal People in Bank-Financed Projects'

The Operational Manual Statement on 'Tribal people' (OMS 2.34),[10] was rather brief but emphasised the need for 'special measures' in projects intended for beneficiaries other than tribal people and likely to harm such people. The Bank should avoid financing projects encroaching upon traditional territories used or occupied by tribal people unless 'adequate safeguards' were provided. If projects involved undesired effects for tribal people, there should be measures taken to prevent or mitigate such effects.

While the 'special measures' logic was a big step forward for the protection of indigenous peoples, the overall approach in OMS 2.34 followed the 'integrationist' and 'protectionist' assumptions of the International Labour Organisation (ILO) Convention No. 107 (1957).[11] The main objective at the time was to ensure the integration and adap-

---

8   Wade (note 5) p. 630.
9   Ibid.
10   OMS 2.34 (note 6). At the time the Bank's operational documents were not made public. Information was available to external observers mainly through various reports, working papers and articles written by Bank staff, such as the writings of the Bank's Legal Counsel Ibrahim Shihata. Shihata broke new ground in 1994 when he included as appendixes to his book on the World Bank Inspection Panel a number of relevant operational documents of the Bank. See I. Shihata *The World Bank Inspection Panel* (Oxford: Oxford University Press, 1st edition, 1994). Since the late 1990s, the whole Operational Manual is available at the website of the World Bank www.worldbank.org as are many of the reports and working papers produced in the organisation.
11   International Labour Organisation, Convention concerning the protection and integration of indigenous and other tribal and semi-tribal populations in independent countries, C 107

tation of tribes into the wider political economies and rural societies of their country.[12]

OMS 2.34 defined tribal people as ethnic groups that have 'stable, low-energy, sustained-yield economic systems' and had in varying degrees the following characteristics:

– Were geographically isolated or semi-isolated
– Were 'unacculturated' (or 'partially acculturated') into the societal norms of the majority
– Were non-monetised (or partially monetised)
– Were non-literate and without a written language
– Were linguistically distinct
– Identified closely with one particular territory
– Had an economic lifestyle highly dependent on a specific natural environment
– Exhibited poor political organisation and representation
– Had loose tenure over traditional lands, which was often disrespected by the dominant society and its institutions.[13]

We recognise in this list many of the elements of ILO Convention No 107,[14] including the understanding of tribal people mainly as economic production units, the assumption of a strong link to isolated territories, the emphasis on 'underdevelopment' both economically and culturally.

The policy was not concerned with projects designed specifically for tribal peoples as the direct beneficiaries, but rather with other projects having an impact on tribal people. Indeed at the time, the thought of projects designed to benefit primarily indigenous peoples seems to have been unthinkable. At the time, and according to the policy, development projects should have provided 'adequate time and conditions for acculturation', a process that needed to be 'slow and gradual'. The policy tried further to highlight the opportunities tribal people could offer to the wider society 'by increasing

(1957). ILO Conventions are available at www.ilo.org/ilolex/ Both ILO conventions on indigenous peoples (C. 107 and C. 169) are included as annexes in Thornberry (note 2), pp. 432-452.

12   S. Davis, The World Bank and Indigenous Peoples, Paper presented at the Denver Initiative Conference on Human Rights, University of Denver Law School, April 1993, (Washington: World Bank).

13   J. Martinez Cobo Study of the Problem of Discrimination against Indigenous Populations, UN Document E/CN.4/Sub.2/1986/7 and Adds. 1-4. The characteristics described appear identically in the Goodland study, see above (note 7). In addition, Goodland included in his study 'Notes on terminology' (p. vii) which clarified inter alia that 'indigenous' meant 'native', which implies birth or origin in the region, and, further, the implication 'of not having been introduced from another region of the country'. In contrast to other approaches (such as those often encountered in the UN system, including the Martinez Cobo study) Goodland's and the World Bank's understanding of indigenousness does not include necessarily a reference to invasion and colonisation. In this sense, it is a wider understanding of indigenousness not limited to the first (and presumably) sole inhabitants of a particular territory.

14   Convention No. 107 (note 11).

the national society's knowledge of proven adaptation to and utilization of fragile and marginal environments'.[15] In order to be able to prevent or mitigate harmful effects on tribal peoples, the policy requested four steps:

1)   the recognition, demarcation and protection of tribal areas containing the resources required to sustain the tribal people's traditional means of livelihood;

2)   appropriate social services, especially with regard to diseases and protection of health;

3)   the maintenance, to the extent desired by the tribe, of its cultural integrity; and

4)   a forum for the participation of the tribal people in decisions affecting them, and providing for adjudication and redress of grievances.[16]

Finally, the policy tried to identify the steps Bank staff needed to take at various stages of the project cycle (design, preparation, appraisal, implementation, monitoring and evaluation). Crucial in this respect was the effort to introduce anthropological knowledge into the work of the Bank.

It is ironic that the Bank adopted the Operational Manual Statement and the Goodland study at a time when many Latin American indigenous organisations and anthropologists were criticising the strong integrationist approach for not adequately recognising the historical persistence of indigenous identities and cultures.[17]

In 1989, the Office of Environmental and Scientific Affairs reviewed the Bank's experience in implementing OMS 2.34.[18] The effects of the tribal policy were mainly identified as an increase over time in the number of projects that were found to have consequences for the health, cultural integrity and economic wellbeing of tribal groups. It was also reported that the policy was applied mainly to small, isolated groups in South America and Central and South Africa, and not to larger and complex tribal peoples in India, Southeast Asia or East and West Africa. The review also indicated that the Bank was not particularly successful in ensuring the integration of all four protective elements identified in the policy (land demarcation and protection, health and social services, protection of tribal cultural integrity and tribal participation). Very few projects incorporated components of land demarcation and protection, and then only at a late stage of the project cycle. Participation was found to be extremely poor and health and social services were not designed in accordance with the needs and preferences of the groups concerned. With reference to the United Nations Study by Jose Martinez Cobo on Discrimination against Indigenous Populations (1986)[19] the review concluded that the most effective way

15   OMS 2.34 (note 6) para. 4.
16   Ibid. para. 7.
17   Davis (note 12) p. 3.
18   It should be noted that the review was done as a desk review by the Office of Environmental and Scientific Affairs, and not by the Operations Evaluation Unit which had been established by McNamara in 1970. This can perhaps be seen as a sign of the institutional isolation of indigenous matters in the Bank as a whole.
19   Cobo study (note 13).

of strengthening Bank-financed tribal components was by convincing borrower governments to include tribal and indigenous peoples in project design and execution.

At about the same time the ILO was reassessing the international standards set in Convention No. 107, and it adopted the new Convention concerning Indigenous and Tribal peoples in Independent Countries (Convention No. 169)[20] in June 1989. This came into force in 1991. Self-identification was now introduced as a fundamental criterion for determining the groups to be covered by the Convention.[21] Even though the emphasis on economic subsistence persisted, numerous provisions were introduced concerning participation of indigenous peoples in decisions affecting them, on education (including education in the traditional languages), as well as on land and natural resources.

Returning to the World Bank, the complexity of the Bank-financed projects along the Narmada River added to the experience from the Polonoroeste in Brazil and meant that the World Bank Legal Department became much more involved in trying to ensure the incorporation of the tribal policy in Bank projects and loan agreements.[22]

The participation era: Operational Directive 4.20 on Indigenous Peoples

Internal reassessments and external pressures on the Bank (as a consequence of projects like Polonoroeste and Narmada), combined with the international reassessment of indigenous issues, led to a revision of the old Operational Manual Statement on tribal people, resulting in the preparation of an Operational Directive entitled *Indigenous Peoples* (OD 4.20)[23] in September 1991.

The directive changed the basic assumptions about indigenous peoples in fundamental ways. Development projects should not only take into account the situation of affected indigenous groups and mitigate possible negative impacts, but should 'ensure that indigenous peoples *benefit* from development projects' (my emphasis).[24] The Bank's broad objective is said to be to 'ensure that the development process fosters full respect for their dignity, human rights, and cultural uniqueness'.[25]

While the basic link to land rights in geographically defined areas, economic activities[26] and other 'productive resources' is maintained, the Directive also emphasised that development plans should be 'culturally appropriate' and that project components *could*

---

20 International Labour Organisation, Convention concerning Indigenous and Tribal Peoples in Independent Countries, C. 169 (1989). For further references see above note 11.

21 Ibid. Article 1(2).

22 I. Shihata (note 10).

23 Operational Directive 4.20 (1991) is available at www.worldbank.org and has been published as an appendix to I. Shihata (ibid).

24 OD 4.20 Ibid. para. 2.

25 Ibid. para. 6.

26 OD 4.20 (note 23) encompasses a wider range of indigenous economic activities than the previous policy, including shifting agriculture in or near forests, wage labour, or even 'small-scale market oriented activities' (see para. 5).

include not only health services, entitlement to land and natural resources and productive infrastructure but equally *education* and '*linguistic and cultural preservation*' (my emphasis).

OD 4.20 applies to all 'projects that affect indigenous peoples'. According to the section on definitions[27] the term 'indigenous peoples' covers also 'indigenous ethnic minorities', 'tribal groups' and 'scheduled tribes'. All these terms describe 'social groups with a social and cultural identity distinct from the dominant society that makes them vulnerable to being disadvantaged in the development process'. The distinctiveness and vulnerability are linked to a set of characteristics possessed in varying degrees:

- a close attachment to ancestral territories and to the natural resources in these areas;
- self-identification and identification by others as members of a distinct cultural group;
- an indigenous language, often distinct from the national language;
- customary social and political institutions;
- primarily subsistence-oriented production.

The directive does not elaborate on the difference between those terms, but some assistance is given by the characteristics described above.

The table below tries to identify the core elements and the shifts in the understanding of indigenousness as reflected in the two policy documents of the World Bank. In summary, one can see that the economic production aspects are toned down in the latter policy, while cultural distinctiveness is emphasised. The autonomy of indigenous peoples is underlined through the introduction of self-identification, although in an interplay with identification by the surrounding society. All elements of 'acculturation' are excluded from the latter document.

Table 1: Understandings of indigenousness in OMS 2.34 and OD 4.20

OMS 2.34 characteristics	OD 4.20 characteristics
Geographically isolated or semi-isolated and identified closely with one particular territory	Close attachment to ancestral territories and to the natural resources in these areas
–	Self-identification and identification by others as members of a distinct cultural group
Non-monetised	–
Linguistically distinct but non-literate and without a written language	Indigenous language, often distinct from the national language
'Unacculturated' (or 'partially acculturated')	Culturally distinct and vulnerable
Economic lifestyle highly dependent on a specific natural environment	Primarily subsistence-oriented production
Poor political organisation and representation	Customary social and political institutions

---

27   Ibid. paras. 3-5.

Operational Directive 4.20 is still in force, even though it has been under revision since the late 1990s (see below). The directive identifies the tension between policies of 'isolation' and policies of 'acculturation'. This unfortunate, but not uncommon, dichotomy excludes the possibility and viability of the preservation of cultural distinctiveness without complete isolation.[28]

In trying to avoid this dilemma, the Bank chooses the path of *informed participation* (emphasis in the original).[29] This may of course be criticised for not being a true response to the original dilemma, but it introduced into the Bank's work the basic idea that indigenous peoples themselves should consider and respond to this dilemma. Types of informed participation are given as examples: direct consultation, incorporation of indigenous knowledge into projects, and appropriate use of 'experienced specialists' in projects.

The reference in the Directive to 'experienced specialists' has its background in debates about the need to integrate anthropological and sociological insights into Bank operations. Indeed already under the section on definitions, it is specified that '[t]ask managers must exercise judgment in determining the populations to which this directive applies and should make use of specialised anthropological and sociological experts throughout the project cycle'.[30] Similarly, in the provisions on Project Processing and Documentation it is provided that '[e]arly involvement of anthropologists and local NGOs with expertise in matters related to indigenous peoples is a useful way to identify mechanisms for effective participation and local development opportunities'.[31] One could therefore argue that the increased interest in indigenous and resettlement issues within the Bank was at least in part the result of new academic disciplines and professional groups entering the sphere of the Bank, people like ecologist Robert Goodland and sociologist Michael Cernea. The increased interest in indigenous peoples resulted in its turn in a further accentuation of the need to broaden the professional body of the Bank, this time mainly with anthropologists.

The 1991 Operational Directive also gives details with regard to the practical implications of the policy during the project cycle. For investment projects that 'affect indigenous peoples' the borrower has to prepare an Indigenous Peoples Development Plan (IPDP) that is consistent with the Bank's policy. When the whole project envisages indigenous peoples as direct beneficiaries, the provisions of the OD apply to the project in its entirety (and a specific IPDP is not required). It is clear at this point that OD 4.20, as is the case with very many policy documents, and especially those recently elevated to be called Safeguard Policies do not create obligations only for the World Bank and

---

28   Thornberry discusses 'indicia of indigeousness' as an open-ended notion and points to the importance of the 'land-spirituality nexus' as well as the co-existence of cultural and economic relationships. Thornberry (note 2) p. 409.

29   OD 4.20 (note 23) para. 8.

30   Ibid. para. 5, last sentence.

31   Ibid. para. 17.

its staff, but equally for borrowing countries.[32] In most cases this is legally based on the incorporation of the main requirements of Safeguard Policies into the loan agreement signed between the Bank and the borrower. As such those requirements form part of the conditionality attached to bank loans and grants. If the borrower does not fulfil its obligations under the agreement, the Bank can interrupt the disbursement of funds and even cancel the agreement.

In addition to the provisions on informed participation mentioned earlier, a characteristic element of OD 4.20 is the effort towards empowerment and capacity building for the benefit of indigenous peoples. An IPDP should 'avoid creating or aggravating the dependency of indigenous people' on the project and planning should 'encourage *early handover* of project management to local people' (my emphasis). In order to be able to fulfil this goal, plans should include general education and training in management skills for indigenous people from the onset of the project.[33] It is recognised by the policy that all this takes time, and successful planning should be afforded long lead times as well as arrangements for extended follow-up.

The implementation of Operational Directive 4.20: mixed achievements

Operational Directive 4.20 adjusted the World Bank's policy on indigenous peoples to be in line with ILO Convention No. 169 and opened up development projects for increased indigenous participation. It recognised the cultural specificity of indigenous groups and adopted a flexible and dialectic approach to the inclusion of the processes of self-identification and identification by others in the recognition of groups as indigenous. But how did the Directive work in practice? What was its status, not solely in the normative hierarchy of the Bank, where it has been recognised since 1997 as one of the ten Safeguard Policies, but in the mindset of Bank staff and borrowers?

The Operations Evaluation Department (OED) of the Bank decided to evaluate the implementation of this particular directive in two phases. The evaluation reports were issued in January and April 2003.[34] The evaluation was prompted by the fact that the directive had been under revision since 1996, that there already exists a Draft Opera-

---

32   The notion of Safeguard Policies was introduced into the World Bank in 1997. Ten specific Bank policies have been included in this hierarchically higher level of operational policies. They concern: environmental assessment, natural habitats, pest management, involuntary resettlement, indigenous peoples, forestry, safety of dams, cultural property, international waterways and projects in disputed areas.

33   OD 4.20 (note 23) para. 14 (para. 14 deals with the prerequisites of a successful development plan).

34   *Implementation of Operational Directive 4.20 on Indigenous Peoples: An Independent Desk Review*, Report No. 25332, January 10, 2003, World Bank, Operations Evaluation Department (OED Evaluation I); and *Implementation of Operational Directive 4.20 on Indigenous Peoples: An Evaluation of Results*, Report No. 25754, April 10, 2003, World Bank, Operations Evaluation Department (OED Evaluation II).

tional Policy (OP 4.10) on Indigenous Peoples[35] circulated by the Bank for comments and external consultation in March 2001 (see below) and that external consultations were held in late 2001 and early 2002 with a number of indigenous peoples and non-governmental organisations (NGOs) in order to discuss the new draft policy.

The OED *Evaluation I* reviewed projects in 34 countries between January 1992 and May 2001. A total of 234 projects were reviewed, out of which 89 projects were found to affect indigenous peoples.[36] The OD was applied only in 55 of the 89 projects that affected indigenous peoples. The second phase of the evaluation looked more closely at the achievements and weaknesses in the 55 projects where the OD was applied. Eight projects were cancelled, although it is unclear whether this was solely due to problems involving indigenous issues.

The implementation of the Directive across different regions varied greatly. The regions with most projects affecting indigenous peoples, East Asia and Pacific Region (EAP; 20 projects) and Latin America and Caribbean Region (LCR; 50 projects) had few projects with a full Indigenous Peoples Development Plan (IPDP) or at least elements thereof (7 for EAP and 15 for LCR). In total, only 32 projects (out of the 89 which affect indigenous peoples) had an IPDP or elements thereof. The OED also made an effort to evaluate the knowledge and quality of work of regional teams in issues of indigenous peoples, resulting also in this respect in great differences among regions, with the Latin America and Caribbean region showing some positive, although modest, results.[37]

Not only were IPDPs seldom developed, but they were also rarely included among the clauses of loan agreements. Such clauses were incorporated in loan agreements only if there was a full IPDP. This meant that if there was no IPDP, e.g. when the indigenous peoples were considered as beneficiaries, or there were only elements of an IPDP the responsibilities of the borrower are seldom reflected in the loan agreements.[38] Out of the 47 projects studied in depth in the evaluation's second phase, only seven had IPDPs and another 21 projects had elements of IPDPs.[39]

The OED *Evaluation I* concluded that the Bank works most often with the borrowing country's legal framework as a starting point, as is envisaged in the OD itself. However, problems arise when there are no domestic legal provisions or when those provisions are not in line with the main principles in the Bank Directive. In such cases, the Bank either did not raise the issue, or did so in country discussions and in the loan agreements. In China, for instance, the Bank works with the definition of 55 national minorities

---

35   World Bank, draft Operational Policy 4.10 and draft Bank Procedures 4.10 on Indigenous Peoples (2001), available at www.worldbank.org.

36   The OED has used a narrow definition of 'affected' which covers only those directly harmed or where they are among the intended beneficiaries.

37   OED Evaluation II (note 34) p. 8, Table 2.1.

38   Ibid. pp. 14-15.

39   Ibid. p. 20.

in Chinese legislation.[40] Similarly, in loan agreements with Vietnam the term 'Ethnic Minorities' is used. The evaluation found a wide range of opinions among Bank staff and managers on how the OD is to be applied, particularly with regard to the groups and individuals to be covered by it. Some considered that the OD applies only to indigenous groups, others considered that both indigenous and tribal groups are covered, while a third group believed that ethnic minorities were covered as well as indigenous and tribal groups.[41] The evaluation reveals that the international obligations of a country (such as ratifications of ILO conventions or human rights treaties) are in principle taken into consideration in the assessment by Bank staff of the existence of indigenous groups.

In specific case studies highlighted in the review, the OED reviewers and the Bank's Management had different views on the application of the Operational Directive. While the review, on the basis of its own assessment and expert views, concluded that Berbers in Morocco and Somalis in Ethiopia should be covered by the OD, the Bank's staff and Management did not think so. The evaluation also revealed that, in spite of the Directive's specific provisions regarding consultation with experts, only a limited number of projects indicated that anthropologists or sociologists were involved during project participation.[42]

This can be linked to the issue of participation and capacity-building for indigenous peoples. Whilst participation in design and implementation was fairly high in projects where the OD was applied, participation in actual decision-making (which presumably includes the decision of who is covered by the OD and who is not as well as the decision of who is affected and who is a beneficiary) only existed in about half of the projects where the OD applied (51%).[43] In addition, it was found that only 52% of the projects that applied the OD involved 'some form of capacity-building' of indigenous peoples.[44] It is thus concluded that, with the exception of social fund projects, capacity building effort 'was weak overall'.[45] The evaluation found that 'informed participation' was most effective when:

1)   accountable and representative institutional structures were well integrated within the local governance structures;

2)   project guidelines were formulated and effectively disseminated to indigenous peoples;

---

40   OED Evaluation I (note 34) para. 3.8 and Memorandum to the Executive Directors and the President.

41   Ibid. p. 3. It should be noted that the staff survey was answered by only 206 out of 2,485 staff members who received it. Assuming that those that responded are those most interested and familiar with indigenous issues, it can be argued that only a small number of staff members feel truly familiar with the Operational Directive (see Box 4.2. on Results of Staff Survey, p. 26).

42   Ibid. p. 16.

43   Ibid. p. 20, Table 3.4.

44   Ibid.

45   OED Evaluation II (note 34) p. 34.

3)   capacity building was carried out on project objectives, management, implementation and monitoring;
4)   there was a credible dispute settlement mechanism accessible to indigenous peoples;
5)   mechanisms were in place for internal and independent monitoring and auditing.[46]

Capacity-building and participation are undoubtedly linked to the level of education and language skills of indigenous peoples, both in the traditional language as well as in the language use for official decision-making and consultations. Four of the 47 projects which were studied in depth concerned education. Language was, however, considered in only one of those four projects. It can be argued that this confirms the view of indigenousness primarily in terms of subsistence-patterns and economic activity rather than in terms of cultural distinctiveness. In spite of the policy's provisions on participation and capacity building it seems that the Bank still persists in an understanding of indigenous peoples as small, isolated, subsistence-based and fully distinct groups.[47] These groups need in other words to combine the impossible: both participation and isolation.

With respect to the quality of implementation of the policy, the evaluation noted an improvement in implementation in more recent years. It is clear it took the Operational Directive at least five years to get internalised and embedded in Bank operations.[48] However, the number of projects to which the OD was applied (out of the projects that affect indigenous peoples) has remained the same, both in closed and open projects (62 percent).

The main findings and recommendations of the OED evaluation (both phases) were that the Bank:
1)   needed to clarify the intent, scope and requirements of the revised policy;
2)   should distinguish the safeguard (so called *do no harm*) aspects of the revised policy from the *do good* aspects in order to delineate its own responsibilities;
3)   should use the policy not only at a project level, but also in Country Assistance Strategies and other country dialogue;
4)   should design regional and sub-regional strategies to implement the policy;
5)   should increase the relevance and effectiveness of IPDPs.

In the light of the above findings and recommendations of the Operations Evaluation Department, and taking into account the external consultations held by the World Bank

---

46   Ibid. p. 41.
47   See response of Management with regard to the Somalis in Ethiopia. OED Evaluation I (note 34) Box 3.1.
48   OED Evaluation I (note 34) Table 3.3 compares the quality of OD application in closed and open projects where the OD was applied. There is an increase from 58% to 77% satisfactory or highly satisfactory application moving from closed to open projects.

in 2001-2002, it is possible to assess the results of the Draft Operational Policy 4.10 made public by the Bank in March 2001.[49]

Backlash? The on-going revision of OD 4.20

The revision of a number of the Bank's policies in recent years has prompted some commentators to ask whether the current comprehensive revisions entail, in reality, a lowering of Bank standards. Such a lowering could be explained by the unwillingness of some borrowers to accept wide conditions on issues such as the environment, indigenous peoples or resettlement. This could result in the cancellation of projects (as mentioned earlier, there were eight projects cancelled among the 55 in which OD 4.20 was applied) or in borrowers finding alternative sources of funding, or in a combination of both situations (both the Sardar Sarovar dam and the so called Qinghai-component of the China Poverty Reduction Project were finally pursued only after the cancellation of Bank loans and with alternative funding[50]). There are those both inside and outside the Bank who argue that the high transaction costs involved in projects involving Safeguard Policies lead to 'risk aversion' by the Bank as well as by borrowers, resulting in a sharp decrease in infrastructure projects financed by the Bank in the 1990s as well as middle-income countries (who can find alternative funding from regional development banks or from private sources) avoiding loans from the World Bank.[51]

A comparison of OD 4.20 and Draft Operational Policy and Bank Procedures 4.10 (OP/BP 4.10)[52] on Indigenous Peoples illustrates a number of important differences.

The structure of a policy accompanied by Bank Procedures is intended to keep apart the mandatory safeguard obligations of the Bank (what the OED review called 'do no harm aspects') from procedural aspects, which are not mandatory and which mainly concern the respective roles of the Bank and the borrower. Another effect of the distinction is the increased emphasis on the role of the borrower, an emphasis in line with the wider policy of 'country ownership' which has become one of the pillars of present development thinking.

---

49 It should be clear from the dates given above that the 2001 draft was issued before the conduct of the evaluation review, and therefore does not incorporate the recommendations of the OED. It is hard to explain why the review was carried out only after the original draft was made public. One possible explanation is that the external consultation directed a number of critical comments against the draft, and the Bank needed to find a way to dilute external criticism and rework the draft.

50 On indigenous issues in the work of the Inspection Panel see below.

51 D. Kapur *Do As I Say Not As I Do: A Critique of G-7 Proposals on reforming the Multilateral Development Banks* (UNCTAD and Center for International Development, Harvard University: G-24 Discussion Paper Series, No. 20, February 2003) pp. 8-9.

52 Draft O.P/B.P 4.10 (note 35). http://www.worldbank.org has a comparative chart of O.P/B.P. 4.10. However, I find that the comparison does not highlight adequately the major differences, something I try to compensate for in the present analysis.

While the definition of indigenous peoples is largely identical – covering also 'indigenous ethnic minorities', 'tribal groups' and 'scheduled tribes' – there is a strengthened emphasis on land rights in Draft OP/BP 4.10. Thus draft paragraphs 4 and 5 describe not only 'the close attachment to ancestral territories and the natural resources in them' but argue also that such groups have 'a social and economic status that limits their capacity to defend their interests in and rights to land and other productive resources'.

Draft paragraphs 12 and 13 concern rights to land and resources and state that the borrower needs to take into account both individual and *collective rights* to use and develop the lands they occupy (my emphasis) and to give particular attention to the right of indigenous peoples to be protected against encroachment. There is, however, a weakening of the text as regards the legal recognition of such land rights, especially when the lands have been brought into the domain of the state. During the consultations of the World Bank concerning the draft policy the provisions on land and protected areas were heavily criticised.[53]

Comparison of provisions on land related legislation

OD 4.20 – Paragraph 15 on Indigenous Peoples Development Plan (IPDP)	Draft OP 4.10 – Paras. 12-13 entitled Lands and Resources
15. The development plan should be prepared in tandem with the preparation of the main investment. In many cases, proper protection of the rights of indigenous people will require the implementation of special project components that may lie outside the primary project's objectives. These components can include activities related to health and nutrition, productive infrastructure, linguistic and cultural preservation, entitlement to natural resources, and education. The project component for indigenous peoples development should include the following elements, as needed: (a) *Legal Framework*. The plan should contain an assessment of (i) the legal status of the groups covered by this OD, as reflected in the country's constitution, legislation, and subsidiary legislation (regulations, administrative orders, etc.); and (ii) the ability of such groups to obtain access to and effectively use the legal system to defend their rights. Particular attention should be given to the rights	12. The economies, identities and forms of social organization of indigenous peoples are often closely tied to land, water and other natural resources. Therefore, in Bank-assisted projects which affect indigenous peoples, the Borrower takes into account their individual and collective rights to use and develop the lands that they occupy, to continue to have access to natural resources vital to their subsistence, to the sustainability of their cultures, and to their future development. 13. In order to avoid or minimize adverse impacts of Bank-assisted projects on affected indigenous groups, and to determine measures which may be needed to enhance their security over lands and other resources, in the design of the project the Borrower gives particular attention to: a) the cultural, religious and sacred values that these groups attribute to their lands and resources; b) their individual and communal or collective rights to use and develop the lands they occupy and to be protected against

53   See several comments in Summary of Consultations with external Stakeholders regarding the World Bank Draft Indigenous Peoples Policy April 18, 2002 (Updated October 7, 2002).

of indigenous peoples to use and develop the lands that they occupy, to be protected against illegal intruders, and to have access to natural resources (such as forests, wildlife, and water) vital to their subsistence and reproduction.

(b) *Baseline Data.* Baseline data should include (i) accurate, up-to-date maps and aerial photographs of the area of project influence and the areas inhabited by indigenous peoples; (ii) analysis of the social structure and income sources of the population; (iii) inventories of the resources that indigenous people use and technical data on their production systems; and (iv) the relationship of indigenous peoples to other local and national groups. It is particularly important that baseline studies capture the full range of production and marketing activities in which indigenous people are engaged. Site visits by qualified social and technical experts should verify and update secondary sources.

(c) Land Tenure. When local legislation needs strengthening, the Bank should offer to advise and assist the borrower in establishing legal recognition of the customary or traditional land tenure systems of indigenous peoples. Where the traditional lands of indigenous peoples have been brought by law into the domain of the state and where it is inappropriate to convert traditional rights into those of legal ownership, alternative arrangements should be implemented to grant long-term, renewable rights of custodianship and use to indigenous peoples. These steps should be taken before the initiation of other planning steps that may be contingent on recognized land titles.

encroachment; c) their customary use of the natural resources vital to their culture and ways of life; and d) their natural resources management practices and the long-term sustainability of these practices.

Where a Bank-assisted project has an impact on the lands and resources occupied or used by indigenous peoples and taking into account the Borrower's legislation, consideration is given to establishing legal recognition of the customary or traditional land tenure systems of affected indigenous peoples or granting them long-term renewable rights of custodianship and use.

14. *Commercial Use of Lands and Resources.* When Bank-assisted projects involve the commercial exploitation of natural resources (including forests, mineral, and hydrocarbon resources) on lands owned, or customarily used by indigenous groups, the Borrower: a) informs these groups of their rights to such resources under statutory and customary law; b) informs them of the potential impacts of such projects on their livelihoods, environments and use of natural resources; c) consults them at an early stage on the development of the project, and involves them in decisions which affect them; and d) provides them with opportunities to derive benefits from the project. e) As in all projects which affect indigenous groups, adverse impacts upon them are avoided or minimized, and benefits should be culturally appropriate.

15. *Parks and Protected Areas.* In many countries, the lands set aside for legally designated parks and protected areas may overlap with lands and natural resources customarily owned or used by indigenous peoples. The Bank recognizes both the significance of these customary rights and the need for long-term sustainable management of critical ecosystems. For these reasons, where Bank-assisted projects introduce new arrangements in legally designated parks and protected areas to ensure that natural resources are not depleted, the Borrower introduces a process, acceptable to the Bank, to ensure the informed participation of those indigenous peoples with customary rights of use, in project design and implementation. Preference is also given to collaborative arrange-

ments that enable them to continue to use such
resources in a sustainable manner and to maintain their ways of life.

From the comparison above, it becomes clear that the World Bank's wish to distinguish between the obligations of the Bank and those of the borrower, at the same time
as strengthening 'country ownership' of projects, has resulted in less clear obligations
for the Bank itself, particularly with regard to the preparation of the document entitled until now the Indigenous Peoples Development Plan (IPDP) and in the future the
Indigenous Peoples Plan (IPP). An Indigenous Peoples Plan is to be prepared, at least
in theory, by the Borrower alone and only after a social assessment has been completed
(again by the Borrower) showing that 'a project has adverse impacts upon particular
indigenous groups', in other words quite late during project preparation.[54] However, the
Draft Operational Policy is also far less rigorous as to the precise contents of such plans,
leaving aside all requirements for a detailed account of the legal framework as well as
the evaluation of the ability of indigenous peoples to use the described legal framework.
One could therefore well argue that this new approach contradicts the conclusions of
the OED evaluation which emphasised the beneficial effects of comprehensive IPDPs.

As already noted earlier, OD 4.20 currently requires that in cases 'where the traditional lands of indigenous peoples have been brought by law into the domain of the state
and where it is inappropriate to convert traditional rights into those of legal ownership,
alternative arrangements should be implemented to *grant long-term, renewable rights of
custodianship and use* to indigenous peoples' (my emphasis). This general obligation has
now disappeared, allowing the take-over of indigenous lands by states, for commercial
or protective purposes. It is replaced by the combination of provisions regarding the
commercial use of lands, resources, parks and protected areas (paragraphs 14-15) which
do not grant indigenous peoples any explicit compensatory rights but recognise only
guarantees of information, consultation, 'opportunities to derive benefits' and 'collaborative arrangements that enable them to continue to use such resources'.

Another important difference concerns the emancipatory potential of Bank
projects. OD 4.20 recognises among the prerequisites of a successful IPDP that the
plan avoids creating or aggravating the dependency of indigenous peoples on projects
stating that 'planning should encourage *early handover* of project management to local
people'. It also states that the plan should include 'general education and training in
management skills for indigenous people *from the onset* of the project' (my emphasis).[55]
Similarly, OD 4.20 envisages technical assistance in order to build up the institutional
capacity not only of the Borrower's institutions but also to support development initiatives taken by indigenous peoples themselves.[56] In the draft policy Borrowers '*may*

---

54   This is provided for in paragraph 6 of the Bank Procedures 4.10 (note 35).
55   OD 4.20 (note 23) para. 14(f).
56   Ibid. para. 12.

provide indigenous peoples an opportunity to be more fully included' through measures such as 'building the capacity of indigenous groups to participate on an informed basis in the development process' and the Bank can provide technical assistance for this purpose *at the Borrower's request.*[57]

While the strengthened emphasis on inclusiveness, *consultation* and *informed participation* has been welcomed during the external consultations that the Bank has held in 2001-2002, it has also been pointed out that there undoubtedly remains a great deal of confusion about the relation between the two concepts of consultation and participation. Some commentators have required that the Bank incorporates instead the principle of *informed consent*, for instance with regard to the provisions on parks and protected areas. As mentioned earlier, the OED evaluation of the implementation of OD 4.20 concluded that participation of indigenous peoples in decision-making was weak and recommended specific measures, including capacity building for indigenous peoples as a core element of IPDPs. It seems that these recommendations of the evaluation have been sidelined during the revision process.

The selective comparison of the OD 4.20 with draft OP/BP 4.10 seems all in all to give support to the arguments of those seeing a lowering of standards, first of all as far as concerns the obligations of the Bank itself, but also in terms of the precision of obligations of borrowers. This is perhaps the reason for the great delay in the final discussion of the new policy by the Executive Board.

Indigenous issues before the Inspection Panel

The decade-long experience of the Inspection Panel of the World Bank – the first internal organ in an international organisation providing recourse for private parties who claim to have been adversely affected by the organisation's activities – shows that the effects of projects on indigenous peoples is one of the most controversial aspects of World Bank activities. A lowering of standards would indeed limit the jurisdiction of the Inspection Panel in indigenous issues which have been among the core concerns of the Panel (together with the policy on environmental assessment).

Out of 27 requests received by the Inspection Panel in 1994-2002, 13 requests have alleged a violation of OD 4.20 concerning indigenous peoples and 14 requests have alleged a violation of OD 4.30 concerning involuntary resettlement.[58] In most of these cases (10 requests in total) there is an overlap with allegations of violation of both the above mentioned policies.[59] The Inspection Panel has had occasion to examine the implementation of OD 4.20 not only in Latin America (Brazil, Chile, Argentina, Paraguay, and Ecuador) and Southeast Asia (Nepal and India), but also in China (in

---

57   OP/BP 4.10 (note 35) paras. 19-20.
58   The World Bank, Operational Directive 4.30: Involuntary Settlement (1990).
59   The World Bank *Accountability at the World Bank. The Inspection Panel 10 years on* (Washington: The World Bank, 2003).

the Western Poverty Reduction Project) and Africa (Chad and Cameroon in the recent Petroleum Development and Pipeline Project, and Uganda). Failings in requirements of participation seem to be the most frequent claim in the above mentioned requests. The obligation of the World Bank to supervise the implementation of participatory requirements cuts through the separation of Bank/Borrower spheres.

The experience of the Inspection Panel illustrates vividly the difficulty in separating the obligations of the Bank and the obligations of the borrower. Indeed Richard Bissell, former Chairman of the Inspection Panel, has argued that the Resolution establishing the Inspection Panel 'attempted to restore a formal relationship between the Bank and the Borrower governments that all observers knew had been breached for decades'.[60] The same could now be said about the Draft Operational Policy on Indigenous Peoples.

Conclusions

I have argued that the World Bank has worked over a long period of time and in parallel with the International Labour Organisation and the United Nations in order to incorporate indigenous issues into development work and to adopt standards concerning indigenous peoples for its operations. This process shows how the Bank, in spite of the conscious distance it keeps from other international organisations (with the exception of the International Monetary Fund and the OECD), is part of the normative process of international law, both as regards standard setting and supervision mechanisms. In Thornberry's terms, one may argue that the Bank has developed into a dialogic space of indigenous discourse.[61]

The conclusions and suggestions of the OED evaluation on the implementation of the directive on indigenous peoples have given us much food for thought concerning the challenges of incorporating an indigenous perspective into development and pursuing development work for the benefit of indigenous peoples. These conclusions are particularly important as regards participation, arguing *inter alia* for early information, capacity building for indigenous peoples and appropriate dispute settlement mechanisms.

The long-lasting efforts for a revision of the policy on indigenous peoples seem, however, to show proof of persisting limitations in this process in spite of assurances given by the Bank that the revised policy will not fall below the standards of the now valid operational directive.[62] The Executive Board has been delaying a discussion on a revised draft, which is expected to be adopted later in 2004 after a new round of public

---

60   R.E. Bissell 'Institutional and Procedural Aspects of the Inspection Panel' in G. Alfredsson and R. Ring (eds.) *The Inspection Panel of the World Bank: A Different Complaints Procedure* (The Hague: Martinus Nijhoff, 2001) p. 113.

61   Thornberry returns repeatedly to the importance of dialogue and participation and the conduct within international law of multiple indigenous discourses. See (note 2) pp. 8-10; 61-88 (chapter 3 entitled 'Ambiguous discourses') and pp. 406-429.

62   This assurance was given during a telephone interview with Navin Rai, responsible for coordination of indigenous issues in the World Bank on 14 April 2004.

consultations. Whether this will be possible remains to be seen. More important, however, is whether the World Bank, donors and borrowers will be interested in implementing the recommendations of the OED in order to improve the record of development sensitivity to indigenous concerns, with or without a new policy document.

Chapter 7

Economic Solutions to Political Problems: The Case of the Chittagong Hill Tracts

Chandra Roy [1]

Little is known of the Chittagong Hill Tracts region in Bangladesh, and even less of its indigenous peoples, the Jummas. This is a brief overview of their struggle to maintain their identity as distinct peoples with a clear vision of their future development.

I. Introduction

Bangladesh has gained distinction as a country steering from natural disasters through famine and flooding to political turmoil and general strikes (*hartals*), a common form of protest used by the opposition forces to bring the country to a grinding halt. It is also on the brink of economic disaster with each strike costing the country approximately $ 60 million. A country of some 141,340,476 (July 2004 estimate), [2] with over 98% of the country of Bengali ethnicity and of the Islamic faith, Bangladesh is a largely homogenous country. The credo of one-people, one-faith, was the basis for its creation in December 1971 with Bengali hegemony as the driving force.

There are an estimated 2.5 million indigenous peoples in the north and south-east of the country. They belong to 45 different peoples who are struggling to maintain their culture and identity as separate peoples, and who pose a challenge to the integrating forces of nationalism. How these demands can be addressed, while preserving the *raison d'être* for Bangladesh's secession from Pakistan which followed a civil war that claimed thousands of lives, is the key question that has yet to be resolved.

This chapter explores the erosion of the rights of the indigenous peoples of the Chittagong Hill Tracts (CHT) with the paradigm of economic development. It also describes the struggle of these peoples to gain recognition of their rights as distinct peoples with their own identity, culture and traditions. Developments at the interna-

---

1   An Indigenous lawyer from the Chittagong Hill Tracts, Bangladesh, Chandra Roy holds an LL.M in international law from The American University, Washington D.C.

2   From the CIA: *The World Factbook-Bangladesh* at www.cia.gov (accessed 29 July 2004).

Nazila Ghanea & Alexandra Xanthaki (eds.), Minorities, Peoples and Self-Determination, pp. 113-135.
© *2005 Koninklijke Brill NV. Printed in The Netherlands. ISBN 90 04 14301 7.*

tional level including the UN Committee on the Elimination of Racial Discrimination (CERD) – of which Patrick Thornberry is a member, are also included as part of this exploration.

2.   Historical Background

The Chittagong Hill Tracts is in south-eastern Bangladesh along the border with India's Tripura and Mizoram States and covers a land area of approximately 13,189 square kilometres (5,089 square miles).[3] It is bordered by the Chin and Arakan Hills of Burma (Myanmar) to the south. Nearly 90% of the terrain is hilly or mountainous, as its name implies. The ranges are part of the Himalayan chain.

The Hill Tracts was historically an independent area with its own economic, social and political systems administered by the traditional authorities who ruled as rajas or 'paramount chiefs'. The erosion of independence began with the Mughal emperors in the 17th century. Attracted by the natural resources of the region, they made efforts to bring the CHT under the sway of successive administrations. In 1760, the region was ceded to the East India Company, the forerunner to British rule in India and in 1860 formally annexed to Bengal. This process is described as follows by Mr. J B Larma, President of the Parbatya Chattagram Jana Samhati Samiti (PCJSS):

> Before the colonization, the indigenous Jumma people of CHT were independent. During the whole period of the Mughal rule in this Indian sub-continent, the Chakma Kings were internally supreme and externally free. Only in 1712 there were several encounters between the forces of Chakma King and the Mughal Governor of Chittagong because of a border dispute. These were followed by a truce and by dint of which the Jumma people were allowed commercial transaction with the Bengali traders in exchange for a stipulated amount of cotton. Henceforth, there had been no external interference by any outside power in the affairs of the CHT until 1787 when an agreement was signed with the British and the British colonization started since 1860. So the Kings of the CHT reigned independently during the whole pre-British Era.[4]

The British were responsible for a set of rules to administer the area, namely Regulation 1 of 1900 known as the Hill Tracts Manual or CHT Regulations. These regulations remain

---

3   The total area of Bangladesh is 144,000 square kms. of which the land mass is 133,910. Thus, the CHT is approximately 1/10th of the total land area of Bangladesh.

4   Jyotirindra Bodhipriya Larma, 'The CHT Issue and its Solution', paper presented at Regional Training Program to Enhance the Conflict Prevention and Peace-Building Capacities of Indigenous Peoples' Representatives of the Asia-Pacific" held in Chiang Mai, Thailand from 7-12 April 2003 organized by United Nations Institute for Training and Research (UNITAR). Mr. J. B. Larma is the Chairperson of the Chittagong Hill Tracts Regional Council. He is also the President of the Parbatya Chattagram Jana Samhati Samiti (PCJSS) and Member of the CHT Accord Implementation Committee.

in force to this day, albeit with amendments which have diluted the original intent and purpose. The regulations recognize the CHT as an indigenous area by curtailing and limiting the extent and scope of external interference.

When India was divided in 1947 between India and Pakistan, the latter was composed of the two provinces of East and West Pakistan. The Chittagong Hill Tracts was allotted to East Pakistan. This was against the wishes of the indigenous peoples who had demanded to be included in secular India and for the CHT to be accorded the status of 'princely state' as was the case for other such states in India. This demand was ignored. The reason given for the rejection was that the port city of Chittagong, which is contiguous to the Hill Tracts, hence the eponymous name Chittagong Hill Tracts, needed a protection zone as it is so close to the border.[5]

When Bangladesh was created in 1971, the CHT became a part of this new state. Continuing the policy of divide and rule, the CHT is currently divided into three administrative districts – Rangamati, Khagrachari and Bandarban Hill Districts.

3. The Indigenous Peoples

The Chittagong Hill Tracts is the traditional homeland of an estimated 600,000 indigenous people. They consist of 11 ethnic groups namely the Bawm, Chakma, Chak, Khyang, Khumi, Lushai, Marma, Pankhu, Mro, Taungchangya and Tripura.

These groups have their own history, culture and traditions which differ from the majority Bengali population and their members are of Austro-Mongolian, Tibeto-Burman or Mon Khmer extraction. Most of them are Buddhists, while some, mainly the Tripura, are Hindus, and a few have converted to Christianity. Most also include customary rites and practices in their spiritual beliefs.

To demonstrate national unity and pride the indigenous peoples use the term 'Jummas' to refer to themselves. This comes from the word 'jum', i.e. rotational agriculture, which is common to most of the indigenous peoples. It differentiates them from their plains neighbours and was initially used in a derogatory manner.

Many of the indigenous peoples have their own languages, although many of the scripts are being lost entirely due to disuse. This is due to the use of the official language Bengali as the medium of instruction in the national educational system. Indigenous language instruction is non-existent, with the result that many of the indigenous people cannot read or write in their mother tongues. Many of these languages are under threat of extinction. Recently, some indigenous peoples' organisations have taken the initiative and introduced indigenous language instruction at local schools.

---

5   The name Chittagong Hill Tracts originated after the British annexed the region in 1860. Previously it was known as *Jum Bungoo* or *Kapas Mahal* in Mughal and British revenue records. Due to the lack of detailed knowledge about the region, in addition to the fact that its revenue administration came to be controlled by the Chief of the Chittagong Council, and later by the Collector of Chittagong, it came to be regarded as part of the revenue administration of the Chittagong Collectorate; hence its present name.

The table below details the current CHT population by ethnicity, language and religion:

Ethnic Groups, Language, Religion and Population[6]

Ethnic Group	Language	Script	Religion	Rangamati District	Khagrachari District	Bandarban District	Total Population
Bengali	Bangla	Bangla	Muslim & Hindu	178,065	174,969	120,000	473,034
Indigenous peoples							
Chakma	Chakma	Chakma	Buddhist	157,385	77,869	4,163	239,417
Marma	Marma	Burmese	Buddhist	40,868	42,183	59,288	142,339
Tripura	Kok Borok	Undecided	Hindu & Christian	5,865	47,072	8,187	61,124
Mro	Mro	Mixed	Krama & Buddhist	164	40	21,963	22,167
Tanchangya	Tanchangya	Chakma	Buddhist	13,718	–	5,493	19,211
Bawm	Bawm	Roman	Christian	–	–	6,429	6,429
Pankhua	Pankhua	Roman	Christian	3,128	–	99	3,227
Khyang	Khyang	Roman	Buddhist & Christian	525	–	1,425	1,950
Chak	Chak	Burmese	Buddhist	–	–	1,681	1,681
Khumi	Khumi	-	Krama & Buddhist	91	–	1,150	1,241
Lushai	Lushai	Chakma	Christian	436	–	226	662
TOTAL				400,245	342,133	230,104	972,482

---

6   Source: Asian Development Bank *Chittagong Hill Tracts Region Development Plan (ADB TA # 3328-BAN), Rangamati, February 2001* (Dhaka-Rangamati: ADB, 2001).

4.   The Process of Disempowerment[7]

The Hill Tracts region is one of the most marginalised and least developed regions of Bangladesh. It is also one of the most heavily militarised regions in the world, and remains so despite an agreement to end a twenty-five year period of violent conflict.

This situation has its roots in the historical process of disempowerment of the indigenous peoples. Policies implemented during the British and Pakistani period and carried over to present times continue to have a major bearing. At the heart of the conflict is the question of land and the struggle for self-determination, as in almost all such situations involving indigenous peoples.

Successive administrations have sought to address this political problem through economic measures. These have aimed at bringing the Hill Tracts and its people into the mainstream of national development, with a total disregard for the economy and production systems, socio-cultural values and political aspirations of the indigenous peoples. Problems emerging from each historical period have continued to have an effect on the present, and have added further to the marginalisation of the indigenous peoples. The following is a brief summary of this process:

4.1. British period (1860-1947)

Prior to the arrival of the British in the region, the CHT had always maintained its independence. Having succeeded in bringing the Hill Tracts within its administrative regime, the British – the pioneers of entrepreneurial conquest – began to institute a policy of afforestation. This was primarily for financial gain, with conservation only an auxiliary objective. Section 3 of the Forest Act of 1927 was the foundation for this strategy:

> 3.   Power to reserve forests – The Government may constitute any forest-land or waste-land or any land suitable for afforestation which is the property of the Government, or over which the Government has proprietary rights, or to the whole or any part of the forest-produce of which the Government is entitled, as reserved forest in the manner hereinafter provided.

Through this legislative mechanism, large areas of the Hill Tracts were respectively declared:

(a)   Reserved Forest – with a total prohibition on use and access to the forest and natural resources;

(b)   Protected – with limited extraction and use allowed;

(c)   Unclassified – a third category introduced for areas which had not yet been identified as either reserved or protected.

---

7   For more details see R.C.K. Roy *Land Rights of the Indigenous Peoples of the Chittagong Hill Tracts, Bangladesh* (Copenhagen: IWGIA, 2000) Document No. 99.

This process ignored the rights of the indigenous peoples to these lands and natural resources and effectively brought the forests under government ownership, control and management. The indigenous peoples' rights to ownership and possession of the lands and natural resources in these areas was not recognised. The process brought into effect without any discussions or consultations with the indigenous peoples who were faced with a *fait accompli.*

This act drastically reduced the resource-base of the indigenous peoples, and made their traditional subsistence activities a criminal act (in the reserved forests), or restricted their access and the use of the areas for daily activities (in the protected forests). The indigenous peoples, dependent on the forest and their resources for their survival, were evicted from these forests or prevented from using and accessing them for jum and other subsistence activities. The indigenous peoples' protests over this mechanism were ignored. With their traditional lands being increasingly appropriated by the state and declared to be 'government forests', the sense of injustice and frustration of the indigenous peoples grew stronger. Successive administrators maintained this mechanism and it remains in use.

> This process continues and in 1992, 1996, and 1998 the Ministry of Environment and Forests initiated a process to enlarge the existing reserved forests through a series of gazette notifications. The Committee for the Protection of Forests and Land Rights in the CHT, created to mobilise support to prevent the affected indigenous peoples (approximately 200,000) from being evicted off these lands, is against these orders which it believes will convert forests and grazing commons, homesteads and agricultural lands into industry-oriented plantations with the effect of destroying the biological and cultural diversity of the region. The indigenous peoples will receive no benefits whatsoever. The proposed areas amount to 7,411,286.30 acres (Bandarban: 7,28,0917.17 acres; Khagrachari: 41,907.50 acres; and Rangamati: 88,461.63 acres).[8] These notifications remain in force despite repeated demands by the Forest Committee for their repeal.[9]

Current reports from the CHT document that the afforestation policies of the Government continued unabated. 'Thus, the Khyang ethnic people, the smallest and most deprived and disadvantaged Jumma group in the CHT, are on the verge of total eviction from their ancestral land where they have been living and cultivating *Jum* from generation to generation.'[10] The following table indicates the amount of forest land in the CHT:

---

8   Committee for the Protection of Forests and Land Rights *Mobilise Support to Stop the Eviction of Indigenous Peoples from Ancestral Lands in the Chittagong Hill Tracts, Bangladesh in the name of Afforestation and Protection of the Environment* (Chittagong Hill Tracts: CPFLR, 2001).

9   See Jumma Peoples' Network, 'Bangladesh' in *The Indigenous World 2002-2003* (Copenhagen: International Work Group for Indigenous Affairs, 2003) p. 301.

10   PCJSS *Report on the CHT Accord, April 2004* (Rangamati: PCJSS Information Department 2004).

Forest Land Classification in CHT[11]

	Classification	Area (Hectares)			
		Rangamati	Bandarban	Khagrachari	Total CHT
1	Gazetted Reserved & Protected forest (RF + PF)	234,520	74,841	23,151	332,5120
2	Estimated remaining Reserved Forest (RF)	49,613	—	4,018	53,373
3	Encroached RF[12]	2,176	—	—	2,176
4	Estimated remaining protected forest (PF)	0	0	0	0
5	Planted forests (private)	22,259	26,184	8,930	57,373
6	Unclassified State Forest (USF)	322,521	292,522	94,656	709,699
7	USF 'notified' for reclassification to RF	23,680	27,000	12,660	63,340
8	Total in district under control of Forest Department (1-7 including 'notified' land not formally 'gazetted')	258,200	101,841	35,811	395,852
9	Forest area controlled by Ministry of Land (i.e. USF)	322,521	292,522	94,656	709,699
10	Private forest land				
	TOTAL (rows 1,5,6)	579,300	393,547	126,737	1,099,584

The impact on the indigenous peoples of this forestation policy is significant, especially on the indigenous women who bear the major responsibility for the family's daily needs:

> Researchers have pointed out that in developing countries it is women who are the most dependent on forests for their sustenance (Shiva, 1989:18). The traditional division of labour in forest-dependent societies has allocated hazardous tasks as well as those requiring physical strength to men, and work that requires sustained effort and endurance has been assigned to women. The division is strengthened with taboos and beliefs. Deforestation affects indigenous women more than indigenous men because

---

11   R.D. Roy, 'Land and Forest Rights in the Chittagong Hill Tracts, Bangladesh' paper presented at the International Centre for Integrated Mountain Development (ICIMOD), Nepal, February 2002.

12   Similar activities occurring in Bandarban and Khagrachari on non-RF lands.

women's primary responsibilities such as cooking, fetching water and gathering fire-
wood pose hardships when ecological degradation of forests occurs. This is equally
true in the CHT.

...Indigenous women, through their traditional role as *de facto* managers of the rural
household are involved virtually in the entire household and outside activities...[it is]
usually women who have the most intricate knowledge about forest food items, their
nutritional value and about herbal medicinal plants. The degradation of natural forests
results not only in the extinction of many plants, but the indigenous women's knowledge of their natural resources. Moreover, women have to bear the burden of fetching
water and food items, which are farther and farther removed from their homes. Thus
the impact of deforestation on indigenous women is not only upon their knowledge
systems, economic well-being and health, but on their status in society. [13]

In 2000, the Forest Act 1927 was amended by the Forest (Amendment) Act of 2000.
Contrary to international standards, this act does not provide any mechanisms for
participation or consultation of the peoples concerned, and gives arbitrary power to
the forest department. It is criticised as being 'anti-people and anti-environment and
because it vests the Forest Department officials with draconian powers that are liable to
be misused.'[14] The indigenous peoples have demanded its repeal and the amendment of
the Forestry Master Plan, National Forestry Policy, the Forest Act of 1927 and related
laws and policies through a democratic and transparent process.[15]

In the meantime, the environmental degradation and devastation in the CHT is
progressing at an alarming rate and large areas of the region are totally devoid of any
forest cover.

4.2. The Pakistan Period (1947-71)

The key issue during this period was the construction of a hydro-electric power project
on the River Karnaphuli at Kaptai (1959-63) creating a reservoir of 256 square miles.[16]

54,000 acres of farmlands went underwater (approximately 40% of the agricultural
land), and as a result, brought about a situation of constant food insecurity which con-

---

13   R.D. Roy and S. Halim 'Valuing Village Commons in Forestry' in 5.2 *Indigenous Perspectives*
       (2002) Tebtebba Foundation, Baguio City, p. 21.

14   *Dhaka Forests Declaration*, adopted at a Workshop on 'Forests and Indigenous Peoples'
       organized by Jatiyo Adivasi Parishad (Bangladesh Indigenous Peoples Forum), SEHD (Soci-
       ety for Human Rights and Development) and Taungya et al, Dhaka, 9 June 2001.

15   For more details see R.D. Roy & S. Halim 'A Critique to the Forest (Amendment) Act of
       2000 and the (draft) Social Forestry Rules of 2000' in Philip Gain (ed.) *The Forest (Amend-
       ment) Act 2000 and the (draft) Social Forestry Rules, 2000: A Critique* (Dhaka: Society for
       Environment and Human Development, 2001) pp. 5-45.

16   *CHT Gazetteer* (1971) p. 99.

tinues to this day. In addition to submerging what amounted to the rice bowl of the Hill Tracts, over 100,000 indigenous peoples were rendered homeless and lost their homes, farms, temples, and spiritual sites forever. Many of the indigenous people sought refuge in India and remain there to this day. As reported in official Government records:

> According to the survey undertaken by the Rehabilitation Officer, about 10,000 ploughing families having land in the reservoir bed and 8,000 landless *jumia* families comprising more than one lakh[17] people were displaced. The reservoir submerged a vast area comprising 125 *mouzas*…The inundation threw over 54,000 acres of plough land out of cultivation. This area constitutes 40 per cent of the total settled cultivable land of the district. The fertile valleys of the district, *viz.*, Karnafuli, Chengi, Kassalong and Maini have been inundated.[18]

Although indigenous leaders raised strong objections to the dam, they were informed that it was necessary for the development of the plains areas.[19] It is described as follows:

> Completed in 1963 at a cost of Rs. 4.9 crores,[20] with funding from the US development agency – USAID – the Kaptai power plant supplied electricity to the plains districts, mainly to the port city of Chittagong. There were no arrangements to provide electricity to indigenous homes, or for them to participate in any manner in the benefits of this huge development project, yet their loss in terms of emotional and economic impact is incalculable. As a result of the loss of their ancestral lands, some 40,000 Chakmas migrated to Arunachal Pradesh in India, and remain stateless up to this day.[21]

Most of the indigenous peoples received little or no compensation. As an alternative, the indigenous peoples were encouraged to turn to horticulture of pineapples and cashew nuts, but without adequate storage and transportation facilities, this plan too was a failure, and added to the indigenous peoples' impoverishment and marginalisation.

There is a recent plan to increase the power of the dam and thereby the level of water of the lake. It is with funding from the Japanese Government, a major aid contributor to Bangladesh. The indigenous peoples have protested against this as it would

---

17   A local method of counting. One lakh is 100,000.

18   (note 16) p. 42.

19   The Chakma Chief, Raja Tridiv Roy met with the Minister in Charge to explain the tremendous damage the project would have on the lives and lands of the indigenous people. He was told that if an arm had to be amputated (in order to save the entire body) then that arm had to go. Mr. Manobendra Narayan Larma, who was later to become a member of Parliament (MP) and lead the Parbatya Chattagram Jana Samhati Samiti (PCJSS), was arrested by the police for demonstrating against the decision to construct the dam.

20   (note 16) p. 155.

21   (note 7) p. 96.

decrease their land and resource base even further, but there has not been any response so far.[22]

4.3. *Bangladesh period (1971 to present day)*

With the emergence of Bangladesh, a fragile new state vulnerable to the demands of nation-building, the question of the indigenous peoples of the Hill Tracts was not an urgent issue. As indigenous peoples were perceived as 'backward segments of the population' their demands for regional autonomy went unheeded and were equated to secession:

> As a state, Bangladesh was the outcome of an intensely nationalist movement, and Bengali nationalism was seen by policymakers as all-encompassing.[23] Having successfully led the country to independence, the Awami League could perceive the dangers of secession inherent within such demands for autonomy.'[24]

The indigenous peoples were advised to forget such demands and to integrate.

Between 1979 and 1984, the then president, Major General Zia-ur Rehman began a population transfer programme whereby landless families from the plains were settled in the Hill Tracts. Through this programme, aimed at diluting the indigenous composition of the region by making them a minority in their own lands and concurrently ensuring the assimilation of their culture and traditions, some 450,000 persons were brought into the Hill Tracts. In addition to cash and other such benefits, each family was also provided with 7.5 acres of land – which had belonged to the indigenous peoples. The following table illustrates the economic implications of this programme, purely in terms of land as the primary resource base for the indigenous peoples.[25]

Estimate	Families (est. 5 persons)	Lands	Total
Minimum	40,000	11.5 acres	460,000 acres
Maximum	80,000	11.5 acres	920,000 acres

---

22   For more details, see C.K. Roy *Impact of Development in the CHT: Ways Forward* paper presented at the Forum for Development Corporation, Trømso, Norway, October 2003.

23   A. Mohsin *The Chittagong Hill Tracts, Bangladesh: On the Difficult Road to Peace,* International Peace Academy Occasional Paper Series (Boulder: Lynne Rienners, 2003) p. 23: Author interview on 19 May 1993 with Kamal Hussein, the main architect of the Bangladesh constitution. Hussein argued that ethnicity was not in currency at the time of Bangladesh independence and that policymakers could not foresee its consequences.

24   Ibid.

25   (note 7) p. 114.

Having already lost much of their land with the dam, and trying to eke out a living from the little that remained, the indigenous peoples' now had their lands taken from them, often forcibly, and almost always illegally, and given to settler families.

This situation was exacerbated further when the government began a policy of militarisation of the CHT known as Operation Dabanal (wildfire). A 1991 fact-finding mission by the International CHT Commission made a detailed report on the situation prevailing in the Hill Tracts and described the CHT as being under military control.[26] The 24th Infantry Division of the Bangladesh Army is in control of the CHT, with over-all command vested in the General Officer Commanding (GOC) in the cantonment in Chittagong. Although exact figures are unknown with numbers ranging from 30,000 to 80,000, a large portion of the Bangladesh forces are deployed in the Hill Tracts (approximately 1/3), with some analysts regarding the ratio of Jummas to military personnel to be as much as 6:1.[27]

In this volatile and ethnically charged environment, many human rights abuses have been committed against the indigenous peoples. The main perpetrators were the armed forces working in close cooperation with the sponsored settlers. To add to this tense situation, the government decided to provide arms to the settlers, who then organized into voluntary civil patrol units known as Village Defence Parties (VDPs). There were a number of massacres of the indigenous peoples during this time of which the Kalampati massacre (1980), Panchari (1986), Logadu (1989), Logang (1992), Naniachar (1993) are illustrative of the level and extent of the violence in the Hill Tracts. This has been documented by human rights organisations such as Amnesty International.[28] The Committee on the Elimination of Racial Discrimination also commented on this situation when examining Bangladesh's compliance with the provisions of the convention in 1993, as did the International Labour Organisation's Committee of Experts while supervising the application, in law and practice, of ILO Convention No. 107 on Indigenous and Tribal Peoples (1957) by Bangladesh. The ILO expert committee made the following comment in relation to Logang:

> It continues to receive allegations from various sources, including information submit-
> ted to the United Nations bodies, of persistent human rights violations in this region
> including detailed allegations that on 10 April 1992 the [indigenous] village of Logang
> (about 600 houses) was destroyed by non-[indigenous] settlers, civilian defence forces

---

26   See CHT Commission *Life is not Ours: Land and Human Rights in the Chittagong Hill Tracts, Bangladesh* (Copenhagen: International Work Group for Indigenous Affairs (IWGIA) and Netherlands: Organizing Committee CHT Campaign, 1991) p. 112.

27   For more details see, 'Military Resistance in the CHT' at www.geocities.com/jummanation.com (accessed 29 July 2004)

28   For details see *The Chittagong Hill Tracts: Militarization, Oppression and the Hill Tribes* (London: Anti-Slavery Society, 1984) and *Unlawful Killings and Torture in the Chittagong Hill Tracts* (London: Amnesty International, 1986).

(Village Defence Party, VDP) and paramilitary forces (Ansars). Some reports state that hundreds of [indigenous] villagers were killed and that the military took no preventive action.[29]

The Asian Development Bank's report on the CHT describes the situation as follows:

Ethnic cleansing:	[The] army would participate or look on. At the height of the conflict after Shanti Bahini attacks on settlers in mainly Khagrachari, a reign of settler terror unleashed on indigenous villages with looting, burning and massacres. It made 75,000 people flee the country. People who returned 5 to 15 years later would find their land occupied by settlers, often with forged documents.[30]

Another major upheaval caused by the Kaptai dam, the creation of reserve forests and the settlement programme was the displacement of thousands of indigenous peoples. A government task force created in 1998 – Taskforce for Chittagong Hill Tracts Refugee Rehabilitation Affairs – estimated there are some 128,364 internally displaced families in the CHT numbering some 500,000 persons, of which 90,208 are indigenous while 38,156 are of non-indigenous/settler origin. The inclusion of the settlers as 'internally displaced' was strongly condemned by the indigenous peoples who blame the settlement programme itself for being a major cause for their situation.[31] The Global Internal Displacement Project gives the above figures while clarifying that it is difficult to know the actual number of internally displaced in the CHT.[32]

Many of the internally-displaced remain homeless to this day. With reports of the military's plans to expand into their areas, the indigenous peoples are threatened with continuing dispossession and displacement:

Further, the military authority and the government have taken initiative to acquire 9,560 acres of land for the expansion of Ruma Cantonment, 183 acres of land for the expansion of Bandarban Brigade Headquarters, 30,000 acres of land to open a new Artillery Training Centre, 26,000 acres of land to open a new Air Force Train-

29   International Labour Office *Report of the Committee of Experts on the Application of Conventions and Recommendations* International Labour Conference, 80th session Report III (Part 4 A) (Geneva: ILO, 1993) pp. 308-310.

30   CHT Region Development Plan 2001: Social and Indigenous Peoples Issues, Report 7.

31   4.236 *The Daily Star* Internet Edition of 22 January 2004: 'CHT taskforce meets after 4 years, winds up without success'.

32   Global IDP Project, Norwegian Refugee Council, Report on: *Bangladesh: land disputes perpetuate internal displacement,* 1 December 2003 at www.idpproject.org (accessed 29 July 2004).

ing Center and 50 acres of land for the expansion of Longadu Military Zone without any prior consent either from the Hill District Councils or from the CHT Regional Council. By now 11,886 acres of land have already been acquired in the Bandarban Hill District for the Artillery Training Center violating this provision. The land illegally acquired by the government in the name of various authorities in Bandarban Hill district alone is given in the following table:[33]

Land Acquired For:	Quantity in acres
Ruma Cantonment	9,560
Expansion of Bandarban Brigade Headquarters	183
Establishment of a new Artillery Training Center	30,000
Establishment of a new Air Force Training Center	26,000
Reserved Forest	72,000
Lease given by DC	18,333
Total:	156,076

In the examination of Bangladesh's report, the Committee on the Elimination of Racial Discrimination raised the issue of the arrangements under the Forest Act of 1927 which placed the indigenous peoples in a precarious position.[34]

The major issue in the CHT is land. Land is the economic resource base for the indigenous peoples and they are dependent on it for their economic and cultural survival. Without their land, they cannot maintain their identity as a separate people. The rate at which the indigenous peoples are being divested of their lands in the CHT is alarming. This is the result of projects and programmes carried out in the name of development and modernisation. The end result for the indigenous peoples has been dispossession, deprivation and poverty. Today, the majority of the indigenous peoples live below the poverty line, and many are under employed or unemployed.

The Asian Development Bank (ADB) survey assesses the CHT population in the following categories:

---

33 PCJSS *Report on the CHT Accord, April 2004* (Rangamati: PCJSS Information Department, 2004).

34 This comment was raised by Prof. Thornberry, see Summary Record of the 1457th meeting, CERD (Geneva: UN CERD/C/SR.1457).

Various groups in the CHT (ADB:CHT 2001 Report)

Rough estimations and unknowns

1. Displaced people	
Indigenous	Some 150,000 – 200,000
Settlers	Some 60,000 – 100,000
2. People affected by possible changes in land use and current policy	
People affected by land converted to military use	25,000 people
People affected by the conversion of land to reserved forest	> 100,000 people
People affected by the current Forestry policy	> 400,000 people
People affected by an increase in the minimum level of Lake Kaptai: Lakeside people	~ 85,000 people
People affected by the government sponsored settlement programme	~ 80 – 100,000 families
3. Socio-cultural groups	
Indigenous people:	*> 550,000*
Two dominant indigenous communities, Chakma and Marma	> 420,000 people
Two medium-size ethnic groups (Tripura and Tanchangya)	> 90,000 people
Nine minority ethnic groups (including Nepali and Assamese), least integrated in over-all society and power structure	> 45,000 people in total
Non indigenous people:	*> 550,000*
Long time settlers ("adibashi")	Growing group, because of co-option
Refugee settlers (from India), said to be accepted	Small number
Recent settlers (1960s, and the early 1980s), not accepted by indigenous people.	400,000

5.   Indigenous Resistance

The indigenous peoples of the CHT have been slowly but surely divested of their traditional lands through various strategies. This has been in response to their struggle for self-determination which found expression in a demand for autonomy and self-rule. This demand, voiced by the increasingly politicised and organised indigenous peoples' movement from the beginning of the colonial period (1930s onwards), has largely been ignored. The end result has been conflict and violence, which has served to draw the attention of the government and of the world to the CHT region.

The indigenous peoples have been politically organised through their traditional institutions under the rajas, and as political parties from 1915 onwards with the formation of the Chakma Jubo Samiti (Chakma Youth Party) followed by the Parbattya

Chattagram Jana Samiti (CHT Peoples Party) in 1920, and others.[35] They have made consistent demands for self-determination and for autonomy and protested regarding the devastation of the dam and settlement programme and the forestation policy. They have also participated in national politics through representation at the national and provincial assemblies.[36]

When Bangladesh was created in 1971, because it had itself exercised its right to self-determination by seceding from Pakistan, the indigenous peoples of the Hill Tracts hoped their demands for self-rule would find some accommodation:

> The political life of the Hill people of the CHT in the state of Bangladesh thus began with a feeling of indifference and to a certain extent apprehension. This was to turn into an acute sense of alienation as the state went ahead with its political project of creating a culturally homogenous population on the image of Bengalis, the dominant ethnic community in the state.[37]

In the words of the PCJSS leader, Mr. J.B. Larma:

> The indigenous Jumma people hoped that the new rulers of Bangladesh would realize their hopes and aspirations as Bangladesh rulers also struggled against the oppression and suppression of Pakistani ruler and the Jumma people would be free from oppression and discrimination. So the Jumma people demanded of the then government for autonomy in a democratic way. Unfortunately the government of Bangladesh did not respect their fundamental rights and did not write even a single word in the constitution regarding the entity and safeguard of the Jumma people. Rather immediately following the independence of Bangladesh in early 1972 the CHT underwent militarization. Three cantonments were established in Dighinala, Ruma and Alikadam during Sheikh Mujib period…Against this backdrop, on 16 February 1972, a delegation of the Jumma people led by *Manabendra Narayan Larma*, then a member of parliament, called on the Prime Minister *Sheikh Mujibur Rahman* and submitted a written memorandum with four-point charter of demands consisting of –
> (1)   Autonomy for the CHT;
> (2)   Retention of the CHT Regulation 1900;
> (3)   Recognition of the three Chiefs of the Jummas and
> (4)   Ban on the influx of the Bengali Muslim into the CHT.[38]

---

35   B.K. Choudhury *Genesis of the Chakma Movement (1772-1989): Historic Background* (Agartala: Tripura Darpan Prakashani) p. 30.

36   For more details, see R.C.K. Roy 'Indigenous Peoples and Elections: Case Study: The Chittagong Hill Tracts' in T. Kristiansen (ed.) *And the Winner Might Be…Democratic Elections and Independent Journalism* (Kristiansand: International Reporter, 2004) pp. 141-160.

37   (note 23) p. 56.

38   (note 4).

When the demands of the indigenous peoples for regional autonomy were ignored the then MP for the CHT, Manabendra Narayan Larma formed the Parbatya Chattagram Jana Samhati Samiti (PCJSS) in March 1972.

The army was brought into the CHT the same year, 1972, as a counter-insurgency strategy with full scale militarization occurring in 1975 – the Ministry of Defence took over the Hill Tracts portfolio in 1977. As a response to the militarisation and settlement programme, and to protect the rights of the indigenous peoples, an armed wing of the PCJSS known as the Shanti Bahini (Peace Brigade) was formed in 1973 and began operations in 1975. The PCJSS and the Shanti Bahini lead the indigenous peoples' movement and in the ensuing civil war, many lives were lost and thousands fled to refugee camps. Many indigenous peoples were also abducted, tortured and imprisoned.

It was during this time, that a clearly defined economic policy as a response to the political movement was initiated. This was under the presidency of Zia-ur-Rahman (who had a military background and its support), and the military was tasked with economic development to be implemented through the CHT Development Board which was formally established in 1976. This was an inappropriate and inadequate response to the CHT crisis, and only served to further marginalise and isolate the indigenous Jummas, especially since the major thrust of the development went towards benefiting and entrenching the army and the settlers deeper in the CHT:

> Although the army is said to be there for counter-insurgency and national security, when the Chittagong Hill Tracts Development Board was created, the General Commanding Officer in charge of the Hill Tracts was its chairperson in 1982. The CHTDB was established for the 'welfare' of the hill people, in actual practice, it was part of the counter-insurgency strategy, and most of its work has been oriented to furthering this objective. For instance, it has engaged in expanding the road networks, which in effect has opened up the Hill Tracts to commercial enterprise, and to bringing in more troops. The CHTDB was also involved in the relocation of the indigenous peoples into 'model' or 'cluster' villages where they were under surveillance by the military, and movement restricted.[39]

Economic development has had little positive impact or influence on the indigenous peoples who demand control of their economy. They have had very little input into the policy and activities of the CHTDB which is insurgency-oriented even to this day, as well as being influenced by development paradigms formulated for the plains areas of Bangladesh which are culturally inappropriate for the CHT. As Raja Devasish Roy stresses 'You cannot protect a culture unless the whole economy is taken care of.'[40]

---

39   (note 22).
40   (note 23) p. 74.

5.1 Impact on Indigenous Women

In the Hill Tracts, as in many other indigenous areas where there is or has been conflict, the indigenous women are a particular target:

> In the 20 years or more of violent conflict which claimed hundreds of lives, the indigenous women were targeted for their ethnicity and gender, which centred on their central role as the transmitters of their culture to future generations. There are countless reports of rape, forced marriages and abductions of indigenous Jumma women. Although the Peace Accord of 1997 has paved the way for a return to normalcy in the Hill Tracts, with the military remaining a constant and continuous presence in the region, indigenous women do not feel secure, and there are continuing reports of rape and sexual violence, committed by the armed forces, and/or the settlers. For instance, in August 2003, in Mahalchari[41] in an attack by settlers a number of indigenous villages were set on fire, people injured and property damaged. Ten indigenous women were raped.[42]

A research project on the issue of violence of indigenous women in the CHT analyses the use of rape as an instrument in the struggle for power:

> Militarization, which still continues in the CHT, in the name of keeping peace in the region, is resulting in much misery of innocent people, both men and women. Before the end of organized warfare in the CHT, many instances of rape of indigenous women by security personnel were widely reported, if discreetly. The cessation of hostilities may have decreased the risk of such sexual offences, but women are still at risk. Although the 1997 Accord provides for the dismantling of military camps (except for some specified large garrisons), this provision is still to be implemented in substance by the Government of Bangladesh... Furthermore, state-sponsored Bengali in-migration (1979-1984) not only led to the displacement of the hill people in the CHT but also created security problems for them, for both the men and the women...
> As in the case of security forces, instances of rape and violence against indigenous women by the state-sponsored Bengali settlers also took place during the insurgency period. However, such instances seem to have risen in the post-conflict period. This may be because the settlers, who were mostly confined in military-protected "cluster villages" before are now far more mobile because of the end of the guerrilla war.[43]

---

41 PCJSS Report: *An Account of Communal Attack in Mahalchari upon the indigenous Jumma people* by the Bengali settlers with full backing of the Army (Rangamati: PCJSS Information Department, 2003).

42 R.C.K. Roy 'Indigenous Women: A Gender Perspective' (Guovdageaidnu/Kautokeino: Resource Centre for the Rights of Indigenous Peoples 2004) at www.galdu.org (accessed 29 July 2004).

43 *Violence against women in the CHT* (working title) by Dr. Sadeka Halim, Associate Professor, Department of Sociology & Women's Studies, Advocates Susmita Chakma and Rajib

In a well known case, the organising secretary of the Hill Women's Federation, Kalpana Chakma, was abducted from her home by security personnel in June 1996. This issue was raised by the Working Group on Enforced and Voluntary Disappearances to the Commission on Human Rights,[44] and mentioned by the Committee on the Elimination of Racial Discrimination (CERD) when considering Bangladesh's report under the Convention in March 2001.[45]

5.2   Demographic Changes

The population transfer programme has brought about radical changes in the demographic composition of the Hill Tracts:

Indigenous people and Bengali Population
Chittagong Hill Tracts (1872 – 1991)[46]

Census Year	1872	1901	1951	1981	1991
Indigenous	61,957	116,000	261,538	441,776	501,144
Non-Indigenous	1,097	8,762	26,150	304,873	473,301
Total	63,054	124,762	287,688	746,649	974,445
Indigenous %	98%	93%	91%	59%	51%
Non-Indigenous %	2%	7%	9%	41%	49%

The European Union has offered the Government financial assistance to rehabilitate and resettle the settler families to areas outside the CHT,[47] but no steps have as yet been taken in this regard.

6.   1997 Peace Accord

A number of attempts were made to negotiate with the PCJSS and the Shanti Bahini and to resolve the conflict, the first one being initiated in 1977 under President Zia-ur Rahman. After a series of protracted and complex negotiations, conducted with successive governments, the Government and the PCJSS agreed a peace accord in December

---

Chakma, both practicing lawyers in Rangamati Bar, Chittagong Hill Tracts, commissioned by FFOWSIA, Freedom Foundation, Dhaka, Bangladesh to be published by Freedom Foundation, 2004. Cited with the authors' permission.

44   UN Document E/CN.4/1998/434.

45   Summary record of the 1457th meeting (CERD/C/SR.1457) 19 March 2001.

46   R.D. Roy *Background Study on the Chittagong Hill Tracts Land Situation*, Prepared for CARE-Bangladesh, Dhaka, Bangladesh 5 August 2002. Source: B. H. Suhrawardy, 'Outline of the CHT Economy: An Analysis' (in Bengali) in Arunendu Tripura et al (eds.) in *Vision* (Rangamati, 15 June 1995) p. 38.

47   European Parliament Resolution on Bangladesh, adopted on 17 January 2001.

1997. This accord provides the framework for limited autonomy and has been welcomed as a respite from over twenty years of violent conflict.

The accord provides the elements for limited self-rule in the CHT through an apex Regional Council, three District Councils (established in 1989), and a Land Commission. It also provides for the creation of a central ministry on CHT affairs (MOCHTA). Although these institutions have been established and are nominally operational, they have not been granted their full powers and all lack both institutional capacity and resources, and urgently need financial and technical assistance to ensure they can execute their tasks and responsibilities. For instance, the Land Commission began functioning recently with a retired judge as the chair. However, the other members including the traditional leaders have not been formally included and thus it is not fully operational. In the interim period, thousands of claims have been filed with the commission, all regarding land disputes between the indigenous peoples and the settlers:

> A major concern is that many of the settlers have documents, allegedly falsifications, while many of the indigenous peoples have lost their documents and records during the civil war. This is especially true for those who fled the violence in the Hill Tracts and took refuge in India (approximately 55,000). They have returned to the Hill Tracts on the basis of rehabilitation-repatriation agreements with the government (1992 and 1997), but the terms of these agreements have not been met, and many of the returnee refugees remain in temporary venues waiting to have their lands restituted to them as agreed.[48]

The 1997 accord also provides for the de-militarisation of the CHT stipulating the withdrawal of all temporary camps of military, Ansar and Village Defense Party, with the exception of the border security forces (BDR) and six permanent cantonments (one each at district headquarters of Bandarban, Khagrachari and Rangamati, and at Alikadam, Dighinala and Ruma). However, there are no signs of the army withdrawing from the CHT, instead it has leased lands as shown above. The JSS reports that only 35 army camps of the 500 in the CHT have been dismantled so far, despite repeated demands for the armed forces to withdraw from the CHT because of their involvement in past and continuing human rights' violations. This was reiterated by CERD while examining Bangladesh's obligations under the Convention on the Elimination of Racial Discrimination:

> The Committee is concerned about reports of human rights' violations by security forces present in the Chittagong Hill Tracts affecting the tribal population, including reports of arbitrary arrests and detentions, and ill treatment. The Committee recommends that the State party implement effective measures to guarantee to all Bangladeshis, without distinction based on race, colour, descent or national or ethnic origin, the right to security of person and protection by the State against violence or bodily harm.[49]

---

48   (note 22).

49   UN Document No. CERD/C/304/Add. 118, CERD *Concluding Observations of the Committee on the Elimination of Racial Discrimination: Bangladesh. 27/04/200*, para. 9.

There are some indigenous peoples who believe the Accord does not fulfil their demands for self-determination. They formed an anti-Accord group known as the United Peoples Democratic Front (UPDF) in 1998. This internal hostility has added to the already complicated situation in the Hill Tracts. There are ongoing efforts to try and resolve the differences between the two parties, but so far, they have not been successful.

The slow implementation of the Accord has been a cause of concern both locally, nationally and internationally. There have been repeated demands for its rapid implementation from the indigenous peoples, the PCJSS, the UN, donors and development agencies. CERD has also expressed its concern as follows:

> Nothwithstanding certain positive developments, the Committee is concerned about the slow progress in implementing the Chittagong Hill Tracts Peace Accord. The Committee urges the State party to intensify its efforts in this regard and recommends that the State party provide in its next report details regarding, *inter alia*, the work of the Land Commission, the repatriation and rehabilitation of refugees and internally displaced persons in the CHT, the work of the Special Task Force on Internally Displaced Person, the resettlement of Bengali settlers outside the Chittagong Hill Tracts…and the process of withdrawal of security forces from the CHT.[50]

7. Conclusion

This chapter provides a brief glance at the situation of the indigenous peoples of the Chittagong Hill Tracts. It is not exhaustive and hopes to stimulate greater interest and action in strengthening the rights of the Jummas.

The Jummas have their own vision of development and of peace, one which is in accordance with their values and practices, and based on their systems for decision-making, which is consensus-oriented. This has to be respected and with it their right to self-determination to ensure their survival as distinct peoples. The 1997 Peace Accord provides the elements towards this process and its speedy implementation is a necessary first step forward.

The Accord provides the framework for economic development and for political self-rule. It can be used as leverage by the indigenous peoples, their support agencies and by concerned donors to secure a stable environment in the Hill Tracts, one where the rule of law prevails, the peoples' voice is heard and heeded, and their rights to their lands recognised and protected.

Past injustices cannot be undone, but they can be corrected and steps taken to ensure they do not recur again. The international community can utilise the Accord to initiate this reconciliation process and as a confidence-building measure call for the urgent removal of the armed forces from the CHT, and the rehabilitation and re-settle-

---

50   Ibid.

ment of the state-sponsored settlers to other regions in the country. This should be done on a voluntary basis and the help humanitarian agencies such as the United Nations High Commissioner for Refugees (UNHCR) could be sought in this regard, with financial assistance from the European Commission among others. In this process, the Government could continue to provide these families with the food and other cash-in-kind handouts as it has done since their arrival in the CHT.

Taking into account the emphasis placed on economic development as a solution to the political problems of the CHT, international agencies and donor countries can focus on the economic aspects of the CHT problem, however from the perspective of the indigenous peoples rather than that of the Government or the agencies. Any economic development should be indigenous-driven and lead, with the peoples concerned in full control of their destiny. Only then can there be sustainable peace and development in the CHT. This is the challenge facing the CHT today.

Annex 1:
Map of Hill Tracts and Neighboring Regions

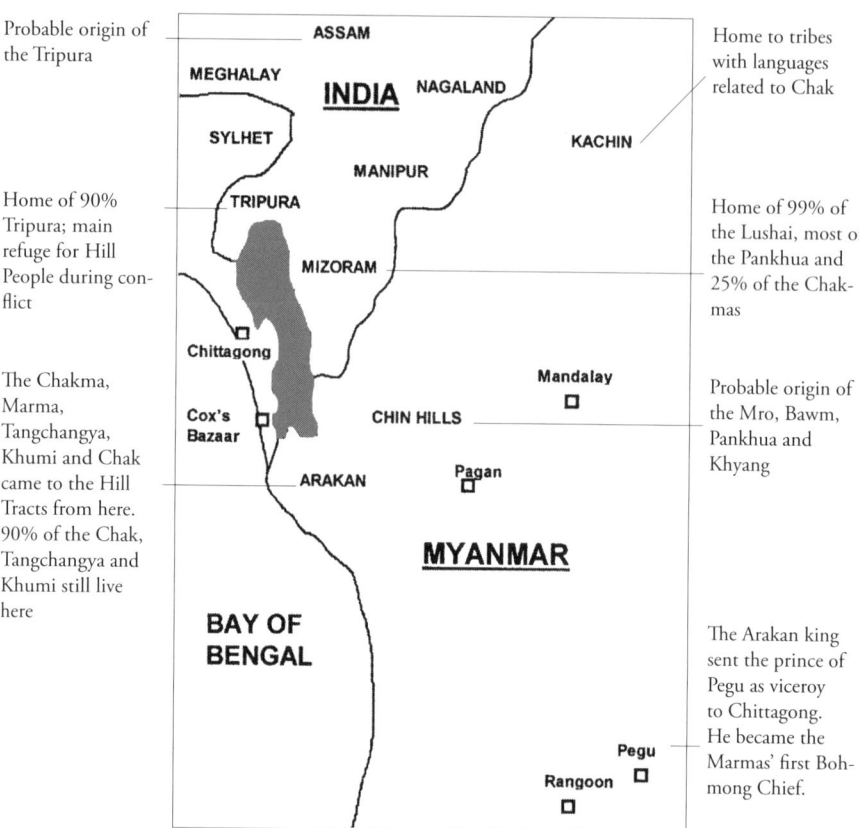

Probable origin of the Tripura

Home of 90% Tripura; main refuge for Hill People during conflict

The Chakma, Marma, Tangchangya, Khumi and Chak came to the Hill Tracts from here. 90% of the Chak, Tangchangya and Khumi still live here

Home to tribes with languages related to Chak

Home of 99% of the Lushai, most of the Pankhua and 25% of the Chakmas

Probable origin of the Mro, Bawm, Pankhua and Khyang

The Arakan king sent the prince of Pegu as viceroy to Chittagong. He became the Marmas' first Bohmong Chief.

Source: Report: Chittagong Hill Tracts Region Development Plan (ADB TA No. 3328-BAN), February 2001, Asian Development Bank.

Annex 2
Ethnic Composition of Population, Chittagong Hill Tracts (1991 Census)[51]

	Bandarban Hill Tracts	% of Dist Pop	Khagrachari Hill Tracts	% of Dist Pop	Rangamati Hill Tracts	% of Dist Pop	Total Pop CHT	% of Total Pop CHT	% of Ind Pop CHT
Bawm	6,431	2.78					6,431	0.65	1.28
Chak	1,681	0.72					1,681	0.17	0.33
Chakma	4,163	1.80	77,869	22.73	157,385	39.32	239,417	24.57	47.92
Khyang	1,455	0.63			525	0.13	1,980	0.20	0.39
Khumi	1,150	0.49			91	0.02	1,241	0.12	0.24
Lushai	226	0.09			436	0.10	662	0.06	0.13
Marma	59,291	25.70	82,183	23.99	40,868	10.21	142,342	14.60	28.49
Mru	21,963	9.52	40	0.01	164	0.04	22, 167	2.27	4.43
Pankhua	99	0.04			3,128	0.78	3,227	0.33	0.64
Tanchangya	5,499	2.38			13,718	3.42	19,217	1.97	3.84
Tripura	8,237	3.57	47,072	13.74	5,865	1.46	61,174	6.27	12.24
Bengali	120,241	52.12	174,969	51.08	178,065	44.48	473,275	48.56	
Others	229	0.09	355	0.10			584	0.05	
Indigenous	110,195	47.77	167,164	48.80	222,180	55.51	499,539	51.26	
Total	230,665		342,488		400,245		974,445		

Source: Revised Estimate of 1991 Census based upon records of the Hill District Council, Rangamati Hill Tracts (courtesy: Arunendu Tripura, Public Relations Officer)

51   R.D. Roy, 'Challenges for Juridical Pluralism and Customary Laws of the Indigenous Peoples: The Case of the Chittagong Hill Tracts, Bangladesh' in Chandra Roy (ed.), *Defending Diversity: Case Studies* (Utsjoki: The Saami Council, Swedish Section, 2004) p. 156.

Section II

Minorities

Chapter 8

Individuals, Collectivities and Rights

Geoff Gilbert[1]

Introduction

Throughout the 1990s, international organizations, the United Nations,[2] the Organization for Security and Co-operation in Europe[3] and the Council of Europe,[4] all promulgated minority rights instruments. In fact, the various documents gave rights to persons belonging to minorities, not to the minority groups themselves. Some of the instruments expressly *did* call on the State to protect the minorities and promote their cultural identities, and even recommended autonomy as one means of achieving that end, but no extant instrument dealing with minorities accords them rights. Nevertheless, the question has arisen as to primacy between the individual and the minority. While this may seem a redundant debate, it reflects the underlying context in which minority rights are played out in States. The State stands in a dual role *vis-à-vis* the minority group and the individual persons belonging to the minority; it is the guarantor of international obligations and duties owed to each separately, but it must also work in both a trilateral relationship where individual rights need to be measured against the obligation to protect the group, preserve its existence and promote its identity – it is this issue that has given rise to the questions about primacy.[5]

---

1 I am grateful to my colleague, Professor Jane Wright, for her insightful comments on an earlier draft.

2 United Nations General Assembly Declaration on the Rights of Persons Belonging to National or Ethnic, Religious or Linguistic Minorities, 1992, GA Res.47/135, Annex, 47 UNGAOR Supp. (No.49) p. 210, UN Doc.A/47/49 (1993); see also, the commentary by Asbjørn Eide, E/CN.4/Sub.2/AC.5/1998/WP.1, 13 May 1998, and comments thereon, E/CN.4/Sub.2/AC.5/1999/WP.1.

3 See Copenhagen Document, 11 HRLJ 232 (1990), and T. Buergenthal, 'A new public order for Europe', 11 *HRLJ* 217 (1990) p. 217.

4 Framework Convention for the Protection of National Minorities, 34 ILM 351 (1995); see also, H. Klebes, 'The Council of Europe's Framework Convention for the Protection of National Minorities', 16 *HRLJ* 92 (1995) p. 92.

5 In this chapter, the term obligation (other than in quotations) is used with respect to States where there is no correlative right. Rights indicate correlative duties. An obligation owed to

Nazila Ghanea & Alexandra Xanthaki (eds.), Minorities, Peoples and Self-Determination, *pp. 139-161.*
© 2005 *Koninklijke Brill NV. Printed in The Netherlands. ISBN 90 04 14301 7.*

Thus, this chapter seeks to address several different but related questions: the nature of minority rights and the identity of the right-holder; the relationship between the individual member's rights and the rights, if any, of the minority itself; and, the role of the State *vis-à-vis* the minority and the individual member. Moreover, when these questions are addressed, it is usually by political scientists or legal theorists, whereas this chapter will include case and treaty-based analysis as to practice. These questions obviously also overlap and do not form a simple series of subheadings for the chapter.

The Nature of Minority Rights

Article 1 of the Framework Convention for the Protection of National Minorities 1995[6] provides as follows:

> The protection of national minorities and of the rights and freedoms of persons belonging to those minorities forms an integral part of the international protection of *human rights*, and as such falls within the scope of international co-operation. [Emphasis added]

In that opening provision of what is still the only extant minority rights treaty regime on the international or regional plane, are raised all the issues that explain why the study of the protection of minority rights in international law presents so much that is vague and unclear. While minority rights are declared to be human rights in many international instruments, the relationship between the individual member of the minority group, the collectivity and the State, respectively, is often explored only in part.

At one level, one could argue that minority rights cannot be human rights except to the extent that they are a specialised regime for persons belonging to minority groups. If it were truly a *minority* rights regime, then it is not, by definition, *human* rights: human rights attach to individuals, whereas minority rights ought to attach to the minority *qua* minority group.[7]

> The doctrine of human rights affirms two fundamental principles of Western liberalism. The first is that the human individual is the most fundamental moral unit. The second is that all human individuals are morally equal.

---

one actor might, however, be indirectly enforceable through the enforcement of a right held by another actor.

6   (note 4).

7   M. Freeman, 'Are there Collective Human Rights?', 43 *Political Studies* Special Issue (1995) p. 25; J. Donnelly, 'Human Rights, Individual Rights and Collective Rights' in J. Berting *et al.* (eds.) *Human Rights in a Pluralist World* (Westport CT: Meckler 1990). It is not part of this chapter to try and define what constitutes a minority.

Moreover, as Patrick Thornberry noted over a decade ago, the corollary is that the individual's rights must trump those, if any, of the minority group.[8]

There may be a problem in general, however, as to what lengths cultural 'authenticity' and 'identity' may be carried. The answer suggested in [this book] is that minority rights need to be brought into balance with human rights or, more correctly, to be seen as part of human rights. Whatever respect must be paid to the rights of groups, the stance of modern international law is clear in according primacy to individual choice: respect for group rights does not justify 'group determinism', the overriding of individual choice by claims of the group.

Therefore, are minority rights as presently constituted simply human rights for persons belonging to specific groups within the State, or have there been developments since the end of the 1980s that have given the minority group a legal status? And, if so, has the minority group become the holder of *human* rights?

The principal international guarantee of minority rights is Article 27 of the International Covenant on Civil and Political Rights;[9]

Article 27. In those states in which ethnic, religious, or linguistic minorities exist, persons belonging to such minorities shall not be denied the right, in community with the other members of their group, to enjoy their own culture, to profess and practice their own religion, or to use their own language.

As can be seen, it protects persons belonging to minority groups. However, more importantly for the present argument, the rights it protects are guaranteed to all individuals in other provisions of this covenant and the International Covenant on Economic, Social and Cultural Rights.[10] For instance, freedom of religion is provided for by Article 18 ICCPR,[11] while the right to use one's own language or enjoy one's own culture in com-

---

8   P. Thornberry *International Law and the Rights of Minorities* (Oxford: OUP, 1991) p. 394. See also, P. Thornberry *Indigenous Peoples and Human Rights* (Manchester: MUP, 2002) pp. 113-14.

9   UNGA Res.2200A(XXI), UNGAOR, 21st Sess., Supp.No.16, 52 (1966); 999 UNTS 171; 6 ILM 368 (1967); 61 AJIL 870 (1967): hereinafter, ICCPR.

10   ICESCR, UNGA Res.2200 A (XXI), 16 December 1966

11   Article 18 ICCPR

1.   Everyone shall have the right to freedom of thought, conscience and religion. This right shall include freedom to have or to adopt a religion or belief of his choice, and freedom, either individually or in community with others and in public or private, to manifest his religion or belief in worship, observance, practice and teaching. ...

3.   Freedom to manifest one's religion or beliefs may be subject only to such limitations as are prescribed by law and are necessary to protect public safety, order, health or morals, or the fundamental rights and freedoms of others.

munity with others can be derived from the rights to freedom of expression,[12] the right to take part in cultural life,[13] the right to education[14] and freedom of association.[15] To the extent that those rights can be restricted, Article 27 makes clear that special preference has to be given to allowing persons belonging to minority groups to exercise these rights.[16] On the other hand, given that the European Court of Human Rights, without any provision corresponding to Article 27 in the European Convention for the Protection of Human Rights and Fundamental Freedoms,[17] has still extended guarantees to minority groups, it can easily be argued that minority rights is simply shorthand for human rights that are of particular relevance to persons belonging to minority groups who wish to preserve their own identity.[18] For John Packer, for instance:

> [it] is perhaps necessary to recall at this point that, in so far as minority rights are considered to be part of human rights, the point of departure for consideration of the international standards of minority rights must be the Charter of the United Nations which in its Preamble, article 1(3) and Article 55 entrenches 'universal respect for human rights and fundamental freedoms for all without distinction as to race, sex, language or religion' as a basic objective of the organization.[19]

---

12   Article 19 ICCPR

   2.   Everyone shall have the right to freedom of expression; this right shall include freedom to seek, receive and impart information and ideas of all kinds, regardless of frontiers, either orally, in writing or in print, in the form of art, or through any other media of his choice.

13   Article 15 ICESCR

   1.   The States Parties to the present Covenant recognize the right of everyone:
   (a)   To take part in cultural life.

14   Article 13 ICESCR

   1.   The States Parties to the present Covenant recognize the right of everyone to education. They agree that education shall be directed to the full development of the human personality and the sense of its dignity, and shall strengthen the respect for human rights and fundamental freedoms. *They further agree that education shall enable all persons to participate effectively in a free society, promote understanding, tolerance and friendship among all nations and all racial, ethnic or religious groups*, and further the activities of the United Nations for the maintenance of peace. [Emphasis added].

15   Article 22 ICCPR

   1.   Everyone shall have the right to freedom of association with others ….

16   *Viz.* Thornberry 2002 (note 8), pp. 154 *et seq.*, especially pp. 158-9.

17   ETS/5 (1950) p. 5.

18   See J. Packer, 'On the Content of Minority Rights' in J. Räikkä (ed.) *Do We Need Minority Rights?* (Dordrecht: Kluwer Law International, 1996) p. 122.

19   Packer (note 18) p. 145. See also Jules Deschênes (Canadian member of the UN Sub-Commission), Proposal Concerning a Definition of the Term 'Minority', UN Doc E/CN.4/Sub.2/1985/31.

Packer goes on to assert[20] that relying on the advisory opinion of the Permanent Court of International Justice in the *Minority Schools in Albania* case[21] is misconceived because it was decided pre-Charter and the institutionalisation of international human rights law in the post-second world war period. No-one would allege that the minority rights regime of the inter-war years was reawakened after 1945. Nevertheless, to the extent that decisions of the PCIJ interpreted non-discrimination, unquestionably part of the post-1945 international human rights law regime, in the context of minorities wishing to preserve their identity (as opposed to one where the State is viewed as consisting of so many individuals)[22], that analysis found in the *Minority Schools* case cannot easily be dismissed. As Capotorti put it:

> 241. It can, therefore, be stated that the two concepts are distinct in the sense that the concept of equality and non-discrimination implies a formal guarantee of uniform treatment for all individuals – who must be ensured the enjoyment of the same rights and accept the same obligations – whereas the concept of protection of minorities implies special measures in favour of members of a minority group. None the less, the purpose of these measures is to institute factual equality between the members of the minority group and other individuals. This confirms the thesis that prevention of discrimination, on the one hand, and the *implementation of special measures to protect minorities*, on the other, are, merely two aspects of the same problem: that of defending fundamental human rights. [Emphasis added][23]

---

20   (note 18) pp. 145-6. See also Thornberry 1991 (note 8) p. 220, challenging the less than cautious approach of Y. Dinstein.

21   Advisory opinion of 6 April 1935, PCIJ (XXXIVth Session), Series A-B, No. 64. The essence of the decision can be found at p. 17 where it is argued that two things were needed for the protection of minorities, equal treatment of persons belonging to minority groups, and 'to ensure for the minority elements suitable means for the preservation of their … peculiarities, their traditions and their national characteristics'.

These two requirements are indeed closely interlocked, for their would be no true equality between a majority and a minority if the latter were deprived of its own institutions, and were consequently compelled to renounce that which constitutes the very essence of its being as a minority.

22   See the ideas of Hobbes and Locke on the State as merely 'a multitude of men' or 'any number of men' – cited in V. Van Dyke, 'The Individual, the State and Ethnic Communities in Political Theory' in W. Kymlicka *The Rights of Minority Cultures* (Oxford: OUP, 1995) pp. 34-35.

23   F. Capotorti, *Study on the Rights of Persons Belonging to Ethnic, Religious and Linguistic Minorities, 1977*, 1991. And see paragraph 585, too, in Conclusions and Recommendations. *Cf.* E-I. A. Daes, Working paper on the relationship and distinction between the rights of persons belonging to minorities and those of indigenous peoples II, E/CN.4/Sub.2/2000/10, para. 30:

For these reasons, most previous attempts to define 'minorities' and 'indigenous peoples' have emphasized their non-dominant status in national society, either as a sufficient crite-

The Human Rights Committee expressed the underlying principle in *Lovelace v Canada*.[24] Having found *prima facie* that the difference in treatment between men and women of the Maliseet Indian tribe was contrary to Articles 2 and 3 of the ICCPR read with Article 27, it immediately stated that:

> 7.2 … On the other hand, article 27 of the Covenant requires States parties to accord protection to ethnic and linguistic minorities and the Committee must give due weight to this obligation.

Thus, even post-1945, it is clear that the collectivity is not ignored and is seen as having a direct relevance to a full understanding of equality and the defence of fundamental human rights. The question is whether in theory and in law the minority group can be a right holder or is the minority group simply the context in which rights of persons belonging to that group are to be viewed and applied?

For philosophers and legal theorists like Michael Hartney,[25] 'morally speaking there can be no such rights' if that means a right that 'inheres in a group or collective entity *rather than in an individual*' [emphasis added]; he regards the lack of clarity as to terminology as not conducive to clear thinking on the subject. On the other hand, Van Dyke[26] is prepared to live with the lack of absolute certainty in order better to reflect practical reality:

> Stressing individualism, liberals have no proper theory of the state. … If, in principle, communities as well as individuals were accepted as right-and-duty-bearing units, the chance would be increased that a coherent and intellectually defensible doctrine or set of doctrines could be developed, which would respond to *practical problems*. Individuals want freedom and equality, to be sure, but there is also a 'quest for com-

---

rion, or in conjunction with the criterion of numerical inferiority. This solution poses both methodological and logical problems. The measurement of dominance can be challenging. A group may nominally control the State apparatus yet be subordinate to another group that controls, for example, the lands, finances or military institutions of the country. *De jure* dominance may be de facto subordination. More seriously, applying non-dominance as a key characteristic of minorities or indigenous peoples results in the paradox that a group ceases to be a minority or an indigenous people when it realizes its human rights, or attains social and political equality. We are faced with a logical dilemma. Either we admit that the goal of equality will never be achieved fully, or we accept terms such as 'minority' as purely situational and transitory. No minority or indigenous people has admitted that its legal status exists only at certain times, and in certain situations.

See Thornberry 2002 (note 8) p. 53.

24 *Sandra Lovelace v Canada*, Communication No. 24/1977 (30 July 1981), U.N. Doc. CCPR/C/OP/1 para. 83 (1984).

25 M. Hartney, 'Some Confusions Concerning Collective Rights' in Kymlicka (note 22) p. 219.

26 (note 22) p.34 and p. 49.

munity'. To focus only on the rights of individuals is to focus only on forces making for atomization and estrangement and to ignore primordial collective sentiment and group loyalties. Because of the failure to consider the appropriate role of communalism in the scheme of things, *theory and doctrine go along one line and practice often goes along another*; and individualism is assumed while anomie is bewailed. The thinking that occurs is compartmentalized – or cynical or naive. [footnote omitted, emphasis added]

Michael Freeman is also prepared to accept that collective rights can be understood within the paradigm of human rights;[27]

Collective human rights are rights the bearers of which are collectivities, which are not reducible to, but are consistent with individual human rights, and the basic justification of which is the same as the basic justification of individual human rights. ... [There] are non-derivative collective human rights which are justified by the grounding value of the interest that individuals have in the quality of their own lives.

Nevertheless, Freeman is aware of the difficulties of promulgating rights for collectivities that avoid

conceptual confusion and political danger. The implication of this is not that the concept of collective human rights should be rejected, but that the conceptual and practical relations between collective and individual human rights should be made as clear as possible.[28]

Therefore, theoretically it is not impossible to conceive of human rights that are specific to the collectivity and which cannot be reduced to human rights for persons belonging to minority groups. However, for international lawyers, the problem is not just one of defining the rights, but of deciding on how, if at all, those rights might be asserted. For international lawyers, it is not the case that there is no right unless there is a remedy.

The correlation of rights with justiciability is an understandable attitude from the domestic-law point of view. But, of course, international lawyers are very familiar with the phenomenon that, for a variety of reasons (sometimes jurisdictional, sometimes more substantive), it is not possible to bring claims in vindication of rights held in international law. The absence of the possibility of recourse to third-party judicial procedures is certainly not the test of whether the right exists or not. To the international lawyer, the existence of the right is tested by reference to the sources of international law.[29]

---

27   (note 7) p. 38.
28   Ibid. p. 39.
29   R. Higgins *Problems and Process: International Law and How We Use It* (Oxford: OUP, 1994) p. 100.

Related to, but separate from the issue of justiciability, is the question of the standing of the minority group, both domestically and internationally. Moreover, even if one has a true collective right and a tribunal to adjudicate upon it that gives the minority group standing, there is always the question of how the minority group is to be represented.[30] Having accorded recognition to the group, that is but the first step because one then has to decide how to identify the representatives of the group – what if certain persons are excluded from deciding on who should represent the group because they are excluded from the group by other members of the selfsame group? Democratic elections to choose the government of a State are premised on the idea that it will not represent the views of every member of the population, but somehow the representatives of the minority group have to be more inclusive. One should not expect all members of the minority group to be in total agreement on every issue,[31] for that is to see the group as some sort of unchangeable, homogeneous monolith, but those representing the minority group are more in the position of trustees than of elected politicians. On the other hand, the larger and more autonomous the group, the more likely that it will have to use elections to choose its representatives – and the State cannot interfere in such a process.[32]

---

30   The Human Rights Committee can only receive communications under Optional Protocol I from individuals. Thus, no claim can be made by any group with respect to self-determination under Article 1. See *Communication No.167/1984, Bernard Ominayak, Chief of the Lake Lubicon Band v Canada*, Views adopted 26 March 1990, UNGAOR, 45th Sess., Supp. No.40, A/45/40, 11 *HRLJ* 305 (1990) para. 13.3; and, *Communication No.413/1990, A.B. v Italy, South Tirol Case*, Decision on Admissibility, 2 November 1990, 12 *HRLJ* 25 (1991) para. 3.2. Nevertheless, a complaint by an individual representing the group in an Article 27 claim can, in appropriate circumstances, rely on Article 1 to give true meaning to the 'enjoyment of culture' – *Communication No.547/1993, Apirana Mahuika v New Zealand*, Views adopted 15 November 2000, where the Human Rights Committee held that 'the provisions of Article 1 may be relevant in the interpretation of other rights protected by the Covenant, in particular Article 27' – para. 9.2.

31   *Viz. Apirana Mahuika* (note 30) para. 5.7.

32   *Hasan and Chaush v Bulgaria* 30985/96, European Court of Human Rights (Grand Chamber), 26 October 2000.

> 62   Where the organization of the religious community is at issue, Article 9 must be interpreted in the light of Article 11 of the Convention which safeguards associative life against unjustified State interference. Seen in this perspective, the believer's right to freedom of religion encompasses the expectation that the community will be allowed to function peacefully free from arbitrary State intervention. Indeed, the autonomous existence of religious communities is indispensable for pluralism in a democratic society and is thus an issue at the very heart of the protection which Article 9 affords. It directly concerns not only the organization of the community as such but also the effective enjoyment of the right to freedom of religion by all its active members. Were the organisational life of the community not protected by Article 9 of the Convention, all other aspects of the individual's freedom of religion would become vulnerable.

> See also M.D. Evans, 'Believing in Communities, European Style' in N. Ghanea (ed.) *The Challenge of Religious Discrimination at the Dawn of the New Millennium* (Leiden: Martinus Nijhoff, 2003) pp. 146-7.

Questions regarding recognition, autonomy and other rights that might inhere in the collective are addressed in the rest of this chapter as part of the overall analysis of the relationship between the State, the minority group and the individual.

The triangular relationship – the rights of the member of the minority group in relation to the rights of the minority and the multiple roles of the State

The most complex issue is how the individual, the minority group and the State interact and, logically, the discussion of that interaction precedes analysis of the rights, duties and obligations of the State with respect to the individual and the minority group.

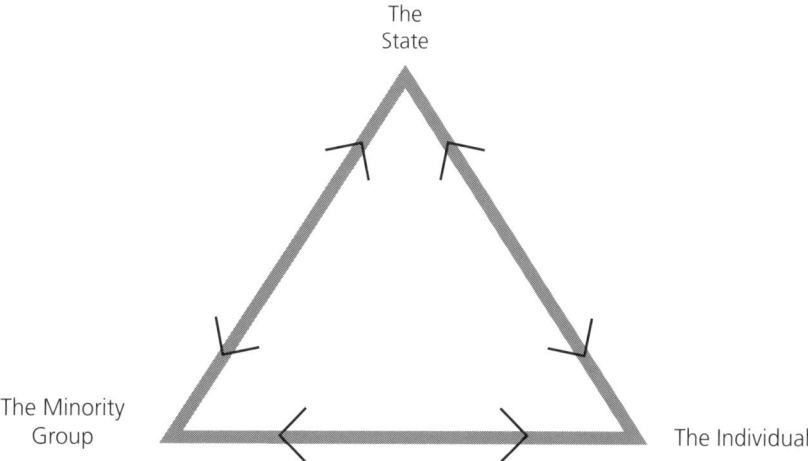

If there are collective rights, then the State has duties toward the minority group as well as the individual. Equally, international law dictates that all rights emanate from State duties in international law at some level. However, the persons belonging to the minority group have a relationship with the State and with the minority group which both, to some extent, confer benefits. In the case of the minority group, though, it can also openly make demands of the individual in the cause of preserving the minority identity. The degree of authority that can be asserted by the minority group over its members is also part of the complex relationship between the individual, the minority group and the State.[33]

---

[33]   See L. Green, 'Internal Minorities and their Rights' in Kymlicka (note 22) p. 257, citing C. Isherwood:

> *Because* the persecuting majority is vile, says the liberal, *therefore* the persecuted minority must be stainlessly pure. Can't you see what nonsense that is. What's to prevent the bad from being persecuted by the worse?

See also, the discussion of *Lovelace* (note 24).

Under extant international instruments, the State owes duties to persons belonging to minority groups as individuals within the jurisdiction of the State and as members of the minority; in addition, it has obligations to the minority group *qua* minority. As things stand, only the individual persons belonging to a minority group have rights. Thus, it is almost a given that the State would enforce the individual's rights where the minority's practices infringed them, even if that were not written into the pertinent international instruments. Article 32 of the, now, OSCE's Copenhagen Document[34] provides as follows:

> (32) To belong to a national minority is a matter of a person's individual choice and *no disadvantage may arise from the exercise of such choice*. ...Persons belonging to national minorities can exercise and enjoy their rights individually as well as in community with other members of their group. *No disadvantage may arise for a person belonging to a national minority on account of the exercise or non-exercise of any such rights*. [Emphasis added]

The Council of Europe's Framework Convention for the Protection of National Minorities[35] is similarly constructed.

> Article 3
> 1 Every person belonging to a national minority shall have the right freely to choose to be treated or not to be treated as such *and no disadvantage shall result from this choice* or from the exercise of the rights which are connected to that choice. [Emphasis added]

With respect to the ICCPR, obligations to the minority group are not express, so, unsurprisingly, the Human Rights Committee has given priority to the individual over the group's interests. In *Lovelace*,[36] Canada, in consultation with the tribal elders, had drafted a law that denied benefits of membership of the minority group to women who married outside the group – there was no similar disenfranchisement for men who married outside. The Human Rights Committee acknowledged in paragraph 7.2 that Article 27 required 'States parties to accord protection to ethnic and linguistic minorities and the Committee must give due weight to this obligation'. Nevertheless, the Committee went on to hold that Sandra Lovelace's Article 27 rights had been breached:

> 14. The rights under Article 27 of the Covenant have to be secured to 'persons belonging' to the minority. At present Sandra Lovelace does not qualify as an Indian under Canadian legislation. However, the Indian Act deals primarily with a number of privileges which, as stated above, do not as such come within the scope of the Covenant. Protection under the Indian Act and protection under article 27 of the Covenant

---

34   (note 3).
35   (note 4).
36   (note 24).

therefore have to be distinguished. Persons who are born and brought up on a reserve, who have kept ties with their community and wish to maintain these ties must normally be considered as belonging to that minority within the meaning of the Covenant. Since Sandra Lovelace is ethnically a Maliseet Indian and has only been absent from her home reserve for a few years during the existence of her marriage, she is, in the opinion of the Committee, entitled to be regarded as 'belonging' to this minority and to claim the benefits of Article 27 of the Covenant. The question whether these benefits have been denied to her, depends on how far they extend.

15. ... The Committee recognizes the need to define the category of persons entitled to live on a reserve, for such purposes as those explained by the Government regarding protection of its resources and preservation of the identity of its people. However, the obligations which the Government has since undertaken under the Covenant must also be taken into account.

Prima facie, therefore, whenever there is a conflict of interest between the minority group and the individual that lacks a reasonable and objective justification,[37] the State should prefer the individual over the minority.[38] Political scientists explain the balancing act in the following terms:[39]

> The liberal State may intervene in illiberal communities for the sake of individual rights or tolerate a partly illiberal pluralism in order to keep the peace between different *communal conceptions of the good*. [Emphasis added]

As Thornberry has noted, though, the position is not necessarily that simple in practice. Article 27 protects the rights of the individual persons belonging to the minority group and to try and directly derive a right of the group therefrom would be unjustified – the protection of the group through Article 27 can only ever be derivative of a benefit to persons belonging to the minority group. For instance, '[when] cultural or linguistic character or identity is lost or degraded, the change tends to be irreversible'.[40] As such, one is comparing the interests of some of the persons belonging to the minority group as against the interests of the others. It is an acknowledgement that the preservation of group identity is an individual good.

---

37   *Lovelace* (note 24) para. 16; *Apirana Mahuika* (note 30) para. 9.6.

38   For the reverse situation where the group is complaining because the state has favoured the individual, see *Muonio Saami Village v Sweden* 28222/95, European Court of Human Rights (First Section), 15 February 2000 – Friendly Settlement, European Court of Human Rights (First Section), 9 January 2001.

39   M. Freeman (note 7) p. 37 summarizing C. Kukathas.

40   See P. Thornberry, 'The UN Declaration: Background, Analysis and Observations' in A. Phillips and A. Rosas, *The UN Minority Rights Declaration* (Turku/Åbo: London, Åbo Akademi University Institute for Human Rights/Minority Rights Group International, 1993) p. 22, citing I. Brownlie.

To what extent, however, would autonomy for the minority group readjust the balance and limit the State's sovereign jurisdiction within its own territory? If there is a collective right that could be held by a minority group *qua* group, it would be autonomy; other rights that might inhere in the minority discussed below, the right to recognition and the right to continuation of pre-existing rights, can be held by persons belonging to the minority group, but autonomy would have to be a right of the minority group itself. The scope and content of any emerging right to autonomy are unclear. At the beginning of the 1990s, the potential remit of self-determination beyond decolonization was hardly ever asserted.[41] It is now clear, however, that self-determination has relevance internally as well as externally.[42] For appropriate groups, including minorities, internal self-determination consists of autonomy sufficient for the group to control its own affairs. Does that indicate that the collectivity now has value as a right-holder independent of the benefit to members derived from its continued existence, a value that has to be weighed against the rights of the individual member? Moreover, does it demand a balancing of rights between the individual and the minority group? If autonomy is a right for the minority group *qua* group, then it changes the context in which the triangular relationship is to be understood. So far, the relationship has been understood in terms of obligations owed by the State to minority groups, but rights only for the individual persons belonging to the minority group. If autonomy is a right for the minority group, then the State will have a duty to balance the rights of the individual and the group in the same

---

41   See H. Hannum, 'Rethinking Self-Determination', 34.1 *Va.J Int'l L* (1993) p.23. *Cf.* I. Brownlie, 'The Rights of Peoples in Modern International Law' in J. Crawford *The Rights of Peoples* (Oxford: OUP, 1988) p. 16.

> [The] issues of self-determination, the treatment of minorities, and the status of indigenous populations, are the same, and the segregation of [these] topics is an impediment to fruitful work. The rights and claims of groups with their own cultural histories and identities are in principle the same – they must be. It is the problems of implementation of principles and standards which vary, simply because the facts will vary. ... This association of categories is not generally accepted, and the separation of categories is one reason for the hesitant approach to the definition of 'peoples' or 'minorities' or 'indigenous populations'.

NB. Even H. Gros Espiell held that the law on self-determination might develop to include minorities – *The Right to Self-Determination – Implementation of United Nations Resolutions*, E/CN.4/Sub.2/405/Rev.1 (1980) para. 56.

42   See F. Kirgis, 'The Degrees of Self-Determination in the United Nations Era', 88 *AJIL* 304 (1994); A. Rosas, 'Internal Self-Determination' and J. Salmon, 'Internal Aspects of the Right to Self-Determination: Towards a Democratic Legitimacy Principle', both in C. Tomuschat, *Modern Law of Self-Determination* (Dordrecht, Martinus Nijhoff, 1993) at p. 225 and p. 253, respectively. See also, I. Brownlie, 255 *Hague Recueil* (1995) pp. 55-61, A. Cassese *Self-determination of peoples: a Legal Reappraisal* (Cambridge: CUP, 1995), P. Alston *Peoples' Rights* (Oxford: OUP, 2001) and G. Gilbert, 'Autonomy and Minority Groups – A Right in International Law?' 35.2 *Cornell Int'l LJ* 307 (2002) p. 307.

way that it balances conflicting rights held by different individuals.[43] However, in exercising this balancing function, there is a significant difference. In assuming autonomous control over its own internal affairs, the minority group must do so in conformity with international human rights law standards.[44] As Freeman opines:[45]

> Liberal theory accords collective rights to nation-states but not to nations without states. However, nation-states have rights because they protect interests. Collectivities within nation-states have rights for the same reason …

Therefore, even if the State were to accord autonomy to the minority group or the minority group could assert the developing right to autonomy, the individual persons belonging to the minority group should notice little or no difference in practice. Under the traditional view, the balancing by the State would have been between the interests of some members of the minority group as against that of other members with respect to the preservation of group identity, while the new approach granting collective rights to the minority group only grants those rights so that the group can protect the interests of the members of the minority group – once again, any conflict between the individual member and the minority group would turn on whether there was an interest for other members of the minority group in preserving the *status quo*.[46]

The closest that international human rights law has come to dealing with this issue is in the Lund Recommendations[47] and the European Court of Human Rights case of

---

43   M. Freeman (note 7) p. 29. As he goes on to write, '[conflicts] of rights, with their consequent indeterminacy, are, however, stubborn facts of human rights politics'.

44   Where traditional practices might violate those standards, it is patronizing in the extreme to assume that the group will not change how it behaves in response to discussions about developments in international law that States have only adopted since the end of the second world war. It also seems to view minorities as set in stone and places them in some false historical ghetto.

45   (note 7) p. 32.

46   See M. Freeman (note 7) at 35.
      Some restriction of the individual rights of insiders may also be justified to prevent actions that would undermine communities which are necessary for autonomous choices. What makes this justification of community restriction of individual rights liberal is that its purpose is to protect a rights-supporting community.

47   Lund Recommendations on the Effective Participation of National Minorities in Public Life, promulgated at the request of the OSCE HCNM, (The Hague: Foundation on Inter-Ethnic Relations, September 1999); see also, K. Myntti's *Commentary*, (Turku/Åbo: Institute for Human Rights, Åbo Akademi University, 2001). Although mere recommendations with respect to a non-legally binding document, Copenhagen 1990 (note 3) the United Nations Sub-Commission Working Group on Minorities has promoted their relevance to enhanced minority relations in States – in no way could one assert that they are customary international law, but they should be borne in mind by all States grappling with the issue of effective participation by minority groups.

the *Jewish Liturgical Association Cha'are Shalom Ve Tsedek v France*.[48] The Lund Recommendations on Effective Participation were drafted under the auspices of the OSCE's High Commissioner on National Minorities 'to encourage and facilitate the adoption by States of specific measures to alleviate tensions related to national minorities and thus to serve the ultimate conflict prevention goal …'.[49] Recommendation 21 provides that 'autonomous authorities must respect and ensure the human rights of all persons, including the rights of any minorities within their jurisdiction'. As well as addressing the responsibility of the minority group granted territorial autonomy *vis à vis* other minority groups within its jurisdiction, Recommendation 21 requires the minority group to respect and ensure the human rights of *all* persons, those who belong to the group and those who do not. Simply because the individual is a person belonging to the minority group with autonomous authority does not mean that s/he has to forgo her/his human rights. Those human rights flow from the obligations of the State, but the minority group has to respect them, too, and, like the State, will need to engage in a balancing exercise. Autonomy is a collective right, but it generates an individual good, the preservation of the collectivity.

The *Jewish Liturgical Association* case[50] can be read as conforming too much to State interests – the European Court of Human Rights allowed France to ignore a minority within a minority for administrative convenience. The right to license ritual slaughter (*shechitah*) to fulfil *kashrut* was granted by France to the 'Joint Rabbinical Committee [which] is part of the Jewish Consistorial Association of Paris, which is an offshoot of the Central Consistory, the institution set up by Napoleon I by means of the Imperial Decree of 17 March 1808 to administer Jewish worship in France. … The rabbinical court, or Beth Din, which rules on questions of religious law (marriage, divorce and conversions), supervises observance of the dietary laws and appoints and monitors the *kashrut* slaughterers and inspectors employed by the Consistory'.[51] The Central Consistory, which represents 700,000 Jews in France, derived half its income from a levy of eight francs per kilo on ritually slaughtered meat. The applicants in the Strasbourg case were a group of Jews, numbering about 40,000, who followed stricter dietary requirements and who wanted to establish their own slaughterhouse so as to guarantee that the meat they ate was *glatt*. Some of the meat from Central Consistory slaughterhouses was *glatt* and meat of that quality could also be imported from Belgium. The applicant association had established illegal slaughterhouses and levied a tax of four francs per kilo.[52]

> 58. The applicant association, whose arguments were endorsed by the Commission, submitted that by refusing it the approval necessary for it to authorize its own ritual

48   27417/95, European Court of Human Rights (Grand Chamber), 27 June 2000.
49   Lund Recommendations (note 47) p.6.
50   (note 48).
51   Ibid. paras. 22 and 25. For a full background to Jewish ritual slaughter, see paras. 13-26.
52   The applicant association could have sought authorization from the Jewish Consistorial Association of Paris.

slaughterers to perform ritual slaughter, in accordance with the religious prescriptions of its members, and by granting such approval to the [Jewish Consistorial Association of Paris] alone, the French authorities had infringed in a discriminatory way its right to manifest its religion through observance of the rites of the Jewish religion. It relied on Article 9 of the Convention, taken alone and together with Article 14.

The majority of the Court found that ritual slaughter was part of 'manifestation' within Article 9 of the ECHR's guarantee of freedom of religion.[53] In line therewith, ritual slaughter was permitted in France and the only difference between the Jewish Consistorial Association of Paris' slaughterhouses and those run by the applicant was in the thoroughness of the examination of the dead animal afterwards. If the adherents of the applicant association had not been able to obtain meat that was *glatt*, that might have been an interference with Article 9, but such meat was available from authorised slaughterhouses and from Belgium.[54] Even if there had been a violation in principle of Article 9.1, paragraph 2 would have relieved France of liability. The second complaint, that France discriminated between the two Jewish 'minorities', contrary to Article 14, was dismissed because of the limited impact of the difference in treatment which also had a reasonable and objective justification.

The dissenting members of the Court found that there had been a violation of Article 9 alone and with Article 14. They argued that the obligation of the State is to permit pluralism.[55] It was not permissible, as the majority judgment provided, for France to rely on the applicant reaching a deal with the larger Jewish minority group in France, which would not necessarily be unbiased. The fact that *glatt* meat could be obtained from elsewhere was irrelevant. The minority opinion, however, was principally based on Article 9 read with Article 14.

> [The] majority should not have confined their reasons to the assertion that the inter-ference was of 'limited effect' and that the difference of treatment was 'limited in scope'. Where freedom of religion is concerned, it is not for the European Court of Human Rights to substitute its assessment of the scope or seriousness of an interfer-ence for that of the persons or groups concerned, because the essential object of Article 9 of the Convention is to protect individuals' most private convictions.

They first held that the two groups, the applicant association and the Jewish Consistorial Association of Paris, were comparable. The government had tried to justify the differ-ence in treatment on the number of adherents of the Jewish Consistorial Association of Paris and of the applicant association, but the minority opinion, acknowledging that

---

53   (note 48) para. 74. The French government had also argued that the applicant association was only interested in commercial matters, the slaughter and sale of *kashrut* meat.
54   Ibid. paras. 80-3.
55   *Viz. Serif v Greece*, 38178/97, European Court of Human Rights (Second Section), 14 December 1999, paras. 49-53.

States have a legitimate interest in not having to negotiate with multifarious unrepresentative organisations, found that there was a corresponding obligation:

> to secure true religious pluralism, which is an inherent feature of the notion of a democratic society…. In the light of the foregoing considerations, we consider that the difference in treatment between the applicant and the [Jewish Consistorial Association of Paris] – one of which received the approval that the other was denied – had no objective and reasonable justification and was disproportionate. There has therefore been a violation of Article 14 taken together with Article 9 of the Convention.

Although phrased in terms of a dispute between two groups, it needs to be remembered that the ECHR only provides individual human rights: there is no equivalent to Article 27 ICCPR offering persons belonging to a minority group the right to enjoy their culture in community with other members of that group. Nevertheless, groups of individuals can bring complaints under Article 34 ECHR. In having to intervene between the Paris Consistory and the applicant association, France has favoured the larger group and the reasoning of the majority in the Grand Chamber balances not rights, but ease of access to suitable meat. The reasoning of the dissenting minority is more thorough and is to be preferred. The decision of the European Court of Human Rights does not even provide the individuals within the minority association the minimum guarantee that theory demands, the right of exit.[56]

The final issue to be addressed within the triangular relationship concerns whether persons belonging to the minority group can waive their rights. There are some rights that can never be waived, most obviously the non-derogable rights. An individual who belongs to a minority group cannot agree to torture or slavery, for instance, even if the group's practices include either or both and the individual freely consents. On the other hand, some groups will make demands of their adherents that if the State were to do the same would leave it in breach of its human rights commitments – groups that discriminate on grounds of gender place women in a situation where they either leave or suffer discrimination. It is clear that international human rights law accepts that members can waive certain rights. In *McGuinness v United Kingdom*,[57] newly elected members of the British Parliament had to swear an oath that they would bear faithful and true allegiance to the Queen and her heirs. As a member of Sinn Féin, a party dedicated to the principle that the Irish people have the right to self-determination, the applicant refused to take such an oath and fought the election knowing he would not be allowed to take his seat. However, after the election the Speaker of the House of Commons ruled he could have no access to the facilities of the House, including an office, staff allowances and research facilities. He complained of violations of Articles 10 (oath contrary to his political principles), 9 (oath contrary to his religion as a Roman Catholic, since

---

56   See M. Freeman (note 7) p. 39. It will be interesting to see whether Protocol 12 to the ECHR, that provides for a free standing right to non-discrimination encourages the European Court of Human Rights to address difference in treatment *per se*, rather than, as it has to do at present, difference as regards enjoyment of another Convention right.

57   39511/98, European Court of Human Rights (Third Section), 8 June 1999.

the monarch can never be a Roman Catholic), 3 of Protocol 1 (the new ruling by the Speaker prevented him properly representing his constituents), 13 (no effective remedy) and 14 (discrimination). The Court held that freedom of expression is especially important for elected representatives of the people. Nevertheless, the restriction in paragraph 2 of Article 10 relating to the 'protection of the rights of others' could extend to the protection of effective democracy.[58] The entire complaint was dismissed as inadmissible due to being manifestly ill-founded. Much seemed to turn on the fact that the applicant was not required to swear or affirm allegiance to a particular religion, that he would be able to retain his republican views and pursue them in Parliament, and that he *and his electors* had known throughout that as a matter of principle he would never be allowed to sit in Parliament if elected. To that extent it seems the Court accepted that one can waive some rights to some extent. However, while Sinn Féin supporters can be assumed to have acquiesced in their loss of representation, a Member of Parliament represents all her/his constituents and those voting for other parties definitely did not agree that they should have no MP if their candidate lost. While the actual decision in *McGuinness* can be questioned, the principle that voluntary membership might entail a diminution in rights cannot be doubted.[59]

The parallel relationships – the position of the State *vis-à-vis* the persons belonging to the minority group and the minority group

As stated, the State has a continuing duty under its human rights commitments in international law, including non-discrimination. The persons belonging to the minority group should not suffer for being members of the group, nor be labelled as members of the group – group membership should be a matter of free choice with no negative consequences *vis-à-vis* the State.[60] The content of the obligation to the minority group is still

---

58   See *Ahmed v United Kingdom*, European Court of Human Rights, 2 September 1998, para. 52.

59   It is beyond the scope of this paper to justify a diminution of rights for children who are members.

60   There is an argument that previous entrenched discrimination towards minority groups should entail that individual persons belonging to minority groups require affirmative action to ensure equality. In order to rectify the worse position the Roma find themselves in by comparison with most other minorities in Europe, the Framework Convention Advisory Committee has recommended to several States that particular steps be taken. The argument that history cannot be rectified is defeatist – *viz.* Albania's response to the Advisory Committee opinion, paragraph 35 (ACFC/SR (99) 6; government response received 18 February 2003):

> With regard to the Advisory Committee concern for the assimilation of Vlachs/Aromanians in Albania, experts should have in mind that this process of integration is not an event of today, but a result of a long historical process and the passed situation cannot be returned artificially. This does not mean that the particularities of that community of Vlachs which has still preserved its linguistic, cultural, etc. features, be not taken in consideration.

unclear and any rights that might be possessed by the collectivity are open to dispute. Nonetheless, it is uncontrovertible that the State has parallel relationships with persons belonging to the minority group and the minority group itself.

The State

The Individual   The Minority Group

Albanian state undoubtedly should take measures and encourage the preservation of these features. It is not easy for the Albanian Government to realise the return of the historical assimilating processes happened in centuries, but anyhow it supports the remaining elements of their linguistic identity....

The starting point in relation to the position of the State with respect to the individual persons belonging to the minority group is well set out in Recommendation 4 of the Lund Recommendations.[61]

> Individuals identify themselves in numerous ways in addition to their identity as members of a national minority. The decision as to whether an individual is a member of a minority, the majority, or neither rests with that individual and shall not be imposed on her or him. Moreover, no person shall suffer any disadvantage as a result of such a choice or a refusal to choose.

Self-identification is an essential aspect of being a member of a minority. Usually, the individual will want to be able to identify herself/himself as a member of the minority group without any negative consequences, but it should not be forgotten that persons belonging to minority groups also have the right to opt out of the group without fearing that the State will continue to label them as members thereof. Self-identification has its limits, however. In *Kosteski v Macedonia*,[62] the applicant had been dismissed for non-attendance at work which, he asserted, was due to his observance of Muslim religious holidays, as guaranteed by the Macedonian Constitution. The Court adjourned the case to let the Government respond to complaints under Article 9 alone and with Article 14. The Article 14 complaint is based on the fact that the Macedonian authorities required him to prove he was Muslim, unlike other Muslims in Macedonia – given that his parents were Christian and, up until the events that led to his dismissal, he had always celebrated the Christian holidays, this case may require the European Court of Human Rights to examine how one proves one belongs to a particular minority group.[63]

As regards the minority group, it is less clear that they possess rights as against States; the above discussed right to autonomy is *de lege ferenda* at best. That having been said, international law clearly recognises the existence of minorities. It protects them through the Genocide Convention 1948 from acts 'committed with intent to destroy,

---

61   (note 47).

62   55170/00, European Court of Human Rights (Second Section), 3 May 2001.

63   *Cf. Rights of Minorities in Upper Silesia (Minority Schools)*, PCIJ Series A No.15, 26 April 1928, p. 34.

> There is reason to believe that, in the conditions which exist in Upper Silesia, a multitude of cases occur in which the question whether a person belongs to a minority particularly of race or language does not clearly appear from the facts. Such an uncertainty might for example exist, as regards language…where he knows and makes use of several languages, and, as regards race, in the case of mixed marriages. If the authorities wish to verify or dispute the substance of a declaration by a person, it is very unlikely that in such cases they would be able to reach a result more nearly corresponding to the actual state of facts. Such a proceeding on the part of the authorities would, moreover, very easily assume in public opinion the aspect of a vexatious measure which would inflame political passions and which would counteract the aims of pacification which are also at the basis of the stipulations concerning the protection of minorities.

in whole or in part, a national, ethnical, racial or religious group…'.[64] The 1992 UN Declaration[65] and the Framework Convention for the Protection of National Minorities both call for the protection of minorities. Does this mean that at minimum, the minority group has a right to self-identification and, possibly, a concomitant right to recognition?[66] Since the time of the League of Nations, international law has held that the 'existence of communities is a question of fact', 'not a question of law'.[67] As such, the acknowledgement of minorities by the State is not determinative.[68] That, however, does not entail there is a right to recognition.

While the Human Rights Committee will not entertain communications from individuals against France under Article 27 because of the French declaration with respect thereto,[69] in dealing with the French periodic reports it demands that France address minority issues.[70] Furthermore, Martti Koskenniemi has averred that internal self-determination has 'conferred the right on religious, ethnic or linguistic groups to

---

64   78 UNTS (1951) p. 277. The term genocide was coined by Lemkin in his 1944 book Axis Rule in Occupied Europe. On the right to exist, see J. Packer, 'United Nations Protection of Minorities in Time of Public Emergency: the Hard-Core of Minority Rights' in D. Prémont (ed.) *Non-Derogable Rights and States of Emergency* (Brussels: Émile Bruylant, 1996).

65   (note 2).

66   Even if there is no concomitant right to standing before any tribunal to assert it – see Higgins (note 29).

67   *Greco-Bulgarian Communities Case*, PCIJ, Series B, No.17, at 22. See also, Capotorti (note 23) paras. 204-05.

68   Domestic law cannot be used to deny international duties and obligations – see Article 27 Vienna Convention on the Law of Treaties, 1969, 8 ILM (1969) p. 679. And see Capotorti (note 23) para. 570; P. Thornberry and M.A. Martin-Estébanez *Minority Rights in Europe* (Strasbourg: Council of Europe, 2004) pp. 13-14.

69   See *TK v France*, Communication No. 220/1987 CCPR/C/37/D/220/1987, 8 December 1989, para. 8.6.

70   See Concluding Observations of the Human Rights Committee, CCPR/C/79/Add.80, 4 August 1997.

> 24.   The Committee takes note of the declaration made by France concerning the prohibition, prescribed under article 27 of the Covenant, to deny ethnic, religious or linguistic minorities the right, in community with members of their group, to enjoy their own culture, to profess and practise their own religion or to use their own language. The Committee has taken note of the avowed commitment of France to respect and ensure that all individuals enjoy equal rights, regardless of their origin. *The Committee is, however, unable to agree that France is a country in which there are no ethnic, religious or linguistic minorities.* The Committee wishes to recall in this respect that the mere fact that equal rights are granted to all individuals and that all individuals are equal before the law does not preclude the existence in fact of minorities in a country, and their entitlement to the enjoyment of their culture, the practice of their religion or the use of their language in community with other members of their group. [Emphasis added]

have their identity recognised'.[71] Indeed, the European Court of Human Rights has never required that the applicant have official recognition from the State before it can have *locus standi* in Strasbourg. In *Agabaloglu v Turkey*,[72] although the case was eventually declared inadmissible for non-exhaustion of domestic remedies, the First Section entertained a case brought in the name of the Armenian Protestant Church and School of Gedikpasa for dispossession, despite the fact that it was not properly registered in Turkey. Indeed, it can be inferred that, had the Foundation sought compensation for improvements in the property before the Turkish courts and failed, then a case under Article 1 of Protocol 1, on its own and in combination with Article 14, would have been declared admissible. The Court again declared the matter an admissible issue under Article 11 in *Gorzelik et al. v Poland*.[73] The applicants had sought to form an association named the 'Union of People of Silesian Nationality' which had been denied by the higher Polish courts partly on the basis that there was no Silesian *nation*, only an ethnic group. The government's argument was that national minority status confers privileges under domestic law and that no group should have the right to self-declare that it is a nation – the European Court of Human Rights declared the issue admissible, but at the hearing on the merits rejected the applicants' claim. The case seemed to turn on the preferential treatment accorded to 'national minorities' under Polish electoral law. The Court held that the group should have been prepared to compromise on, *inter alia*, its name, and that Poland was accorded a wide margin of appreciation with respect to democracy within the State.

> 67. … Likewise, practice regarding official recognition by States of national, ethnic or other minorities within their population varies from country to country or even within countries. The choice as to what form such recognition should take and whether it should be implemented through international treaties or bilateral agreements or incorporated into the constitution or a special statute must, by the nature of things, be left largely to the State concerned, as it will depend on particular national circumstances.

However, what is implicit in that paragraph from the judgment of the Grand Chamber is that States ought to recognise national minorities, subject only to restrictions necessary in a democratic society. The corollary of the obligation to protect minorities under international instruments is a duty to recognise them. To deny that there are minorities on the territory of the State is partly to question their existence.[74] Furthermore, even

---

71   M. Koskenniemi, 'National Self-Determination Today: Problems of Legal Theory and Practice' 43 *ICLQ* (1994) p. 267.

72   31134/96, European Court of Human Rights (First Section), 8 June 1999.

73   44158/98, European Court of Human Rights (Fourth Section), 17 May 2001 (admissibility); 20 December 2001 (Merits, especially para. 64); 17 February 2004 (Grand Chamber).

74   Connected therewith is the right of minority groups to maintain contacts across borders – see Article 17 Framework Convention and paragraph 32.4 Copenhagen Document.

if the group has no standing to assert this duty on its own behalf, individual members of the group will not be able to enjoy their culture unless the group continues to exist. Therefore, this right of the minority group to recognition must vicariously be part of the claim by individual persons belonging to the group to their rights.

Finally, while the minority group might not be able to claim rights *qua* group, where the State has granted rights in the past, there would appear to be a legitimate expectation that they will continue and that they might be asserted before international bodies. Strasbourg has recognised that non-discrimination assumes a level playing field for all groups in society. To that end, positive measures by the State that favour the minority are sometimes held to have a reasonable and objective justification. Strasbourg would refrain from interfering on behalf of a majority where the State took steps to promote the interests of the minority group, particularly where this would allow the minority to express its opinion in elections more freely – Article 3, Protocol 1.

> Rather on the contrary, a system taking into account the specific situation as to majority and minority …must be seen as making it easier for the people to express its opinion freely.[75]

Furthermore, in *Cyprus v Turkey*[76] the Commission radically held that it might be a violation in certain circumstances to deny mother-tongue education even at the secondary school level. However, one has to have regard to the particular situation in Northern Cyprus: the prior existence of such schools and their abolition by the Turkish authorities; an international agreement (UN Doc. S/11789, Vienna, 31 July-2 August 1975) to allow the Greek Cypriot authorities to provide such education in the North, fulfilment of which the Turkish authorities prevented; and, the denial of the right to return to Northern Cyprus of Greek Cypriot children who went to the southern part of the island for their education, even though, by the time of the hearing, this denial was limited to males over 16.

> 478. … However, education in [Turkish or English-speaking] schools does not correspond to the needs of the persons concerned *who have the legitimate wish to preserve their own ethnic and cultural identity*. While it is true that Article 2 of Protocol No. 1 guarantees access only to existing educational facilities, it must be noted that in the present case such educational facilities have in fact existed in the past and have been abolished by the Turkish Cypriot authorities. … In the Commission's opinion the total absence of appropriate secondary schools for Greek Cypriots living in northern Cyprus cannot be compensated for either by the authorities' allowing the pupils concerned to attend such schools in southern Cyprus. … In these circumstances the

---

75   *Lindsay et al. v United Kingdom* 8364/78, 3 *CMLR* (1979) pp. 170-1. See also, *The Liberal Party et al. v United Kingdom*, 4 *EHRR* (1982) p. 106.

76   25781/94, European Commission of Human Rights, adopted on 4 June 1999 para. 474-79; European Court of Human Rights (Grand Chamber), 10 May 2001.

practice of the Turkish Cypriot authorities amounts to a denial of the substance of the right to education. [Emphasis added]

The Court upheld this reasoning: 'It cannot be maintained that the provision of secondary education in the south in keeping with the linguistic tradition of the enclaved Greek Cypriots suffices to fulfil the obligation laid down in Article 2 of Protocol No. 1, having regard to the impact of that option on family life.'[77] Accepting the peculiar situation that applies in Northern Cyprus, these arguments may be of relevance wherever there is that slow decline in inter-communal relations between the State and the minority and pre-existing domestic rights are withdrawn.

Conclusion

The picture that was completely clouded in the late 1980s and early 1990s has gained a little focus, but there are still no sharply defined features. This chapter did not set out to argue that there are already existing collective rights, just that there could be, that they might be human rights and, that if that were the case, the State has a dual role: that of regulating the relationship between the individual persons belonging to the minority group and the group, even if the minority group were to have a right to autonomy; and of guaranteeing rights to the individual members of the group and to the group – in the latter case, the minimum seems to be a right to recognition and a right to no arbitrary removal of pre-existing rights. Finding the right balance in regulating the relationship is undoubtedly the most difficult task, but international law cannot keep denying standing to sub-state entities.

---

77   (Ibid.) para. 278; see also para. 292.

Chapter 9

Minorities, Indigenous and Tribal Peoples, and Peoples: Definitions of Terms as a Matter of International Law[1]

Gudmundur Alfredsson[2]

1. Introduction

In the international human rights instruments, comprehensive definitions of the beneficiaries of group rights and peoples' rights are missing. This affects individuals, like those belonging to minorities and indigenous and tribal peoples, when members of the groups want to benefit from special measures which are available for overcoming discrimination and achieving equal rights and dignity. The use of the term 'collective rights' is intentionally avoided here since group rights and peoples' rights, albeit both collective, are still fundamentally different in respect of substantive rights, available forums and applicable procedures.

Despite this general lack of legal definitions, the international instruments contain several significant indications. For example, with regard to minorities, reference is often made to national and/or ethnic origins, languages or religions as the necessary objective characteristics of the groups concerned (see below). For 'peoples' as beneficiaries of the right of self-determination, relevant texts often refer to territories and countries. More importantly, indications of the necessary characteristics and additional elements of the meaning of the terms are created and confirmed in the practice of States and international organisations.

Diverse as the groups and peoples are, certain categories and specific situations may indeed cause difficulties for standard-setting. Nevertheless, it is my opinion that the definitions are incomplete largely because States are reluctant to deal with rights of groups and peoples. In part, as far as group rights are concerned, ignorance, lack of tol-

---

1   This piece is a draft chapter (here without footnotes or country examples) from a manuscript which the author is preparing, with the working title: 'Textbook on Minority Rights'. It is a privilege to submit this chapter to a Festschrift in honour of Professor Patrick Thornberry, a good friend and colleague who is the leading authority on minority and indigenous rights in international law.
2   Director of the Raoul Wallenberg Institute of Human Rights and Humanitarian Law and Professor at the Law Faculty of Lund University in Sweden.

Nazila Ghanea & Alexandra Xanthaki (eds.), Minorities, Peoples and Self-Determination, pp. 163-172.
© *2005 Koninklijke Brill NV. Printed in The Netherlands. ISBN 90 04 14301 7.*

erance and undoubtedly racism play a role in the lack of codified definitions. This reluctance has to do with the unfortunate but frequent (mis)conception that such rights may lead to separatist claims which would threaten the sovereignty and territorial integrity of States. Minorities who share identities with populations across borders particularly touch upon government sensitivities, due to perceived threats to territorial integrity.

Peoples' rights may indeed constitute a threat as far as the right of self-determination is concerned, but minority and indigenous and tribal rights do not. By and large, in existing international law minority and indigenous rights are about keeping groups happy within States. This is evident, for example, in the increasing emphasis on respect for minority rights as tools for the prevention and resolution of violent ethnic conflicts. By guaranteeing equal rights and non-discrimination to everyone within a State, and by offering special measures when necessary for achieving the same, the intention is to improve the quality of life, avoid tensions and thus prevent or reduce the likelihood of State dismemberment. Another purpose of rights for groups and their members is obviously the maintenance of cultural diversity in terms of identities, customs, languages, and so on.

Both the instruments and the practices of States and international organizations make clear distinctions between group rights and peoples' rights. The significance of this differentiation is obvious when one considers that peoples have the right of self-determination with the option of independence, that is self-determination in an external sense; while groups generally do not possess the right of self-determination, at least not in a manner that lists independence as one of the options.

Some groups and academic authors maintain that minority, indigenous and tribal groups should also have the right of self-determination but in an internal sense, meaning self-government or autonomy within States. This is a very different story. In the 1999 Lund Recommendations on the Effective Participation of National Minorities in Public Life, the use of self-determination language in presenting standards on non-territorial and territorial autonomies is clearly and intentionally avoided.

It is remarkable in this modern world of ours that there does not exist a complete directory of minorities and indigenous and tribal peoples. The United Nations University produced in 1988 the first volume of a World Guide of Ethnic Minorities and Indigenous Peoples, but subsequent volumes never came out because too many governments were displeased about the results. The Minority Rights Group International (MRG), a non-governmental organization in London, has published a long series on several hundred minorities in all parts of the world and a World Directory of Minorities which, despite the title, is far from complete. Of course, the lack of clear definitions does not make the job any easier. It does not help that the United Nations and, for example, the MRG seemingly employ different definitions.

How many groups are there? How many individuals belong to these groups? On the basis of the definition elements below, and after a country-by-country survey, it is my rough estimate that there are some 12-14,000 minority, indigenous and tribal groups in the world. By another estimate of mine, about 1.5 billion individuals belong to these groups or 25% of the world's population. In addition to usefulness for standard-setting as well as for national implementation and international monitoring, more complete directories based on the definition elements would deliver a powerful message to the effect that the groups, and their rights and the rights of their members, are not a marginal phenomenon.

And how many peoples are awaiting the opportunity to exercise the right of (external) self-determination? One could suggest at least a few dozen, that is the non-self-governing territories still on the UN decolonization lists. Other colonial entities, formerly listed as non-self-governing territories, belong to a similar listing if they have been integrated into administering powers without the free and informed approval of the peoples concerned.

Below, on the basis of references in the international instruments and in the practices of States and international organisations, attempts will be made to define the terms 'minorities', 'indigenous peoples', 'tribal peoples' and 'peoples'.

2.   Minorities

As stated above, no comprehensive definition of the term 'minority' has been adopted in the international standards. Such definitions have, however, long been sought in connection with international standard-setting and monitoring efforts. In 1987, as secretary of the UN working group drafting the Declaration on the Rights of Persons belonging to Minorities, which was adopted in 1992, I made a compilation of definition proposals which had been submitted to the League of Nations and the United Nations during 50-60 years of debates (UN document E/CN.4/1987/WG.5/WP.1). A number of additional proposals have been tabled subsequently.

On the basis of that experience, I am convinced that the unwillingness of governments to adopt codified definitions has often served as a convenient device for tactically delaying substantive discussions. It is much more comfortable to keep talking about definitions rather than about actual groups, their rights, available special measures and access to international monitoring procedures; let alone to addresss national implementation. Much of the time, after all, it is self-evident which groups qualify for protection. The former Organisation for Security and Co-operation in Europe (OSCE)High Commissioner on National Minorities, Max van der Stoel, has been quoted as saying that he knows a minority when he sees one.

The necessary elements of a definition of the term 'minority' emerge quite clearly in national and international practices. Furthermore, most of the above-mentioned definition proposals have common components. These essential components of a definition are certain objective characteristics, self-identification, the numbers, and long-term presence on the territory concerned. Other suggested elements, like vulnerability or government recognition, are presumably not worthwhile (see below).

2.1. Objective Characteristics

The objective characteristics relate to joint affiliation or affinity of the members of a minority as far as national or ethnic origin, language and/or religion are concerned. The requirement appears in instruments such as the title of the 1992 UN Declaration on the Rights of Persons belonging to National or Ethnic, Religious and Linguistic Minorities.

The reliance in European instruments on the term 'national minorities' does not change or limit this element concerning objective characteristics. While different interpretations have been attached to this term, it should and is indeed likely to cover the same groups as the international standards. This understanding is confirmed by the practice of the OSCE High Commissioner on National Minorities and the Advisory Committee under the Framework Convention for the Protection of National Minorities.

For the allocation of rights, diverse geographical and cultural settings also play a role. It may be assumed, for example, that an ethnic minority with a broad range of its own characteristics is in need of more extensive rights protection than a religious minority which, apart from the religion, shares the identity of the majority population. Non-discrimination provisions already work in their favour, and freedoms for manifesting and professing a religion together with special measures for preserving and maintaining religious characteristics and institutions are well-established. If these groups possess other characteristics, such as linguistic ones, they would of course qualify for the more extensive minority rights.

National or ethnic origin, language and/or religion are the objective characteristics to which the international instruments refer. Political minorities do not come under the heading of minority rights, as they may be the majority after the next elections. The inclusion of social (for example untouchables) and sexual (for example gays and lesbians) minorities has not been agreed upon.

2.2. Self-Identification

The subjective element of a definition is a necessary addition to the objective characteristics, as acknowledged in some instruments. Nobody should be forced to belong to a minority group, but at the same time individuals must have a free and informed choice to make and a government must certainly refrain from forced assimilation. The subjective element presumably comes in two layers. An individual can decide whether he/she is a member of a minority. Secondarily, the group must accept the individual concerned on the basis of the facts (common characteristics) and in a non-arbitrary fashion.

For example, ILO Convention No. 169 concerning Indigenous and Tribal Peoples in Independent Countries specifies in article 1, paragraph 2, that self-identification shall be regarded as a fundamental criterion for determining the groups to which the Convention applies. UN Special Rapporteurs have also recommended the same. One such example comes from Francesco Capatorti in his 1977 report to the Sub-Commission for the Prevention of Discrimination and Protection of Minorities.

2.3. *The Numbers*

This is inherent in the term 'minority' and almost unnecessary for the purposes of the definition, but a minority group must constitute less than one half of the State population. An actual minority cannot designate and treat the majority as if it were a minority.

A country may be composed of only minorities if no group makes up more than 50% of the population. Several States around the world meet this characterisation. In such a situation, all the different groups of the country would be entitled to minority protection in terms of equal rights, non-discrimination and special measures.

2.4. *The Time Element*

Perhaps the most difficult and controversial component of the definition is the requirement that a minority must have a long-term presence in the territory concerned. In other words, a group should be well-established in a country over a significant period of time before it is accorded the status of a minority. The time element applies also to religious minorities, thus excluding newly established sects for the purposes of minority rights (while the sects, of course, still possess the freedoms of assembly, association, expression and religion).

Migrant workers, immigrants, refugees, stateless persons and other foreigners who enter and remain in a country on a temporary basis are, with some notable exceptions, generally entitled to the enjoyment of human rights without discrimination. Their protection is already attended to by other means in human rights instruments designed for their benefit. They may find themselves in circumstances not dissimilar to those facing minorities, but they are nevertheless exercising a 'free' choice and should accept the drawbacks and not only the benefits of that selection.

There are good policy reasons for this approach regarding the time element. If we did not have it, we would see the inclination of governments to either water down minority rights or close the doors to immigrants and asylum seekers. The Human Rights Committee (the treaty body which monitors compliance with the International Covenant on Civil and Political Rights), in General Comment No. 23 of 1994, may have adopted a different and broader point of view. However, it would not be realistic or sustainable to grant/demand instant minority protection to actual cases of recent arrivals in a country.

At some point, however, the newcomers become minorities. How much time is required for this? At least two countries have talked of about 100 years being required for this. In my opinion, drawing on the practice of many other States, a likely and reasonable turning point is when the individuals concerned identify more closely with the new territory or country (where they now live) than the old territory or country (where their parents or grandparents came from). We are thus talking about the time it takes for the offspring to go through the school system, that is one or two generations or thereabouts.

2.5. *Unnecessary or Undesirable Definition Elements*

If a group in a given country meets the definitional elements, States do not and should not have a say on the identification or recognition of that group by way of legislation, registration or other means. The Human Rights Committee, in paragraph 5.2 of General Comment No. 23, agrees on this point. When ratifying the Framework Convention for the Protection of National Minorities, several States have in declarations listed the groups which they see as entitled to protection under that Convention. There is every reason to challenge this type of practice which would allow governments to arbitrarily deny rights to certain groups.

Some lawyers have argued that the wording of article 27 of the International Covenant on Civil and Political Rights requires official recognition of a minority prior to its enjoyment of the rights in question. The acceptance or non-acceptance by governments is simply irrelevant if groups in a given country meet objective, subjective and other definition elements. Non-acceptance by governments should automatically be considered suspect, to the degree that it is arbitrary and that it leads to discrimination between and unequal treatment of groups. Calling groups by other names, such as cohabiting nations or nationalities or tribes, is likewise insufficient for depriving them of minority protection.

Similarly, a State should not be allowed to escape its minority rights responsibilities by denying citizenship to members of a group on an arbitrary or discriminatory basis, provided of course that they have lived on the territory concerned long enough to meet the time element of the definition. In grey areas, and possibly in certain historical circumstances, delimitation can be left to States, as with the implementation of human rights and minority rights in general. However, such determinations, in order to overcome arbitrariness, should be subject to supervision by international organisations in accordance with existing standards and within available monitoring procedures. In other words, a margin of appreciation may enter the picture, but it must be a narrow one.

Vulnerability or a non-dominant position have been mentioned in the UN debates and in scholarly literature as possible elements of a minority definition. To this author, these are about the point in time when the application of minority rights becomes necessary. A non-vulnerable or privileged minority does not need minority rights, but it is still a minority group; five or 50 years later, if vulnerability enters the picture or when privileges come to an end, that group should be entitled to protection.

3. Indigenous Peoples

A clear distinction has by now been made in international human rights law between 'minorities' and 'indigenous peoples'. The rights of both are about protection within a State, without interruption of sovereignty and territorial integrity. The distinction appears in terms of the drafting and adoption of different standards and the creation of separate forums and monitoring procedures. There are overlaps to the degree the rights and available measures are the same, but there are also differences.

Indigenous rights involve not only equal rights and non-discrimination but also special measures extending, among other things, to possession of land and to benefits from natural resources. Autonomy or self-government, not least with reference to language on the management of land and resources in ILO Convention No. 169, sometimes referred to as internal self-determination, may also be more readily available to indigenous peoples than to minorities.

As to objective characteristics, the subjective element and the numbers factor, the definitions of minorities and indigenous peoples overlap. Indigenous peoples have national, ethnic, linguistic and religious characteristics which distinguish them from the majority population. Self-identification is applicable, as spelled out in article 1 of the ILO Convention No. 169. If indigenous peoples constitute the majority of a State population, they need full and equal human rights, not minority or indigenous rights.

When compared with the minority definition, it is the time element which is fundamentally different. A crucial factor in the definition of indigenous peoples is their original inhabitation of the land on which, unlike the minorities, they have lived from time immemorial or at least from before the arrival of later settlers. In addition, the indigenous ways of life much of the time also depend on or are closely interwoven with land, including the links of traditional economies to the land, such as for fishing, gathering, herding or hunting.

4. Tribal Peoples

The definition situation is less clear when it comes to 'tribal peoples' who are covered by ILO Convention No. 169. Article 1 defines them as groups 'whose social, cultural and economic conditions distinguish them from other sections of the national community, and whose status is regulated wholly or partially by their own customs or traditions or by special laws or regulations'. Again, as to objective characteristics, the subjective element and the numbers factor, the definitions of minorities and indigenous and tribal peoples overlap.

In addition, and that must be the real reason for addressing the rights of tribal peoples together with those of indigenous peoples in the ILO Convention, tribal peoples rely on the land for their ways of life and traditional economies. The term tribal peoples will also extend to nomadic groups who, if only seasonally, depend on land for camping or otherwise.

In the United Nations, where the term is not used in human rights instruments, tribal peoples are likely to be classified as minorities. As far as Europe is concerned, it has been suggested that, with reference to their ways of life and corresponding needs, the Roma and Travellers constitute tribal peoples in the countries where they live. In an African context, the question of whether the term can be used instead of the term 'peoples' rights' in the African Charter on Human and Peoples' Rights, is now being entertained.

At this juncture, it is important to make a distinction between minorities and indigenous and tribal peoples on the one hand and the term 'peoples' on the other. In addition to self-determination, the term 'peoples' has found its way into a few human rights instruments and resolutions, notably with regard to natural resources, development and peace. It was much in vogue at UNESCO which has organised a series of conferences on the topic and at the African Union (previously the Organisation of African Unity) which proclaims peoples' rights in the title and several articles of the African Charter on Human and Peoples' Rights.

5.   Peoples

Like the other terms we have been looking at, the term 'peoples' has not been comprehensively defined in international law. For the purpose of self-determination in general and decolonisation in particular, the term has in practice been limited to the populations of fixed territorial entities, more often than not without regard to the ethnic composition and cultural characteristics of the people living there.

In the context of the right of (external) self-determination, it flows from the instruments and from practice that a people means the population of a distinct territorial or geographical entity. As a rule, these entities have external or internal borders and/or natural boundaries (rivers, islands) which, as separate units, enjoy a significant degree of acceptance by their surroundings. In international law instruments and discourse, the term 'peoples' has for all practical purposes replaced the more ethnically loaded term 'nations'. Instead of national self-determination, the reference today would be to the right of peoples to self-determination.

The emphasis on a distinct territorial entity appears in many international texts. This is true in particular in connection with the process of political decolonisation, as evidenced by provisions in the UN Charter on trust and non-self-governing territories, rather than on non-self-governing peoples. This is also clear in the title of the 1960 Declaration on the Granting of Independence to Colonial Countries and Peoples, with the reference to countries coming before peoples. This reliance on territory is reflected in General Assembly resolution 1541 (XV) which accompanied the 1960 Declaration and lays down the practical guidelines for its realisation.

In addition to these and other international instruments, the same emphasis is repeatedly confirmed in the practice of States and international organizations, including case-law of the International Court of Justice. 'Peoples' in the context of political decolonisation thus refers to the populations of distinct territories, with only a few exceptions, like the one hundred or so overseas colonies which have successfully exercised the right of self-determination by becoming new and independent States. This has happened for the most part without any respect to the composition or characteristics of the populations living within the former colonial boundaries, even when borders have been drawn with straight lines which have arbitrarily divided ethnic groups between two or more States.

In addition to decolonisation, the international community has agreed to the emergence of new States in response to occupation by force (provided it took place after 1945 or maybe 1928) and in cases of agreed-upon separation or divorce. As attempts to redraw borders, like in the former Yugoslavia, are likely to generate more problems than solutions, that experience will only reinforce the reluctance of the international community to accept separation without agreement of the parties.

When defining the term 'peoples', as stated above with regard to the decolonisation process but also beyond, no demands are made for the uniformity of national or ethnic composition, the language spoken or the religion practiced. On the contrary, the practice so far mostly follows borders irrespective of the composition of the population. It is noteworthy that that the underlining of territorial distinctions stands in clear contradiction to the definition of the terms 'indigenous peoples', 'tribal peoples' and 'minorities'. For these groups, the emphasis is on the composition of the group.

The distinction from groups (that is minorities and indigenous and tribal peoples) and the consequent importance of the term 'peoples', relates for the most part to the right of self-determination. Peoples have access to forums and procedures at the United Nations designed for decolonisation purposes.

Peoples entitled to external self-determination have a number of free, impressive choices:

a)   The creation of an independent, sovereign State, in charge of internal and external matters, with access to full membership in international and regional organizations;

b)   The establishment of a sovereign entity in personal union with another State. The details of the relationship and any division of labour, as well as means of amendment and termination, depend on the deal made by the parties;

c)   Free association or commonwealth with another country. In the UN listing of minimum options which should be made available to colonial countries and peoples, free association is the middle station between independence and integration. It can lead to a variety of arrangements, including membership in selected international and regional organisations, but the people concerned continues to possess the right of external self-determination;

d)   Integration into a State, be it a unitary or a federal one. Such a move is, at some point, likely to become irreversible; and

e)   Following integration, a people is likely to be seen as a group, opening the door to self-government within a State. A number of possible variations arise in terms of both autonomous institutions and delegated powers or functions. As a rule, these functions will not encompass foreign affairs, defence and monetary issues. The 1999 Lund Recommendations on the Effective Participation of National Minorities in Public Life offer suggestions as to which functions could be handed over to minority groups.

The terms minorities, indigenous and tribal peoples and peoples will at times create confusion, inasmuch as, and also when, some of the same claims will surface. Some groups may qualify for the concept and broader rights of peoples when they have been incorrectly designated as minorities or indigenous peoples or systematically denied representation and victimised at the national level. On the other hand, apart from exceptional situations, we must keep in mind that the very idea of minority and indigenous and tribal rights, as they are pursued by the international community, implies continued sovereignty and territorial integrity of States.

Finally, beyond the right of self-determination, the term 'peoples' also appears in instruments of the United Nations and the African Union on the right to development, the right to peace and other solidarity rights. It would appear that the term in these contexts applies to the population of a State, thus confirming the territorial approach, but these references to peoples' rights are not much liked by the human rights community. The objections are based on the argument that these either constitute State rights which do not belong to the human rights arena or that they allow governments to sit on both sides of the table, representing the State as guarantor and the people as a beneficiary which is not likely to bring significant human rights results.

6.   Concluding Remarks

In this chapter, rather than to come up with comprehensive definitions, I have attempted to highlight the definition elements which appear in the practices of States and international organisations. These elements come a long way towards establishing the meaning of the terms and the distinctions between them. The absence of complete definitions should not allow Governments arbitrarily to get away from group protection where it is called for. After all, in line with Max van der Stoel as quoted above, much of the time it is self-evident which groups constitute minorities and what category of groups.

Finally, minorities, indigenous and tribal peoples, and peoples are already subjects of international law, albeit in limited and often inconsistent capacities, to the degree they have rights, duties and procedural standing before international forums. Increasingly in the work of international organisations, they are significant actors which have to be engaged with the aim of keeping the peace, ensuring prosperity and maintaining diversity in law and practice. To that goal, it helps to know what we are talking about.

Chapter 10

INTEGRATION AND SEPARATION: LEGAL AND POLITICAL CHOICES IN IMPLEMENTING MINORITY RIGHTS

Tom Hadden[1]

There is a tendency among some human rights lawyers and activists to think of human rights as a guarantee of fixed minimum standards. In practice the implementation of most human rights is more often than not a flexible process. This is partly due to the need to balance the delivery of conflicting rights and partly to shifts over time in the interpretation and relative importance of particular rights.

Flexibility in minority rights

Both these factors are especially significant in the implementation of minority rights. A substantial margin of appreciation is granted to states in the implementation of minority rights under all the main international conventions and instruments. Most are formulated in very general terms and many contain significant qualifications. A striking example is the frequently asserted and clearly important right to minority language education. Article 4.3 of the United Nations Declaration on the Rights of Persons Belonging to National or Ethnic, Religious and Linguistic Minorities[2] (United Nations Declaration) includes significant qualifications in respect of 'appropriate measures' so that 'wherever possible'

---

1   Professor of International Law, Human Rights Centre, Queen's University, Belfast, U.K. This contribution, as is appropriate, had its origin in a paper delivered at a seminar organised by Patrick Thornberry at the University of Keele on 28 February 1996. It has been developed in a series of presentations and working papers for the United Nations Working Group on Minorities. This version draws heavily on the Working Paper presented at the Tenth Session of the Working Group in March 2004, 'International and National Action for the Protection of Minorities', UN Doc E/CN.4/Sub.2/AC.5/2004/WP.3. Patrick Thornberry may not have approved of all that was said in the original version and would probably not agree with everything in this version. But I would like to acknowledge his unwitting contribution to the development of my thinking.
2   UN Doc. A/47/49 (1993). Article 4.3. reads:

> States should take appropriate measures so that, whenever possible, persons belonging to minorities may have adequate opportunities to learn their mother tongue or to have instruction in their mother tongue.

Nazila Ghanea & Alexandra Xanthaki (eds.), Minorities, Peoples and Self-Determination, pp. 173-191.
© 2005 Koninklijke Brill NV. Printed in The Netherlands. ISBN 90 04 14301 7.

persons belonging to minorities may have 'adequate opportunities' to learn their mother tongue or to have instruction in their mother tongue. The more developed provisions of article 14.2 of the European Framework Convention on the Protection of National Minorities[3] (European Framework Convention) are even more circumspect:

> In areas inhabited by persons belonging to national minorities traditionally or in substantial numbers, if there is *sufficient demand*, the Parties shall *endeavour* to ensure, *as far as is possible* and *within the framework of their education systems*, that persons belonging to those minorities have *adequate* opportunities for being taught the minority language or for receiving instruction in this language.[4]

Formulations of this kind clearly give national governments a good deal of discretion on whether and, if so, how, to make provision for minority language education.

In addition there is an established tendency in the field of minority rights for there to be significant movement to and fro over time in the national and international consensus on the proper balance between individual and communal rights.[5] At some times the primary emphasis has been on the rights of individuals and the validity of group rights of any kind has been challenged. At others there has been equal stress on the need to recognise the legitimacy and even the primacy of the rights of minorities and communities as such. Despite the best efforts of some theorists to conceal this ambivalence by focusing attention on the rights of individual members of minorities or communities, there is a real difference between policies and practices that emphasise individual equality and non-discrimination and those that emphasise the rights of minorities not only to communal equality but also to distinctive rights as such. One of the most contentious areas is the choice between policies that are designed to achieve equality in public or private employment for a minority community as a whole, whether by imposing quotas or other positive measures, and policies that emphasise the prior right of all individuals to selection on merit.

Separation or integration

There is a further important choice, both for states and for individuals, between the objectives of communal separation and communal integration.[6] The choice for states is between policies and practices that are designed to permit or even encourage minorities to establish a degree of communal separation, for example by providing separate schools for religious and linguistic minorities, and those that are designed to promote greater

---

3   CETS No. 157 (1995).
4   Emphasis added by author.
5   This point is developed at greater length in T. Hadden, 'The Pendulum Theory of Individual, Communal and Minority Rights', 3 *Critical Review of International Social and Political Philosophy* (2000) pp. 77-90.
6   UN Doc E/CN.4/Sub.2/AC.5/2001/WP.6, Tom Hadden with Ciaran O Maolain *Integrative Approaches to the Accommodation of Minorities* (2001).

integration between members of different communities, for example by providing state funding only for common schools. There is a tendency for representatives of minorities to demand separate institutions for education and for various forms of regional or functional autonomy. Many governments, on the other hand, prefer to work towards greater integration of members of all communities whether by assimilation or various forms of multi-culturalism. In practice a combination of policies for both separation and integration in different spheres is required.

The choice for individuals is equally important. Some members of minorities regard the preservation of their separate identity and culture as paramount. Others prefer to integrate with the wider community, to pursue their own economic and cultural goals and to break away from what they may regard as the constraints of their communal culture. Here too the preferred choice for many will involve a combination of maintaining their communal identity for some purposes while also establishing their economic and social independence.

The lack of clarity in international instruments

The main international conventions and declarations on minority rights do not provide much assistance in making these choices, either on what priority is to be given to individual versus group rights or on the related choice between separation and integration. The first post-war provision for minorities in article 27 of the International Covenant on Civil and Political Rights (ICCPR) does not point clearly in either direction. The more detailed provisions of the United Nations Declaration and the European Framework Convention are usually taken to point towards the development of separate facilities rather than integration. The right of members of minorities to participate effectively in decisions concerning them is often regarded as akin to the right of peoples to self-determination and has frequently been elevated into a right to autonomy. The heavily qualified right to education in or through minority languages is likewise taken to support a claim to separate schools at state expense. And the rights to protection of the existence of minorities, to protection from forced assimilation and to positive action to promote their identity, culture and development can be portrayed in a similar way. But the right to effective participation, as will be seen, can equally be treated as pointing towards effective integration in national decision-making processes. The right to education in or through a mother tongue can be respected in integrated as well as separate schools. and the right of minorities to protection from assimilation against their will in article 5.2 of the European Framework Convention is expressly stated to be 'without prejudice to measures taken in pursuance of [a State's] general integration policy'.[7]

---

7   See above (note 3). Article 5.2 reads:

 Without prejudice to measures taken in pursuance of their general integration policy, the Parties shall refrain from policies or practices aimed at assimilation of persons belonging to national minorities against their will and shall protect these persons from any action aimed at such assimilation.

Permissible policy choices

The effect of these careful formulations is to leave a considerable degree of freedom to States to pursue substantially different policies in respect of minorities within their territory.[8] The deliberate elimination or expulsion of a minority by genocide or ethnic cleansing is clearly prohibited, as is forcible assimilation. But that leaves at least three strategic policy options for governments to decide between: encouragement of assimilation, integration with diversity and various forms of separation and autonomy.

It may assist in clarifying the nature of each of these approaches to attempt a descriptive definition of the longer term objectives that they incorporate:

- *assimilation* can be taken to cover structures and policies aimed at eliminating the separate identity and culture of members of minority communities and absorbing them on an equal basis into a wider national identity and culture;
- *integration* can be taken to cover structures and policies aimed at securing full recognition of the identity and culture of members of minority communities and their full participation as such in national or regional society and government;
- *separation or autonomy* can be taken to cover structures and policies designed to permit members of minority communities to maintain their distinctive identity by exercising effective control over their own political, economic, social or cultural affairs on a regional, local or functional basis.

The inclusion of any form of assimilation as a permitted policy option may seem strange to some minority activists. But there is a crucial distinction between forced and voluntary assimilation. As already indicated, many members of minorities, especially immigrants and those with mixed parentage, want to be assimilated into the wider society and to be treated in exactly the same way as everyone else. This desire is reflected in the right not to be treated as a member of a minority that is expressly provided for in article 3.1 of the European Framework Convention and less directly in article 3.2 of the United Nations Declaration. It is also indirectly recognised in the inclusion in most definitions of minorities of the idea that there should be a subjective commitment to maintaining a separate identity and culture. If there is no such commitment, there is likely to be a gradual process of assimilation and there is nothing inherently wrong with that. The concept of a 'melting pot' from which a distinctive 'American' identity has emerged has always been one of the strengths of the United States of America. A similar process of nation-building by the merging of previously distinctive tribal communities is the underlying objective in many ex-colonial territories, notably in Africa. Any such objective must, of course, be balanced with the obligation under article 1 of the United Nations Declaration and articles 1 and 5.1 of the European Framework Convention to

---

8   J. McGarry and B. O'Leary (eds.) *The Politics of Ethnic Conflict Regulation* (Oxford: Oxford University Press, 1993) Chapter 1; and A. Eide *A Review and Analysis of Constructive Approaches to Group Accommodation in Divided or Multicultural Societies*, Forum for Peace and Reconciliation in Ireland, Consultancy Studies 3 (Dublin: Stationery Office, 1996).

protect the existence and promote the identity of minorities. But those obligations could not legitimately be implemented or enforced against the wishes of those involved. It will then be a matter for political debate as to what combination of state encouragement for voluntary assimilation and state encouragement for the maintenance of distinctive communal identities is the best way of meeting the wishes of all sections of the population and in so doing of achieving peace, stability and prosperity.

These broad policy options may then be related to a further set of widely used terms, notably those of multi-cultural or inter-cultural policies and practices. Since these are often used in a variable and confusing way within the human rights community,[9] it is desirable to establish greater precision and clarity in their use:

- societies and policies based on assimilation could best be described as *mono-cultural*;
- societies and policies based on the recognition and accommodation of various distinctive communities and cultures within a broadly integrated and socially inclusive framework could best be described as *multi-cultural*;
- societies and policies based on the provision of separate or autonomous institutions or structures for each distinctive community or culture could perhaps be best described as *auto-cultural*;
- policies based on the development of direct relationships between otherwise separate or autonomous communities might then be described as *inter-cultural*.

Practical policy choices

The practical implementation of these distinct policy options can be illustrated in a wide range of different areas. But it is important to recognise that they are not mutually exclusive. There is no requirement that governments should be consistent in the pursuit of one or other of these broad policy objectives. In many cases the preferred approach will be a complex combination of different policies in different areas with a view to achieving an acceptable balance over time between the conflicting political, social and economic pressures in multi-ethnic societies. The following issues can affect that balance.

(a) Constitutional or legislative recognition

One of the primary demands of many well-established minority and indigenous communities is for some form of constitutional or legislative recognition of their existence and rights in national law.[10] This form of recognition provides a formal guarantee of

---

9   The proposed use of the words 'multicultural' and 'intercultural' at the Montreal International Seminar on Intercultural and Multicultural Education is an example of a different and somewhat confusing approach; UN Doc E/CN.4/Sub.2/AC.5/2000/WP.4, Sub-Commission on the Promotion and Protection of Minorities, *Montreal International Seminar on Intercultural and Multicultural Education* (2000), para. 6.

10   This issue is discussed, with examples from national constitutions in the annex, in UN

the continued protection of their existence and provides a firm basis for other measures to promote their identity and ensure their effective participation in the structures of government, as is now prescribed in the United Nations Declaration and the European Framework Convention. In states where there are two or more major ethnic, religious or linguistic communities there is a general trend to include some reference to this fact in the national constitution and a similar approach has been adopted in a number of states in North and South America in respect of their indigenous communities or peoples. In appropriate cases it can therefore be considered to be good practice. Where minorities are less well-established or less numerous, as in the case of many immigrant communities, specific constitutional recognition may be less practicable. In such cases an alternative approach may be to include a general reference to the multi-ethnic or multi-cultural nature of the population, as for example in Canada.[11] This may likewise provide a firm foundation for more detailed legislative recognition and protection for identified groups, such as measures to prohibit discrimination and to provide for monitoring of fair participation in employment or in the structures of government. In some cases the formal recognition of the multi-ethnic composition of the population may also be linked to policies to encourage greater integration. But there is no requirement in international law to adopt measures of this kind. In many states, notably those in Africa that have inherited colonial boundaries that include a large number of diverse and potentially divisive ethnic, linguistic or religious communities, the primary governmental objective has been to build a single national identity and to discourage or even prohibit ethnic or linguistic separatism. In a few West African states, for example, the formation of ethnic political parties has been formally prohibited.[12]

(b) Membership and representation

In cases where rights and duties have been created in respect of minorities or their members the issues of membership and representation cannot be avoided. Who is to be treated as a member of the protected group and who is to be entitled to represent it in political negotiations or legal proceedings?

Three interlocking approaches have emerged by which membership of a designated minority or indigenous community may be determined:[13]

Doc E/CN.4/Sub.2/AC.5/2001/WP.6, T. Hadden and C. O Maolain (note 6) and UN Doc E/CN.4/Sub.2/AC.5/2001/CRP.9, *Appendix to working paper* (2001).

11   See article 26 of the Canadian Charter of Rights and Freedoms, Part I of the Constitution Act (1982): 'This Charter shall be interpreted in a manner consistent with the preservation and enhancement of the multicultural heritage of Canadians'.

12   UN Doc E/CN.4/Sub.2/AC.5/2001/WP.2, S. Slimane *Peoples' Rights in Africa: towards the recognition and protection of ethnic, religious and linguistic specificities* (2001).

13   The issues are discussed in M. Salomon and A. Sengupta *The Right to Development: Obligations of States and the Rights of Minorities and Indigenous Peoples* (London: Minority Rights Group International, 2003).

–   reliance on objective or factual criteria;
–   self-identification;
–   acceptance by other group members.

The choice between these may have significant implications not only for the individuals and communities concerned, but also for wider national policies.

Exclusive reliance on supposedly objective or factual criteria is likely to be associated with broader policies of separation rather than of integration, notably those involving the creation of separate voting rolls, as until recently in Pakistan,[14] or the formal recording of ethnic affiliation on individual identity cards, as in the *propiska* system in the former Soviet Union. It may also prove difficult to implement in practice, especially where inter-marriage and the resulting mixed identities are prevalent. And it runs counter to the principle of individual choice in the United Nations Declaration and the European Framework Convention. So too would exclusive reliance on communal acceptance. On the other hand, exclusive reliance on self-identification may result in perverse claims of membership. A combination of objective criteria and an acceptance that individuals may choose not to be identified as a member of any group but to assert an individual or integrated identity is likely to fit most easily with general policies of integration or progressive voluntary assimilation. In almost every case, however, policies involving positive measures to promote communal or group equality require some form of monitoring which in turn requires some method of allocating individuals to one or more communal groups. In the absence of any firm rules or guidelines in international human rights or minority law prescribing how these problems are to be resolved, it is left to individual states to develop their own procedures, which will in turn be influenced by their broader policy objectives.

Similar issues arise in respect of the representation of a protected minority or indigenous community in consultations, negotiations or legal proceedings. This is especially important where the rights or duties are formulated not in respect of individual members but of the group or community as a whole. In such cases some formal provision is required to ensure effective and genuine representation of the group, not least because there is a risk that unrepresentative individuals or organisations will seek to pursue objectives or activities that are not supported by or in the interests of the group as a whole. The activity of 'ethnic entrepreneurs' in promoting exclusive or separatist agendas against the wishes of most of their communities has been identified as a contributory factor in a number of recent ethnic or communal conflicts, as for example in Bosnia in the early 1990s.[15] Nor can it be assumed that all the members of an ethnic or linguistic community share the same objectives. There is some evidence that the major-

---

14   Constitution of the Islamic Republic of Pakistan, art. 51(4A); this provision was repealed in 2001; see generally UN Doc E/CN.4/Sub.2/AC.5/2003/WP.5, International Centre for Ethnic Studies, *Statement of Principles on Minority and Group Rights in South Asia*, (2003) pp. 23-26.

15   D. Horowicz *Ethnic Groups in Conflict* (Berkeley: University of California Press, 1985).

ity of members of minority communities may be less interested in pursuing separatist objectives than some of their political leaders. Mechanisms or procedures to enable all the members of groups or communities to express their views, whether by the election of representatives or by referendums, on issues such as separate or integrated provision for schooling and other communal facilities, may play an important part in the development of agreed national policies.

(c)   Effective participation

Both the United Nations Declaration and the European Framework Convention seek to guarantee effective participation by members of minorities in decisions which affect their interests. But it is not clear how this obligation is to be implemented. Some activists and commentators, as indicated above, have sought to elevate this provision into a form of internal self-determination by asserting a right to regional, local or functional autonomy for established minorities.[16] Others have questioned the legitimacy and practicality of any such claim and most states have reacted negatively to the extension of the concept of self-determination into this area.

In practice there is a wide range of ways in which the principle of effective participation can be implemented, each of which may be linked to broader national strategies.[17] If the underlying objective is to achieve greater integration of representatives of minorities in governmental structures, measures may be taken to ensure more effective representation of members of minorities in national or regional legislatures or councils, whether by the introduction of appropriate forms of proportional representation, the reservation of seats, or encouragement for national or regional parties to select a proportion of candidates from minority communities. Formal or informal provision may also be made to ensure that appointments to non-elected public bodies are made in such a way as to ensure that their composition is representative of society as a whole. If, on the other hand, there is general acceptance of the principle of autonomy for established minority or indigenous communities, provision can be made for the devolution of legislative or administrative powers to regional or local councils in areas where members of minorities are concentrated, or alternatively for the creation of autonomous councils with executive or consultative authority on economic, cultural or linguistic affairs on a

---

16   UN Doc E/CN.4/Sub.2/AC.5/2001/CRP.5, G. Gilbert *Autonomy and Minority Groups: a legal right in international law?* (2001); and H. Hannum *Autonomy, Sovereignty and Self-Determination: The Accommodation of Conflicting Rights* (Philadelphia: University of Pennsylvania Press, 1996).

17   Some of the possibilities are discussed in UN Doc E/CN.4/Sub.2/AC.5/1999/WP.4, *Towards Effective Participation of Minorities: Proposals of an Expert Seminar organised by the European Centre for Minority Issues (the Flensberg Proposals)* (1999); see also W. Kymlicka *Multicultural Citizenship* (Oxford: Oxford University Press, 1995) and A. Lijphart *Democracy in Plural Societies* (New Haven: Yale University Press 1977).

functional as opposed to a territorial basis. In some cases a combination of both forms of effective participation may be found appropriate.

(d) Religion and language

The right of members of minority and indigenous communities to practise their religion and use their own language is guaranteed under article 27 of the International Covenant on Civil and Political Rights.[18] But this is in a sense no more than is already guaranteed by general provisions on freedom of religion, private life and protection from discrimination on the grounds of religion or language under the main human rights conventions. So it is not surprising that most of the cases under article 27 have concerned the right to enjoy culture rather than language or religion.[19] For present purposes the main issues in respect of minority religions and languages arise over the impact of formal provisions on state religions and official languages.

There is no requirement in human rights law that states should be founded on secular principles or that they should insist on a strict separation between secular and religious institutions. Nor is there any bar on the recognition of a state religion. But the more extreme forms of both secular and religious states clearly tend towards a monocultural and thus a broadly assimilationist objective, in which those who do not accept the prevailing values may feel excluded or disadvantaged by the requirements of public office or the education system. The pursuit of greater integration in a multi-cultural environment, on the other hand, is likely to involve either the formal recognition of a number of different religions or the adoption of less extreme forms of secularism in which the expression of different religious symbols or practices in schools or public bodies is accepted. Some forms of official recognition of minority religions, however, may contribute to greater separation. The reservation of a number of parliamentary seats for Christians in the Islamic Republic of Pakistan, for example, was tied to the maintenance of separate voting rolls and has recently been abandoned in response to pressure for greater integration.[20]

---

18   Article 27 states:

> In those States in which minorities ethnic, religious or linguistic minorities exist, persons belonging to such minorities shall not be denied the right, in community with other members of their group, to enjoy their own culture, to profess and practice their own religion, or to use their own language.

International Covenant on Civil and Political Rights, UN Doc. A/6316 (1966). General Assembly resolution 2200 A, XXI session, 16 December 1966, Article 27.

19   *Kitoc* v. *Sweden*, Communication No. 197/1985, CCPR/C/33/D/197/1985, 10 August 1988; *Lansman* v. *Finland*, Communication No. 671/1995, CCPR/C/58/D/671/1995, 22 November 1996; *Mahuika* v. *New Zealand*, Communication No. 547/1993, CCPR/C/70/D/547/1993, 15 November 2000.

20   Horowicz (note 15).

The recognition and regulation of the use of minority languages is often an even more contentious issue. Under some more extreme policies of assimilation a single national language may be prescribed for all official purposes and the use of minority languages may be prohibited, as for example until recently in Turkey in respect of the Kurdish language in the media.[21] Even where there is a single official language, however, it is more usual for some leeway to be afforded to the use of minority languages for official purposes where that is necessary for effective communication and this approach has been incorporated in the United Nations Declaration and the European Framework Convention. Under more developed forms of multi-cultural integration several languages may be granted official status and their use regulated for prescribed purposes, as for example in Canada, Wales and Ireland. In such cases the underlying pressures of commercial and political life are likely to result in official or voluntary encouragement for bilingualism. Language recognition and regulation may also be associated with separatist pressures or policies, if the exclusive use of a particular official language is prescribed on a territorial basis. Language regulation in Belgium provides a striking example of both these possibilities, in that the exclusive use of Flemish or French is prescribed in the autonomous regions of Flanders and Wallonia respectively, while there is a bilingual regime in the Brussels Capital region.[22]

(e)   Education

The choice between the provision of common, integrated or separate schooling is equally contentious. It is widely recognised that the provision of separate schools is one of the most effective means of preserving or promoting the language, culture and communal solidarity of any minority. But there are also well-founded concerns in some countries, especially those with historically deeply divided societies, that maintaining separate and mutually exclusive educational systems can contribute to the perpetuation of communal misunderstanding, antagonism and conflict, as in Northern Ireland.[23] In such cases, the provision of education in common state-funded schools attended by the vast majority of pupils is widely recognised as one of the most effective means of promoting an integrated multi-cultural society, provided that the curriculum is designed to respect and provide for all major communal groups. The curriculum of common schools may also, of course, be designed to achieve the progressive assimilation of members of minority communities.

---

21   The prohibition was repealed in 2003 as part of the reform package agreed with the European Union in preparation for possible accession by Turkey.

22   For a more detailed account see T. Hadden and E. Craig *Integration and Separation: Rights in Divided Societies* (Belfast: Centre for International and Comparative Human Rights Law ,2000).

23   C. Moffat (ed.) *Education Together for a Change: Integrated Education and Community Relations in Northern Ireland* (Belfast: Fortnight Educational Trust, 1993).

Neither the United Nations Declaration nor the European Framework Convention, as has been seen, provide any clear guidance on the choice between these alternative approaches. The Declaration provides in article 4.3[24] that members of minorities should wherever possible have the opportunity to learn or have instruction in their mother tongue, thus leaving open the choice between separate 'immersion' schools or the provision of minority language classes in common schools. It also emphasises in article 4.4[25] the desirability of encouraging members of both majority and minority communities to learn about their respective histories, traditions, languages and cultures, which may again be achieved either in common or in separate schools. There is a similar ambivalence in the Framework Convention. It recognises in article 13 the right of members of minorities to maintain 'their own private educational and training establishments' but expressly excludes any obligation on the State to provide funding for them.[26] The heavily qualified obligation under article 14 to provide adequate opportunities to be taught or receive instruction in a minority language may also be fulfilled in either separate or common schools.[27]

The practical implementation of these provisions will usually depend on the size and concentration of the relevant minority. In cases where an ethnic, religious or linguistic minority or indigenous community is concentrated in a well-defined area the claim for separate schools as of right is probably strongest. In cases where members of one or more well-established or immigrant minorities have moved to major cities or where there is a long history of communal antagonism the arguments for integrated or common schools with a multi-cultural, and if necessary a multi-lingual, curriculum may be more compelling. The dominant considerations for national governments will

---

24 See above (note 2).

25 Ibid. Article 4.4 reads:

> States should consider appropriate measures so that persons belonging to minorities may participate fully in the economic progress and development in their country.

26 Ibid. Article 13 reads:

> 1. Within the framework of their educational systems, the Parties shall recognise that persons belonging to a national minority have the right to set up and manage their own private educational and training establishment.
>
> 2. The exercise of this right shall not entail any financial obligation for the Parties.

27 Ibid. Article 14 reads:

> 1. The Parties undertake to recognise that every person belonging to a national minority has the right to learn his or her minority language.
>
> 2. In areas inhabited by persons belonging to national minorities traditionally or in substantial numbers, if there is sufficient demand, the Parties shall endeavour to ensure, as far as possible and within the framework of their education systems, that persons belonging to those minorities have adequate opportunities for being taught the minority language or receiving instruction in this language.
>
> 3. Paragraph 2 of this article shall be implemented without prejudice to the learning of the official language or the teaching of this language.

quite properly be centred on finding the arrangements that are most likely to lead to long-term peace and stability rather than on attempting to find conclusive guidance in the relevant international human rights instruments.

(f) Employment

There is a well-established tendency for members of minorities who migrate to large cities or other centres of employment to cluster together in particular areas and to be concentrated in particular occupations or types of work.[28] There is also an associated tendency for them to experience systematic discrimination and to be excluded from many mainstream occupations and activities. Discrimination on grounds of race, ethnic origin, religion or language is of course prohibited both in the main human rights conventions and in the more recent minority rights instruments. But there remains a good deal of discretion as to what further measures national governments may wish to adopt to promote the effective participation of members of minorities in social and economic life, as prescribed in the United Nations Declaration, or to promote full and effective equality in all areas of social and economic life, as prescribed in the European Framework Convention.

It is in respect of employment that the strongest case for measures to promote integration, as opposed to separation, can usually be made. The twin complaints of discrimination and more general economic disadvantage typically lead to calls for a fair share of jobs in the public service, not least in the army and police, and effective measures to secure a similar result in at least the more modernised private sector companies. A variety of measures can be adopted to move towards and eventually achieve these objectives. Major public sector bodies can be required to monitor the ethnic or religious balance in their workforces and to work towards some measure of proportionality in their composition. In some cases a formal quota system may be adopted to ensure that this is achieved, as for example in respect of the German and Italian speaking communities in the South Tyrol in Italy[29] or the 'scheduled castes' in India.[30] Similar obligations can be imposed, where appropriate, on major private sector employers. Any proportionate positive measure of this kind can then be protected from allegations of discrimination in accordance with the terms of article 8.3 of the United Nations Declaration[31] or article 4.3 of the European Framework Convention.[32] The underlying objective of measures of this kind in most cases is not to eliminate discrimination and disadvantage by creating

---

28   Horowicz (note 15) chapter 4.

29   Hadden and Craig (note 22).

30   Indian Constitution, art. 335.

31   See above (note 2). Article 8.4. states that 'measures taken by states to ensure the effective enjoyment of the rights set forth in the present Declaration shall not prima facie be considered contrary to the principle of equality contained in the Universal Declaration on Human Rights.

32   See above (note 3). Article 4.3 states that any positive measure 'shall not be considered to be an act of discrimination'.

segregated workplaces composed exclusively of members of one or other community, as might be the objective in a separatist approach. It is rather to work towards balanced employment in the public service, the army and the police and in so doing to emphasise the commitment of the state to an integrated multi-cultural ethos in those areas. It may be noted that this general principle has been formally adopted within the United Nations in respect of all forms of law enforcement: '... like all agencies of the criminal justice system, every law enforcement agency should be representative of and responsive and accountable to the community as a whole'.[33]

(g) Development

A rather different focus will often be required in respect of national development plans.[34] Though the United Nations Declaration refers in article 4.5 to the need for appropriate measures to ensure that members of minorities can participate fully in national economic progress and development,[35] more attention is likely to be paid to the requirement in article 5.1 that 'national policies and programmes shall be planned and implemented with due regard for the legitimate interests of persons belonging to minorities'.[36] Representatives of minority and indigenous communities typically complain of the disruptive and disadvantageous impact of national development policies and projects on their traditional economies and lifestyles, the displacement of large numbers from their traditional lands and the failure to provide effective compensation for those affected.

The dominant focus is thus on the essentially separatist demand by rural minority or indigenous communities for protection from interference, rather than any form of integration in the processes of development. The related demand for more effective consultation during the preparation of the plans is similarly likely to be aimed at reducing the disruptive impact of development projects or activities that cannot be prevented. This is also evident in the claims to protection for the continued enjoyment of traditional culture in most of the cases decided by the Human Rights Committee under article 27 of the ICCPR.[37] In a series of cases concerning the indigenous Saami people in Scandinavia and the Maori people in New Zealand, the Human Rights Committee has accepted that indigenous herding and fishing communities have a *prima facie* right to maintain their traditional practices.[38] But it has added that some reasonable limitation or regulation of these practices may be legitimate, provided there is effective consultation with representatives of the communities affected. It must always be remembered that the purpose of

---

33   Code of Conduct for Law Enforcement Officials, adopted by General Assembly Resolution 34/169 of 17 December 1979.

34   UN Doc E/CN.4/Sub.2/AC.5/2002/WP.6, Minority Rights Group International, *Minority Rights and Development: Overcoming Exclusion, Discrimination and Poverty.*

35   See above (note 2).

36   Ibid.

37   See above (note 18)

38   See above (note 19).

human rights instruments is not to fix patterns of land use and distribution or communal cultures at some arbitrary point in time, whether past or present. Minority and indigenous communities are not to be excluded from participation in all forms of development. But they have a right, along with other sectors in society, to seek forms of development that will assist in the preservation of their separate cultures and lifestyles.

Minorities and indigenous peoples

No attempt has been made thus far to draw a distinction between minorities and indigenous peoples or communities. This is partly because it is often difficult to establish satisfactory criteria on which to make a clear distinction, as has been made clear in a number of international seminars in Africa and Asia.[39] Though indigenous peoples typically assert a different formal status as 'first peoples' with a right to self-determination, and have managed to create a series of separate institutions within the United Nations, in more practical terms the rights and obligations owed to indigenous and minority communities are best described as a continuum depending on their particular circumstances and lifestyles. It is clear, for example, that while most indigenous communities have a particular attachment to their traditional lands, many rural minorities also assert similar claims for their lands and both assert a right to protection from incursion or appropriation by outsiders. The fact that some indigenous communities have been able to achieve as much by relying on the general terms of article 27 of the ICCPR[40] as they have under more specific instruments relating to indigenous peoples emphasises the point. The list of additional issues on which some form of special status and provision is claimed, such as formal constitutional recognition, effective rules on membership and representation, a right to some form of territorial or functional autonomy, full social and economic equality, and protection from inappropriate national development, is the same for both groups. The recent report of the Working Group of the African Commission on Human and Peoples' Rights, though, has proposed a somewhat restrictive definition of indigenous populations or communities as 'first and foremost (but not exclusively) different groups of hunter-gatherers or former hunter-gatherers and certain groups of pastoralists'.[41] The Working Group has confirmed this approach by stressing

---

39   UN Doc E/CN.4/Sub.2/AC.5/2001/3, *Report of the Workshop on Multiculturalism in Africa, held in Kidal, Mali 8-13 January 2001*, (2001) para. 61; UN Doc E/CN.4/Sub.2/AC.5/2003/2, *Conclusions and Recommendations of the Sub-regional Seminar on Minority Rights: Cultural Diversity and Development in Southeast Asia, held in Chiang Mai, Thailand, 4-7 December 2002*, (2002) para 10; and UN Doc E/CN.4/Sub.2/2000/10, A. Eide and E-I. Daes, *Working Paper on the relationship and distinction between the rights of persons belonging to minorities and those of indigenous peoples* (2000).

40   See above (note 18).

41   *Report of the African Commission's Working Group of Experts on Indigenous Populations/Communities*, adopted by the African Commission on Human and Peoples' Rights at its 34th Ordinary session in Banjul, The Gambia (2003), p. 76.

that indigenous populations or communities are not entitled to special rights as such, but to the enjoyment of the full range of individual and group rights recognised by the African Charter on Human and Peoples' Rights.[42] In practical terms the precise form of protection and the most appropriate positive measures will in every case depend on the particular circumstances of the minority or indigenous community concerned. Hunter-gatherers, pastoralists and some traditional agriculturalists clearly require different forms of protection and development than other rural and urban communities. The history of human communities has always been one of continuous interaction, change and development. Within that framework it is the task of human rights instruments and institutions and national legislative and administrative authorities to select the particular forms of recognition, protection and positive development that are most appropriate in each particular case.

A table of choices

The essentials of the position that has been developed thus far are summarised in the accompanying table, which draws together some of the various permissible measures that might be adopted in pursuit of the key strategic objectives of assimilation, integration or separation. Though this form of presentation is inevitably schematic and hides the difficulty in drawing firm lines between the measures under each main heading, it has the advantage of highlighting the wide range of measures that governments must consider in developing their policies for their minority and indigenous communities.

---

42   OAU Doc. CAB/LEG/67/3 rev.5, Organisation of African Unity, *African (Banjul) Charter on Human and Peoples' Rights* (1981).

	Assimilation	Integration	Separation
Recognition	All citizens are equal; there are no minorities	Recognition of minorities with equal status	Recognition of minorities with separate status
Membership	Denied	Choice for each individual	Assigned by law
Political participation	Simple majority rule	Special measures to ensure fair representation	Regional or functional autonomy
Religion	Secularism or state religion	Various religions formally recognised	Separate status, e.g separate voting rolls
Language	Single national language for all official purposes	Several languages formally recognised for public purposes; support for bilingualism	Designated areas for exclusive use of each language
Education	Common schools; prescribed national curriculum	Integrated schools with multi-cultural curriculums	Separate schools for minorities
Employment	Recruitment on merit; prohibition of discrimination	Provision to ensure fair participation in public/private sectors	Separate employment structures
Development	National development plans	Participation of minorities in development plans	Separate development structures

Some conclusions

This tabular presentation, and the preceding discussion on which it is based, suggests a number of more general conclusions.

(a) There is a genuine choice

The first is that there is a genuine choice for governments in dealing with minority and indigenous communities between the broad policy objectives summarised in the table. The main human rights conventions and declarations, as has been shown, do not prescribe any particular approach or any particular set of measures. Nor do they provide any clear differentiation between the various types of minority and indigenous communities. Some of the major factors that may quite properly influence the choice of policy are the size of the community, its concentration or dispersal, whether it is predominately centred in rural or urban localities (or both), how long it has been established and what kind of social and economic lifestyle it has preserved or developed.

In simpler terms, size matters. So do history and location. So too does the level of communal solidarity and commitment to a particular lifestyle.

Size matters because larger minorities are generally entitled to greater recognition and more extensive special measures to ensure the promotion of their identity and culture and their effective participation in decision-making. Very small minorities, on the other hand, may have to be satisfied with more limited protections for their identity and culture. And in cases where two or more major communities are vying for political or economic control comprehensive measures to ensure communal equality and political power-sharing may be required, as for example in Belgium and Northern Ireland and potentially in Afghanistan and Iraq.

History matters because length of settlement or status as indigenous or 'first peoples' clearly contributes to the legitimacy of claims for special recognition and special protections, as in the case of native peoples in North America or nomads, herders or hunter-gathers in Africa and elsewhere. A legacy of marginalisation, domination and discrimination may also require more extensive measures to correct past wrongs and to achieve communal equality and inclusion, as in the case of the Roma in Europe. More recent immigrant populations, on the other hand, may have to be satisfied with measures to eliminate discrimination and to promote individual equality, cultural accommodation and more general integration.

Location matters because a substantial concentration of members of a minority in one area in which they constitute nearly the whole population may strengthen a claim for territorial autonomy. Cases in which a minority is dispersed over the whole of a state's territory, on the other hand, are likely to require a different set of measures to ensure effective participation. There is also likely to be a substantial difference in the measures needed to protect and promote the identity of minorities whose members are predominately located in rural or urban areas. Special measures, such as bilateral treaties, are also likely to be required in respect of minorities whose members occupy border areas between two states, as is expressly recognised in article 18 of the European Framework Convention.[43] But the nature of any such treaty will differ, depending on whether the minority in one state shares an identity with the majority in the other, as for example in the case of the minority Catholic population in Northern Ireland, the minority Albanian population in Macedonia or the minority Tamil population in Sri Lanka, or whether both are minorities, as in the case of the Basque population in Spain and France and the Kurdish population in Turkey, Syria, Iraq and Iran.

Communal solidarity matters because without it there would be little basis for the adoption of special measures. If no appreciable body of those who might be considered to constitute an ethnic or linguistic minority expresses any desire for or commitment to the preservation of its historic culture or language and prefers to be integrated or assimilated into the wider national society, measures to prohibit discrimination and to facilitate that preference would seem to be entirely appropriate. The same may be said of a religious community that is content to be treated on an equal and non-discriminatory basis in the exercise of its right to religious freedom but otherwise to be indistinguish-

---

43   See above (note 3).

able from the rest of the population. As has already been indicated, the very existence of a minority community for the purposes of international human rights obligations is dependent on some degree of communal commitment to the maintenance of a distinctive language or culture.

Only a few of these factors are expressly or even implicitly dealt with in the main human rights instruments. And it is not immediately obvious that they should be. Human rights lawyers usually have limited training and experience in the political and economic skills which are needed in developing appropriate policies and programmes of action in this area. They may legitimately establish some basic principles and propose some guidelines for their possible implementation.[44] But the decision on how they are actually to be implemented is probably best left to others.

(b)   A mix of objectives and measures may be best

The second conclusion is that it should not be assumed that a single-minded pursuit of one or other of the main objectives identified in the table is likely to be a good idea. There is an obvious risk that an open and deliberate commitment to assimilation or separation as a long-term objective will generate an adverse reaction from either the majority or minority communities. Too much focus on assimilation may provide the leaders of minority or indigenous communities with just the ammunition they need to develop their position and power as communal defenders or ethnic entrepreneurs. Too much emphasis on separation or autonomy, on the other hand, may contribute to demands for even greater degrees of self-determination and possible secession. It may also contribute to increased inter-communal conflict based on allegations of unfair and discriminatory special treatment. And too much emphasis on middle-of-the-road policies of integration may not be enough to satisfy the demands and aspirations of particular communities. In matters of this kind a mixture of policies and a large degree of flexibility may be the best way to manage the conflicting pressures and demands of different groups and communities.

(c)   Effective participation in decision-making is a key component

A third conclusion is that one of the key elements in the successful development and implementation of any policy is likely to be effective consultation with those most directly affected. This is highlighted in the concept of effective participation that is included in all the main human rights conventions and declarations and also in many of the rulings by the Human Rights Committee and other adjudicatory bodies. It is also an important component in the overall and generally successful strategy of the High

---

44   UN Doc E/CN.4/Sub.2/AC.5/2003/WP.1, T. Hadden *Towards a Set of Regional Guidelines or Codes of Practice on the Implementation of the Directive* (2003).

Commissioner for Minorities within the Organisation for Security and Co-operation in Europe.

(d) Managing perpetual change

A final point is that it should not be assumed that a single set of policies will be appropriate over a long period. The political, social and economic circumstances of every community and particularly of minority and indigenous communities are subject to constant change and development, whether from demographic changes, physical movement or the impact of governmental policies. The task facing national governments in this sphere is to find a way of managing the conflicting and ever-changing communal pressures for assimilation, integration and separation in response to changing circumstances rather than to apply a simple set of minority or indigenous rights. As I have argued elsewhere, the best analogy may be that of the management by economists and politicians of the economic cycle between 'boom and bust'.[45] To adapt a phrase used there: just as economists have to come to terms with the need to understand and manage the business cycle as best they can, so must human rights lawyers and political scientists and advisers come to terms with the need to understand and manage the swings of the pendulum between assimilation, integration and separation rather than seek to adjudicate on, and implement, fixed and unchanging rights.

---

45   Hadden (note 5) p. 90.

Chapter 11

Repressing Minorities and Getting Away with It? A Consideration of Economic, Social and Cultural Rights

Nazila Ghanea[1]

Why this Focus?

This chapter outlines how the persecution of minorities seems to become largely invisible, and therefore apparently condoned, when their treatment falls within deprivations of Economic, Social and Cultural Rights (ESCR) rather than Civil and Political Rights (CPR).

It is a fact, for example, that within the arena of human rights the denial of the right to food attracts less attention than the question of the death penalty, hunger receives less attention than torture, education less than the right to vote and cultural rights less than the freedom of association or expression. This remains the case despite the formal equality and indivisibility of economic, social, cultural, civil and political rights – as upheld by the Vienna Declaration and Programme of Action adopted at the 1993 UN World Conference on Human Rights.[2]

But why is the focus of this chapter on minorities rather than more broadly on the denial of ESCR? Firstly, it is acknowledged that it is not *only* when the denial of ESCR is carried out against minorities that there seems to be little outcry against it, there is the wider fact of muted responses to abuses of ESCR in general. However, the issue is being examined in relation to minorities here because denial, or severely reduced, access to ESCR sometimes constitutes intentional governmental policy against minorities. Despite this intentional discrimination, this often escapes international condemnation. Secondly, the denial of ESCR has a cumulatively negative impact when it is focused on

---

1   Senior Lecturer in International Law and Human Rights, University of London, Institute of Commonwealth Studies. The author was very grateful of the conducive and friendly research environment of the Lauterpacht Research Centre for International Law at the University of Cambridge, where she was a Visiting Fellow whilst completing this chapter and co-editing this collection.

2   'All human rights are universal, indivisible and interdependent and interrelated.' UN Doc A/CONF.157/23, Vienna Declaration and Programme of Action, World Conference on Human Rights, (1993), Article 5.

Nazila Ghanea & Alexandra Xanthaki (eds.), Minorities, Peoples and Self-Determination, pp. 193-209.
© *2005 Koninklijke Brill NV. Printed in The Netherlands. ISBN 90 04 14301 7.*

minorities. Here there is not only the immediate impact on the concerned individuals, but also the longer-term impact on the group as a whole. This cumulative impact is currently not given sufficient recognition in the framework of international human rights law. Furthermore, politically it seems that not only is the acuteness of the impact of such denial over time not recognised, but it also seems to be a fact that such treatment becomes habitual to the international community and attracts even less attention with the passage of time. Finally, the psychological impact of such habitual denials of ESCR goes largely unnoticed. This psychological impact, of course, also affects individuals, but it is the group dimension of it on the collective that will be focused on here.

This chapter therefore argues that there are serious shortcomings in the international protection of ESCRs as it extends to minority groups. Present standards and mechanisms are inadequate in the face of this multi-faceted challenge. This means that the slow suffocation of a minority group can largely be dismissed whilst only particularly cruel, short, sharp, sudden and bloody episodes against them attract attention.

International Standards and Procedures

This chapter therefore focuses on this issue as 'the persecution of minorities through the ongoing denial of ESCR'. The reason for this terminology is that the concern of this research is with particularly severe denial of ESCR that is targeted and imposed on minorities. It will therefore go beyond incidental disadvantages and discriminatory behaviour suffered due to the action of others or the general ESC deprivations also suffered by the wider population in that territory.

When it comes to existing international standards and procedures that may offer protection, we find that minorities fall through the gaps between a number of instruments and procedures. Those that will be addressed here are five-fold: the Refugee Convention,[3] the Genocide Convention,[4] the International Convention on Economic, Social and Cultural Rights (ICESCR),[5] the procedures of the UN Commission on Human Rights and the UN Declaration on Minorities.[6]

---

3   *Convention relating to the Status of Refugees* (1951) United Nations Conference of Plenipotentiaries on the Status of Refugees and Stateless, http://www.unhchr.ch/html/menu3/b/o_c_ref.htm (accessed 1 May 2004).

4   *Convention on the Prevention and Punishment of the Crime of Genocide*, UNGA Resolution 260 A (III) (1948), http://www.unhchr.ch/html/menu3/b/p_genoci.htm (accessed 1 May 2004)

5   *International Covenant on Economic, Social and Cultural Rights*, UNGA Res.2200 A (XXI), 16 December 1966.

6   *Declaration on the Rights of Persons Belonging to National or Ethnic, Religious or Linguistic Minorities*, UN Doc.A/47/49 (1993), United Nations General Assembly Res.47/135, Annex, 47 UNGAOR Supp.(No.49) p. 210.

Definitions

1. Refugee Convention's definition – difficulty in qualifying as 'persecution'

The distinction between 'discrimination' and 'persecution' is one that is critical in determinations that have to be made in Refugee Law. The United Nations High Commissioner for Refugees (UNHCR) has determined that

> [I]t is only in certain circumstances that discrimination will amount to persecution. This would be so if measures of discrimination lead to consequences of a substantially prejudicial nature for the person concerned, e.g. serious restrictions on his right to earn his livelihood, his right to practise his religion, or his access to normally available educational facilities.[7]

It is the sustained or systemic denial of core human rights that is the standard that needs to be reached. Interestingly, many jurisdictions recognise 'that various threats to human rights, in their cumulative effect, can deny human dignity in key ways and should properly be recognized as persecution for the purposes of the Convention'.[8] It is also worthy of note that refugee law has established that the 'well-founded fear of persecution' threshold that needs to be reached does not have to be in the physical sense. The climate of fear and insecurity that a victim suffers can itself be recognised as having been persecutory; and forms of psychological and mental harm are also to be included in the concept of persecution.[9]

Despite such permissible understandings, there are enormous challenges facing those minorities who would wish to seek refugee status on the grounds of targeted, continued and severe denials of ESCRs facing their minority group. The main difficulty is the need to individualise the 'well-founded fear of persecution'.[10] Whereas with torture and the death penalty it is fairly clear how this individualised 'well-founded fear of persecution' may be proven, what is the equivalent for denial of ESCR? The confiscation of one's property, dismissal from one's employment, the denial of one's pension, the inability to educate one's children – all due to one's minority status – these would be the counter proofs in the arena of ESCR. However, it would be unlikely that such instances

---

7   Handbook on Procedures and Criteria for Determining Refugee Status under the 1951 Convention and the 1967 Protocol relating to the Status of Refugees, document HCR/IP/4/Eng./REV.1, UNHCR, (1979), para. 54.

8   See New Zealand's Refugee Appeal No. 2039/93 Re MN (12 February 1996) 16 quoted in Refugee Status Appeals Authority, Refugee Appeal No. 71404/99 at Auckland (29 October 1999), http://www.refugee.org.nz/rsaa/text/docs/71404-99.htm (accessed 12 May 2004).

9   Refugee Status Appeals Authority, Refugee Appeal No. 71404/99 at Auckland (29 October 1999), http://www.refugee.org.nz/rsaa/text/docs/71404-99.htm (accessed 12 May 2004).

10   This stands at the opposite end of the spectrum to victims of the Genocide Convention where the victim is 'a member of a group, chosen as such, which, hence, means that the victim of the crime of genocide is the group itself and not only the individual'. See ICTR, Prosecutor v. Jean-Paul Akayesu, Case no. ICTR-96-64-4-T, decision of 2 September 1998, para. 521.

would be deemed as sufficiently grave for the recognition of refugee status. It is for this reason that we can note that minorities such as the Ahmadiyya of Pakistan and Copts of Egypt for example are primarily leaving their respective countries in their multitudes through immigration channels rather than obtaining refugee status.

Jackson argues that 'the degree of precision'[11] that is required to establish the individual well-founded fear of persecution is now interpreted in a much more stringent fashion than it ever has been. In its historical and legal precedents, he finds much greater appreciation of the group character and determination of some refugee movements. In larger-scale situations 'an objective evaluation of the reasons for departure'[12] would have dominated 'individual status determination'.[13] What should be noted here is that members of minorities under discussion in my study are *not* purely leaving for economic reasons, for personal convenience or in order to escape the indiscriminate consequences of general situations of violence or conflict – these being persons excluded from the Refugee Convention.[14] They are being especially targeted for their membership of a minority group for particular and serious denials of ESCR – measures from which the general population are excluded. However, the targeting of the minority group as a whole, the economic consequences of this denial, and the difficulty in establishing a causal relationship between such denials and minority status – all act as hindrances in arguing for refugee status. Jackson's argument that the present requirement of '"singling out" – if valid at all – is not applicable in large-scale group situations'[15] is therefore helpful in this regard.

Contextualising this challenge in the light of the original language of the non-refoulement principle of the 1951 Refugee Convention[16] is also informative. Article 33(1) of the 1951 Convention states that no refugee is to be expelled or returned 'in any manner whatsoever to the frontiers of territories where his life or freedom would be threatened on account of his race, religion, nationality, membership of a particular social group or political opinion'. The inclusion of 'freedom' being threatened is more inclusive than 'life' – and its scope arguably covers the combined impact of severe ESCR denials of, for example, education, livelihood, employment and participation.

2.   *Genocide Convention's definition* – scope of genocide and question of ethnocide

Whereas for Lemkin the terms genocide and ethnocide were interchangeable, and referred to the destruction of a nation or of an ethnic group,[17] there have been distinc-

---

11   I.C. Jackson *The refugee concept in group situations* (The Hague: Martinus Nijhoff, 1999) p. 463.
12   Ibid. p. 466.
13   Ibid.
14   Ibid. p. 469.
15   Ibid. p. 472.
16   (note 3).
17   R. Lemkin *Axis Rule in Occupied Europe* (Carnegie Endowment for International Peace, 1944) p. 79.

tions between these two terms suggested by other writers. There is a sense in which eth-nocide can be considered a sub-type of genocide rather than interchangeable with it.

Where processes prohibit or interfere with the continuity of a culture or nation but do not include the type of 'murderous oppression directly under the generic concept of genocide', Charny[18] prefers the term ethnocide. This is defined as 'intentional destruc-tion of the culture of another people, not necessarily including destruction of actual lives'.[19] He reserves the term genocide for 'actual mass murders that end the lives of people'.[20] UNESCO, however, recognises ethnocide as the denial to an ethnic group of 'the right to enjoy, develop and transmit its own culture and its own language, whether collectively or individually'.[21] More significantly, it recognises ethnocide as being 'equiv-alent to genocide'.[22]

What is clear is that the Genocide Convention of 1948[23] excluded ethnocide from its specification of crimes from which it offers legal protection.[24] If the right of a group to protection from destruction is taken to primarily mean its immediate physical exist-ence, rather than its longer-term and continued existence as a group, what does this imply for our concern here with the protection of minorities from targeted, ongoing and severe persecution through the denial of ESCR, especially where the intent to destroy the group through such measures can be demonstrated?

The definition of genocide in the Convention is focused on physical and biological destruction of a 'national, ethnical, racial or religious group'. The exhaustive list of acts committed with intent to destroy the group include the killing, serious bodily or mental harm, imposition of conditions of life calculated to bring about its physical destruction, the prevention of births or the forced transfer of children. Article 2(b) regarding serious bodily or mental harm to members of the group, with intent to destroy the group in whole or part, would seem to be the most amenable to our subject matter. The inclusion of both this act in 2 (2)(b), as well as that contained in 2(e) regarding the transfer of children, would seem to suggest some recognition of the manners in which a group may face 'destruction' other than exclusively through physical destruction. The International Criminal Tribunal on Rwanda (ICTR) has recognised that bodily or mental harm in

18 I.W. Charny, 'Toward a Generic Definition of Genocide,' in G.J. Andreopoulos (ed.) *Genocide: Conceptual and Historical Dimensions* (University of Pennsylvania Press, 1994).

19 Ibid. p. 85.

20 Ibid. p. 84.

21 UNESCO DOC. FS82/2F.32 (1981), UNESCO, Declaration of San José, December 1981, preamble, para. 2.

22 Ibid. operative para. 1.

23 (note 5).

24 See Morsink's detailed study of discussions surrounding ethnocide during the drafting of both the Universal Declaration of Human Rights and the Genocide Convention. J. Mors-ink, 'Cultural Genocide, the Universal Declaration, and Minority Rights,' 21.4 *Human Rights Quarterly* (1999) p. 1009.

2(b) does not necessarily have to be 'permanent and irremediable'.[25] Reference is made by the ICTR to the Eichmann case's delineation of serious bodily or mental harm as 'enslavement, starvation, deportation and persecution ... designed to cause their degradation, deprivation of their rights as human beings, and to suppress them and cause them inhumane suffering and torture'.[26] The ICTR itself takes Article 2 (2)(b) to include bodily or mental torture, inhumane or degrading treatment.

What is punishable under genocide is the act itself, or the conspiracy to commit it, the incitement to commit it, the attempt to commit it and complicity in genocide.[27] It is interesting that whilst the 19 April 2004 Krstic judgement of the International Criminal Tribunal for the former Yugoslavia (ICTY) takes into consideration the impact of such practices on the wider *continuity of the group* as a whole, it does so only in assessing whether the physical destruction of the group 'in part' has been substantial enough to merit the determination of the intent to destroy that part – thereby reaching the threshold of genocide.[28] In the Jelisic judgement, the ICTY made a distinction between two forms of intent.

> It may consist of desiring the extermination of a very large number of the members of the group, in which case it would constitute an intention to destroy a group en masse. However, it may also consist of the desired destruction of a more limited number of persons selected for the impact that their disappearance would have upon the survival of the group as such. This would then constitute an intention to destroy the group 'selectively'.[29]

25   ICTR, Prosecutor v. Jean-Paul Akayesu, Case no. ICTR-96-64-4-T, decision of 2 September 1998, para. 502.

26   Attorney General of the Government of Israel v. Adolph Eichmann, District Court of Jerusalem 12 December 1961, in 36 *The International Law Reports* (1968) p. 340, quoted by the ICTR, Prosecutor v. Jean-Paul Akayesu, Case no. ICTR-96-64-4-T, decision of 2 September 1998, para. 503.

27   See ICTY, Prosecutor v. Goran Jelisic, Case No: IT-95-10-A, judgement of 5 July 2001, para. 44(3).

28   The judgement was based on the criterion that the destruction of the part needed to be substantial enough to affect the group in its entirety. 'The determination of when the targeted part is substantial enough to meet this requirement may involve a number of considerations. The numeric size of the targeted part of the group is the necessary and important starting point, though not in all cases the ending point of the inquiry. The number of individuals targeted should be evaluated not only in absolute terms, but also in relation to the overall size of the entire group. In addition to the numeric size of the targeted portion, its prominence within the group can be a useful consideration. If a specific part of the group is emblematic of the overall group, or is essential to its survival, that may support a finding that the part qualifies as substantial within the meaning of Article 4. [of the Genocide Convention relating to intent]' ICTY, Prosecutor v. Radislav Krstic, Case No: IT-98-33-A, judgement of 19 April 2004, para. 12.

29   ICTY, Second Amended Indictment against Goran Jelisic and Ranko Cesic, Prosecutor v. Goran Jelisic, decision of 14 December 1999, para. 82.

Again, this is important in its, albeit indirect, recognition of the relevance of the non-physical survival of a group to genocide.

Considering the Genocide Convention remains one of the few treaties that specifically protects the existence of groups, the exclusion of ethnocide does not bode well. If a minority group is impoverished, goes underground or is dispersed, and is forced to relinquish its identity in the interests of escaping ongoing and severe denials of ESCR, then it seems that there cannot be any recognition of this as being a genocidal act in the strict legal sense. However, in line with obligations enshrined in Article 1 towards the *prevention* of genocide, States Parties should be alert to ethnocide as often signalling an early warning sign of a forthcoming genocide – hence the need to arrest such occurrences. As Morsink argues, cultural genocide 'is more often than not a preparatory stage for the physical or biological genocide that soon follows'.[30]

A particularly vivid illustration of the difficulties in dealing with the destruction of a group in the light of genocide relates to the case of the Tibetans. Despite an almost 55 year period of diplomatic lobbying, the situation of human rights in Tibet has thus far only led to the adoption of four UN General Assembly resolutions, a UN Sub-Commission resolution, a report by the UN Secretary-General and a mention in reports from various UN bodies.[31] Annual attempts at censuring China through the public 1235 procedure of the Commission on Human Rights fail through the manipulative use of the Commission 'no-action' motion.[32] The situation of human rights in Tibet has been noted by the Tibet Justice Center[33] as being one of a 'persistent and progressive pattern of human rights abuses against the Tibetan people'.[34] They suggest that this pattern 'points to an imminent threat of destruction of the Tibetans as a people.'[35] The Center therefore just stops short of utilising the term genocide. It is interesting that the Legal Inquiry Committee on Tibet set up by the International Commission of Jurists in 1960 found that genocide *had* been committed in Tibet 'in an attempt to destroy the Tibetans as a religious group'.[36] This Committee based its assessment on the following four principal facts:

---

30   Morsink (note 24) p. 1029.

31   See Tibet Justice Center website, UN legal materials on Tibet http://www.tibetjustice.org/materials/#un (accessed 21 April 2004).

32   For more information on no-action motions see Rules of Procedure of the Functional Commissions of the Economic and Social Council, initially adopted by the Economic and Social Council in resolution 100 (V) of 12 August 1947 and adapted a number of times since. Rule 65(2). They can be found on-line on http://www.unhchr.ch/html/menu2/2/rules.htm (accessed 25 April 2004).

33   Formerly known as the 'International Committee of Lawyers for Tibet'.

34   Interventions drafted by the Tibet Justice Center and submitted to the UN Sub-Commission on the Prevention of Discrimination and Protection of Minorities (now known as the UN Sub-Commission for the Promotion and Protection of Human Rights), forty-ninth session, found at http://www.tibetjustice.org/reports/un/unint2.html (accessed 21 April 2004).

35   Ibid.

36   International Commission of Jurists, Tibet – Tibet and the Chinese People's Republic, 1960, ICJ Catalog number 837. Excerpts of this report can be consulted on the Government of Tibet in Exile

(a)   that the Chinese will not permit adherence to and practice of Buddhism in Tibet;

(b)   that they have systematically set out to eradicate this religious belief in Tibet;

(c)   that in pursuit of this design they have killed religious figures because their religious belief and practice was an encouragement and example to others;

(d)   that they have forcibly transferred large numbers of Tibetan children to a Chinese materialist environment in order to prevent them from having a religious upbringing.[37]

3.   *The International Convention on Economic, Social and Cultural Rights*

The next aspect with regard to the protection of minorities from the targeted and continued denial of ESCR relates to the protection of ESCR in general. Whereas formally CPR and ESCR are indivisible and inter-dependent, there are numerous ways in which ESCR continue to be subordinated in fact.

There has been a draft of the Optional Protocol to the International Convention on Economic, Social and Cultural Rights (ICESCR) on the table since 1996, but as yet there are no procedures in place to enable consideration of complaints regarding violations of that Convention. Estimates are that, at best, it will take another four to five years before an Optional Protocol to the Convention can be adopted at the UN General Assembly.[38] Even when adopted, the considerations of 'progressive realisation', 'to the maximum of available resources', the 'highest attainable standard' and with 'a view to achieving the full realization' may be invoked in compromising the realisation of ESCR for all, including for minorities. Should the Committee on ESCR pursue the same track followed by the Human Rights Committee in relation to Article 27 of the International Covenant on Civil and Political Rights (ICCPR), even when an Optional Protocol to the ICESCR is adopted the Committee would only allow minorities to complain about violations of the ICESCR as individuals belonging to such minorities and not as minorities as such. Therefore, again, it would only be the rights of individual members belonging to the minority group – in relation for example to freedom from hunger and the highest attainable standard of physical and mental health – which would be of concern and not the gradual impoverishment and decimation of the minority community as a whole.

Article 27 of the ICCPR is the most widely accepted international legally-binding provision on minorities. Article 27 confers on 'persons belonging to minorities' the right to 'national, ethnic, religious or linguistic identity, or a combination thereof,

---

website on http://www.tibet.com/Resolution/icj60.html (accessed 21 April 2004). The report can also be purchased from the ICJ http://www.icj.org.

37   Ibid.

38   MINBYUN-Lawyers for a Democratic Society, Concise Background Document on the Optional Protocol to the International Covenant on Economic, Social and Cultural Rights, http://minbyun.jinbo.net/un/intero3/59chr/Background%20Document%20on%20the%20Optional%20Protocol.doc (accessed 26 April 2004).

and to preserve the characteristics which they wish to maintain and develop'.[39] General Comment 23 (1994) on Article 27 explains that the rights enshrined in Article 27 are individual rights, but that they depend 'on the ability of the minority group to maintain its culture, language or religion' and that it may therefore be necessary to 'protect the identity of a minority'.[40] Donders observes that the collective reference to minorities as such in Article 27 is in relation to State duties rather than rights for the minority group. 'Thus, the latter [the communities involved] are not the subjects of these provisions, but their beneficiaries'.[41]

The case law from the Human Rights Committee on Article 27[42] seems to support the presumption mentioned above, that the gradual decimation and impoverishment of a minority community as a whole would not come under the scope of the protection of Article 27. Since the Committee on ESCR does not have a minority provision like the ICCPR's Article 27, it will be even more constrained in to the way in which it can deal with the protection of minorities who are collectively and intentionally being denied their covenantal rights.

A vivid example of the selective blindness through which the international community neglects human rights sufferings of the ESC kind in relation to minorities is the present-day case of the Baháʾís in Iran. Whereas the persecution against the Baháʾís was recognised in repeated condemnations of the Iranian government through resolutions adopted by the international community between 1980 and 2001 at the United Nations, this condemnation has largely slowed down.[43] The persecution this religious community of over 300,000 suffers is clearly government-instigated and remains government-propelled. The most vivid indication of the intentional government policy against the Baháʾís in Iran, and particularly its focus on economic, social and cultural denials targeting them, stems from a 1991 governmental directive. This directive was uncovered in the 1993 report of the UN Special Representative of the Human Rights Situation in Iran to the United Nations Commission on Human Rights. Whilst the Iranian delegation dis-

---

39   It states: 'In those States in which minorities ethnic, religious or linguistic minorities exist, persons belonging to such minorities shall not be denied the right, in community with other members of their group, to enjoy their own culture, to profess and practice their own religion, or to use their own language.' International Covenant on Civil and Political Rights, UN Doc A/6316 (1966). General Assembly resolution 2200A, XXI session, 16 December 1966, Article 27.

40   UN Doc HRI\GEN\1\Rev.1 at 38, Human Rights Committee, General Comment 23, 50th session, (1994), para. 6(2).

41   Y.M. Donders *Towards a Right to Cultural Identity?* (Antwerp: Intersentia, 2002).

42   For cases see, for example: Kitok v. Sweden, UN Doc CCPR/C/33/D/197/1985, Human Rights Committee, (1985); Lubicon Lake Band v. Canada, UN Doc CCPR/C/38/D/167/1984, Human Rights Committee, (1990); and Lovelace v. Canada., UN Doc CCPR/C/13/D/24/1977, Human Rights Committee, (1981).

43   For a detailed discussion of this see N. Ghanea *Human Rights, the UN and the Baháʾís in Iran* (The Hague: Kluwer Law, 2003). No resolution condemning Iran's human rights situation has been adopted at the UN Commission on Human Rights since April 2001, but such a resolution was adopted by the UN General Assembly in December 2003.

missed it as a forgery, many other observers acknowledged its accuracy in relation to the Bahá'í situation. The Circular had been issued by the Supreme Revolutionary Cultural Council on 25 February 1991 and concerned official policy to be followed in relation to the Bahá'ís.[44] Its main thrust was encapsulated in section (a)(iii), 'the Government's treatment of them shall be such that their progress and development shall be blocked', through severe educational, ideological, cultural, propaganda and economic pressures. With regard to their legal and social status, the directive allowed them the possibility of leading 'a modest life' in so far as this, (c)(ii): 'does not constitute encouragement for them to persist in their status as Baha'is'. The UN Special Representative had commented that the directive included some 'slightly positive elements' in relation to the previous sufferings, but that the rule on limiting their progress and development limited all such positive readings of it.[45] As Afshari has argued, the intention of Iranian government policy against the Bahá'ís has been to 'destroy the conditions needed for their [the Bahá'ís] survival as a community with a distinct religious identity'.[46]

This Iranian secret memorandum on the destruction of the Bahá'ís can be considered as an extremely ingenious plot to engineer a very bleak, entrenched and deteriorating position for the whole of the Bahá'í community in Iran in the long-term future. Whilst the outright killing, torture and imprisonment of large numbers of Bahá'ís had diminished somewhat by the late 1980s, the present kind of assault on the community may actually crudely be described as a much more effective ploy than 'merely' killing them. That strategy had strengthened the resolve of the Bahá'ís and triggered support for them both nationally and internationally. The fact that the persecution of the Bahá'ís is embedded, ongoing and institutionalised, and that the Iranian Government itself has been instrumental in maintaining such severe political, socio-economic and cultural levels against them, is widely acknowledged. The silence of the international community in relation to this method of destroying the largest religious minority community in Iran is therefore ominous.

4.   *The procedures of the UN Commission on Human Rights*

If we move our consideration to UN Charter-based rather than Treaty-based mechanisms, the record is not much more promising. Despite the 1235 and 1503 procedures

---

44   The directive was summarised by the Special Representative in: Doc.E/CN.4/1993/41, Commission on Human Rights, 49th session, 28 January 1993, Item 12 of the provisional agenda, Question of the violation of human rights and fundamental freedoms in any part of the world, with particular reference to colonial and other dependent countries and territories, Final Report on the situation of human rights in the Islamic Republic of Iran by the Special Representative of the Commission on Human Rights, Mr. Reynaldo Galindo Pohl, pursuant to Commission resolution 1992/67 of 4 March 1992, para. 310.

45   Ibid. para. 311.

46   R. Afshari *Human Rights in Iran, The abuse of cultural relativism* (Philadelphia: University of Pennsylvania Press, 2001) p. 124.

being designed to be able to deal with consistent patterns of gross and reliably attested violations of human rights,[47] their record in the protection of ESCRs is dismal. As the strongest sanctions of the UN Commission on Human Rights, and the main procedures of the UN human rights machinery designed to address patterns of violations against large numbers of people, it is of serious concern that neither procedure has ever primarily been triggered due to violations of ESCRs. This has certainly not been due to lack of need. As Alston has observed, 'alleged violations of economic, social and cultural rights have never been examined seriously'.[48] It seems that only 'episodic' bloodshed, which is primarily as a result of the denial of civil and political rights, is considered worthy of consideration, rather than any equivalent suffering or even loss of life due to denial of ESCRs.

Perhaps the main underlying reason that ESCRs have not triggered the 1503 and 1235 procedures is that since ESCR have more obvious resource implications in the eyes of states, and since many states have poor records themselves in the field of ESCRs, they are reluctant to get involved in criticising the records of other states in this field.

5.   The UN Declaration on Minorities

Despite Morsink's claim that 'the greatest problem in international affairs today [is] the treatment of members of minority groups',[49] the only international provision exclusively concerned with the rights of minorities is the 1992 UN Declaration on the Rights of Persons Belonging to National or Ethnic, Religious or Linguistic Minorities. As a Declaration, this is legally non-binding and there are no plans to see it developed into a binding Covenant.

The Declaration addresses ESCR in Articles 2 and 4. Article 2(2) notes that 'Persons belonging to minorities have the right to participate effectively in cultural, religious, social, economic and public life.'[50] Article 4(5) notes that 'States should consider appropriate measures so that persons belonging to minorities may participate fully in the economic progress and development in their country.'[51] It seems obvious that the targeted and ongoing denial of ESCR against minorities goes against the standards in the Declaration of 'effective' and 'full' participation.

However, further policy recommendations and guidelines – elaborating minimum standards of conduct legally required by states – are needed in this area. There is some

---

47   The 1235 procedure came into being through ECOSOC resolution 1235 (XLII) of 6/6/67 and the 1503 procedure came into being through ECOSOC resolution 1503 (XLVIII) of 27/5/70.

48   P. Alston, 'The Commission on Human Rights,' in P. Alston (ed.) *The United Nations and Human Rights, A Critical Appraisal* (Oxford: Oxford University Press, 1992) p. 151.

49   Morsink (note 24) p. 1010.

50   UN Doc A/47/49, Declaration on the Rights of Persons Belonging to National or Ethnic, Religious or Linguistic Minorities, (1993), Article 2(2).

51   Ibid. Article 2(5).

mobilisation towards the development of such standards in the area of the economic self-determination of indigenous peoples and indigenous peoples and development.

Working Group of Minorities, of the UN Sub-Commission on Promotion and Protection of Human Rights

The Working Group on Minorities was established in 1995[52] in order to promote the rights set out in the Minorities Declaration, as well as to elucidate and elaborate upon them. The Working Group does not deal with complaints by minorities. It meets for just five working days a year. Its aim is to be a forum for dialogue – through facilitating awareness, understanding and respect between minorities and governments and between minorities themselves. Suggestions and recommendations are invited during the session in order to come to 'peaceful' and 'constructive' solutions to problems concerning minorities.

The Working Group recognises that minority–state problems are often related to 'the existence of structures or systems that have the effect of either perpetuating the marginalisation of minority communities from decision-making or of unfairly benefiting majority populations or dominant groups in the economic, social and political life of the country'.[53] They also note the problem of economic inequality between communities as a root cause of conflict; and instead they call for inclusive development.[54]

The Working Group would be a good arena in which to pursue the elaboration of policy recommendations and guidelines regarding the critical need for the respect of the ESCR of minorities. Such guidelines could then be elaborated through a Sub-Commission study and then passed on to the Commission on Human Rights to possibly consider creating a mandate to advance reporting on this issue.

Three-fold Consequences of the denial of ESCRs on minorities

Three dimensions can be highlighted in relation to the delineation of the particular burden imposed by the targeted, ongoing and severe denials of ESCR to minorities. Each of these will be examined in turn below.

(1)   The targeted denial of ESCRs against minorities

A typology of various kinds of discrimination may highlight a number of different factors, but it is clear that as far as tracing governmental responsibility is concerned: (i) direct discrimination which continues over a significant period, (ii) that is discriminatory in intent as well as in effect, (iii) that is institutional and institutionalised, and (iv)

---

52   As a result of ECOSOC resolution 1995/31 of 25 July 1995.
53   See United Nations, Sub-Commission on Promotion and Protection of Human Rights, Working Group on Minorities http://www.unhchr.ch/minorities/group.htm (accessed 12 May 2004).
54   Ibid.

active and systematic – is certainly of the gravest category. Such discrimination may be in a number of fields, including the political, cultural, social and socio-economic spheres. The focus of this chapter is the latter.

Makkonen recognises the negative consequences of discrimination in stating that 'Discrimination is a direct denial of the equal worth of the victim, and as such, acts of discrimination have a dual negative effect: the denial of a right, service or good that the person is entitled to, and the denial of the full and equal worth of that person. As such, it is a violation of a persons' identity.'[55] Here we recognise discrimination – or, in its more severe form, 'persecution' – as, in Makkonen's words, having a causal relationship with 'alienation, exclusion, radicalization, and decreasing psychological well-being'.[56]

(II) The cumulative impact of such denials

Having discussed the gravity of discrimination above, we are led to a question that receives surprisingly little attention in the human rights field. Does embedded and ongoing persecution create its own dynamics and difficulties? More crucially, does even an *unchanging* level of persecution create increasing suffering for its victims? And what impact does this have on the group as a whole when such persecution is targeted against minorities? It is suggested in this chapter that there is a particular edge to cumulative persecution, and this needs to be fully appreciated and addressed. This 'edge' is not only on the existing impact of such cumulative persecution, but even more on the effort required to eradicate the negative impact of such persecution.

The particularities of cumulative discrimination have recently been given recognition in the UN Committee on the Elimination of Racial Discrimination (CERD) on which Patrick serves with distinction. CERD's work on descent and the Roma. In their General Recommendation on descent, CERD recognises the need to 'eliminate the scourge of descent-based discrimination and empower communities affected by it'.[57] In remedying the consequences of this discrimination, a range of legislative and policy-oriented measures are proposed, including special measures in favour of those suffering from descent-based discrimination, creating specialised institutions to promote their equality and periodic surveys to assess their situation on the ground. The General Recommendation further recognises the very broad impact of such severe discrimination against a group – from segregation in all spheres of life to discrimination in marriage and inheritance, limitations in occupational choice and conditions, and subjection to lack of respect in human dignity and equality in all spheres.

---

55   T. Makkonen 'Main Causes, Forms and Consequences of Discrimination,' in *IOM Helsinki and The European Union Against Discrimination, Awareness Raising and Legal Training on Discrimination Practices*, 2002, http://www.iom.fi/anti-discrimination/pdf/CH%20I%202003%20FINAL. pdf (accessed 12 May 2004), p. 3.

56   Ibid.

57   CERD General Recommendation 19, Article 1, para. 1 of the Convention (Descent), 1 November 2002, on Article 1 para. 1, adopted at the 61st session.

In a further General Recommendation on the discrimination faced by the Roma,[58] CERD recognises that legislation alone is not enough in tackling the problem. Their rights in the fields of education and the media and their participation in public life need promotion. The wider discrimination also has to be tackled to allow their social integration, to guarantee them equality of opportunity and to encourage the reinforcement of their identity and culture.

Both these examples, of descent and the Roma, illustrate the tremendous longer-term difficulties in reversing the negative consequences of cumulative persecution against minority groups. It is therefore surprising that there is not much serious concern in human rights standards and mechanisms with trying to prevent the onset of such patterns of persecution against minorities.

(III) The Psychological Consequences

When the psychology of minorities is discussed, it is often in the context of the purpose they serve as scapegoats for the majority. But what about the psychology of the victimised minority group itself? According to Makkonen, 'Discrimination is about exclusion and subordination and it effectively conveys an explicit message of differentness and inferiority of the victim.'[59] He notes that experiences of discrimination have a direct bearing on psychological wellbeing, and such experiences have been found to increase symptoms related to anxiety and depression. Victims cope and respond to discrimination in a number of ways. All victims develop, whether consciously or subconsciously, a strategy of survival. These response strategies are of two types according to Makkonen[60] – denial and avoidance, or fighting back.

In the first category, victims may deny the discrimination by explaining discriminatory incidents and practices in terms other than discrimination. Victims may even come to believe that the discriminatory framework was legitimate, blaming themselves for what happened. They may also seek to avoid situations where there is a high probability of ending up being discriminated against. At the extreme, this strategy may involve self-denial, whereby a victim may seek to hide, soften up or even completely give up the discriminated aspect of his or her identity. The whole avoidance strategy goes some way towards fulfilling the aims of those that are upholding the discrimination – the exclusion of 'the different' from society is achieved and the disadvantages against the group are perpetuated.

In the second category, however, victims adopt an active strategy of fighting discrimination. They stand up for the rights and security of themselves as victims. This strategy is the most beneficial in the long-term, as it makes discrimination visible, provides a positive example to other victims and has emancipatory power. Very few minori-

---

58   CERD General Recommendation 27, Discrimination against Roma, 16 August 2000, adopted at the 57th session.
59   Makkonen (note 55) p. 14.
60   Ibid. p. 15.

ties that suffer targeted, severe and continual denials of ESCR retain the energy and resolve to maintain such a fight. Cohen discusses how denial can be a 'habitual coping strategy'.[61] He examines how intolerable facts and images shift from being disturbing to becoming normal and tolerable. Whilst his excellent study of denial and 'normalization and routinization' of the intolerable is focused on perpetrators of or bystanders in atrocities, it raises issues which are even more pertinent to victims themselves.

Further to this issue of the survival strategy adopted by the minority in response to discrimination, is the question of the impact of long-term discrimination in and of itself. The CERD General Recommendations on the Roma and descent go some way towards recognising this long-term impact, but mechanisms and procedures need to be set up to prevent, or at least to reduce, the expanding list of such entrenched cases of total diminishment of minority groups. Makkonen notes that discrimination often causes a chain reaction of disadvantages.[62] For example, being denied a job for discriminatory reasons may lead to poorer housing in perhaps a deprived area and hostile living environment, and this in turn can reduce the victim's ambitions and ability to be in the social environment where networks may lead to job opportunities. Therefore, disadvantages tend to reinforce each other and discrimination at one stage can have a profound impact on life opportunities as a whole.

When these processes of disadvantage take place for a long period of time and on a large scale, one enters a situation in which the negative attitudes towards a group and events of discrimination against the members of that group start to reinforce each other. Prejudices fuel discriminatory acts against the group, leading to social distance from that group, which in turn results in socio-economic distance – leading to a 'vicious circle of discrimination'.[63] The general public is often blind to the real causes of the socio-economic differences, so they begin to see these differences as a proof of inferiority or defect on the part of the victimised minority group.

Statistics bear witness to the impact of socio-economic distance and social exclusion from society at large. For example:

Ethnic minorities in the US are
– 3-5 times more likely to be homeless than the rest of the population;
– 2-3 times more likely to suffer from serious mental illnesses;
– 2-3 times more likely to suffer from alcohol or drug abuse.

The Native Americans
– Are one and a half times more likely to commit suicide;
– have over twice the possibility of exposure to violent crime.

Hispanic men in the US are
– 4 times more likely than white men to spend a period of their lives in prison.

---

61   S. Cohen *States of Denial, Knowing about Atrocities and Suffering* (Cambridge: Polity, 2001) p. 54.
62   Makkonen (note 55) p. 15.
63   Ibid.

Similar statistics hold for other countries and other minorities. Whereas not *all* the blame can be placed on the majority, clearly it is a dominant factor in the explanation of such figures.

The impact of long-term persecution on minorities as a whole is similarly grave. They may suffer, for example, from the breakdown of their culture, customs and self-esteem, leading to problems in relation to health, family breakdown, violence and possibly substance abuse and child abuse.

Numerous studies of Holocaust survivors show the residual effect of such persecution is retained through unresolved issues of mistrust, feelings of persecution, isolation and anxiety. Such research is indicative of the long-term consequences of psychological trauma resulting from periods of extreme persecution. For example, even many of those who experienced the Holocaust as children had adjustment problems as adults and suffer from the so called 'survival syndrome'. So persecution has long-lasting ramifications because of the *internalisation* of that persecution. Some research even questions the effects of this on the children of survivors.[64]

Stated simply, the record shows minorities succumbing to their diminished status and no longer really considering themselves as an integral or equal part of mainstream society.

The gravity of this fact comes into focus when one considers that it takes generations just to reverse purely the *economic* consequences of such entrenched discrimination. Freedom House has noted regarding the Copts in Egypt, for example, that prejudice, abuse and restrictions have created 'an atmosphere of persecution', raising the fear that 'during the 21st century the Copts may have a vastly diminished presence in their homeland'.[65] Freedom House also notes that thousands of Copts convert to Islam each year, many under pressure; and the Copts have an emigration rate 3 to 4 times that of Muslims, leading to estimates that over a million Copts have left Egypt in the past thirty years. They report that even economically-motivated emigration by some Copts 'is partially due to underlying religious concerns'.[66]

Because of the communal suffering, it is clear that redressing such human rights violations has to relate to the larger community where the violations have occurred. The whole community needs to recognise the harm and take a part in the offer of reparation for victims. Recovery from the inequality and persecution heaped upon minorities over long decades will likely need affirmative action in the immediate aftermath, special legislative and policy-oriented measures, and reparations.

---

64   On the question of the psychopathological behaviour of children from families with a history of political suppression and torture, see, for example: N. Bilanakis, E. Pappas and M. Dinou 'The impact of political suppression and torture on the second generation, A comparative study' 8.1 *Torture, Quarterly Journal on Rehabilitation of Torture Victims and Prevention of Torture* (July 1998).

65   Freedom House, Center for Religious Freedom *Egypt's Endangered Christians Report, Summary of Findings*, http://freedomhouse.org/religion/publications/endangered/ (accessed 12 May 2004).

66   Ibid.

Conclusion

In conclusion then, this chapter argues that the repercussions of targeted, ongoing and severe violations of ESCR focused on minorities needs particular attention because of its impact, the ease with which it becomes entrenched, and the difficulty in subsequently eradicating its corrosive influences. Furthermore, international attention to this matter has been notable in its absence. Existing standards and procedures seem inadequate in fully appreciating its various aspects and being able to deal with its human rights implications. In fact, the international community seems to become 'hardened' to such entrenched and habitual denials of the human rights of minorities; (and subsequently the international community comes to welcome relative improvements in such human rights rather than insisting on international standards).

Present provisions and practices are inadequate and insufficiently victim-centred to appreciate the devastating long-term consequences of such neglect.

This chapter has argued that the slow silencing of a minority group through the severe denial of ESCR is no less discriminatory or cruel than sudden and bloody episodes against them. It has suggested that even the standard 'course' of cumulative persecution has an increasingly negative impact on minority groups and that its effects are collective and apparently invisible to the international community, since the nature of such economic, social and cultural persecution seems to have made it too subtle for the mobilisation of the international community. This is of serious concern since it seems to indicate the 'satisfaction' of the international community with formal equality rather than actual equality.

It is time the international community responded to this void – through mobilisation, activism, normative developments and international action. It is not a new instrument that is being proposed by this author, but a greater appreciation of the dynamics of this suffering by existing mechanisms and procedures. The most suitable and amenable avenues for the pursuit of this matter would seem to be the following. Firstly, it is suggested that this matter be put to further consultation at the UN Working Group on Minorities. Subsequently, it is suggested that it be passed to the Sub-Commission for further study, and then submitted to the Commission on Human Rights for pursual through the adoption of a thematic mandate to examine and report on the matter to the international community. Within the Treaty-based bodies it is suggested that CERD adopt a broader General Recommendation addressing this matter and the Committee on ESCR explore it through a day of general discussion. Provision would have to be made in the draft Optional Protocol on the ICESCR to be able to heed the collective dimension of this burden on minorities. Last, but not least, mobilisation, studies and activism are necessary to facilitate the emergence of the above.

Chapter 12

Multiculturalism and Its Discontents

Dominic McGoldrick[1]

1. Introduction

This chapter examines the roles played by the concept of *multiculturalism* in human rights discourse. It considers how multiculturalism has been contested in theory, applied in practice and come under sustained challenge. The purposes of the chapter are to assess the concept of multiculturalism and to judge its value in human rights discourse. Part 2 addresses definitional issues. It also considers why multiculturalism has moved to the centre stage of political and legal agendas. Part 3 considers the factual premises of multiculturalism and the use of human rights discourse in responding to them. Part 4 explains how multiculturalism has been challenged in political and social theory and in practice. Part 5 gives a specific practical context to the discussion in terms of the dissolution of the leading Islamic political party in Turkey (*Refah Partisi*) and how the European Court of Human Rights assessed this. Finally, Part 6 concludes with some observations on the roles played by the concept of multiculturalism in human rights discourse.

The focus of the chapter is on multiculturalism in the public space and in immigrant states, particularly in Western Europe. Multiculturalism in Central and Eastern Europe arguably raises some different issues where national minorities have inhabited particular territories for long historical periods. European Union expansion in 2004 will likely raise many of the practical issues considered in this essay, as what have previously been foreign policy issues (minority rights) for the EU become internal issues (human rights).[2]

---

[1] Professor of Public International Law and Director of the International and European Law Unit, University of Liverpool. I am grateful to Gerard Delanty, Steve Wheatley and Kevin Boyle for their comments on a draft of this essay, and to Eric Donnelly for his research assistance. Responsibility for the views expressed is mine alone.

[2] F. Van Den Burghe, 'The EU and the Protection of Minorities: How Real is the Alleged Double Standard', 22 *Yearbook of European Law* (2003) p. 155. See also C. Wallace and J. Shaw, 'Education, Multiculturalism and the Charter of Fundamental Rights of the European Union' in T. Hervey and J. Kenner (eds.) *Economic and Social Rights under the EU Charter of Fundamental Rights – A Legal Perspective* (Oxford: Hart, 2003) p. 223.

Nazila Ghanea & Alexandra Xanthaki (eds.), Minorities, Peoples and Self-Determination, pp. 211-235.
© 2005 Koninklijke Brill NV. Printed in The Netherlands. ISBN 90 04 14301 7.

2. Multiculturalism

Like pretty much everything in our post-modern world, *multiculturalism* is a contested concept[3] with multiple meanings[4] at different societal levels.[5] The term multiculturalism has been widely used as a tool of analysis since the end of the 1960s. However, it is hard to define multiculturalism because cultural identity is itself a dynamic evolving organism that is often blurred with political identity and political ideology.[6] We may accept that many social and political communities have an imagined sense of community.[7] Many of them also have an imagined sense that they are multicultural. Even if a credible understanding of multiculturalism can be reached, considering it in human rights terms can be problematic. It is widely accepted that it there are severe difficulties in formulating cultural issues as human rights issues.[8]

Nonetheless, a series of events and issues have combined to put the concept of multiculturalism back at centre stage. These include the attacks on the United States on 9-11 and the measures taken in response by many states around the world. It has been alleged that many of these measures have disproportionately affected particular cultural groups and have weakened the degrees of respect and tolerance accorded to them by other groups.[9] Secondly, there is the issue of the rise of religious fundamentalism particularly when allied to political Islam. The war on terrorism and controlling extreme religious groups are daunting challenges that attract much political and legal attention. However, the real practice of multiculturalism is found in the way hundreds of aspects of daily life are resolved. Among the practical issues are the application of personal religious laws

---

3   See C.W. Watson *Multiculturalism* (Buckingham: Open University Press, 2000); M. Parris, 'Multiculturalism. A dangerous word...just like apartheid', *The Times*, 24 January 2004.

4   See G. Delanty *Community* (London: Routledge, 2003) pp. 92-110 which discusses ten main models of multiculturalism (monoculturalism, republican multiculturalism, pillarisation, liberal multiculturalism, communitarian multiculturalism, liberal communitarian multiculturalism, interculturalism, radical multiculturalism and transnational multiculturalism); G. Delanty, 'The Limits of Diversity: Community Beyond Unity and Difference', in F. Christiansen and U. Hedetoft, *The Politics of Multiple Belonging, Ethnicity and Nationalism in Europe and Asia* (Aldershot: Ashgate, 2004).

5   M. Wieviorka, 'Is Multiculturalism the Solution?', 21.5 *Ethnic and Racial Studies* (1998) pp. 881-910.

6   'Any attempt to talk about cultural issue in terms of rights may be slippery and difficult. Culture is not a static concept: cultures change all the time' L. Prott, 'Cultural Rights As Peoples Rights', in J. Crawford (ed.) *The Rights of Peoples* (Oxford: OUP, 1988) p. 95.

7   See B. Anderson *Imagined Communities: Reflections On The Origin And Spread Of Nationalism* (London: Verso, 1991, Rev. ed.).

8   Prott, (note 6) pp. 105-6.

9   For example, the arrest of thousands of Muslims in the US and elsewhere, the rise of far right parties in Western Europe accompanied by an increasing number of racist attacks.

concerning families, children and property,[10] the application of employment and health and safety law to religious groups, the dissolution of Islamic political parties (e.g., in Turkey), the regulation of Islamic clothing in the workplace or in educational facilities (e.g. the hijab (headscarf)/ jilbab debate in France, Germany,[11] the UK,[12] Turkey[13] and many other countries) and the control of burials (e.g., in Switzerland).[14]

3.   Multiculturalism and Human Rights

3.1   Multiculturalism in Context

The three basic factual premises for multiculturalism are clear. Firstly, in the twentieth century, many more states became permanently ethnically diverse because of territorial changes, population movements, immigration and refugee flows.[15] With over 120 million immigrants and over 20 million refugees, this necessarily made states more multicultural in a narrow statistical sense. More significantly though, there has been a 'politicisation of migration' in which multiculturalism has been deployed negatively. In this context, multiculturalism has been merely a tool for the management of cultural diversity. It has meant a minimalist recognition of a different 'other', but not an acceptance of it or respect for its different values. Secondly, the technological and information advances expressed in the concept of globalisation have made the interdependence and connections between states and their populations much closer.[16] As the world has gone 'glocal' identities are both local and global. One consequence of this has been that defi-

---

10   See the constitutional case law considered in F. Raday, 'Culture, Religion, and Gender', 1.4 *International Journal of Constitutional Law* (2003) pp. 663-715; *Ludin v. Baden Württemberg*, (September 2003) (State Parliaments could pass laws banning the headscarf). A number of them subsequently did so. In June 2004, the Federal Administrative Court upheld the action by one of the states.

11   D. Schiek, 'Just a Piece of Cloth? – German Courts and Employees with Headscarves', 33.1 *Industrial Law Journal* (2004) pp. 68-73.

12   *R. on the application of Shabina Begum (through her litigation friend Sherwas Rahman) v The Headteacher And Governors Of Denbigh High School*, [2004] EWHC 1389 (Admin), [2004] ELR (upholding a school's uniform policy that did not allow for the wearing of the jilbab (long cloak).

13   See the decision of the European Court of Human Rights, fourth Section, in *Leyla Sahin v. Turkey*, Judgment of 29 June 2004 (headscarf prohibition in University of Istanbul did not violate Article 9 ECHR).

14   R. Toivanen, 'Death, Ri(gh)tes, and Institutions in Immigrant Switzerland', in M. Scheinin and R. Toivanen (eds.) *Rethinking Non-Discrimination and Minority Rights* (Turku/ Abo: Institute for Human Rights, 2004) pp. 201-17.

15   J. MacLaughlin, 'Racism, Ethnicity and Multiculturalism in Contemporary Europe: A Review Essay', 17.8 *Political Geography* (1998) pp. 1013-24.

16   See P. Kivisto *Multiculturalism in a Global Society* (Oxford: Blackwell, 2002); UN Sub-Commission on the Promotion and Protection of Human Rights, E/CN.4/Sub.2/2003/14 *Globalization and its Impact on the Full Enjoyment of Human Rights*, Final Report (25 June 2003).

nitions or understandings of what constitute groups or cultures have been even more amorphous and contingent. The issue of what is deemed to constitute 'culture' in the first place obviously forms part of any credible debate on multiculturalism.[17]

Thirdly, there has been the rise of the political and legal status of minorities and indigenous peoples. A greater understanding of and respect for their distinctive cultures, and some measure of guilt at their treatment by dominant majorities, have accompanied this.[18] From this has flowed a more positive understanding of multiculturalism, which recognises a positive value in diversity, a meaningful acceptance of other cultures and respect for their values, traditions and deep moral differences.

3.2   Multiculturalism and International Human Rights Law

Throughout the twentieth century international human rights lawyers primarily responded to these changing factual premises by reference to the concept of minority rights.[19] States responded along a spectrum that is often categorised as running from integrationist, assimilationist, separatist, to paternalistic. For much of the period since 1945 the development of minority rights has been partly located in a discourse on self-determination – the rights of peoples – a group right *par excellence*.[20] However, many states reject the very idea of group rights in general and of self-determination for minorities in particular. They have followed an assimilationist policy because they feared that accommodating minority rights carried the risk that minority groups would proceed with claims to self-determination that, if realised, could entail the destruction of the state.[21] That context of discourse placed minorities in a negative and destabilising light. As the twentieth century drew to a close, the Organization for Security and Co-operation in Europe (OSCE) led the way in seeking to persuade states to view minorities in a much more positive light and to reflect on past injustices against them.[22] There has also

---

17   C. Taylor *Multiculturalism and the Politics of Recognition* (Princeton: Princeton University Press, 1992); M. Mayo *Cultures, Communities, Identities* (Basingstoke: Palgrave, 2000) pp. 1-35. 'Culture is a macroconcept because it is definitive of human society', Raday, (note 10).

18   See P. Thornberry *Indigenous Peoples and Human Rights* (Manchester: Manchester University Press, 2002); E.A. Povinelli *The Cunning of Recognition: Indigenous Alterities and the Making of Australian Multiculturalism* (Durham: Duke University Press, 2002); Prott, (note 6).

19   See P. Thornberry *International Law and the Rights of Minorities* (Oxford: Oxford University Press, 1991).

20   See M. Freeman, 'Past Wrongs and Liberal Justice' 5 *Ethical Theory and Practice* (2002) pp. 201-20.

21   See G. Welhengama *Minorities' Claims: From Autonomy to Secession* (Aldershot: Ashgate, 2000); P. Thornberry 'Self-Determination, Minorities, Human Rights: A Review of International Instruments' 38 *ICLQ* (1989) pp. 867-89.

22   D. McGoldrick, 'The Development of the Conference on Security and Co-operation in Europe after the 1992 Conference' 42 *ICLQ* (1993) pp. 411-33. The High Commissioner for National Minorities has acknowledged that there is a norm deficit when it comes to the practical application of minorities provisions in such spheres as elections, education, and

been a strong emphasis on rights of participation.[23] At the risk of oversimplification, the attractive orthodox position was reached that only 'peoples' had a right to self-determination and that minorities were not 'peoples' for this purpose, and therefore minorities did not have a right of self-determination.[24] What they did have were minority rights. These were principally articulated in Article 27 of the International Covenant on Civil and Political Rights (ICCPR) (1966), the United Nations Declaration on the Rights of Persons Belonging to National or Ethnic, Religious and Linguistic Minorities (1992) and the Council of Europe's Framework Convention for the Protection of National Minorities (1995).[25] Indigenous people(s) have pursued a strategy which sees them claiming minority rights but also additional rights as a 'peoples'.[26]

3.3   *Where Does Multiculturalism Fit Into This International Human Rights Landscape?*

Interestingly, the concept of *multiculturalism* is rarely discussed as such.[27] It does not appear as a term in the major international human rights instruments[28] or in academic human rights texts. It may be considered to be implicit in the right of everyone to take part in cultural life (Article 27 of the Universal Declaration of Human Rights (UDHR); Article 15(1) of the International Covenant on Economic, Social and Cultural Rights (ICESCR)),[29] or the right of ethnic, religious or linguistic minorities to enjoy their own culture (Article 27 ICCPR). There is also a discourse on cultural relativism. Although this can have implications for multiculturalism, it is primarily concerned with the valid-

---

language. For attempts to address the deficit see A. Eide, 'Cultural Rights and Minorities', in G. Alfredsson and M. Stavropoulou (eds) *Justice Pending: Indigenous Peoples and Other Good Causes* (The Hague: Nijhoff, 2002) pp. 83-97.

23   See M. Koenig 'Democratic Governance in Multicultural Societies: Social Conditions for the Implementation of International Human Rights Through Multicultural Policies' 2.11 *Management of Social Transformations*, Discussion Paper No. 30 (2003) <www.unesco/most/ln2pol2.htm>; S. Wheatley, 'Deliberative Democracy and Minorities', 14.3 *EJIL* (2003) pp. 507-27.

24   See C. Tomuschat (ed) *Modern Law Of Self-Determination* (Dordrecht: Nijhoff, 1993); Eide (note 22) at pp. 95-6. See the critique of K. Knop *Diversity and Self-Determination in International Law* (Cambridge: Cambridge University Press, 2002).

25   See P. Thornberry and M. Amor Estébanez *Minority Rights in Europe* (Strasbourg: Council of Europe, 2004).

26   See P. Thornberry *Indigenous Peoples and Human Rights* (Manchester: Manchester University Press, 2002).

27   Habermas identifies religious toleration as an early model of multiculturalism, see J. Habermas, 'Intolerance and Discrimination', 1.1(2) *International Journal of Constitutional Law* (2003) pp. 2-12.

28   The obvious explanation is that the term was not widely used before the late 1960s. The two international covenants on human rights were adopted in 1966.

29   See also Article 15(2) ICESCR referring to the diffusion of culture by states; Article 13(c) CEDAW and Article 31 CRC.

ity of the source of a moral rule or, in a weaker form, with interpreting human rights norms with sensitivity to the cultural specificities of a particular state.[30] Its focus is more on culture as distinct from multiculturalism.[31] In some instances the cultural relativist approach might mean interpreting texts in a less multiculturalist way.

The term 'multiculturalism' does appear in some UNESCO texts on culture.[32] UNESCO's approach to culture has been the subject of a powerful critique by Thomas Eriksen.[33] He argued that using the general concept of culture tends to obscure rather than to clarify:

> Since the concept of culture has become so multifarious as to obscure rather than clarify understandings of the social world, it may now perhaps be allowed to return to the culture pages of the broadsheets, to the world of Bildung. Instead of invoking culture, if one talks about say, local arts, one could simply say local arts; if one means language, ideology, patriarchy, children's rights, food habits, ritual practices or local political structures, one could use those or equivalent terms instead of covering them up in the deceptively cozy blanket of culture. In a continuous world, as Ingold puts it … "the concept of culture … will have to go".
>
> To be more specific:
>
> (i)   What are spoken of as cultural rights in *Our Creative Diversity*, whatever they may be, ought to be seen as individual rights. It is as an individual I have the right to go to the church/mosque/synagogue or not, speak my mother-tongue or another language of my choice, relish the cultural heritage of my country or prefer Pan-Germanism, French Enlightenment philosophy or whatever. As an individual I have the right to attach myself to a tradition and the freedom to choose not to.
>
> (ii)   There is no need for a concept of culture in order to respect local conditions in development work: it is sufficient to be sensitive to the fact that local realities are always locally constructed, whether one works in inner-city Chicago or in the Kenyan countryside. One cannot meaningfully rank one locality as more authentic than another. What is at stake in development work is not cultural authenticity or purity, but people's ability to gain control over their own lives.

---

30   See A.D. Renteln *International Human Rights: Universalism Versus Relativism* (Newbury Park Calif.: Sage, 1990); S. Harris-Short 'International Human Rights Law: Imperialist, Inept and Ineffective? Cultural Relativism and the UN Convention on the Rights of the Child', 25 *HRQ* (2003) pp. 130-81.

31   See A.A. An-Naim (ed) *Human Rights in Cross-Cultural Perspectives – A Quest for Concensus* (Philadelphia: Philadelphia University Press, 1992).

32   See *World Commission on Culture and Development – Our Creative Diversity* (Paris: World Commission on Culture and Diversity, 1995); UNESCO Universal Declaration on Cultural Diversity (2 November 2001).

33   See T.H. Eriksson 'Between Universalism, and Relativism: A Critique of the UNESCO Concepts of Culture?', in J. Cowan et al *Culture and Rights: Anthropological Perspectives* (Cambridge: Cambridge University Press, 2001) pp. 127-48.

(iii) Finally, it is perfectly possible to support local arts, rural newspapers and the preservation of historical buildings without using mystifying language about "a people's culture". Accuracy would be gained, and unintended side-effects would be avoided, if such precise terms replaced the all-encompassing culture concept. The insistence on respect for local circumstances, incidentally, would alleviate any suspicion of crude Enlightenment imperialism à la Finkielkraut. And naturally, Radovan Karadzic and Jean-Marie Le Pen would not be pleased with such a level of precision.

If the mystifying and ideologically charged culture concept can be discarded, the case for a global ethics also seems stronger.[34]

3.4 *The circumstances of multiculturalism*

For most states in the world, multiculturalism is a statistical fact, even if they deny the legal existence of minorities.[35] This factual multiculturalism – what Paul Kelly has described as the 'circumstances of multiculturalism'[36] – presents many social and political challenges for states. States and communities may 'imagine' their communitarian basis and national identity but these imagined communities are a social reality for their dominant majority populations or their powerful political groupings. Their imagined communities can appear threatened by multiculturalism.

Human rights norms have played an important part in providing states with a framework to meet the challenges of multiculturalism. Most human rights apply to everyone and so rights to freedom of expression, association, assembly, religion, property, education, use of language and, perhaps most significantly, the right to equality and the right not to be discriminated against,[37] all have a role in ensuring multiculturalism and accommodating diversity.[38] Cultural rights are often grounded in arguments

---

34   Ibid.
35   For example, as does France. See UN Doc. CCPR/C/79/Add.80, HRC's Concluding Observations on France, para. 24 (4 August 1997).
36   P. Kelly 'Introduction: Between Culture and Equality' in P. Kelly (ed.) *Multiculturalism Reconsidered* (Cambridge: Polity, 2002) p. 3.
37   See Scheinin and Toivanen, (note 14); A. McColgan, 'Principles of Equality and Protection From Discrimination in International Human Rights Law' 7 *EHRLR* (2002) p. 24.
38   See P. Jones, 'Human Rights and Diverse Cultures: Continuity or Discontinuity?' in S. Caney and P. Jones (eds) *Human Rights and Global Diversity* (Ilford: Cass, 2001) ('The rights commonly claimed for human beings would include rights to express and to pursue … differences … it is not human diversity in general that is troublesome for a theory of human rights. The troubles are caused by a particular type of diversity: diversity of belief and value', pp. 27-28). Cf. C. Kukathas, 'Are There Any Cultural Rights' 20 *Political Theory* (1992) pp. 105-39, which stresses the liberty to exit a group.

based on dignity or autonomy.[39] Often the multiculturalism aspect of a human rights discourse is subliminal or taken for granted. For example, for the European Court of Human Rights, a 'democratic society' for the purposes of the European Convention on Human Rights is characterised by 'pluralism, tolerance, and broadmindedness'. These same essential characteristics are exhibited by states that claim to be multiculturalist. Alexandra Xanthaki has argued that:

> Multiculturalism can only exist in a pluralist society, where an array of choices and opportunities would maintain a marketplace of goods, ideas, cultural and political options. In this context, individuals that are not hopelessly dependent on specific cultural attachments will be able to make their own choices.[40]

In addition, the specific rights of minorities and indigenous peoples (and some claimed group rights) are directed to recognising and ensuring the continuing existence of their distinctive cultural identity and their own contribution into aspects of the majoritarian culture.[41]

The above account of multiculturalism is over-simplified but largely orthodox. It might also be suggested that international human rights lawyers have largely taken multiculturalism as a given social reality and, by and large, assumed that it was an inherently positive concept, a 'human good'. The more 'multicultural' a state's policies, the more likely it was to respect the human rights of more of its population. Indeed, a small number of states have specific reference to multiculturalism in their Constitutions or constitutional documents. For example, Article 27 of the Canadian Charter of Rights and Freedoms (1982) states that, 'This Charter shall be interpreted in a manner consistent with the preservation and enhancement of the multicultural heritage of Canadians'. Other states stress the importance of the participation in cultural life. For example, Section 30 of the South African Constitution (1996) states that, 'Everyone has the right to use the language and to participate in the cultural life of their choice, but no one exercising these rights may do so in a manner inconsistent with any provision of the Bill of Rights'. Since 1986 a number of Latin American Constitutions or amendments have referred to the multi-ethnic or pluricultural nature of their societies.[42]

---

39   See E.R. Gill, 'Autonomy, Diversity and the Right to Culture', in B. M. Leiser and T. D. Campbell (eds.) *Human Rights in Philosophy and Practice* (Aldershot: Ashgate, 2001) pp. 282-302 ('Cultural membership as an expression of autonomy implies the presence of critical reflection', p. 298).

40   A. Xanthaki 'Collective Rights: The Case of Indigenous Peoples', in B. M. Leiser and T. D. Campbell (eds.) *Human Rights in Philosophy and Practice* (Aldershot: Dartmouth, 2001) p. 311.

41   See Eide (note 22).

42   R. Sieder 'Introduction' to R. Sieder (ed.) *Multiculturalism in Latin America* (Basingstoke: Macmillan, 2002) p. 4.

4. Challenges to Multiculturalism

4.1 Theoretical Challenges

At the turn of the new millennium it was relatively safe to state that multiculturalism has become the dominant discourse, particularly as part of liberal and communitarian theory. However, it has been increasingly contested. The fundamental challenge for the theory has been the issue of supporting illiberal cultures, particularly those that do not have at least a formal premise of gender equality.[43] One of the most influential contributors, Will Kymlicka, has argued that the politics of difference have to be contained within a model of liberal justice.[44] He has developed a liberal theory of limited group rights (accompanied by a right of exit).[45] Kymlicka's approach has been criticised as too tied to liberal Western values and insufficiently sensitive to cultural differences, an inadequate starting point for safeguarding communal goods and justifying collective rights.[46]

There have been an increasing number of challenges by political philosophers to the orthodox positive assessment of multiculturalism.[47] Communitarians challenge the narrowness, individualism and atomistic nature of liberalism. They give primacy to the community and stress the place of an individual in a social context. The (purer) communitarians have challenged the defensiveness of liberal multiculturalism. They have argued for a more positive multiculturalism that gives greater recognition for communities in general, and for group rights in particular, as instruments for the protection of communities. Bhikhu Parekh considers that liberalism alone is an inadequate as a basis for multiculturalism.[48] He has argued for the public recognition of cultural minorities. He sees culture as constitutive of individual choice. Culture cannot be viewed in the context of choice alone. Cultural membership is not an optional extra. Communitarian multiculturalists would argue that cultural membership must be recognised as a basis for legitimate differentiation. States would be required to allow minority groups to opt out of general laws, including constitutional guarantees of equality and fundamental rights.

---

43   See J. Rawls *The Rights of Peoples, with, The Idea Of Public Reason Revisited* (Cambridge, Mass: Harvard University Press, 1999); A.A. An-Naim 'Towards a Cross-Cultural Approach to Defining International Standards of Human Rights: The Meaning of Cruel, Inhuman, or Degrading Treatment or Punishment', in An-Naim, (note 31) pp. 19-43.

44   W. Kymlicka *Liberalism, Community and Culture* (Oxford: OUP, 1989).

45   W. Kymlicka *Multicultural Citizenship: A Liberal Theory of Minority Rights* (Oxford: OUP, 1995). See also M. McDonald 'Should Communities Have Rights? Reflections on Liberal Individualism', in An-Naim, (note 31) pp. 133-61.

46   See M. Malik 'Communal Goods as Human Rights' in C. Gearty and A. Tomkins *Understanding Rights* (London: Mansell, 1996).

47   See Freeman (note 20).

48   B. Parekh *Rethinking Multiculturalism: Cultural Diversity And Political Theory* (Basingstoke: Macmillan, 2000).

Multiculturalism has been attacked from all sides of the political spectrum. Feminist writers have starkly asked if *Multiculturalism is 'Bad For Women?'*[49] They have argued that a multicultural ideology has been oppressive on struggles for equality in spheres such as gender, race, ethnicity and sexuality.[50] In 1998, Yasmin Alibhai-Brown argued for a need to move beyond multiculturalism.[51] In 2004, Trevor Phillips, the Chairman of the United Kingdom's Race Relations Commission caused controversy by suggesting that the UK abandon its policy multiculturalism completely. He submitted that everyone, including migrants and asylum seekers, should be encouraged to embrace English culture and history as their own.[52]

The liberal case against multiculturalism has been strongly re-stated by Brian Barry in *Culture and Equality: An Egalitarian Critique of Multiculturalism.*[53] He defended a liberal-democratic conception of justice that was blind to cultural differences. He criticised the toleration of injustice in the name of multiculturalism. He argued that culture and equality are fundamentally incompatible commitments and that the turn to multiculturalism was ultimately a 'dead end'. The preoccupation with culture was a distraction from unequal treatment, discrimination and injustice. Barry's thesis has attracted a sustained response from the defenders of multiculturalism.[54] However, it has highlighted the essential issue on which many multicultural disputes turn: *is equality to be given a higher normative value than culture?* For Frances Raday, 'the cultural relativism implicit in normative communitarianism must displace the value of gender equality as, by definition, traditionalist cultures and religions, in which gender equality is not an accepted norm, are in no way inferior to those social systems in which it is'.[55] Gerard Delanty has similarly argued that: 'Ultimately liberal democracy and multiculturalism are not compatible, since the former is based on equality and the latter on diversity'.[56]

49   See S.M. Okin (ed.) *Is Multiculturalism Bad For Women?* (Princeton NJ: Princeton Univ. Press, 1999). See also S. Mullaly 'Feminism and Multicultural Dilemmas in India: Revisiting the Shah Bano Case' 24 *OJLS* (2004) *forthcoming;* L. Volp 'Feminism Versus Multiculturalism' 101 *Columbia Law Review* (2001) pp. 1181-1218; A. Schachar *Multicultural Jurisdiction: Cultural Differences and Women's Rights* (Cambridge: CUP, 2001).

50   'Multiculturalism not only exacerbates and legitimises the oppression of already oppressed minority groups, but poses threats to liberal democracy and individual human rights', C. Beckett and M. Macey 'Race, Gender and Sexuality: The Oppression of Multiculturalism', 24.3/4 *Women's Studies International Forum* (2001) pp. 309-19.

51   *After Multiculturalism* (Foreign Policy Centre, 1998) <www.fpc.org.uk>

52   'Debate call on "multicultural" UK', BBC News <http://newsearch.bbc.co.uk/1/hi/uk_politics/3599925.stm>

53   (Cambridge, Mass: Harvard University Press, 2002).

54   See Kelly (note 36) which includes a reply by Barry to his critics, pp. 204-38.

55   Raday (note 10).

56   Delanty *Community* (note 4) p. 99.

4.2   Racism and Identity

While multiculturalism emerged in the 1960s and 1970s as a technique for managing the cultural diversity that necessarily resulted from immigration, the subsequent focus in the 1980s and 1990s has became more firmly fixed on race.[57] In the 1990s and the first years of the new century, particularly after 9-11, there has been an increased consciousness of managing religious diversity, particularly its fundamentalist aspects.[58] Claims by Islamic groups to have their practices accepted and respected have become more widespread and have been accompanied by stronger Islamic political organisations in many states. Some have argued for a post-multiculturalist approach that stresses a politics of recognition of cultural difference. Difference and diversity become values in themselves that should be sought and preserved.[59] This stress on recognising and maintaining difference has in turn invited accusations of racism.[60] Minette Marrin has argued that: 'Multiculturalism actually promotes racism. It engenders confusion, resentment and bullying; it encourages division and prevents people developing a shared British identity. This idea should have been dumped long since.'[61]

Multiculturalism is increasingly presented as either dated[62] or as having gone too far in pursuit of its own ideology.[63] Some of the policies adopted in the UK in the name of multiculturalism have been ridiculed. Minette Marrin cites the toleration of racially inflammatory speech by Abu Hamza, a proposal by education authorities in Manchester to set up a school in Bangladesh for British-born Bengali children who missed school when their parents took them to Bangladesh to learn about their heritage and culture and a proposal by Tower Hamlets council to build an old people's block just for Asians.[64]

---

57   This has been the case notwithstanding that the concept of 'race' having any scientific meaning has itself greatly been undermined.

58   C.W. Howland 'The Challenge of Religious Fundamentalism to the Liberty and Equality of Women: An Analysis under the United Nations Charter', 35.2 *Columbia J. of Transnational Law* (1997) pp. 272-377.

59   Cf. K. Mitchell 'Educating the National Citizen in Neoliberal Times: from the Multicultural Self to the Strategic Cosmopolitan' *Trans. Inst. British Geography* (2003) pp. 377-403. This article discusses the strategic use of diversity for competitive advantage in the global marketplace.

60   'Many critics…believe that radical multiculturalsim is racist in conception since its key element is the proposition of essential difference (exactly in contradiction with human rights philosophy which posits sameness or equality)', Delanty *Community* (note 4) p. 105.

61   *'View From The Right'*: Special Report: Race Issues In The UK, *The Guardian*, 29 May 2001.

62   See M. Wieviorka 'Is Multiculturalism the Solution?' 21.5 *Ethnic and Racial Studies* (1998) p. 907; M. Martiniello 'Wievorka's View on Multiculturalism: A Critique' Ibid. pp. 911-16.

63   See T. Makkonen 'Is Multiculturalism Bad for the Fight Against Discrimination' in Scheinin and Toivanen (note 14) pp. 155-77.

64   M. Marrin 'Britain's New Apartheid Makes Strangers of Us All' *Sunday Times*, 9 May 2004, p. 17.

4.3   The Discomfort of Strangers

In 2004, an article by David Goodhart entitled the 'Discomfort of Strangers' sparked an intense debate on multiculturalism.[65] He posed the question of whether Britain was becoming too diverse to sustain the mutual obligations behind a good society and the welfare state. The logic of solidarity, with its tendency to draw boundaries, and the logic of diversity, with its tendency to cross them, at times pulled apart:

> Thanks to the erosion of collective norms and identities, in particular of class and nation, and the recent surge of immigration into Europe, this may be such a time... When solidarity and diversity pull against each other, which side should public policy favour? Diversity can increasingly look after itself – the underlying drift of social and economic development favours it. Solidarity, on the other hand, thrives at times of adversity, hence its high point just after the second world war and its steady decline ever since as affluence, mobility, value diversity and (in some areas) immigration have loosened the ties of a common culture. Public policy should therefore tend to favour solidarity in four broad areas.
>
> **Immigration and asylum...** In return for learning the language, getting a job and paying taxes, and abiding by the laws and norms of the host society, immigrants must be given a stake in the system and incentives to become good citizens... Immigrants from the same place are bound to want to congregate together but policy should try to prevent that consolidating into segregation across all the main areas of life: residence, school, workplace, church. In any case, the laissez-faire approach of the postwar period in which ethnic minority citizens were not encouraged to join the common culture (although many did) should be buried. Citizenship ceremonies, language lessons and the mentoring of new citizens should help to create a British version of the old US melting pot. This third way on identity can be distinguished from the coercive assimilationism of the nationalist right, which rejects any element of foreign culture, and from multiculturalism, which rejects a common culture.
>
> **Welfare policy:** A generous welfare state is not compatible with open borders and possibly not even with US-style mass immigration. Europe is not America...welfare should become more overtly conditional. The rules must be transparent and blind to ethnicity, religion, sexuality and so on, but not blind to behaviour. People who consistently break the rules of civilised behaviour should not receive unconditional benefits.
>
> **Culture:**...The teaching of British history, and in particular the history of the empire and of subsequent immigration into Britain, should be a central part of the school curriculum. At the same time, immigrants should be encouraged to become part

---

65   D. Goodhart 'Too Diverse' *Prospect Magazine* (February, 2004), reprinted in 'Discomfort of Strangers' *The Guardian*, 27 February 2004. See also his reaction to the responses to his article 'Diversity Divide' *Prospect Magazine*, April 2004.

of the British "we," even while bringing their own very different perspective on its formation.

Politics and Language: since the arrival of immigrant groups from non-liberal or illiberal cultures it has become clear that to remain liberal the state may have to prescribe a clearer hierarchy of values. The US has tried to resolve the tension between liberalism and pluralism by developing a powerful national myth. Even if this were desirable in Britain, it is probably not possible to emulate. Indeed, the idea of fostering a common culture, in any strong sense, may no longer be possible either. One only has to try listing what the elements of a common culture might be to realise how hard it would be to legislate for. That does not mean that the idea must be abandoned; rather, it should inform public policy as an underlying assumption rather than a set of policies.

Too often the language of liberal universalism that dominates public debate ignores the real affinities of place and people. These affinities are not obstacles to be overcome on the road to the good society; they are one of its foundation stones. People will always favour their own families and communities; it is the task of a realistic liberalism to strive for a definition of community that is wide enough to include people from many different backgrounds, without being so wide as to become meaningless.

The ensuing debate illustrated many of the arguments deployed in the multiculturalism debate. Some of the responses are described Goodhart as racist and xenophobic. However, most accepted that he had raised fundamental questions about commitment to a state and its common values and that those questions needed answering.[66] For Keith Banting and Will Kymlicka the relationship between diversity and redistribution was highly contingent on factors other than multiculturalism.[67] Some of the countries with the most pro-active multiculturalism policies, like Australia and Canada, had adopted very pro-active citizenship promotion and language training policies. For John Denham, diversity was a challenge to solidarity, but there was, 'nothing inevitable or mechanical that links the scale of diversity with the weakness of solidarity'.[68] Trevor Phillips cited the UK's National Health Service as a world-beating example of the way that ethnic diversity can create social solidarity.[69] There is also the economic argument that the UK needs more immigrants to keep pace with its booming economy and to boost its ageing workforce.[70] Saskia Sasseen has noted that solidarity can evolve quickly:

---

66   See the series of replies from seventeen specialists at http://www.prospect-magazine.co.uk/HtmlPages/replies.asp (accessed 9 August 2004); T. Phillips, 'Genteel Xenophobia Is As Bad As Any Other Kind: Some Liberals Have Given Up On The Idea Of A Multi-Ethnic Britain' *The Guardian*, 16 February 2004; Editorial, 'Celebrating Diversity', *The Guardian*, 24 February 2004, p. 27 (submitting that Goodhart's arguments are flawed).

67   K. Banting and W. Kymlika 'The worrying American model' http://www.prospect-magazine.co.uk/HtmlPages/replies.asp (note 66).

68   J. Denham '21st-century Britishness' Ibid. Similarly B. Parekh 'What are civilised rules?' Ibid.

69   T. Phillips (note 66).

70   D. Coyle 'More Diversity of Economy' (ibid.).

[H]istorical demography shows us that all our European societies have over time incorporated many if not all the major foreign immigrant groups and, further, that it has often taken no more than a couple of generations to turn them into the we – the community that can experience solidarity in Goodhart's analysis. One third of the French population is second or third generation foreign ancestry; for Vienna's Austrians it is 40 per cent.[71]

For Sarah Spencer: 'There is no reason to think, however, that the vast majority of immigrants and second-generation ethnic minorities are any more unwilling to pay taxes, to vote or contribute economically and socially than anyone else.'[72]

She was the only one of the commentators to make reference to international human rights as a minimum standard against which to assess cultures:

Goodhart rightly suggests that social cohesion requires a level of common values, but that it is difficult to agree what these might be. Yet there is one code of ethics which does have a legitimacy beyond that produced by any single government, to which we can all be expected to adhere regardless of background or faith: international human rights standards. Here we have minimum, agreed standards on the treatment of others which outlaw extreme practices. But we also have a mechanism for balancing the rights of one person, say to freedom of speech, against another, to freedom from incitement to racial hatred. In most cases (excluding torture for instance), human rights standards are not absolute but can be limited by the state, where necessary and proportional, to protect the rights of others. In teaching respect for the human rights of others we thus have a valuable tool for promoting cohesion. In its recent decision to include human rights within the remit of the proposed Commission on Equality and Human Rights, the government recognised the importance of that dimension.
Goodhart questions whether there is a contradiction between universal human rights standards and the exclusivity of citizenship. Not so. Human rights standards set only minimum requirements of protection, and responsibilities towards others, which apply to all. Beyond that minimum, citizenship can accord additional rights and responsibilities to those for whom, residing in the longer term, that deeper level of mutual commitment is appropriate.[73]

Some commentators were supportive of Goodhart's approach or at least of his understanding of the challenge. Bob Rowthorn commented that:

By the middle of the century they will imply the addition of 11.5m foreigners to the population of this country and a net loss of 4.3m British citizens. These numbers represent a huge cumulative transformation. They also understate the scale of change

71   S. Sassen 'Diversity Consumers', (ibid.)
72   S. Spencer '"In" Groups and "Out" Groups', (ibid.).
73   Ibid.

since the immigrants are on average young and many of them come from cultures where fertility is high. If we take into account both the number of immigrants and their higher than average fertility, the transformation of our society implied by present rates of migration is truly dramatic…To admit many millions of immigrants over the course of a few decades is a huge and irreversible social experiment. If it turns out to be wrong then we will be stuck with the consequences. This is not an argument for opposing all immigration, but it is an argument for proceeding cautiously.[74]

Amitai Etzioni stated that:

> Immigrants who wish to become members of our national communities (or the EU, for that matter) must accept certain basics. These include respect for human rights, the democratic form of government, the law, as well as a command of the prevailing language(s) and an acceptance of both the glory and the burdens of our national histories.[75]

Many of the commentators noted the need for shared or common values: 'Shared values and common identities can only emerge through a process of political dialogue and struggle, a process whereby different values are put to the test, and a collective language of citizenship emerges.'[76]

> … it is not entirely clear to me how Goodhart proposes to integrate immigrants and generate a sense of solidarity. Citizenship ceremonies and so on, are fine, but largely symbolic. I do not know what "adopting" British history means, especially for Britain's ex-colonial subjects and their offspring. As for common culture, Goodhart recognises the obvious difficulty of specifying its contents and enforcing them. Common values are more promising, but they can only be public and political in nature. He surely does not want all Britons to share the same set of personal ideals and visions of the good life. An ominous note is stuck when he says that those violating "the rules of civilised behaviour" should be denied the unconditional benefits accruing from citizenship. What are these rules? The most important of them are embodied in laws, which we should obviously require immigrants to observe. Difficulties arise when we go beyond them. Who is to lay down these rules, and what do they exclude? Football hooliganism and racist attacks obviously. But what about corporate fraud? Evasion of taxes? Media lies and demonisation of asylum seekers which poison the wellsprings of civility?[77]

Other commentators stressed the importance of dialogue:

---

74   B. Rawthorn 'The impact of immigration' (ibid.).
75   A. Etzioni 'Diversity within unity', (ibid.).
76   K. Malik 'Diversity of people or values?' (ibid.).
77   B. Parekh 'What are civilised rules?' (ibid.).

we should recognise the value of keeping the conversation about who "we" are open and negotiable. This in turn requires that we should recognise all the participants in this dialogue as possessing equal value, both those of us who have been here for many generations, and those of us newly arrived. It places responsibility on those that are "in" to recognise that they have no special privilege to Britishness based merely on longevity, but it also requires those who arrive into the conversation to identify, to an extent, with the narratives that have emerged out of a history that cannot be wished away.[78]

4.4 The Application of Multiculturalism: Some Recent Controversies

Practical challenges to multiculturalism in the UK have been replicated in many European states. In France in 2003-4, an intense national debate was triggered by a prohibition on schoolchildren wearing an Islamic headscarf (hijab) in state schools. In the Netherlands a Parliamentary inquiry was ordered into the perceived failures of its multicultural policies and an extreme asylum policy was adopted involving the proposed deportation of large numbers of illegal immigrants. The UK also had a number of high profile cases concerning the wearing of Islamic uniforms in school which gave rise to public debate.[79] In *R on the application of Shabina Begum (through her litigation friend Sherwas Rahman) v The Headteacher And Governors Of Denbigh High School* the Administrative Court upheld the legality of the schools not allowing B to wear a jilbab, a full length cloak, which she claimed was required of her under Islamic law.[80] Although the applicant lost the case, the facts illustrated the lengths to which some schools and local education authorities had gone in pursuit of multiculturalism. The contrast with the French ban in 2004 is still striking. The post 9-11 period has also seen allegations of a greater degree of Islamophobia in the UK[81] and recommendations for the UK state education system which is failing to meet the needs of Muslim parents and pupils.[82] In response to practical challenges like these, many states that advocated a multiculturalist ideology, such as Sweden, have become much more pragmatic and less ideological.[83]

---

78   A. Mondal 'New National Myths' (ibid.).

79   See T. Halpin 'Ban on Islamic dress "violated pupil's rights"' *The Times*, 28 May 2004; Debate in *The Times* 1 and 5 June 2004.

80   *Begum Case* (note 12).

81   See Commission on British Muslims and Islamophobia *Islamophobia: Issues Challenges And Action* (Stoke: Trentham Books, 2004); M. Marrin 'Islamophobia: the Making of a Nasty British Myth' *Sunday Times*, 6 June 2004, p. 21.

82   See *Muslims on Education* (Association of Muslim Social Scientists, FED 2000, the Muslim College UK and the Forum Against Islamaphobia and Racism, June 2004); L. Ward 'State Schools "Must Do Better" for Muslims' *The Guardian*, 8 June 2004. There are an estimated one and half million Muslims in the UK.

83   M. Scheinin 'How to Resolve Conflicts Between Collective and Individual Rights', in Scheinin and Toivanen (note 14) pp. 219-38.

4.5 *Beyond Multiculturalism*

In a European context, Gerard Delanty has advocated the need to move to a new model for pursuing social equality or for addressing justice for individuals:

> Multiculturalism emerged in the context of societies that did not experience major questioning of their national identities. In its inception, in the post-second world war period in Europe (earlier in the case of the United States) it was formed out of societies that had to integrate, manage or accommodate exiles, immigrants, indigenous populations and other dislocated people who could be conveniently designated by groups; in a related sense, it also designated anti-racism and, in later practices, citizenship. Multiculturalism was a model of management rather rather than of genuine integration. Western multiculturalism, particularly in Western Europe, was always based on the assumption of liberal tolerance rather than of participation in citizenship. It was constructed on the assumption that there was a dominant cultural identity in the society to which ethnic groups had to adjust but to whom certain concessions could be made. It was never intended as a model for pursuing social equality or for addressing justice for individuals. Today it is a different matter: diversity has penetrated the cultural identity as a whole. Moreover, questions of tolerance have to be reconciled to problems of protecting individuals. Ironically, while there are more and more demands for group differences, it is more and more difficult to define exactly what constitutes a group.[84]

5. Islamic Fundamentalism

5.1 *Assessing Islamic Fundamentalism*

It is important to take a balanced and realistic view of Islamic fundamentalism. There has been a worldwide 'Islamic resurgence'.[85] However, the forces of Islam cannot be homogenised.[86] The term 'Muslim fundamentalist' is widely used but it is often imprecise and misleading. There are millions of devout Muslims around the world who reject the values and the actions of the terrorists who purport to act in the name of their religion. They reject the 'politics of slaughter' from which Al Qaeda emerged.[87] They

---

84   Delanty (note 4).

85   The expression is that of S.P. Huntingdon *The Clash of Civilisations and the Remaking of World Order* (New York: Simon and Schuster, 1996) pp. 109-20. See also P. Berman *Terror and Liberalism* (London: Norton, 2003) pp. 58-76 on the Islamists Movement since the 1930s.

86   See T. Ali *The Clash of Fundamentalisms – Crusades, Jihads and Modernity* (London: Verso, 2002).

87   The expression is that of P. Berman (note 85) pp. 103-20.

maintain their religious beliefs while positively contributing to multicultural and democratic societies.[88] Indeed, the majority of the worlds' Muslims live in democracies.[89] The number of Muslims is growing. Samuel Huntingdon cited a demographic estimate that in 2025, 30% of the world's population will be Muslim.[90]

It is unarguable that the interpretation and application of Islamic principles represents an important challenge for many cultures. For example, it creates difficulties for the idea of a universal human rights law. Major issues have concerned the status of women and unbelievers, family rights and duties, religious rights and criminal punishments.[91] Ideas of privacy do not fit well with a Muslim belief system, which embraces all aspects of life with no public/ private distinction.[92] The liberal idea of church/ state separation is anathema.[93] Nonetheless, Islamic beliefs are probably better understood than at any time in history. The clash of civilisations is not really new. There has long been a struggle between Christianity and the Islamic empire.[94] It was often a military struggle but it has always been a struggle over ideas and values. Such struggles are normal, even healthy. Moreover, some scholars have argued that the theoretical challenges for example to universal human rights law often turn out to be much reduced in practice.[95] In that practice, there is an enormous variety in the interpretation of Islamic law. It is not at all unusual for one Islamic state to deny the validity of the interpretations of another, for example, on criminal punishment such as amputation of limbs and stoning.

Equally, it must be admitted that there can be some severe tensions between Islamic beliefs and the organisation of modern democratic states. These were graphically illustrated by the decision of the Grand Chamber of the European Court of Human Rights in the *Refah Partisi* case against Turkey, in February 2003.

---

88   See 'Tough on Terror – Muslim Leaders Have A Duty To Condemn Extremism', *The Times*, 3 December 2003.

89   Comments of James Woolsey, former CIA Director *Prospect Magazine*, September 2003.

90   S.P. Huntingdon (note 85) p.117. Interestingly, in the US the number of converts to the Islamic faith has risen since '9-11'.

91   'The emancipation of women, more than any other single issue, is the touchstone of the difference between modernisation and Westernization', B. Lewis *What Went Wrong? – Western Impact and the Middle East Response* (London: Weidenfeld and Nicolson, 2002) p.181. Kuwait was 'liberated' in 1991 but women still do not have the vote there.

92   Berman (note 85) p. 66 on the 'notion of Islam as totality'. Many other faiths have a religious code which seeks to govern private as well as public conduct.

93   Ibid. p. 90.

94   I use 'empire' in the limited sense of wide and disparate geographical location.

95   See M. Baderin 'A Macroscopic Analysis of the Practice of Muslim State Parties to International Human Rights Treaties: Conflict or Congruence' 1 *Nottingham Human Rights Law Journal* (2001) p. 265; M. Baderin *International Human Rights and Islamic Law* (Oxford: OUP, 2003).

5.2 The Refah Partisi Case: The Position Under Turkish Law

Under Article 2 of the Turkish Constitution the Republic of Turkey is, 'a democratic, secular and social State ...' In *Refah Partisi (The Welfare Party) And Others v Turkey*,[96] the case was brought by a Turkish political party, Refah Partisi (hereinafter 'Refah') and three Turkish nationals. The applicants alleged that the dissolution of Refah by the Turkish Constitutional Court and the suspension of certain political rights of the other applicants, who were leaders of Refah at the material time, had breached various Articles of the Convention. Refah was a political party founded in 1983. It took part in a number of general and local elections and was increasingly successful. The results of the 1995 general election made Refah the largest political party in the Turkish parliament with a total of 158 seats in the Grand National Assembly (which had 450 members at the material time). On 28 June 1996, Refah came to power by forming a coalition government. In January 1998, the Constitutional Court dissolved Refah on the ground that it had become a 'centre of activities contrary to the principle of secularism'. The Turkish Constitutional Court upheld the dissolution. It observed that secularism was one of the indispensable conditions of democracy:

In Turkey the principle of secularism was safeguarded by the Constitution, on account of the country's historical experience and the specific features of Islam. The rules of sharia were incompatible with the democratic regime. The principle of secularism prevented the State from manifesting a preference for a particular religion or belief and constituted the foundation of freedom of conscience and equality between citizens before the law. Intervention by the State to preserve the secular nature of the political regime had to be considered necessary in a democratic society. The Constitutional Court further observed that in a plurality of legal systems, as proposed by Refah, society would have to be divided into several religious movements; each individual would have to choose the movement to which he wished to belong and would thus be subjected to the rights and obligations prescribed by the religion of his community. The Constitutional Court pointed out that such a system, whose origins lay in the history of Islam as a political regime, was inimical to the consciousness of allegiance to a nation having legislative and judicial unity. It would naturally impair judicial unity since each religious movement would set up its own courts and the ordinary courts would be obliged to apply the law according to the religion of those appearing before them, thus obliging the latter to reveal their beliefs. It would also undermine legislative and judicial unity, the preconditions for secularism and the consciousness of nationhood, given that each religious movement would be empowered to decree what legal rules should be applicable to its members.[97]

---

96 Applications Nos. 41340/98, 41342/98, 41343/98 and 41344/98, 13 February 2003. 37.1 *EHRR* (2003).

97 Ibid. para 27.

5.3   The Challenge Under The European Convention on Human Rights

The applicants alleged that the dissolution of Refah Partisi (The Welfare Party), and the temporary prohibition barring its leaders from holding similar office in any other political party, had infringed their right to freedom of association, guaranteed by Article 11 of the Convention, the relevant parts of which provide:

1.   Everyone has the right to freedom of peaceful assembly and to freedom of association...

2.   No restrictions shall be placed on the exercise of these rights other than such as are prescribed by law and are necessary in a democratic society in the interests of national security or public safety, for the prevention of disorder or crime, for the protection of health or morals or for the protection of the rights and freedoms of others.

There was no question but that Refah's dissolution and the measures which accompanied it amounted to an interference with the applicants' exercise of their right to freedom of association. The key question was whether the interference was justified.

5.4   Democracy, Religion And The European Convention on Human Rights

The Grand Chamber held that the interferences were justified. On the question of the relationship between democracy and the Convention, the Court recalled its judgment in *United Communist Party of Turkey and Others v. Turkey* as follows:

> Democracy is without doubt a fundamental feature of the 'European public order...That is apparent, firstly, from the Preamble to the Convention, which establishes a very clear connection between the Convention and democracy by stating that the maintenance and further realisation of human rights and fundamental freedoms are best ensured on the one hand by an effective political democracy and on the other by a common understanding and observance of human rights...The Preamble goes on to affirm that European countries have a common heritage of political tradition, ideals, freedom and the rule of law. The Court has observed that in that common heritage are to be found the underlying values of the Convention...; it has pointed out several times that the Convention was designed to maintain and promote the ideals and values of a democratic society...
>
> In addition, Articles 8, 9, 10 and 11 of the Convention require that interference with the exercise of the rights they enshrine must be assessed by the yardstick of what is 'necessary in a democratic society'. The only type of necessity capable of justifying an interference with any of those rights is, therefore, one which may claim to spring from 'democratic society'. Democracy thus appears to be the only political model contemplated by the Convention and, accordingly, the only one compatible with it.[98]

---

98   Judgment of 30 January 1998, *Reports of Judgments and Decisions* 1998-I, pp. 21-22, § 45.

The Court also referred to its case-law concerning the place of religion in a democratic society and a democratic State:

> Moreover, in democratic societies, in which several religions coexist within one and the same population, it may be necessary to place restrictions on this freedom in order to reconcile the interests of the various groups and ensure that everyone's beliefs are respected (see *Kokkinakis v. Greece* ... § 33). The Court has frequently emphasised the State's role as the neutral and impartial organiser of the exercise of various religions, faiths and beliefs, and stated that this role is conducive to public order, religious harmony and tolerance in a democratic society. It also considers that the State's duty of neutrality and impartiality is incompatible with any power on the State's part to assess the legitimacy of religious beliefs (see, *mutatis mutandis, Cha'are Shalom Ve Tsedek v. France* [GC], no. 27417/95, § 84, ECHR 2000-VII) and that it requires the State to ensure mutual tolerance between opposing groups (see, *mutatis mutandis, Metropolitan Church of Bessarabia and Others v. Moldova*, no. 45701/99, § 123, ECHR 2001-XII).[99]

5.5   A Plurality of Legal Systems

On the merits, the Court saw no reason to depart from the Chamber's conclusion that a plurality of legal systems, as proposed by Refah, could not be considered to be compatible with the Convention system. In its judgment, the Chamber gave the following reasoning:

> The Court considers that Refah's proposal that there should be a plurality of legal systems would introduce into all legal relationships a distinction between individuals grounded on religion, would categorise everyone according to his religious beliefs and would allow him rights and freedoms not as an individual but according to his allegiance to a religious movement.
>
> The Court takes the view that such a societal model cannot be considered compatible with the Convention system, for two reasons.
>
> Firstly, it would do away with the State's role as the guarantor of individual rights and freedoms and the impartial organiser of the practice of the various beliefs and religions in a democratic society, since it would oblige individuals to obey, not rules laid down by the State in the exercise of its above-mentioned functions, but static rules of law imposed by the religion concerned. But the State has a positive obligation to ensure that everyone within its jurisdiction enjoys in full, and without being able to waive them, the rights and freedoms guaranteed by the Convention (see, *mutatis mutandis,* the *Airey v. Ireland* judgment of 9 October 1979, Series A no. 32, p. 14, § 25).
>
> Secondly, such a system would undeniably infringe the principle of non-discrimination between individuals as regards their enjoyment of public freedoms, which is one of the fundamental principles of democracy. A difference in treatment between

---

99   *Refah*, para 86.

individuals in all fields of public and private law according to their religion or beliefs manifestly cannot be justified under the Convention, and more particularly Article 14 thereof, which prohibits discrimination. Such a difference in treatment cannot maintain a fair balance between, on the one hand, the claims of certain religious groups who wish to be governed by their own rules and on the other the interest of society as a whole, which must be based on peace and on tolerance between the various religions and beliefs (see, *mutatis mutandis*, the judgment of 23 July 1968 in the '*Belgian linguistic*' case, Series A no. 6, pp. 33-35, §§ 9 and 10, and the *Abdulaziz, Cabales and Balkandali v. the United Kingdom* judgment, Series A no. 94, pp. 35-36, § 72).[100]

5.6 *The Sharia and Democracy*

The Court similarly concurred in the Chamber's view that sharia was incompatible with the fundamental principles of democracy, as set forth in the Convention:

> Like the Constitutional Court, the Court considers that sharia, which faithfully reflects the dogmas and divine rules laid down by religion, is stable and invariable. Principles such as pluralism in the political sphere or the constant evolution of public freedoms have no place in it. The Court notes that, when read together, the offending statements, which contain explicit references to the introduction of sharia, are difficult to reconcile with the fundamental principles of democracy, as conceived in the Convention taken as a whole. It is difficult to declare one's respect for democracy and human rights while at the same time supporting a regime based on sharia, which clearly diverges from Convention values, particularly with regard to its criminal law and criminal procedure, its rules on the legal status of women and the way it intervenes in all spheres of private and public life in accordance with religious precepts....In the Court's view, a political party whose actions seem to be aimed at introducing sharia in a State party to the Convention can hardly be regarded as an association complying with the democratic ideal that underlies the whole of the Convention.[101]

5.7 *Religious States and Secular States*

The decision in *Refah* is a challenging piece of jurisprudence.[102] Turkey is relatively unusual in adopting the model of a secular state.[103] As we have noted, many Muslims

---

100   Ibid. para 119.
101   Ibid. para 123.
102   See the criticisms of K. Boyle, 'Human Rights, Religion and Democracy: The Refah Party Case', 1 *Essex Human Rights Review* (2004).
103   See generally M.D.A. Freeman, 'The Problem of Secularism in Human Rights Theory' 26 *Human Rights Quarterly* (2004) pp. 375-400.

can successfully and freely practice their faith in democratic states. However, for the European Court of Human Rights, the adoption of a wholly Islamic state system is incompatible with European democracy.[104]

6. Conclusions

To return to the initial questions of this essay: *What roles has the concept of multicultural-ism played and what has been its value in human rights discourse?* The exercise of many human rights is entirely consistent with, and indeed is fostered by, multiculturalism. Human rights often supports the right to be different in terms of language, religion, lifestyle and many other forms of social conduct. However, while international human rights is a universalising doctrine, multiculturalism can appear to be a localising doc-trine.[105] In normative terms the international law answers to the apparent conflicts between human rights and culture, or between equality and culture, are answered in favour of the former in each case. Formally, international human rights treaty obliga-tions prevail over national constitutions and customary practice.[106] This can be so even where international treaties recognise a right to use traditional or customary law.[107] There is no express defence of multiculturalism.[108] Equality in general, and gender equality in particular, are of powerful normative status in international human rights law.[109] The Human Rights Committee, in applying and interpreting the International Covenant on Civil and Political Rights (1966) has made it clear that a failure to comply with the obligation to give effect to the Covenant rights cannot be justified by reference to cul-tural considerations.[110] In particular, the right to culture under article 27 cannot be used as a justification for violating the rights of others. This is particularly the case where the conduct involves harm or violence to bodily integrity. A clear example is the asserted

---

104 See generally A.R. Mowbray 'The Role of the European Court of Human Rights in the Promotion of Democracy' *Public Law* (1999) pp. 703-25.

105 On reconciling universalism and cultural diversity see B. Parekh 'Non enthnocentric Uni-versalism' in T. Dunne and N.J. Wheeler (eds) *Human Rights in Global Politics* (Cambridge: CUP, 1999) pp. 128-59.

106 I leave aside the issue of customary international law obligations relating to human rights. See the interesting observations in the Judgment of Lord Steyn in *Re McKerr UKHL* (2004) p. 12, *UKHRR* (2004) p. 385.

107 See R. Yrigoen Fajardo 'Peru: Pluralist Constitution, Monist Judiciary – A Post-Reform Assessment' in Sieder (note 42) pp. 157-83.

108 See Art 5 CEDAW; 'Article 18 (of the ICCPR) may not be relied upon to justify discrimina-tion against women by reference to freedom of thought, conscience and religion', General Comment 28 of the Human Rights Committee (March 2000) para. 21.

109 There are 170 states parties to the Convention on the Elimination of Discrimination Against Women, though a number have made extensive reservations.

110 See General Comment No. 31 UN Doc. CCPR/C/21/Rev.1/Add.13 *Nature of the General Legal Obligation Imposed on States Parties to the Covenant*,(26 May 2004) para 14.

cultural practice of female genital mutilation. However, this rejection of cultural claims also extends to anti-gay laws, polygamy, apostasy and some restrictions on abortion.[111]

Equality and liberty should be the governing norms. Frances Raday has observed that, 'At the level of international tribunals...in all the cases, human rights and gender equality were preferred in the result and religion and cultural differences were rejected'.[112] She also noted that, 'Many of the practices, defended in the name of culture, that impinge on human rights, are gender specific'.[113] The Human Rights Committee has been clear in its view that 'traditional, historical, religious or cultural attitudes' should not be used to justify violations of women's right to equality before the laws and to equal enjoyment of the covenant rights.[114] Human rights discourse may thus assist national judges in reinterpreting or rejecting cultural challenges.[115] It may also help to reform cultures and religions from within.

However, this analysis gives rather a simplistic impression. Human rights law often involves rather sophisticated line-drawing exercises. Moreover, few specific cases are decided by international tribunals. Many states submit extensive reservations to human rights treaties and do resort to cultural relativism as a defence when criticised. Treaty texts are formulated at a high level of abstraction and leave much room for interpretation and the mediation of texts through local cultural standards. Human rights have to be incorporated and applied through a range of legal cultures.[116] Either expressly or implicitly, states are given a significant margin of appreciation.[117] Affirmative action or positive discrimination receives express endorsement in human rights texts and practice.[118] National law exceptions in favour of cultural or religious groups have been accepted as consistent with the principle of non-discrimination.[119] Multiculturalism is a relatively recent concept of social and political theory but it has had wide general support in many parts of the world. States like to be regarded as multicultural. Australia,

---

111   See S. Joseph, J. Schultz and M. Castan (eds.) *The ICCPR – Cases, Materials and Commentary*, 2nd edn (Oxford: Oxford University Press, 2004) pp. 42-3.

112   Raday (note 10). A classic example of this would be the decision of the Human Rights Committee in *Lovelace v Canada* (although the specific decision was based on minority rights rather than equality).

113   Raday (note 10).

114   HRC General Comment 28, para. 5.

115   See Mullaly (note 49), Raday (note 10).

116   See K. Hastrup (ed.) *Legal Cultures and Human Rights: The Challenge of Diversity* (The Hague: Kluwer, 2001).

117   In a European context see Y. Yutak Arai-Takahashi *The Margin of Appreciation and the Principle of Proportionality in the Jurisprudence of the ECHR* (Antwerp: Intersentia, 2002). The HRC continues to maintain that it does not apply a margin of appreciation.

118   See eg. General Comment 23 of the HRC on Article 27.

119   Eg. concerning the Jewish and Moslem practices concerning the killing of animals by slitting their throats.

Canada and Sweden have adopted multiculturalism as a response to ethnic diversity.[120] Its application can often be difficult in practice. National judiciary and administrators may have resort to the language, concepts and methodology of human rights in mediating multicultural disputes. In this sense human rights may be used explicitly or implicitly, as a lowest common denominator. Respect for multiculturalism can be played out but international human rights law can provide a powerful normative weapon that can be used to challenge the illiberal results of multiculturalism.

Finally, there has been one other positive offshoot of multiculturalism. Inasmuch as some multiculturalists stress what is diverse or different between cultures, the analysis has also prompted the question of what values, if any, do connect different cultures. The answer may be found in the language of human rights in terms of substantive rights or at least in procedural modes of resolution.[121] That debate on common values often plays out in the citizenship/ education arena.[122] Some of that debate in turn stresses the importance of human rights in citizenship and in education.[123]

120   See C. Ingles *Multiculturalism: New Policy Response to Diversity* <www.unesco.org/most/pp.4.htm>

121   See Spencer (note 71); Jones (note 37) on human rights as a secondary system of dispute resolution.

122   See E. Craig 'Accommodation of Diversity in Education – A Human Rights Agenda?' 15 *Child and Family Law Quarterly* (2003) pp. 279-94; M. Al-Haj 'Multiculturalism in Deeply Divided Societies: the Israeli Case' 26 *Journal of Intercultural Relations* (2002) pp. 169-83; J. De Groof and G. Lauwers 'Education Policy and Law: The Politics of Multiculturalism in Education' 14 *Education and the Law* (2002) pp. 7-23.

123   On human rights as the basis of citizenship rights for minorities see in Europe see Y. Sogal *The Limits of Citizenship* (Chicago: Chicago University Press, 1994). See also W. Kymlicka and W. Norman (eds.) Citizenship in Diverse Societies (Oxford: Oxford University Press, 2000).

Chapter 13

Colour as a Ground of Discrimination

Michael Banton[1]

States that are parties to the *International Convention on the Elimination of All Forms of Racial Discrimination (ICERD)* have to ensure that persons within their jurisdiction are not treated less favourably on the grounds of race, colour, descent or national or ethnic origin. For the first thirty years of state reporting, doubts remained about whether the Convention's definition of racial discrimination covered less favourable treatment based upon caste or caste-like forms of inequality. These doubts were laid to rest in 2001 when the Committee on the Elimination of Racial Discrimination (CERD), in its concluding observations on reports from Bangladesh and Japan, affirmed that in the Convention 'the term "descent" has its own meaning and is not to be confused with race or ethnic or national origin'. Patrick Thornberry participated in these decisions and went on to play a leading part in the drafting of the Committee's *General Recommendation XXIX* about descent.

CERD has thus differentiated one of the five classes of persons protected under the Convention. The process of differentiating all five classes has some way to run. There are problems rooted in the meanings that are given to the five words in the working languages of the Committee, in particular in the many meanings of the word race. This essay discusses the differentiation of colour as a ground of discrimination.

Misunderstandings on the part of states

From its beginnings, CERD had difficulties with governments whose officials and representatives failed to appreciate the nature of the obligations assumed by states parties because their understanding of racial discrimination derived from the ordinary language meaning given to those two words. Some believed that the Convention was directed against apartheid. Many assumed that it had been adopted solely to prohibit racial discrimination as a state policy. During its third year of operation, in 1972, CERD issued a *General Recommendation* in which it noted the receipt of reports from some states parties that expressed or implied the belief that the information requested in the Committee's

---

[1]   Member of the UN Committee on the Elimination of Racial Discrimination 1986-2001; Chairman of the Committee 1996-98.

Nazila Ghanea & Alexandra Xanthaki (eds.), Minorities, Peoples and Self-Determination, *pp. 237-247.*
© *2005 Koninklijke Brill NV. Printed in The Netherlands. ISBN 90 04 14301 7.*

reporting guidelines 'need not be supplied by States Parties on whose territories racial discrimination did not exist'. It affirmed that states should report on the discharge of their treaty obligations whether or not there was racial discrimination within their territories. Later it noted the preventive aspects of the obligation to make incitement to racial hatred a punishable offence.[2]

Despite these recommendations, misunderstandings continued. In 1999, in its observations on a report from Haiti, CERD reported to the General Assembly 'Concern is expressed at the State party's repeated assertion that there is no racial discrimination as defined in article 1 of the Convention'.[3] Matters were little different in a neighbouring state, the Dominican Republic, which acceded to the ICERD in 1983. Five years later it submitted a document combining its Initial, Second and Third periodic reports. Having received no further reports covering the next fourteen years, CERD in 1997 conducted a brief review of the implementation of the Convention in the Republic without benefit of any report from the government. This stimulated the government to submit a report that combined the five overdue reports. It was considered in 1999 at the Committee's 1364th and 1355th meetings.

The report 'emphasized that racial discrimination between Dominicans, if it ever existed occasionally and selectively, has disappeared from the country as a social pathology' and that therefore 'the Dominican state has never encountered the need to condemn racial discrimination.'[4] CERD expressed concern over these statements by the government because they could not be reconciled with reports from other sources that 'racial prejudices exist not only against Haitians but also against the darker-skinned Dominicans'.[5] As it was not satisfied that the Republic was complying with its obligations to legislate, it indicated the action required.

When members of CERD agree their concluding observations, they are severely constrained by the limited time available to them to secure agreement on draft conclusions. They therefore find it helpful to be able to refer to their reporting guidelines or to any of their general recommendations that detail the Committee's expectations on particular matters. The availability of an already agreed text saves Committee time. I therefore thought the Committee might find it helpful to adopt a recommendation setting out its views on the issue presented by states such as Haiti and the Dominican Republic. It could then be cited whenever CERD had to deal with a government that advanced arguments resembling those of these two states.

---

2   M. Banton *International Action Against Racial Discrimination* (Oxford: Clarendon Press, 1996) pp. 102-108.

3   UN Doc. CERD/C/304/Add.84, CERD, *Concluding Observations of the Committee on the Elimination of Racial Discrimination: Haiti 12/04/2001*, para. 7.

4   UN Doc. CERD/C/331/Add.1, CERD, *Eighth periodic reports of States Parties due in 1998: Dominican Republic. 11/02/1999*, para. 31.

5   UN Doc. CERD/C/304/Add.74, CERD, *Concluding Observations of the Committee on the Elimination of Racial Discrimination: Dominican Republic 26/08/1999*, para. 7.

So at the 56th session in 2000 I circulated a proposed general recommendation 'On the Lesser Forms of Racial Discrimination', which advised such states that they 'should remember that discrimination may be practised by private individuals and by persons who are not nationals of the State'. It observed, 'In some countries there are no distinctive groups based upon race, colour, descent, or national or ethnic origin, but within these societies individuals may nevertheless treat others less favourably because of the significance they attribute to such characteristics.' It went on to indicate the sort of information that might help the Committee form an estimate of the effectiveness of the measures for preventing discrimination of this kind.

My proposed title recalled the reference to 'all forms of racial discrimination' in the title of the Convention, but my colleagues did not approve of this; they preferred the title 'General Recommendation on Racial Discrimination by Individuals'. This formulation reflected the outlook of committee members who were themselves diplomats and inclined to look at problems from the standpoint of the state. I revised my proposal in the light of my colleagues' views and reintroduced it at the 57th session. One of the longest-serving committee members, Mr. Mahmoud Aboul-Nasr, maintained that a general recommendation was unnecessary since CERD had already made it clear that any claim that there was no racial discrimination in a state, and therefore no need to take measures against it, was unacceptable. My experience was that many states did not believe that the Committee was a superior authority in the interpretation of the Convention. They insisted that they could argue on equal terms with the Committee. The states could point to preambular paragraph 10 of the Convention, which declares not just that racial discrimination can be eliminated but that it can be speedily eliminated. The Committee should therefore admit the logical possibility that there may be no racial discrimination in a particular country.

I had drafted my proposal in simple terms that would be understood by the officials who have to prepare their governments' reports and who are not necessarily lawyers; but the many amendments that were proposed robbed it of any simplicity. Some members believed that the request for other kinds of information when individuals were not classified by race, colour, descent, or national or ethnic origin, added to the reporting burden that fell upon states, so opinion in the Committee on the desirability of such a general recommendation was fairly evenly divided. As this was to be my last session as a member of the Committee, I chose not to press the issue.[6]

Responding to observations from Committee members who regretted the paucity of demographic information in the state report, representatives of the Dominican Republic stated that 'the United Nations had recommended that the national statistics office of the Dominican Republic should not include a question in its population census relating to the skin colour of its citizens as the question would itself be discriminatory'.[7] The state's report did not mention identity cards, so CERD members were unaware that all residents in the Republic over the age of eighteen needed a *cédula*, an identity

6   UN Doc.CERD/C/SR.1431, paras. 1-41.
7   UN Doc.CERD/C/SR.1365, para. 18.

card that had to be renewed every five years. This included a record of the person's skin colour. A man might be asked if he was to be described as *blanco, mulato, indio*, or *negro*. Irrespective of their actual complexion, members of the affluent classes were likely to be recorded as *blanco*. The preference for a fair skin colour underpinned a pattern of discrimination that operated on the basis of individual assessment without any reference to racial categories. It was expressed in advertisements for female employees of *buena presencia*. In such ways the nation was coloured. The word *raza* was used in several senses, as in *la raza dominicana*, which was a way of grouping Dominicans in opposition to Haitians.[8]

Had the Committee been aware that the government recorded the skin colour of residents in this manner, it might have wished to consider whether there was any justification for the practice, and whether, indeed, it entailed the very discrimination against persons of darker colour that the state delegation said the government wished to avoid in the census. Comment on this possibility could have provided an opportunity to differentiate discrimination on the ground of colour from other prohibited forms of racial discrimination.

One reason why it is difficult to make such a differentiation is that the Convention uses the word race in two different ways. It is one of five grounds of discrimination, and yet it is also, as *racial* discrimination, a generic name for all five grouped together. As a single ground, it is a subset of itself. If CERD refers to an action as racially discriminatory, it does not have to specify whether it is referring to the set of five grounds or to just one of them. The two possible senses of the word are not distinguished from each other.

The race formula in Britain

This use of the word race to denote both a set of grounds and one member of the set also occurs in British legislation. The Bill introduced in 1965 proposed to make it a criminal offence for the proprietor or manager of any place of public resort to discriminate 'on the ground of colour, race, or ethnic or national origins…' It deliberately aligned its scope with the formula then under discussion in the United Nations.[9] The resulting Act criminalised only incitement to racial hatred; other prohibited forms of discrimination were to be treated as civil wrongs. A fifth ground of prohibited discrimination, of nationality, was added subsequently in the *Race Relations Act 1976*.

Under the current British procedure, a tribunal or court may not have to specify the ground of discrimination. To take an example, in 1986 a young man named D. Smith saw in the Bristol Jobcentre a notice indicating a vacancy for a paint-sprayer in a small privately-owned car repair workshop. The assistant telephoned on his behalf. The

8   D. Howard *Coloring the Nation. Race and Ethnicity in the Dominican Republic* (Oxford: Signal Books; Boulder: Lynne Rienner, 2001) pp. 47-8 and p. 69.

9   See statement by Mr Maurice Foley, Under-Secretary of State, Home Office, in the House of Commons on May 27 1966, 729 H.C. Debates 946.

employer asked if Smith was coloured. She replied in the affirmative. The employer then refused to see him and persisted in this refusal. When these facts were presented to an industrial tribunal, it found that racial discrimination had occurred and awarded damages to Smith.[10] The evidence suggested that the discrimination was on the ground of colour, as are most of the cases of racial discrimination in British workplaces. Had the employer said that he would not employ anyone of a particular race, it might have been possible to conclude that the applicant had been discriminated against on the ground of race rather than colour. As matters presently stand, the tribunal could find that Smith had suffered racial discrimination, using the word race in its generic sense as a denotation of the set of five grounds without considering whether it was on the ground of race as distinguished from that of colour, these being two grounds within the set.

In British terminology Smith's case counted as an example of direct discrimination, as opposed to indirect discrimination. The distinction corresponds to that in the Convention between purpose and effect. The principal British case on the differentiation of the grounds of discrimination arose from an allegation of indirect discrimination, *Mandla v Dowell Lee*.[11] The headmaster of a private school declined to admit a boy who, as a Sikh, wore a turban. The headmaster maintained that the wearing of a turban would accentuate the religious and social distinctions that he sought to minimize in a multiracial school based on the Christian faith. The court had to decide whether Sikhs constituted a 'group of persons' defined by reference to their ethnic origins as a subset of the statute's definition of a racial group.[12] Subsequent to this case, when deciding cases of indirect discrimination courts have adopted the 'but for' test, in which they ask whether the alleged victim would have been treated less favourably *but for* his or her being a member of a particular class of persons.[13] Whether the allegation is of direct or indirect discrimination, the ground is to be decided by reference to objective and not subjective criteria. So in circumstances such as those of Smith's case, any statement made by the employer about why he would not consider the applicant as a potential employee might help a tribunal decide the ground of discrimination, but it would not determine the outcome.

When the 1965 Bill was presented to Parliament it was conventional to refer to coloured people as a class, but since then the trend has been to treat colour as an individual attribute and to use race as the name for a class of persons distinguished by their colour. The employer discriminated against Smith as an individual, in circumstances covered by

---

10   M. Banton 'Racial discrimination at work: Bristol cases, 1980-89', 17.1 *New Community*, (1990) pp. 135-36.

11   *Mandla v Dowell Lee*, 1983 1All ER.

12   A unanimous House of Lords ruled that Sikhs constituted an 'ethnic community' (an expression that occurs nowhere in the statute) and that, as such, were a protected class. I have argued that had the court kept to a strict construction of the expression `class of persons' it would have been led to a different conclusion, see 'Strategic Vision in Combating Racial Discrimination' in M. Anwar, P. Roach and R. Sondhi (eds.) *From Legislation to Integration?* (Basingstoke, Macmillan: 2000) pp. 167-73.

13   *James v Eastleigh Borough Council*, 1990 2 AllER.

Article 5(e)(i) of the Convention forbidding discrimination in enjoyment of the right to work. When someone incites others to racial hatred, which is an offence against public order covered by Article 4(a) of the Convention, the incitement is directed against a class of persons.

In a commentary on the drafting of the first British race relations acts, Anthony Dickey distinguished between a general and a technical meaning of the word 'race'. Of race, he wrote:

> When it is used in its general sense this term connotes any classification of the world's population that is based on one or more personal characteristics which are normally settled once and for all either at conception or at birth and which are thus characteristics over which each individual has no personal control. Examples of such characteristics include skin colour, size of body, shape of head, or type of hair, all of which are normally settled at conception, and culture, language (mother tongue), and national origins, which are normally settled at birth. [14]

He could have added to this list 'ethnic origins' but he could not have added 'race' since that is not a characteristic but a classification. Dickey went on: 'The word "race" in its technical sense, however, is a biological term which connotes "a group of related inter-marrying individuals, a population, which differs from other populations in the relative commonness of certain hereditary traits"'.[15]

The definition he quotes uses the word race as a synonym for subspecies. Following the dictionary definition of 'technical expression' as one requiring specialist knowledge in order to be understood, it can be said that the word 'subspecies' has a technical meaning. While some writers have tried to give a technical meaning to the word race, there has never been any agreement upon what it might be. 'Race' has therefore no technical meaning; it has only a general or popular meaning.

Indeed, much of the trouble started from an attempt to give race a technical meaning. At the end of the eighteenth century the noun *race* was used primarily to denote a line of descent. Those who set out to classify natural objects started with a division into three kingdoms, animal, vegetable and mineral, and then divided living forms into ever-smaller classes ending up with *genus, species* and *variety*. Later, some writers, particularly under the influence of the anatomist Cuvier, tried to insert *race* into the classificatory scheme. Though there was no agreement about where it fitted in, or whether it was a necessary addition, it gave an extra dimension to the popular use of the word. The vertical dimension captured the sense of distinctiveness over time, while the horizontal dimension attempted to classify races in the present. The writers who kept to the older usage employed race as a synonym for *variety*, a class of persons who were the present representatives of a line of descent that must at some time have shared a common ances-

---

14   A. Dickey 'The Race Formula of the Race Relations Acts' *The Juridical Review* (1974) p. 285.
15   Ibid.

tory with persons belonging to other similar classes. This is now more usually called a *subspecies*. Those who believed that race was a key to history contended that a human race was to be equated with a *species*, as a class in the horizontal dimension. Racial classification was to be objectively determined by technical criteria. The definition quoted by Dickey reflected an attempt by geneticists to correct that approach. Nowadays the meaning popularly given to *race* in the English language is closer to that of species than subspecies, as can be seen from the way that individuals of only one-eighth African ancestry have been accounted black.

The European Union's mistake

During the second half of the twentieth century references in Britain to differences of colour were progressively replaced by references to race. In 1950, reviewing the prospects for the protection of human rights around the world, a lawyer in London concluded that 'the greatest discriminations are based on colour distinctions'.[16] In the same year a private member's proposal for legislation used the title *Colour Bar Bill*. In the following years, though the issues were more frequently referred to as matters of race, references to colour remained common. Since the late sixties, however, the idiom of race has dominated, to the extent that there is no reference to differences of colour in the race directive adopted by the EU Council of Ministers in 2000.[17] The directive states that 'direct discrimination shall be taken to occur when one person is treated less favourably than another is, has been or would be treated in a comparable situation on grounds of racial or ethnic origin.'[18] 'Race' as a ground of action has thus swallowed 'colour'.

The Directive's exclusion of colour as a ground of discrimination is the more remarkable in that several EU member states have expressed unease about the continued use of the concept of race. When, in 1999, it appointed a committee to consider new legislation, the Swedish parliament stated: 'The Riksdag has declared that there is no scientific justification for dividing humanity into distinct races and from a biological standpoint consequently no justification for using the word race with reference to humans... the government in international connections should try to see that usage of the word race with reference to humans is avoided in official texts so far as is possible...'

Since 1994, Sweden has had a law against *ethnic* discrimination that prohibits 'unjust or insulting treatment on the ground of race, colour, national or ethnic origin or religious confession.' It uses *ethnic* rather than *race* as the name for the set of grounds. Norway is preparing a new law that is also to be directed against ethnic discrimination.[19]

---

16   L.C. Green 'Human Rights and the Colour Problem' in G. W. Keeton and G. Schwartzenberger (eds.) *Current Legal Problems*, (London: Stevens & Sons, 1950).

17   2000/43/EC.

18   Ibid. article 2.

19   UN Doc.A/58/18, para. 472.

Lacking any technical meaning, the word race has different associations in different languages. It is well known that the Germans, because of the abuses of the Nazi era, are uncomfortable with the expression *Rassismus*, and prefer to speak of *Fremdenfeindlichkeit* (somewhat misleadingly translated as xenophobia). French commentators use *racisme* without hesitation, but are sometimes scandalised by the embodiment in section 3 of the British *Race Relations Act 1976* of a concept of 'racial group'. Any conception of membership in bodies intermediate between the citizen and the state is incompatible with the ideology of the French republic.

That this unease was widely shared among EU member states was demonstrated in 2001 in connection with the World Conference Against Racism. An underlying concern was that action against racial discrimination should not breathe new life into an obsolete conception of race. With the establishment of population genetics in the 1930s, the use of race as a synonym for species among humans had been shown to be misconceived. In the inter-governmental discussions on the text of the conference declaration, the then fifteen states of the European Union stated their shared objection to any wording that might appear to endorse belief in the existence of different human races as this would risk denying the unity of humanity. They could secure little support for their point of view from the representatives of states in other world regions.[20]

A second reason for questioning the omission of colour from the EU directive is the probability that the descendants of immigrants with origins in other world regions will be integrated into European societies by being incorporated into structures of social class. Colour will be one factor in the ranking of individuals by socio-economic status. While some immigrant groups will maintain distinctive community institutions based upon distinctive religious beliefs, ethnic boundaries will be weakened by the processes of upward and downward social mobility affecting the whole population, by the increasing number of people with multiple ethnic origins, and by the effects of official policies. Though in many fields of social life race will be of declining significance, there will be continuing discrimination against individuals on the ground of colour.

In 2003, CERD noted that the scope of the EU directive was more restricted than that of the Convention. In its comments on the United Kingdom report the Committee expressed concern 'that the emerging situation may lead to inconsistencies in discrimination laws and differential levels of protection according to the categorization of protection'.[21] The Committee will presumably question other EU states on the ways in which they give effect to their Convention obligation to provide protection against discrimination on grounds of colour.

---

20   M. Banton *The International Politics of Race* (Oxford: Polity, 2002) p. 7.

21   UN Doc.A/58/18 para. 534. CERD was in error in referring to discrimination on grounds of nationality. The Convention prohibits discrimination on grounds of national origin, not nationality.

Distinguishing colour from race

The two reasons for believing the scope of the EU directive to be unduly restrictive come together in the question of vocabulary. There is now a general belief, widely shared on both sides of the Atlantic, that the contemporary English-language vocabulary for describing and analysing racial and ethnic relations is unsatisfactory.[22] However, ordinary language usage has such a strong grip upon popular conceptions of group identities that it is very difficult to reform this vocabulary. It might be thought that, given the influence of the law in the definition of groups and relationships, the differentiation of colour as a ground of discrimination could be a way to pioneer its reform. Substituting colour for race in certain contexts might resemble the strategy of the women's movement, which has succeeded in substituting the word gender for the word sex when reference is made to social rather than physical differences between men and women.

When the *ICERD* was drafted it might have been better had different words been used for state obligations under Articles 4 and 5 of the *ICERD*. Words like race and racial could have been confined to the prohibition of incitement to racial hatred under Article 4. Under Article 5 states could have been obliged to protect equality in the enjoyment of civil, political, economic, social and cultural rights without distinction as to colour, descent, or national or ethnic origin; there was no need to group these four grounds together as belonging in a category misleadingly named racial. The failure to differentiate these different obligations now restricts the law's potential contribution to the reform of the vocabulary.

The concept of a ground of discrimination is essential to the prohibition of a class of actions, and therefore to the admissibility of a communication to the Committee under Article 14 of the Convention. For example, in dealing with communication 15/1999, *E.I.F. v The Netherlands*, CERD found 'that the decision to dismiss the author from the Police Academy was not the result of discrimination on racial grounds' and therefore it found that the state had not violated its obligations. Using Rule 91(c), CERD could have declared the communication inadmissible because it was not compatible with the provisions of the Convention, but it proceeded to the issue since the state party did not object to the Committee's considering the communication on its merits.[23] Once the Committee moves to the consideration of merits the focus shifts to the obligations of others to protect the rights of a complainant. Since the motives of an action are often mixed, and can be difficult to establish, the test of the action's lawfulness has to be objective. If a tribunal finds that a man has been less favourably treated 'because he is black', or 'because he is a Roma' that is, in each case, to use a proper name for a social category. In the first case a tribunal invokes the popular understanding of social divisions to find

---

22   See M. Banton 'Reforming the Language of Race, Colour and Ethnic Origin' *forthcoming*.
23   UN Doc.A/56/18, Annex IIIA, paras. 6.1 and 6.2.

that there has been discrimination on the ground of colour. In the second case it might find that there had been discrimination on the ground of ethnic origin.[24]

In responding to a complaint about an offensive name used since 1960 for a stand at a sporting stadium in Australia, CERD acknowledged that the offending term was not designed to demean but concluded that its maintenance could be considered insulting and that 'the Convention, as a living instrument, must be interpreted and applied in the circumstances of contemporary society'.[25] These circumstances have been changing dramatically. Few of those who participated in the drafting of the Convention and spoke in the General Assembly debates of 1965 envisaged that it would be used to monitor the sorts of behaviour that now give rise to the kinds of communication that CERD has to consider under Article 14. Apartheid is no more. Decolonisation has run its course. The global focus has shifted to such matters as the consequences of globalisation and the use of the Convention to combat discrimination based upon descent. The focus of individual experience is now upon interpersonal relations. In this developing scenario, discrimination on the ground of colour will come to be more important.

To explain why this is to be expected, it is best to begin by considering what happens when groups of persons distinguished by both colour and other attributes enter into relations with one another. Seen from a sociological perspective, they create a system of exchanges, particularly of labour and of personal services.[26] Members of the two groups will probably prefer, *ceteris paribus*, to associate with those of a colour similar to their own, because similarity of complexion serves as a sign that persons share experience and norms of conduct, just as they can place more trust in those who speak their own language. This preference will normally decline relative to preferences associated with economic and social advancement, such as the prospect of a rewarding business relationship. Among the most important preferences are those regarding suitability as a partner in marriage; these are not limited to considerations of social status but include personal tastes. Research has established that there is a widespread male preference for brides of

---

24   The case of *Lacko v Slovak Republic* could have provided an example. The case arose from an allegation that a waitress had been instructed not to serve Roma. Since the person responsible was penalised, albeit three years after the event, CERD found no violation. See UN Doc. A/56/18, Annex IIIB, para. 10. For another discussion of the differentiation of grounds, see M. Banton, 'Political motives as grounds of racial discrimination' in F. Coomans, F. Grünfeld, I. Westendorp and J. Willems (eds.) *Rendering Justice to the Vulnerable: Liber Amicorum in Honour of Theo van Boven* (The Hague: Kluwer, 2000).

25   Communication 26/2002 (*Hagan v Australia*), UN Doc. A/58/18, Annex IIIA, paras. 7.2 and 7.3.

26   These exchanges have developed most rapidly in capitalist economies. Where distinctive ethnic communities have engaged in mainly subsistence production as, for example, in parts of Macedonia, the pace of change has been much slower. The process of change is also dependent upon the maintenance of order. When this breaks down, the process may be reversed. If in the popular mind there is an association between ethnic distinctiveness and relative wealth, then, as for persons of Chinese origin in SE Asia, a boundary may be drawn more sharply and those within it be attacked.

a fair complexion.[27] Over three generations or so, some males with origins in a more disadvantaged group will become economically successful and marry fair-complexioned women. Some males with origins in the more advantaged group will be downwardly mobile and will marry darker-skinned brides. These processes will produce a colour scale such as that observed in the Dominican Republic, unless, of course, members of the more powerful group utilise their power to transmit their privileges to succeeding generations, as has happened in the USA. There the whites drew a colour line between themselves and the blacks and defined the two groups as races. The so-called 'one drop rule' declared that someone with seven-eighths European and one-eighth African ancestry should count as black.

As a result, within the USA distinctions of ethnic origin are generally treated as creating sub-classes within the two main racial classes. Distinctions of colour are treated as characteristics of individual members of racial classes. In this way a vocabulary of race, colour and ethnic origin has been assembled that differs from the vocabularies of Latin America and Europe. It is so strongly established that people sometimes assume that the North American pattern is the normal one and the Latin American a deviant form. The reverse is the case. In the English-speaking world ideas of race have been used, sometimes deliberately, to support an assumption that there are distinctive inter-racial relations and that they are different from intra-racial relations. This assumption is attributable to the significance humans place upon distinctions of colour, descent and national or ethnic origin.

In the twenty-first century, the tendency to draw colour lines will be challenged by the growth in the numbers of persons who cannot easily be assigned to any racial category because they are of mixed ethnic origin or of an intermediate complexion. Many such persons wish to acknowledge more than one of their lines of ancestry and resist assignment to obsolete racial categories.[28] Because of their colour, they will experience less favourable treatment and will expect this to be recognised in law as discrimination on grounds of colour. This will increase the pressure for the differentiation of colour as a ground of discrimination. CERD should be alert to this development.

---

27   P.L. van den Berghe and P. Frost 'Skin Colour Preference, Sexual Dimorphism and Sexual Selection: a case of gene culture co-evolution?' 9 *Ethnic and Racial Studies*, (1986), pp. 87-113. Preferences vary, so the validity of the findings of this study is not affected by evidence of contrary instances. In many of these studies skin colour has been measured from the amount of light reflected when a spectrophotometer has been placed on a site minimally exposed to sunlight. It is currently proposed to check the identity of individuals by machines that register the special characteristics of eyes, so it is not inconceivable that in the future an individual's bio data may include a measure of skin colour.

28   The growth in numbers of persons of mixed origin will undermine systems of racial assignment, but any growth in the numbers of persons born to persons of different caste will not undermine caste assignment. This form of discrimination on the ground of descent will be particularly difficult to reduce.

Chapter 14

The OSCE High Commissioner on National Minorities: Pyrometer, Prophylactic, Pyrosvestis

John Packer[1]

Prologue

In the best sense of my forgetfulness, I cannot recall when I first met Patrick Thornberry. I am sure that I knew him already through his writings which stood out not only for their scholarly character, but for the humanism which evidently directed them. Professor Thornberry was thus inspirational – indeed, a model. But there was more to this which I came to understand better, as one often does, when I met him. Patrick has passion. With this, he reveals his sense of life with its joys, humour, sadness and injustice. I am not sure which drives him; my professional experience with Professor Thornberry suggests it is his strong objection to the injustices, especially indignities, which some humans so abundantly and perpetually commit upon others, typically victimizing the vulnerable. This no doubt drives Professor Thornberry to fight to defend and protect the vulnerable through law. But I suspect this is the outward sign of a more fundamental passion which derives from Patrick's love of life and its many beauties. It is this combination which I admire and have learned from Patrick Thornberry the person: to seek to join academic discipline and rigour with a full appreciation of the human condition and, thereby, to pursue a better life for all. This is why when one reads Thornberry, there is no mistaking that law does not exist for its own sake but as an instrument of social change and, hopefully, justice. And so both professionally and personally it has been my pleasure to come to know and on occasion work with Patrick Thornberry.

I. Introduction

As international relations have become more numerous and complex, both in terms of governmental and non-governmental entities, the world has become increasingly interdependent. Rapid evolution in technologies has propelled these processes with pro-

---

[1] Fellow, The Carr Center for Human Rights Policy, The John F. Kennedy School of Government, Harvard University; Visiting Assistant Professor of International Law, The Fletcher School of Law and Diplomacy, Tufts University.

Nazila Ghanea & Alexandra Xanthaki (eds.), Minorities, Peoples and Self-Determination, *pp. 249-268.*
© *2005 Koninklijke Brill NV. Printed in The Netherlands. ISBN 90 04 14301 7.*

found effects for human communications, standards of living and security. As a result of this evolution, our common interests have expanded in scope and depth.

It may well be that the factual evolution of our expanded common interests and complex interdependence has so far outpaced our understanding and treatment of its implications. Perhaps most evidently, there appears to be some shortcoming in the nature of political institutions capable of responding in a timely and sufficient manner to the demands which arise. In fact, the institutions (and underlying premises) of contemporary international relations remain rooted in the Westphalian paradigm of the mid-seventeenth century as then agreed by absolute monarchs at the end of religious wars within Europe – before the development of either the nation-State[2] or democracy. At least as a result of modern military capabilities, not to mention forms of group-based or inspired organized violence, it would appear self-evident that our notions of 'sovereignty' and 'security' require some up-dating. Indeed, we have already been forced to rethink security in sometimes surprising terms, such as in relation to the environment – and our understanding of traditional military security has also had to be modified and likely needs to be further modified especially in the light of the contemporary threat of terrorism.[3]

More generally, evolution in international relations has required a transition from *co-existence* to *co-operation* in response to our common interests in managing the global environment, economy and, increasingly, security. This is not only generally so, but it is apparently so even for powers which have chosen to 'go it alone' and then confront the manifold negative implications, risks and costs of such an approach. In any case, conduct *within* States – and not simply *between* States – has increasingly become of necessary and legitimate interest to others. However, the structures and institutional arrangements through which to focus and manage these interests remain somewhat underdeveloped. Nonetheless, some development is taking place in terms of both the transformation of old institutions and the creation of new ones.

Within Europe, various transitions have been taking place. Among the established democracies, there has been a race towards further economic integration in particular within the European Union (EU). Political and economic integration has also been taking place in relation to the EU as membership has expanded and is set to continue

---

2   Of course, the State – defined in Article 1 of the Convention on Rights and Duties of States (Convention of Montevideo, December 1933, L.N.T.S. No. 881) as comprising a permanent population on a defined territory with an effective government capable of entering into relations with other States – has existed for thousands of years. But its organization around 'the nation' (being an ethno-political community) is a Western construction essentially of the 19th Century. The 'nation-State' is, therefore, an historically very recent phenomenon and arguably a passing one.

3   In a sharp article in *The Guardian* newspaper (4 December 2002, p. 7), Jonathan Freedland makes the point that 'War has changed utterly, yet our masters do not see it' and argues for 'a surge in creative thinking' with, among other things, a substantial redirection of military resources to intelligence operations and other activities to address the 'new war – in which only the smart will survive.'

to do so. Indeed, this dynamic has emerged as a central aspect of contemporary inter-governmental relations within Europe. However, while the EU increasingly takes on the attributes of a federal or confederal super-State, it has been struggling to develop an appropriate and generally acceptable foreign and security policy, much less to act coherently and consistently in pursuit of such policy.[4] So far, this has been left essentially to the national policy of individual States and to other European organizations including notably the North Atlantic Treaty Organization (with regard to defence against military threats and, now, some concerted military actions beyond territorial defence), the Council of Europe (with regard to democracy, human rights and certain social and cultural policy) and the Organisation for Security and Co-operation in Europe (OSCE, with regard especially to democratic transition and consolidation, protection of national minorities and related inter-State affairs, and 'soft' security matters). While the afore-mentioned organizations are experiencing their own evolutions, it has been the OSCE which has evolved the quickest and furthest in response to the political changes attending the end of the Cold War. As such, it is the specific subject of this chapter, in particular the institution of the High Commissioner on National Minorities (HCNM) which is a unique institution in international relations as the sole dedicated conflict prevention mechanism working in the field of inter-ethnic relations through quiet diplomacy.

II.   The Development of the OSCE

It should be recalled that the OSCE is principally a *security* organization. Originating in the Conference on Security and Co-operation in Europe (CSCE) which was initiated in the midst of the Cold War as an intergovernmental diplomatic conference aiming to establish common ground between the then opposed blocs of Eastern and Western Europe, the then 35 participating States reached agreement on the *Final Act of Helsinki* on 1 August 1975.[5] By doing so, the two blocs each achieved a measure of satisfaction: the Soviet bloc achieved some formal recognition of post-World War Two frontiers, while the West achieved some formal recognition that human rights and fundamental freedoms were a legitimate international interest and subject of East-West discourse.

The Helsinki process brought together somewhat disparate interests through the evolving notion of 'comprehensive security' whereby the broad areas of interest were divided into three 'baskets' concerning: 1) security questions (meaning mainly military matters); 2) economic and environmental concerns; and 3) 'human contacts, information and human rights' (later to become known as 'the human dimension', including humanitarian concerns). In terms of process, the participating States agreed to the *Final*

---

4   For some views and a discussion of what this could include, *see* 'Foreign Policy for the European Union: Views from Beyond the EU' in *Contemporary International Law Issues: New Forms, New Applications*, Proceedings of the Fourth Hague Joint [ASIL/NVIR] Conference held in The Hague, 2-5 July 1997 (The Hague: T.M.C. Asser Instituut, 1998) pp. 230-245.

5   For the full text of the *Final Act of Helsinki*, *see* http://www.osce.org/docs/english/1990-1999/summits/helfa75e.htm (accessed 6 June 2004).

Act on the basis of consensus which underlined sovereign equality, and has remained the fundamental procedural method.

The *Final Act* expressly states that the participating States share the 'objective of promoting better relations among themselves and ensuring conditions in which their people can live in true and lasting peace free from any threat to or attempt against their security'… and 'the need to exert efforts to make détente both a continuing and an increasingly viable and comprehensive process'. 'Security', therefore, is certainly seen to be about avoiding war, but it is also viewed as much more than that.[6] Specifically, the participating States recognized 'the close link between peace and security in Europe and in the world as a whole and…the need for each of them to make its contribution to the strengthening of world peace and security and to the promotion of fundamental rights, economic and social progress and well-being for all peoples'.

The *Final Act* includes a 'Declaration on Principles Guiding Relations Between Participating States' which, in reaffirming the commitment to develop friendly relations, specifies ten principles 'in conformity with the Charter of the United Nations'. The principles – later to become known as the 'decalogue' – are titled as follows:

I.   Sovereign equality, respect for the rights inherent in sovereignty
II. Refraining from the threat or use of force
III. Inviolability of frontiers
IV. Territorial integrity of States
V.   Peaceful settlement of disputes
VI. Non-intervention in internal affairs
VII. Respect for human rights and fundamental freedoms, including the freedom of thought, conscience, religion or belief
VIII.Equal rights and self-determination of peoples
IX. Co-operation among States
X.   Fulfilment in good faith of obligations under international law

The seventh 'principle' concerning human rights has the most text – comprising eight short separate paragraphs. While underlining in its title the importance of 'the freedom of thought, conscience, religion or belief', it refers to 'the effective exercise of civil, political, economic, social, cultural and other rights and freedoms all of which derive from the inherent dignity of the human person and are essential for his free and full development'. This commitment is further supported by the contents of the eighth paragraph which requires all States to act in conformity with 'the international declarations and agreements in this field'. In addition, the principle states in its fourth paragraph as follows:

> The participating States on whose territory national minorities exist will respect the
> right of persons belonging to such minorities to equality before the law, will afford

---

6   It was already clear (following from the nature of the Cold War) that the goal was to move from the prevailing 'negative peace' to an evolving 'positive peace'.

them the full opportunity for the actual enjoyment of human rights and fundamental freedoms and will, in this manner, protect their legitimate interests in this sphere.

The initial conference yielded an ongoing process which included subsequent 'follow-up' conferences and meetings hosted by various participating States. By 1989, the Cold War had largely thawed and a new period of openness in the Soviet bloc enabled considerable development of the catalogue of accords, including significantly the development of mechanisms of implementation – although these remained essentially diplomatic and quiet in nature.[7] Real progress was achieved in the period 1989-1990 in the course of three meetings on the human dimension held successively in Paris (1989), Copenhagen (1990) and Moscow (1991). At the Copenhagen meeting in June 1990, agreement was reached on a much expanded catalogue of human rights standards, including notably a long list of standards concerning persons belonging to national minorities which at the time was by far the most substantial and progressive text in this field ever adopted at the multilateral level. The CSCE reached perhaps its apex in November 1990 with its second summit of Heads of State and Government when the *Charter of Paris for a New Europe*[8] was signed. According to some commentators, this marked the end of the Cold War as *all* States (including those of Eastern Europe) agreed for the first time to base their societies on the twin principles of: 1) democratic legitimacy of authority; and 2) market economy. In the subsequent eighteen months, the authoritarian regimes of Eastern Europe collapsed one after the other and the Soviet Union itself dissolved.

The euphoria of 1990 was also followed by the shock of the bloody collapse and dissolution of the Socialist Federal Republic of Yugoslavia. It thus became evident that a political commitment to relaxing authoritarian control was not synonymous with guaranteeing respect for human rights, nor with maintaining peace and security. As the lid came off the long simmering caldron of undemocratic and often discriminatory governance, the old nemeses of nationalism and minority grievances soon took centre-stage. A quick survey of unrest in Europe revealed the considerable prospect for problems involving national minorities (i.e. populations constituting a numerical minority in one State, but sharing the same 'nationality'/ethnicity as the population constituting a numerical majority in another, often neighbouring, State)[9] to engulf the continent – especially the

---

7   For developments, including the full texts of the various documents, *see* A. Bloed *The Conference on Security and Co-operation in Europe; Analysis and Basic Documents, 1972-1993* (Dordrecht: Kluwer Academic Publishers, 1993).

8   For the full text of the *Charter of Paris for a New Europe* of November 1990, *see* http://www.osce.org/docs/english/1990-1999/summits/paris90e.htm (accessed 6 June 2004).

9   It is to be noted that there also exist groups which do not enjoy the interest and support of a 'kin-state' (e.g. the Crimean Tatars or the Roma), yet are treated as 'national minorities' by the OSCE. For some considerations on the issue of definition, *see*: J. Packer 'On the Definition of Minorities' in J. Packer and K. Myntti (eds.) *The Protection of Ethnic and Linguistic Minorities in Europe* (Åbo/Turku: Institute for Human Rights, 1993), pp. 23-65; and J. Packer 'Problems in Defining Minorities' in D. Fottrell and W. Bowring (eds.) *Minority and Group Rights In the New Millennium* (The Hague: Kluwer Law International, 1999) pp. 223-274. It

countries of Central and Eastern Europe where democratic experience was short and where the institutions supporting the Rule of Law, civil society and respect for human rights were still to be established or essentially fragile. As evidenced by the collapse of the former Yugoslavia, this situation constituted perhaps the greatest immediate threat to regional peace and security – especially as more and more States (re)acquired their independence and more and more minority situations were created in what are the now 55 participating States of the OSCE.

III. The Institution of the High Commissioner on National Minorities

It was in this context of transition and insecurity that the then CSCE[10] decided at its second Helsinki Summit in July 1992 to establish the institution of the High Commissioner on National Minorities (HCNM) as 'an instrument of conflict prevention at the earliest possible stage'.[11] The HCNM was given a two-fold mandate: 'to provide "early warning" and, as appropriate, "early action" at the earliest possible stage in regard to tensions involving national minority issues which have not yet developed beyond an early warning stage, but, in the judgement of the High Commissioner, have the potential to develop into a conflict in the CSCE area, affecting peace, stability or relations between participating States'. It is notable that the HCNM was created as an instrument of the *security* basket (i.e. not as a mechanism of the human dimension) with a view to preventing possible armed conflict. On this basis, the mandate also placed limits on the HCNM's involvement: he is only to address situations which have the propensity to erupt into international armed conflict; he is not to consider violations of CSCE commitments with regard to an individual person; and he is precluded from considering national minority issues in situations involving 'organized acts of terrorism'.

---

should be noted that the notion of 'national minorities' has no strict meaning in international relations or law, but is rather short-hand reflecting an historically evolving notion which now captures at least 'linguistic, religious and cultural minorities' (to use the language of Article 27 of the 1966 International Covenant on Civil and Political Rights), 'national or ethnic, linguistic and religious minorities' (to use the language of the 1992 UN Declaration on the Rights of Persons Belonging to National or Ethnic, Linguistic and Religious Minorities) and 'certain racial or ethnic groups' or just 'racial groups' (to use the language of the 1965 International Convention on the Elimination of All Forms of Racial Discrimination).

10   The 'Conference on Security and Co-operation in Europe' evolved into the 'Organization for Security and Co-operation in Europe' as a result of a decision taken at the summit meeting held in Budapest in December 1994. For some legal and political considerations on this evolution, *see* M. Sapiro 'Changing the CSCE into the OSCE: Legal Aspects of a Political Transformation', 89.3 *American Journal of International Law* (1995) pp. 631-637.

11   For the mandate of the High Commissioner on national Minorities, *see* http://www.osce.org/docs/english/1990-1999/summits/hels92e.htm (accessed 6 June 2004) at Helsinki Decisions, Chapter II.

Although the mandate of the HCNM has certain expressed restrictions which serve to focus his attentions, it nevertheless remains very wide and, indeed, intrusive.[12] In particular, the HCNM enjoys a right of initiative by which, on the basis of his own judgement, he may take up problems in those situations which he believes merit his involvement. As an independent actor, he may then establish direct contacts with a view to collecting information 'from any source' (with the exception of persons practising or publicly condoning terrorism or violence), including governmental representatives at the highest level. To this end, the HCNM enjoys a virtual right of entry into, and freedom of movement throughout, all participating States. To balance this very wide access to information, the mandate of the HCNM prescribes that he act in a confidential manner and that he report to the Chairman-in-Office and, ultimately, to the Permanent Council in Vienna. As such, the HCNM is to act with great discretion and, thus, to be an instrument of quiet diplomacy aimed at containing – and hopefully de-escalating – tensions. In the event that the intervention of the HCNM is unable to contain tensions, he is required to alert all OSCE States via the Chairman-in-Office and the Permanent Council, such that other means of conflict prevention may be considered.

While the mandate of the HCNM prescribes an *impartial, confidential* and *accountable* approach, it does not prescribe precisely the approach or means through which the HCNM is to fulfil his mandate in preventive diplomacy. It thus fell to the first HCNM, Mr. Max van der Stoel (a former Dutch Foreign Minister), to develop an appropriate approach on the basis of his long experience in diplomacy and his understanding of the Helsinki process. In the first place, the HCNM recognized that his role as an impartial and independent actor required him *not* to act as an advocate for national minorities (N.B. the High Commissioner is a conflict prevention mechanism 'ON' problems involving national minorities), nor as an ombudsman acting on individual complaints. More generally, the HCNM is *not* a mechanism supervising compliance by States with their international obligations and commitments. Rather, the HCNM is to act more as a facilitator cum mediator in an effort to bring disputant parties to some kind of an accord and to avoid problems involving national minorities from turning into 'hot' conflicts.

The HCNM's starting point has been to analyse and approach problems through a logical and practical application of the OSCE notion of 'comprehensive security'. This is to say the HCNM takes a 'root causes' approach to the problems he confronts on the basis of the prescription in his mandate to be 'an instrument of conflict prevention *at the earliest possible stage.*' This follows directly from the linear logic of comprehensive security which informs that peace and security are dependent upon the realization and perception of 'justice', which is itself manifested through respect for human rights, including the rights of persons belonging to minorities; only on this basis is meaningful economic and social development attainable. Consequently, peace and security require

---

12   For a comprehensive analysis of the mandate of the HCNM, *see* R. Zaagman, 'The CSCE High Commissioner on National Minorities: An Analysis of the Mandate and the Institutional Context' in A. Bloed (ed.) *The Challenges of Change; The Helsinki Summit of the CSCE and Its Aftermath* (Dordrecht: Martinus Nijhoff Publishers, 1994) pp. 113-175.

the creation of a 'just order' in the State whereby everyone's human rights may be equally enjoyed and where governance is conducted for the benefit of the whole population and not just some (ethnic or national, linguistic, cultural, religious or racial) part thereof. This means, concretely, that there must be a proper separation of powers to enable the Rule of Law and full respect for human rights. In the absence of these requirements for justice, arbitrariness will no doubt yield discriminatory treatment and the unsatisfied claims of disgruntled persons, including especially persons belonging to national minorities, will sooner or later challenge stability and endanger the peace.

In the OSCE's notion of comprehensive security, peace and security within the State on the basis of a just order respecting human rights is a matter of international concern because of complex interdependence. History has too often demonstrated that systematic violation of human rights within the State has serious effects on other States. Most obvious are the effects of mass outflows of refugees and other persons fleeing conflict. However, as all States become increasingly integrated in their economic, social, environmental and other relations, so insecurity and instability within one State causes disruptions among others. This reflects a global transition. It is only perhaps more noticeable and dynamic (and, thus, more volatile) in the countries of Central and Eastern Europe where there has been at the same time a wrenching transition from centralized Communism to democracy and market economy; this largely explains the HCNM's focus on this part of the OSCE.

IV. The Approach Of The High Commissioner

The HCNM has a wide scope to determine his approach to implementation of his mandate. The mandate is constituted to accommodate great flexibility and expressly relies on the HCNM's 'judgement'. However, aside from the formal possibilities afforded by the mandate, it is to be noted that the institution itself is somewhat of a novelty for which there is little precedence on which to draw for purposes of direction. As a result, the first HCNM blazed a new trail.[13]

The twin objectives of 'early warning' and 'early action' orientate the HCNM's approach in the direction of two functional activities. However, in the first place, he must inform himself about situations and make assessments as to the likelihood of existing tensions heating up and, where they appear uncontainable, the HCNM must sound the alarm and thereby stimulate the closer engagement of participating States, initially

---

13   *See* W. Kemp (ed.) *Quiet Diplomacy in Action: The OSCE High Commissioner on National Minorities* (The Hague: Kluwer Law International, 2001). For updates on the HCNM's work, *see*: S. Holt 'The Activities of the OSCE High Commissioner on National Minorities: January 2001-May 2002' 1 *European Yearbook of Minority Issues* (2001/02) (The Hague: Kluwer Law International, 2003) pp. 563-589; and M. Draper 'The Activities of the OSCE High Commissioner on National Minorities: June 2002-June 2003' 2 *European Yearbook of Minority Issues* (2002/03) (The Hague: Kluwer Law International, 2003) pp. 475-491.

through the Chairman-in-Office. In the more common situation where tension-causing disputes may be brewing and even where there may already be sparks, the HCNM is to act to prevent the disputes from becoming violent and/or destabilizing. Depending upon the nature, stage and intensity of disputes and possible tensions, the HCNM may be required to act more or less urgently and with more or less persuasion. These activities merit further clarification.

1. *The Pyrometer*

The HCNM may be said to function as a pyrometer insofar as he monitors situations with a view to measuring the heat and assessing combustibility. This is a basic and substantial part of the work of the Office of the HCNM.

Prior to making determinations of appropriate action, the HCNM surveys on a daily basis events throughout OSCE participating States. He does this with the assistance of an Office composed of a Director, about a dozen professional staff and a small number of support staff. The professional staff are divided into area-specialist advisers, a few specialized legal advisers and some project officers. On the basis of news reports, NGO submissions and increasing systems of domestic monitoring, along with information received from governments, the HCNM's attention is drawn to situations which may possibly fall within his mandate. In recent years, the HCNM's staff has increasingly travelled to countries to clarify facts on the ground before the High Commissioner may personally become involved. Satisfied that a situation falls (or may fall) within his mandate, the HCNM establishes contacts with relevant actors and arranges an initial visit to the country and location concerned with a view to further orientating him on the whole situation, including the real positions of the parties. In his contacts, the HCNM guarantees confidentiality which encourages the depoliticisation of the issues and reduces the possibility of personalities 'losing face'. The HCNM also undertakes his involvement in a co-operative spirit by which he seeks to be of assistance to the parties and does not employ, nor does he wish to be viewed as employing, coercion. Thus, the HCNM presents himself as a problem-solving aid.

It was the experience of the first HCNM (who took up his duties on 1 January 1993), and continues to be the experience of the second HCNM (Mr. Rolf Ekéus, a retired Swedish diplomat, who took up his duties on 1 July 2001), that many (if not most) of the problems involving national minorities are rooted in the non-respect of human rights (especially discrimination), including the rights of persons belonging to national minorities. Frequently, this includes lack of effective participation in political decision-making processes. This and other issues of concern give rise to inter-ethnic tensions especially in societies where democratic institutions, such as an independent judiciary, are new or fragile – where they lack vigour and where confidence (in particular among minorities) in public institutions, bodies and services is weak.

In order to analyse the problems he confronts, the HCNM regularly turns to the existing standards of human rights. These are many. On the basis of OSCE commitments to uphold all relevant standards, the HCNM may and does refer to any applicable standard irrespective of source, e.g. the United Nations, the Council of Europe, the OSCE, or bilateral accords.[14] These may be of a legally binding nature (e.g. a conventional undertaking) or constitute a political commitment (e.g. texts agreed within the OSCE). It is, of course, useful for the HCNM to be able to refer in his dialogue and ultimate recommendations to established standards freely undertaken by the State concerned; this saves the HCNM from accusations of arbitrariness and furnishes the HCNM with a possible solution on the basis of already prescribed norms and rules agreed to by the State.

2.   *The Prophylactic*

In such a case where, in the High Commissioner's own judgement, a situation exists which merits his active involvement, the HCNM may be said to function as a prophylactic insofar as he engages through actions (largely diplomatic) aimed at preventing or containing tensions from erupting into violence. Through the years, this has become the core of the HCNM's work for which he has developed a number of techniques.

Aside from using existing norms and standards as an analytical tool, these same norms have instrumental value as a pre-existing basis for dialogue and as an important reference for reform or development of policy and law. Upon establishing a direct dialogue with the representatives of all the relevant parties, the HCNM has established a practice of exchanging written letters with the Foreign Minister of the government of the State within whose territorial jurisdiction the situation arises. In this exchange, the HCNM provides his analysis of the situation – taking into account all the legitimate interests at play – and offers his specific recommendations for its resolution. The Foreign Minister then replies. While it was perhaps not foreseen in the HCNM's mandate that such an exchange of letters would become public, neither was it precluded. From the start, it has become the practice that these exchanges are eventually made public after they have been addressed in the Permanent Council with the full attention of all participating States. In this way, confidentiality is maintained (often for months), during which quiet diplomatic activities may be pursued. Ultimately, however, the exchanges are made public with a view to enabling all interested persons (in particular, the representatives of minorities and the affected general public) to know exactly the opinions and recommendations of the HCNM as an impartial and independent actor, together with the opinions and position of the Government *vis-à-vis* those of the HCNM.

---

14   For a general treatment of minority rights in international law, *see*: P. Thornberry *International Law and the Rights of Minorities* (Oxford: Clarendon Press, 1991); and Z. Machnyikova, J. Packer and S. Ratner (eds.) *Contemporary Issues in the Protection of Minorities in Europe* (Kehl am Rhein: N.P. Engel Verlag, forthcoming 2004). For a concise analysis of the catalogue of internationally guaranteed minority rights upon which the HCNM relies in his work, *see* J. Packer 'On the Content of Minority Rights' in J. Räikkä (ed.) *Do We Need Minority Rights? Conceptual Issues* (The Hague: Kluwer Law International, 1996) pp. 121-178.

It is perhaps interesting to note that, of the many situations the HCNM has addressed in over a dozen States, he has so far never used his 'early warning' function – although in exercising the capacity of Personal Representative of the Chairman-in-Office for Kosovo for about one year, Mr. van der Stoel warned of impending serious consequences of intransigence and inaction. But, by focusing his attentions on his function of 'early action', it may well be that the HCNM has attained a certain success. At a minimum, the HCNM has acted to engage disputant parties in dialogue, to assist them to establish ongoing and structured forms of dialogue, to solve specific problems and to work together to find mutually satisfying and enduring solutions thereby avoiding the escalation of tensions.

In the course of ten years of activity, the HCNM has become involved in situations in the following countries, in alphabetical order: Albania, Croatia, Estonia, Georgia, Greece, Hungary, Latvia, Lithuania, the former Yugoslav Republic of Macedonia, Moldova, Kazakhstan, Kyrgyzstan, Romania, Serbia and Montenegro (formerly the Federal Republic of Yugoslavia), Slovakia, and Ukraine. In addition, the HCNM has issued two reports on the situation of the Roma in Europe. More generally, the HCNM has initiated, endorsed and disseminates a series of general recommendations regarding the recurrent issues of the education rights of national minorities, their linguistic rights and their rights of effective participation in public life.[15]

In the course of his work, the HCNM has sought to prevent conflict by various means. In the first place, he has encouraged structured dialogue whereby the parties may find solutions on their own. This has included the organization of ad hoc meetings, the creation of standing consultative bodies (e.g. inter-ethnic councils or round tables), and the expansion of forms of effective participation of national minorities in decision-making processes and bodies (e.g. reserved seats in parliament and decentralization of power). The HCNM also studies existing policy and law from the perspective of analysing the entrenched sources of tensions between minorities and governmental authorities. In this connection, the HCNM uses the relevant international standards as a barometer for his assessments. The HCNM also analyses specific policies and administrative practices by references to relevant domestic law, including notably constitutional provisions. At the same time, the HCNM scrutinizes draft legislation and governmental policies and offers comments thereon; in this way, the HCNM seeks to avoid the adoption of laws and policies which may be difficult to change once they have gone through the political processes and final positions have been declared and fixed. In connection with all of the afore-mentioned, the HCNM may intervene in various ways, e.g. through conversations with relevant interlocutors (or letters addressed to them) or through the HCNM's formal recommendations. In addition, the HCNM makes frequent reference in his work to the evolving standards of good governance which draws

---

15   For a public listing of the HCNM's work, *see* the OSCE's web site at www.osce.org. In addition, the HCNM has been engaged to varying degrees, and in various forms, in an increasing number of countries, sometimes at their invitation, including the United Kingdom (Northern Ireland), Turkey and Uzbekistan/Turkmenistan.

upon the responsibility of democratically elected governments to serve the interests, and respond to legitimate demands (i.e. beyond the minimum standards of human rights), of the whole populations of their States.

A little noticed activity of the HCNM is his quiet efforts to assist in the resolution of problems which owe much to a lack of economic resources or humanitarian aid. This is to say that some problems of inter-ethnic relations may be rooted in competition for scarce jobs or economic benefits, or frustration at the persistence of a difficult humanitarian situation. In many of these situations, the governmental authorities genuinely lack sufficient resources to respond adequately to the problem. The non-resolution of these problems often exacerbates underlying ethnic tensions. Consequently, the HCNM has sought to draw the attention of donor countries and institutions to humanitarian needs and to direct international assistance and investment to such projects as might also contribute to the reduction of tensions. In the former case, the HCNM has encouraged donor countries to fund specific projects undertaken by governments, NGOs and, in a very few cases, the HCNM himself. For example, the HCNM has received financial support from one donor country to fund the publication of new school textbooks in Kyrgyzstan in both the State language and the language of a minority. In the case of international investment, the HCNM seeks to apprise the relevant inter-governmental entities and States of the possibility for their investment, if specifically targeted, to contribute to economic development while at the same time reducing tensions. This may be achieved, e.g., by directing investment to areas of a country where persons belonging to minorities are disproportionately unemployed. Examples where humanitarian aid may play a vital role is in alleviating some of the difficulties experienced by the return of formerly deported Crimean Tatars to their homeland in Ukraine or the HCNM's development programme aimed at assisting the integration of the mainly ethnic Armenian population of the Samtskhe-Javakheti region of Georgia into the broader society of the State of Georgia. These projects have been called 'tension-reducing projects'.[16]

3.   The Pyrosvestis

While the mandate of the HCNM is clearly one of conflict prevention, in fact neither the reality of various situations nor his engagement fall neatly into such a discrete category. More accurately, if one is to imagine a continuum of conflict (and hopefully not a cycle to be repeated), the HCNM has in a number of cases been involved in conflict management and resolution. In this sense, the HCNM may be said to function as a *pyrosvestis* (i.e. a fireman) who acts to stamp out sparks and extinguish small fires or to steer the flames in such a direction that they may burn out or be contained. In this respect, the High Commissioner employs many of the same techniques as used for prevention. Indeed, especially in situations of post-conflict conflict prevention, the notions

---

16   See J. Cohen *Conflict Prevention in the OSCE, An Assessment of Capacities* (The Hague: Netherlands Institute of International Relations, Clingendael, 1999).

of prevention, management and resolution blur and overlap. Good examples of the HCNM's work in such situations include his engagements in Croatia (especially Eastern Slavonia) immediately following the conclusion of the Dayton Peace Agreement,[17] and in the Former Yugoslav Republic of Macedonia during the difficult (and violent) period of spring/summer 2001.[18]

The HCNM has also performed the functions of a fireman in 'ringing the bell' about imminent explosions on two occasions: first, in Kosovo in February 1998 in the face of increased violence on the part of both the Serbian authorities and Kosovar Albanian paramilitary forces,[19] and, second, in the former Yugoslav Republic of Macedonia in May 1999 in the face of a mass influx of ethnic Albanian refugees fleeing the situation in Kosovo.[20] It might be argued that the HCNM in fact provides early warning about such potentials in all situations in which he becomes engaged, since his mere involvement signals his determination that there exists a situation with at least the prospect 'to develop into a conflict within the OSCE area, affecting peace, stability or relations between participating States'. But this is not the same as to 'ring the bell' since to do so means also to signal that the HCNM is not alone capable of containing the situation which has exceeded, or is about to exceed, at least the HCNM's scope for prevention.

V.   The Issues Arising in the Work of the OSCE HCNM

The substantive issues addressed by the HCNM may be divided into several fields. These include the following: 1) identity; 2) culture; 3) education; 4) language; 5) media; 6) political participation; 7) citizenship; and 8) access to resources. While their manifestation and appropriate treatment in a particular situation are a function of important and often determinative case-specific details (including personalities), these recurrent issues may be briefly summarised as follows.

1)   *Identity*. This is often at the root of all disputes, i.e. the equal right of each person to determine, maintain and develop his or her identity free from prescription or coercion. This strikes at the heart of human dignity. It concerns self-esteem. It raises questions concerning the status and use of language, the status and use of names, symbolic concerns, etc. In essence, it is existential and, therefore, not easily surrendered or compromised.

---

17   For a brief summary of the HCNM's involvement in Croatia between 14 December 1995 and early 1999, *see* J. Packer 'The Role of the OSCE High Commissioner on National Minorities in the Former Yugoslavia' 12.2 *Cambridge Review of International Affairs* (1999), pp. 174-176. See also W. Kemp (note 13) pp. 169-175.

18   W. Kemp (note 13) p. 196.

19   Ibid. p. 203.

20   Ibid. pp. 191-192.

2)   *Culture*. Like education, culture is closely related to, and is most probably a fundamental ingredient of, the notion of identity. Notwithstanding the lack of a technically satisfying definition, 'cultural interests' extend to areas both regulated and unregulated by the State. Of course, culture is evident in matters of aesthetics, including notably the arts. To promote the maintenance and development of these interests, there must certainly be the guarantee of liberty, but this is usually not enough: they require economic support. This applies to music academies, art galleries, museums, the maintenance of libraries and archives. To maintain these as living elements of popular life, they may also require the provision of facilities (e.g. auditoria, sports fields and halls, ateliers, community centres) and support of a professional class of artists and artisans to pursue, develop and pass on the elements of culture. Even the establishment of societies[21] and their maintenance requires legal space and economic means. Consequently, disputes have arisen over the equitable division of public economic resources in support of minority cultural interests. Disputes have also arisen over symbolic aspects of culture as reflected (or not) officially at the level of the State. This is to say nothing of how and to which extent culture affects other aspects of social organisation, particular interests and politics in general within the State.

3)   *Education*. This is often a matter of energetic dispute and heated exchange because of the importance of education as a transmitter of identity within a cultural grouping, i.e. from one generation to the next. Education also embodies in its form and content important cultural elements. This applies to curricula (in particular the subjects of language, history and culture) and also the structure of education; an important element of identity is 'world view' which may be reflected in the whole educational process. At the same time, education is critical to general socialization and is, as such, the object of interest (indeed, obligations) on the part of the State. This means that education is, even in the best of situations, the subject of constant tensions between public authorities, parents and interested groups. This applies notwithstanding the possibility of private education in so far as the State may prescribe a measure of standard curricula and may regulate private education. At the same time, minorities may assert a right to a certain accommodation within the public system or claim a measure of support from the State. It also applies at all levels of education: pre-school, primary, secondary, vocational and tertiary. Not surprisingly, education for minorities has been the subject of considerable attention in virtually every situation in which the HCNM has become involved. As such, the issue of education was the focus of an initial set of general recommendations which the HCNM invited a group of internationally recognized independent experts to elaborate: *The Hague Recommendations regarding the Education Rights of National Minorities*.[22]

---

21   For an important judgment on this issue by the European Court of Human Rights see *Case of Sidiropoulos and Others v. Greece* (57/1997/841/1047), judgment of 10 July 1998.

22   For the text of The Hague Recommendations and Explanatory Note (available in several languages) see http://www.osce.org/hcnm/documents/recommendations/hague/index.

4)   *Language.* Perhaps the most recurrent issue concerns the use of language both in public and in private.[23] As many European States define themselves in ethno-linguistic terms (e.g. Germany is the State of Germans who speak German), the place of linguistic minorities within such States, and specifically their linguistic rights, is frequently a source of dispute and tension. In this respect, it must be understood that language has both primordial and instrumental functions. It is primordial in its innate and largely defining nature as a basis and carrier of identity (to *be* German is to speak German); socio-linguists argue convincingly that this is much more than a matter of communication. Of course, language is also instrumental insofar as it functions for purposes of communication to open or close access to other goods. As such, opportunities to use language have important implications for both material and spiritual wellbeing. In open, liberal democracies and markets, language use is important both in private affairs and in public life. In fact, the two spheres sometimes overlap, such as in the conduct and regulation of commerce. Linguistic prescriptions can advantage some and disadvantage others in various domains (e.g. the judiciary and public administration), ways (e.g. quotas and subsidies) and degrees (e.g. totally exclude or just cause difficulty). In an effort to reconcile conflicting linguistic needs, demands and desires in linguistically plural societies – while recognising and affirming the role of a common language in integrating and solidifying the broader society – the HCNM invited a group of internationally recognized independent experts to elaborate the *Oslo Recommendations regarding the Linguistic Rights of National Minorities*[24] and, at around the same time, conducted a survey of all 55 OSCE participating States to see and compare the many and varied ways in which the linguistic rights of minorities are implemented across the region.[25] It is remarkable to observe how much, and in how many different ways, language is regulated across the OSCE region – and how much diversity can and is being accommodated.

---

php3. The Hague Recommendations are also reproduced, together with some scholarly articles (including one co-authored by P. Thornberry), in a dedicated issue of the following journal: 4.2 *International Journal on Minority and Group Rights* (1996/97). With regard to the hotly contested area of higher education, see the special

23   For recent treatments of this issue, see G. Hogan-Brun and S. Wolff (eds.) *Minority Languages in Europe; Frameworks, Status, Prospects* (London: Palgrave, 2003); S. Trifunovska and F. de Varennes (eds.) *Minority Rights in Europe; European Minorities and Languages* (The Hague: T.M.C. Asser Press, 2001); and, with regard specifically to the OSCE, S. Holt and J. Packer, 'OSCE Developments and Linguistic Minorities' 3.2 *UNESCO MOST Journal on Multicultural Societies* (2002), http://www.unesco.org/shs/ijms (accessed 6 June 2004).

24   For the text of the Oslo Recommendations and Explanatory Note (available in several languages), see http://www.osce.org/hcnm/documents/recommendations/oslo/index.php3 (accessed 6 June 2004). The Oslo Recommendations are also reproduced, together with scholarly articles, in a dedicated issue of the following journal: 6.3 *International Journal on Minority and Group Rights* (1999).

25   See the HCNM's *Report on the Linguistic Rights of Persons Belonging to National Minorities in the OSCE Area* (March 1999), available at http://www.osce.org/documents/hcnm/1999/03/239_en.pdf (accessed 6 June 2004).

5)   *Media.* Several aspects of the media have effects upon or other importance for persons belonging to minorities. These include the content of media, its ownership and management, representation of minorities within the media, and its accessibility. A particularly important area in the information age is access to radio and television broadcasting in one's own language and, moreover, from one's own community (i.e., not just re-transmissions in the same language but from a foreign community). Not only is this a significant aspect of cultural cohesion and linguistic maintenance, especially for numerically small or dispersed groups, but it also has significant economic aspects. As a substantially regulated field where, among other things, States have sought to protect official or State languages from being overwhelmed by foreign language broadcasting, perhaps not surprisingly this has given rise to disputes as some governments have stipulated language requirements sometimes with substantial negative effects for minorities.[26] As such, freedom of expression (including use of language) and minority rights have come up against the permitted and necessary regulation of a large field of public communication. In order to address this contentious and complex field, the HCNM commissioned a survey of State practice across the OSCE region[27] and invited a group of independent experts to elaborate *Guidelines on the Use of Minority Languages in the Broadcast Media.*[28]

6)   *Political Participation.* The basic tenet of democracy is that the will of the people be the basis of governmental authority. It is also a fundamental human right.[29] While this generally implies the will of the whole population with regard to authority in the State as a whole, the underlying concept is that the interests of 'the people' (especially the citizenry, but not only)[30] should prevail over other interests and that this prin-

---

26   See S. Holt and J. Packer 'The Use of Minority Languages in the Broadcast Media' *International Journal of Human Rights,* forthcoming.

27   See T. McGonagle, B. Davis Noll and M. Price (eds.) *Minority-Language Related Broadcasting and Legislation in the OSCE.* Programme in Comparative Media Law and Policy, Centre for Socio-Legal Studies, Wolfson College, Oxford University, and Institute for Information Law, University of Amsterdam, April 2003.

28   For the text of the Guidelines and Explanatory Note, see http://www.osce.org/documents/hcnm/2003/10/2242_en.pdf (accessed 6 June 2004).

29   At the universal level, see Article 21 of the Universal Declaration of Human Rights.

30   While international law (notably Article 25 of the International Covenant on Civil and Political Rights) prescribes that 'citizens' have the rights to vote and to stand for election, the broader aspects of political participation (including notably the freedoms of association, assembly and expression) extend to 'everyone' within the jurisdiction of the State. As a matter of State practice, even those particular rights reserved for citizens (i.e. to vote and to stand for election) are increasingly being conferred, typically below the national level, also to non-citizens who may be permanent residents, property owners or taxpayers. Indeed, some international organizations have encouraged this trend as a means of supporting social integration and stability; see, e.g, the work of the now defunct Council of Baltic Sea States Commissioner on Democratic Development, in particular the surveys on the *Rights of Non-*

ciple should apply *a fortiori* for the interests of those citizens who may be specially interested/affected by the exercise of any authority. Thus, a principle of subsidiarity may be deduced from the democratic principle of majority rule. Certainly, this is specified in the OSCE standard that persons belonging to national minorities should enjoy 'effective participation in public affairs, including participation in the affairs relating to the protection and promotion of the identity of such minorities' (paragraph 35 of the 1990 Copenhagen Document).[31] Such participation, in order to be 'effective', may be facilitated through various types of decentralization of governmental authority, including the allocation of specific subject-matter jurisdiction to the minority(ies) as such. Certainly, in an open and democratic society it is neither necessary nor desirable that persons who are not directly affected or interested should hold authority over matters which bear directly or especially on others; in the absence of a demonstrated public interest, minorities could well enjoy a certain autonomy over such matters. At a minimum, minorities should enjoy an adequate say over the development of policies in which they too hold an interest and will be expected to conform. To respond to this key issue, which also encompasses considerations of the organisation and structure of the State especially in terms of division of subject matter jurisdiction, the HCNM invited experts to elaborate the *Lund Recommendations on the Effective Participation of National Minorities in Public Life*.[32] A direct outgrowth of these recommendations was the subsequent elaboration (together with the OSCE's Office for Democratic Institutions and Human Rights and with the International Institute for Democracy and Electoral Assistance) of *Guidelines to Assist National Minority Participation in the Electoral Process*.[33]

---

citizens *Residing Lawfully in the Member States of the CBSS*, Part I, February 1996, 'Voting Rights and the Right to Stand for Public Office' (especially the thoughtful conclusions and recommendations), at http://www.cbss-commissioner.org/surveys/PDF_Documents/ survey_feb_1996_part1.pdf (accessed 6 June 2004), and also Part II, March 1998, 'Right of Association, Access to Civil Service and to other special posts or work', at http://www. cbss-commissioner.org/surveys/PDF_Documents/survey_mar_1998_part2.pdf (accessed 6 June 2004).

31   For the full text of the Copenhagen Document of June 1990, see http://www.osce.org/docs/ english/1990-1999/hd/cope90e.htm (accessed 6 June 2004).

32   For the text of the Lund Recommendations and Explanatory Note (available in several languages), see http://www.osce.org/hcnm/documents/recommendations/lund/index.php3 (accessed 6 June 2004). The Lund Recommendations are also reproduced in addendum to J. Packer 'The origin and nature of the Lund Recommendations on the Effective Participation of National Minorities in Public Life' 2.4 *Helsinki Monitor* (2000), pp. 29-61. See further K. Myntti *A Commentary to the Lund Recommendations on the Effective Participation of National Minorities in Public Life* (Turku/Åbo: Åbo Akademi University Institute for Human Rights, 2001).

33   For the text of the Guidelines (sometimes called 'the Warsaw Guidelines' after the seat of ODIHR where they were elaborated), see http://www.osce.org/documents/ hcnm/2001/01/240_en.pdf (accessed 15 June 2004).

7)   *Citizenship.* In simple terms, this is the question of equality within the polity, in particular equality before the law. But, it raises the larger question of 'insider' versus 'outsider' and, therefore, the legitimacy of interests. Citizenship is both a statement of belonging and also a basis for the enjoyment of certain rights, in particular and importantly political and economic rights. It has become of special significance in States which base citizenship on the criteria of a blood link, i.e. *jus sanguinis*; particularly in the States of restored sovereignty (N.B. the Baltic States of Estonia and Latvia) this is a problem as the new citizenship laws have functioned to exclude the overwhelming majority of persons belonging to national minorities despite very long permanent residence or birth on the territory.[34] It is also a particular problem for the formerly deported persons of the Former Soviet Union who seek to return to their places of origin. It may also become a problem within the EU where the requirement of citizenship to enjoy various rights combined with the so far weak regime for the protection of human rights (and almost absent protection of minorities) leaves non-citizens (even long-term residents and persons born within EU territory) vulnerable.

8)   *Access to Resources.* As noted above in relation to education and culture, access to an equitable share of public resources (usually tax receipts) is often the ultimate subject of dispute. However, this also extends to the more general interest of minorities to enjoy a fair share of economic goods available to the society as a whole. This concerns access to employment within the public service, access to governmental contracts, and an equitable share of government financed investment, development projects and the proceeds from and use of natural resources. For non-citizen but long-term residents (and usually tax payers) belonging to minorities, there may also be the question of access to social security benefits. This is a key but so far under-explored and analysed subject (at least within the work of the OSCE in general, and the HCNM in particular).[35]

Overall, the problems of minorities encountered by the HCNM feature the perception of persons belonging to national minorities that are unfairly prohibited from pursuing their own development or are unfairly precluded from enjoying the benefits of the State. This sense of injustice has been the subject of expressed interest of kin-States. With or without kin-States (indeed, often in their absence), frustrations over such injustices have given rise to self-determination claims which have heightened tensions and sometimes given rise to violence. Unresolved, these disputes have the potential over time to escalate into conflicts within and between States.

---

34   See, e.g., R. Zaagman *Conflict Prevention in the Baltic States: The OSCE High Commissioner on national Minorities in Estonia, Latvia and Lithuania* (Flensburg: European Centre for Minority Issues, 1999).

35   The matter was raised, in the context of promoting social integration, at an OSCE conference held in Locarno in October 1998.

To respond to the above-described issues, the HCNM has contributed his own direct involvement including country-specific recommendations.[36] In addition, he has encouraged the resolution of certain matters in the context of bilateral treaties of friendship and good-neighbourliness. The conclusion of such treaties formed the centre-piece of the first European Stability Pact (i.e. the Balladur initiative).[37] The HCNM has also encouraged internationally recognized independent experts to articulate the further specification of existing standards in regard to the issues of education, use of language (including the broadcast media), and political participation (including forms and structures of governance and elections). In connection with the linguistic rights of minorities, the HCNM has also produced or commissioned public reports surveying and analysing the use of minority languages in all OSCE participating States with a view to making available the breadth of current policies, laws and practices for purposes of comparison and, ultimately, encouraging the adoption by States of the most appropriate and effective ones.

VI. Conclusion

The HCNM is a novel and in large measure effective means of preventing conflict through the promotion of respect for human rights, including the rights of persons belonging to minorities. The existence of the mandate is a logical application of the OSCE notions of comprehensive and co-operative security. It also responds to the reality that all States are (and will foreseeably remain) *plural* in terms of the factual diversity of their ethno-cultural, linguistic, religious and other composition. For this reason, the HCNM has encouraged open and peaceful processes of social integration which accommodate difference through choice drawing on creative solutions and alternatives which are consistent with human rights standards, and he has criticized and rejected policies and laws of coerced assimilation.

Certainly, the relative success of the HCNM owes a lot to the political backing he has enjoyed from all participating States; in particular, the process of European integration has encouraged governments (to varying degrees) to co-operate with him and to implement his recommendations. As a result, the HCNM has succeeded in facilitating numerous processes of political dialogue and reform which have diminished tensions or kept them from escalating. He has also assisted in the clarification and specification of the body of relevant international standards, thereby assisting States to understand

---

36   For the HCNM's country or situation-specific recommendations, *see* http://www.osce.org/hcnm/documents/recommendations/index.php (accessed 6 June 2004).

37   For a review and analysis of contemporary bilateral treaties addressing specifically national minorities see A. Bloed and P. van Dijk (eds.) *Protection of Minority Rights Through Bilateral Treaties* (Dordrecht: Martinus Nijhoff Publishers, 2000); and K. Gál *Bilateral Agreements in Central and Eastern Europe: A New Inter-State Framework for Minority Protection?*, ECMI Working Papers No. 4 (Flensburg: European Centre for Minority Issues, 1999).

and implement better their obligations and commitments.[38] The success of the HCNM appears to owe a great deal to the appropriateness of his approach, to personal skill and care in pursuing it and, ultimately, the quality of specific initiatives and recommendations which have proven in themselves to be of interest to the parties as useful references, if not exact solutions, for the concrete problems they face. This appears to be a testament to the fundamental universality of the values themselves and to the utility of standards of human rights (including minority rights) and good governance as a means of achieving social justice, peace and security and, ultimately, economic and social development.

While the fundamental philosophy of comprehensive security is apparent in the overall approach taken by the HCNM, the choice of his techniques and the emphasis of his recommendations vary together with the speed and intensity of his actions depending upon the nature of the situation confronting the HCNM. From this perspective, the HCNM is variously a monitor, analyst, evaluator, prophylactic and fireman – and throughout a source of early warning for those who watch and listen.

On the basis of over a decade of dedicated activity, it seems now safe to say that the novel idea of the institution of the HCNM has proven to be a successful instrument of conflict prevention. It is increasingly appropriate to the times, where the complexity of disputes and the inappropriateness of alternative means (especially the use of military force) is more and more clear. Simply, the quiet diplomacy of conflict prevention as undertaken by the HCNM works. It is also indisputably cheap, both in terms of human lives saved and suffering avoided and in terms of actual financial expenditures; the annual regular budget of the HCNM is remarkably low at just over Euro 2 million. Certainly, success also depends significantly on the political support the HCNM enjoys in terms of initiatives and for his specific and general recommendations. But, the quality of the approach and the persuasiveness of the person of the HCNM have also proven key elements in the success of the institution so far. There is evidently room for greater utility and effect, for example as an indicator to direct aid and investment which may also contribute significantly (and sometimes determinatively) to the reduction of tensions or even the settlement of disputes. In sum, the institution of the HCNM is now a proven institution which may be an example for the development of similar institutions and approaches elsewhere in the world.[39]

---

38   One observer has thus labeled the HCNM a 'normative intermediary' as he has pursued this work both in general terms and in terms of application in specific situations; *see* S. Ratner 'Does International Law Matter in Preventing Ethnic Conflict?' 32.2 *New York University Journal of International Law and Politics* (2000) pp. 591-698.

39   No less than the UN Secretary-General, Kofi Annan, has called (at the 1999 OSCE Summit in Istanbul) for the rest of the international community to note and emulate the work of the HCNM. Among those pursuing this to various degrees have been the Rockefeller Foundation and the International Peace Academy.

Chapter 15

Council of Europe Policies Concerning the Protection of Linguistic Minorities and the Justiciability of Minority Rights

María Amor Martín Estébanez[1]

1. Introduction

If asked to synthesise Professor Patrick Thornberry's approach to the role of international law in minority protection in one sentence, the present author would do it as follows: the facilitation of the enabling environment where states, persons belonging to minorities, and the groups they belong to, can actively contribute to the development of culturally rich, inclusive and participative societies. It is Professor Thornberry's underlying emphasis on the role of international law in the creation of favourable spaces where existing identities can develop in the context of peaceful and respectful relations, which the present author finds a most inspiring aspect of his work.

This chapter is devoted to linguistic communication, possibly the most intangible and at the same time fundamental of these spaces, as language permeates almost every aspect of minority identity. The chapter focuses on the role of one of the most prominent organisations dealing with human rights protection in Europe, the Council of Europe. The role of the Council of Europe in promoting linguistic minority protection[2] is discussed, its policies explored and the challenges ahead alluded to.

While the importance of linguistic diversity protection may be questioned from some quarters, the protection of linguistic identity is frequently a basic and central

---

1   Centre for Socio-Legal Studies, Wolfson College, University of Oxford.
2   For a previous discussion of this topic see S. Trifunoska 'Protection of Linguistic Rights within the Council of Europe' in S. Trifunoska and F. de Varennes (eds.) *Minority Rights in Europe, European Minorities and Languages* (The Hague: TMC Asser Press, 2001) pp. 145-148. This book contains also a collection of relevant essays and documentation. Introductory remarks on Council of Europe approaches to linguistic minority protection can be found in P. Leuprecht 'Le Conseil de l'Europe et les droits des minorités: les droits des minorités linguistiques' 27 *Cahiers de Droit* (1986) pp. 203-213. On the issue of linguistic minority rights cfr. F. de Varennes *Language, Minorities and Human Rights* (The Hague: Martinus Nijhoff Publishers, 1996).

Nazila Ghanea & Alexandra Xanthaki (eds.), Minorities, Peoples and Self-Determination, *pp. 269-297.*
© *2005 Koninklijke Brill NV. Printed in The Netherlands. ISBN 90 04 14301 7.*

demand of persons belonging to minorities.[3] Linguistic minority issues have become a concern of all Council of Europe organs[4] and of the European Court of Human Rights. The interest of the Council of Europe to this question can be traced back to the introduction of a prohibition of discrimination on the basis of language in the application of the European Convention on Human Rights (ECHR), article 14.[5] Linguistic minority concerns have been linked since then to human rights considerations, as highlighted by the number of 'linguistic cases' brought before the European Commission and Court of Human Rights.[6] However, an explicit 'political' recognition of the fact that minority rights form an integral part of the protection of human rights, even by the Parliamentary Assembly (Assembly) which is the organ which has traditionally echoed minority concerns, had to wait much longer.[7] The reluctant attitude of Council of Europe member states to address minority protection in the framework of the organisation, combined with the need to respond to emerging minority situations where a linguistic component was pivotal, finally resulted in the adoption in 1992 of the European Charter for Regional or Minority Languages (Languages Charter).[8]

---

3   For a thought-provoking collection of essays concerning linguistic diversity protection see M. Kontra, R. Phillipson, T. Skutnabb-Kangas and T. Várady (eds.) *Language: a Right and a Resource, Approaching Linguistic Human Rights* (Budapest: Central European University Press, 1999). A recent, token example of the importance placed on linguistic demands even by minority groups facing situations of material deprivation is provided by the requests for official recognition of the Tartar language in Crimea. See 'Crimean Tartars Mark 60th Anniversary of Deportation', 8 Radio Free Europe/Radio Liberty Newsline No. 94, Part II, 19 May 2004.

4   This also relates to Council of Europe bodies, such as the Commissioner for Human Rights or the European Commission against Racism and Intolerance, and includes also those with a lose institutional setting, such as the European Commission for Democracy through Law (Venice Commission) which is based on an 'enlarged agreement' of the Council of Europe. Given the comparatively lower weight of these bodies in Council of Europe policy-making than that of its political organs (the actions of which the former bodies often aim to influence), the present contribution focuses on the latter.

5   For a recent review of relevant preparatory work on the ECHR see A. Spiliopoulou Åkermark *Justifications of Minority Protection in International Law* (Dordrecht: Kluwer Law International, 1997) pp. 200-203. Aspects of discrimination as an element of minority protection in the linguistic field are discussed in K. Henrard 'The Protection of Linguistic Diversity in Human Rights and Minority Protection Treaties' paper presented at the European University Institute (RSCAS-Law) conference: *'Linguistic Diversity and European Law'* (Florence, 12-13 November 2001), also in the contribution of the same title in B. de Witte and M. Aziz (eds.) *Linguistic Diversity and European Law* (Antwerp: Intersentia, forthcoming).

6   For a recent review of jurisprudence under the ECHR on minority language rights see R. Medda-Windischer 'The European Court of Human Rights and Minority Rights' 25.3 *European Integration* (2003) pp. 256-260.

7   A. Spiliopoulou Åkermark dates in 1990 the first express statement by the Parliamentary Assembly of the Council of Europe 'that minority rights, within the Council of Europe, are regarded as part of human rights'. Spiliopoulou Åkermark (note 5) p. 221.

8   European Treaty Series No. 148. For a presentation of the Charter and the context in which

The Languages Charter's emphasis on 'linguistic' instead of 'minority' protection,[9] aimed to overcome the reluctance of those states who are unwilling to recognise minority rights. However, this has not fully succeeded.[10] One reason behind this may be because the protection of language as such and of linguistic minorities, is not easy to disentangle.[11] The subsequent adoption of the Framework Convention for the Protection of National Minorities (Framework Convention),[12] where linguistic protection occupies a prominent position, was prompted by armed conflicts in the Balkans and further afield. The Framework Convention was the result of the role acquired by the Council of Europe in transforming the political commitments adopted in the framework of the Organisation for Security and Co-operation in Europe (OSCE) into legal obligations.[13] The adoption of the Languages Charter and the Framework Convention has formally configured a dual approach to linguistic minority protection by the Council of Europe, from a 'linguistic protection' and a 'minority right' standpoint. Whilst both approaches easily fit both substantively and procedurally,[14] the question of justiciability remains largely unresolved.

---

it was adopted see J-M. Woehrling 'La Charte européenne des langues régionales ou minoritaires' 95-96 *Terminogramme* (2001), pp. 159-181. See also Spiliopoulou Åkermark (note 5) pp. 233-238, and P. Thornberry and M. A. Martín Estébanez *Minority Rights in Europe, a Review of the Work and Standards of the Council of Europe* (Strasbourg: Council of Europe Publishing, 2004) pp. 137-168.

9   Explanatory Report of the Languages Charter, para. 10.

10   The French approach serves as an illustration. See B. Poignant 'Prospects for ratification of the charter by France' 2 *Regional or Minority Languages* pp. 45-49. On the French approaches to linguistic protection more broadly see further J. Ziller 'Le Droit Français de la Langue entre les Mythes d'une Tradition Interventionniste et la Réalité de Nouvelles Angoisses' in B. de Witte and M. Aziz (eds.) (note 5).

11   This is an aspect of the approach to protection under the Languages Charter discussed by the present author in 'The European Charter for Regional or Minority Languages: on Principles and Approaches' in B. de Witte and M. Aziz (eds.) (note 5). That contribution, as the present one, develops the paper 'Linguistic Diversity and the Council of Europe: The European Charter for Regional or Minority languages and Council of Europe Policies', presented at the European University Institute (RSCAS-Law) conference: *'Linguistic Diversity and European Law'* (Florence, 12-13 November 2001).

12   European Treaty Series No. 157.

13   Following the mandate to this effect given by the first Council of Europe Summit. See Appendix II, Vienna Declaration, First Council of Europe Summit, 9 October 1993, and Explanatory Report of the Framework Convention, para. 10. Among the OSCE documents containing commitments in the field of minority protection, linguistic aspects are treated especially in the 1989 Vienna Concluding Document; the 1990 Document of the Copenhagen Meeting of the Conference on the Human Dimension of the CSCE; and the 1991 Report of the Meeting of Experts on National Minorities in Geneva. See OSCE Human Dimension Commitments, a Reference Guide (Warsaw: ODIHR 2001). See also the 1998 Oslo Recommendations Regarding the Linguistic Rights of National Minorities and Explanatory Note, available electronically on http://www.osce.org/hcnm/recommendations.

14   Convergence on substantive grounds is discussed by the present author in 'The European Charter for Regional or Minority Languages: on Principles and Approaches' (note 11). On

2.   The Policies of the various Organs/Institutions

The approach of the various Council of Europe organs to the question of linguistic minority protection has differed. The existing regulatory framework has resulted from their particular responses to historical, social and political developments and from their interaction. For example, the Assembly has treated linguistic minority protection as an integral element of minority/human rights protection, in spite of its late explicit pronouncement on this issue. The main concern of the Assembly has been the adoption of an additional protocol to the ECHR on minority protection, so its endeavours have largely revolved around the introduction of linguistic protection clauses within a proposed protocol.

Following a number of unsuccessful attempts to adopt a protocol on minority protection, because of the negative response of the Committee of Ministers, the Assembly supported the 'linguistic protection' initiative taken by the Standing Conference of Regional and Local Authorities (later to become the Congress on Local and Regional Authorities: CLRAE). This led to the adoption of the Languages Charter. The Standing Conference's initiative actually finds a precedent in Assembly Recommendation 928 (1981) 'on Educational and Cultural Problems of Minority Languages and Dialects in Europe'[15] which had not led to determined action by the Committee of Ministers. It was almost a decade later, and in the context of transformation and conflict in Central and Eastern Europe, that the Council of Ministers was finally ready to take up the CLRAE's proposals, endorsed by the Assembly, and to engage in the treaty making which resulted in the adoption of the Languages Charter.

2.1.   The approach of the Assembly

The Assembly has been the Council of Europe organ that has brought the issue of linguistic minority protection into the political agenda of the organisation most consistently. Despite the increasing protagonist role acquired by the CLRAE, the role of the Assembly in this field is bound to continue. Especially as current geo-political developments, such as the diminution of violent ethnic conflict in European Union accession candidates, may once again relegate the linguistic minority protection issue to a hidden corner of the inter-governmental co-operation agenda.

---

the procedural aspect, see R. Hoffman, 'A presentation of the Framework Convention for the Protection of National Minorities and its contribution to the protection of minority languages' 2 *Regional or Minority Languages* (1999) pp. 23-24.

15   The content of this recommendation is discussed below. See also P. Thornberry and M.A. Martín Estébanez (note 8) p. 389. The text of the recommendations of the Assembly, as well as other adopted documents, are available electronically on http://assembly.coe.int/Main. asp?link=http%3A//assembly.coe.int/ASP/Doc/ListAT(SQL).asp?Session=2004-S2.

Standard-Setting and Monitoring

As the initial endeavours of the Assembly to introduce a specific article on minor-ity protection in the ECHR did not succeed, the Assembly proceeded to elaborate a draft article aimed at its inclusion in an additional protocol to the ECHR.[16] The text, presented at the Assembly in 1961, and which strongly resembled what later became Article 27 of the International Covenant on Civil and Political Rights (ICCPR), was not adopted.[17] The efforts of the Assembly towards the adoption of an additional protocol to the ECHR which provides an appropriate level of minority protection including its linguistic aspect, have continued.[18]

It was perhaps the Assembly's continued belief in the need for some form of lin-guistic protection guarantees, in the face of perceived resistance by the Committee of Ministers to take up the protocol proposal, that prompted the Recommendation 928 (1981) on the Educational and Cultural Problems of Minority Languages and Dialects in Europe. The recommendation tentatively encourages the Committee of Ministers to consider possible state engagement in the implementation of a series of positive measures, by establishing three pillars for linguistic diversity protection: a) respect for scientific authenticity; b) the right of children to their own language; and c) the right of communities to develop their own language and culture. Thus, in spite of the focus on language in the title of the recommendation, and the demand of respect for it on linguistic, 'scientific' grounds, minority rights are also introduced.[19] Although the Assembly previews the establishment of a monitoring mechanism,[20] it does not pursue a treaty on linguistic diversity, keeping the idea of a general minority protocol on its agenda instead. This will not prevent the Assembly from supporting subsequent efforts by the CLRAE in preparing a 'linguistic diversity specific' instrument.[21]

---

16 It stated that persons belonging to a national minority shall not be denied the right, *inter alia*, to use their own language, and to receive teaching in the language of their choice. See Recommendation 285 (1961) of the Consultative Assembly of the Council of Europe.

17 The ICCPR was adopted and opened for signature on 16 December 1966. It entered into force on 23 March 1976. It can be found in *Human Rights: a Compilation of International Instru-ments* (New York and Geneva: United Nations, 1994) p. 30. On the content of Article 27, see the General Comment of the Human Rights Committee, Report of the Human Rights Com-mittee, vol. I, GAOR, Forty-ninth Session, Supplement No. 40, A/49/40. pp. 107-110.

18 These efforts have occasionally been coupled with parallel initiatives by the inter-govern-mental structures (as discussed below) and even by individual states. As an example of the latter, see the discussion on 'the Austrian Draft Protocol', in P. Thornberry and M.A. Martín Estébanez *The Council of Europe and Minorities* doc. COEMIN pp. 26-27.

19 As described in Thornberry and Martín Estébanez (note 8) p. 389. The European Parliament passed a Resolution on measures in favour of the minority languages and cultures in the same year (O.J. 287/106, 9 November 1981, p. 106).

20 Final para. 5 of the recommendation.

21 See the Assembly's Opinion No. 142 (1988) on Resolution 192 (1988) on Regional or Minority languages in Europe, adopted by the Standing Conference of Local and Regional

Further conceptual development was undertaken by the Assembly in its Recommendation 1134 (1990) 'on the rights of minorities'. The emphasis on linguistic aspects is remarkable, and best illustrated by the special treatment that the rights of 'linguistic minorities' receives as a separate category.[22] Soon after the adoption of the Languages Charter, and in spite of it, the Assembly adopted Recommendation 1201 (1993) 'on an additional protocol on the rights of national minorities to the European Convention on Human Rights'. This was done in view of the persistent lack of progress at the level of the Committee of Ministers in the adoption of such a protocol, not to mention the Assembly's perceived need for a yardstick to assess state performance in the field of minority protection and monitoring compliance with requirements for accession to the organisation.[23] In Recommendation 1201, adopted in a context of mounting inter-ethnic tensions, often including a linguistic element, in a majority of the candidate states,[24] the Assembly puts forward its own protocol proposal, which will subsequently be used as a yardstick.

In this proposal, the number of linguistic aspects identified as requiring subjective minority rights protection by the Assembly is substantially augmented. While the core Article 3 is not far removed from the 1961 proposal (albeit containing a more positive and general wording: 'every person belonging to a national minority shall have the right to express, preserve, and develop in complete freedom his/her religious, ethnic, linguistic or cultural identity ....'),[25] the majority of its remaining substantive provisions relate to 'mother tongue' use.[26] These include its use in: a) the exercise of freedom of expression; b) personal names; c) contacts with administrative authorities; d) place names; e) announcements; and f) language learning and education.

Authorities of Europe. In this Opinion the Assembly notes the parallel interest of the European Parliament, expressed in resolutions adopted on 16 October 1981, 11 February 1983, and 30 October 1987. On the approaches to linguistic diversity in the context of the European Union see N. N. Shuibhne *EC Law and Minority Language Policy: Culture, Citizenship and Fundamental Rights* (The Hague: Kluwer, 2002) and B. de Witte 'Does the European Union have a language policy?' in de Witte and Aziz (eds.) (note 5).

22   See further Thornberry and Martín Estébanez (note 8) p. 397.

23   The extent to which the fulfillment of minority protection standards have become an objective of the Assembly's monitoring is further discussed in Thornberry and Martín Estébanez (note 8) pp. 459-512. For a specific case study see M. Nowak 'Is Bosnia and Herzegovina ready for membership of the Council of Europe?. The Responsibility of the Committee of Ministers and the Parliamentary Assembly' 20 *Human Rights Law Journal* (1999) pp. 285-289.

24   For a description of the subsequent legislative situation from a governmental perspective, see the Report on the Linguistic Rights of Persons Belonging to National Minorities in the OSCE Area, annex, replies from OSCE Participating States (10 March 1999).

25   Note the connection between language and culture established by the Assembly once again.

26   Especially the provisions contained in Articles 7 and 8. A critical review of the content of the protocol proposal is presented in Thornberry and Martín Estébanez (note 8) pp. 402-403.

Since the adoption of Resolution 1201, the Assembly's opinions on accession by candidate states started including references to the Assembly's protocol proposal, soon to be coupled with references to the Languages Charter as well as to the Framework Convention.[27] These standards have later become a quasi-permanent feature of the Assembly's assessment of state performance, in connection with accession, post-accession monitoring and 'post-monitoring dialogue'. Unfortunately, this has not led to satisfactory results in most instances, as illustrated by the continued need to meet linguistic protection standards and by the poor state performance indicated in the various, successive monitoring procedures that have been undertaken.[28]

Often, the Assembly's demands for improved performance with regard to specific states have been met with the signature or ratification of the aforementioned treaties by the states concerned. Occasionally this has also led to direct incorporation, and to the introduction of their provisions, as well as those of the draft protocol, into domestic legislation or bilateral treaties. However, in spite of frequent references in the Assembly's monitoring decisions to state wrong-doings in domestic practice, these have not led to a decision to continue the monitoring. This has been the case despite the acknowledgement of acute problems of linguistic minority protection.[29] This highlights the minor importance given to linguistic minority protection in the Assembly's formalised monitoring. Nominal treaty endorsement often suffices, to the detriment of effective protection.

Encouragement of adherence to relevant treaties has been the object of Assembly decisions not only in conducting formal state monitoring, but also in addressing minority rights protection generally.[30] This has allowed the extension of the Assembly's critique to states in Western Europe, which have been excluded from the formalised monitoring procedures so far. In Recommendation 1492 (2000) 'rights of national minorities' for example, the Assembly named the Council of Europe states which have not yet adhered to the Languages Charter encouraging them to sign or ratify this instrument. It also recommended that publicity be given to the Committee of Experts reports under the Charter, and advocated for the application of the same principles or standards to all member states. The Assembly indirectly endorsed the principle of interculturalism, particularly in the linguistic field, which is upheld by the Charter.[31] Taking an approach which differs from that of the Explanatory Report on the Charter, the Assembly recommendation 'recognises that immigrant populations whose members are citizens of the state in which

---

27   The linguistic provisions of the Framework Convention are discussed in K. Henrard (note 5). See also Thornberry and Martín Estébanez (note 8) pp. 89-135.

28   Ibid. pp. 459-512.

29   The closure of the post-accession monitoring of Bulgaria with Resolution 1211 (2000) serves as an illustration. See Ibid. p. 486.

30   See for example Recommendation 1345 (1997) on the Protection of National Minorities, para. 11. See further the next section in this contribution.

31   The interpretation of this principle under the Charter is discussed in Martín Estébanez (note 11).

they reside constitute special categories of minorities'.[32] While both the Assembly and the Explanatory Report highlight the possibility of specific standards being adopted as regards these groups,[33] the Explanatory Report excludes immigrant protection under the Languages Charter, whilst the recommendation of the Assembly does not.[34]

Another important conceptual step taken by the Assembly concerns sign languages. Following failed attempts to include their protection in the Languages Charter, in Recommendation 1598 (2003) on protection of sign languages in the member states of the Council of Europe, the Assembly supports the drafting of an additional protocol to the Languages Charter to deal with sign languages under the 'non-territorial' category previewed by the Charter.[35] It should be emphasised that in many cases, sign languages would actually qualify as 'territorial' under the Languages Charter,[36] as their use is often concentrated in or confined to specific sections of the state territory. The Committee on the Rehabilitation and Integration of People with Disabilities (CD-P-R) of the Council of Europe, based on a Partial Agreement, noted in its Opinion on Assembly's Recommendation 1492 (in particular on paragraph 12.xiii on sign languages), that some sign languages 'are used in certain geographical areas only and thus meet the definition of regional minority languages'.[37]

In its most recent recommendation on the rights of national minorities, Recommendation 1623 (2003), the Assembly reaffirmed the principle of freedom of expression in minority languages 'in geographical areas where they live in substantial numbers'. This is a principle sustained under the ECHR in connection with the licensing of the broadcast media, as discussed below. The recommendation seems to be geared at counteracting domestic restrictions on the use of minority languages in the broadcast

---

32   Para. 11 of the recommendation.

33   For an analysis of the relevant aspects involved see W. Kymlica *Multicultural Citizenship: a Liberal Theory of Minority Rights* (Oxford: Clarendon Press, 1995).

34   A stand in favour of the protection of the language of migrants in the context of linguistic minority protection is presented in I. Gogolin 'Linguistic Diversity and New Minorities in Europe. Guide for the Development of Language Education Policies in Europe, From Linguistic Diversity to Plurilingual Education', Doc. of the Language Policy Division, Directorate of School, Out-of-School and Higher Education (Strasbourg: Council of Europe, 2002), available electronically on http://www.coe.int/T/E/Cultural_Co-operation/education/Languages/Language_Policy/Policy_development_activities/Studies/List.asp#TopOfPage

35   The Assembly seems to focus on visual sign languages and does not devote specific attention to address non-visual or other unarticulated forms of sound-based language existing in Europe (such as the 'silbo': the whistling-based language characteristic of some of the Canary islands) regardless of its explicit references to Europe's linguistic and cultural heritage.

36   The territorial aspect of the Languages Charter is discussed further in Thornberry and Martín Estébanez (note 8) pp. 144-145 and by the latter author (note 11).

37   Reply from the Committee of Ministers to Assembly Recommendation 1492 (2001), adopted on 12 June 2002, Assembly Doc. 9492, 19 June 2002, Annex 4, para. 8.

media[38] and even in private activities involving communication with the public.[39] In the most recent Recommendation 1589 (2003) on Freedom of Expression in the Media in Europe, a request has been made for the abolition of restrictions on the establishment and functioning of private media broadcasting in minority languages.[40] Regarding the implementation of the Framework Convention and the Languages Charter, the Assembly highlights the problem of restrictive approaches by states to the determination of the beneficiaries of their provisions,[41] and the need to ensure availability not only of their texts, but also of related texts (indirectly referring to the respective state reports) in national minority languages. As the start of the second monitoring cycle of the Languages Charter illustrates, the demands of the Committee of Experts under the Charter do not seem to go as far.[42]

The main concern for the Assembly continues to revolve around the justiciablity of minority rights. It still refers to Recommendation 1201 (1993) in spite of the operation of

---

38   This is also the aim of the Guidelines on the Use of Minority Languages in the Broadcast Media adopted in October 2003. They are available electronically on http://www.osce.org/hcnm/recommendations. See also the collection of studies concerning state practice in a selected group of OSCE states both in Western as well as in Central and Eastern Europe and relevant recommendations elaborated under the auspices of the OSCE Representative on Freedom of the Media: A. Karlsreiter (ed.) *Media in Multilingual Societies, Freedom and Responsibility* (Vienna: OSCE Office of the Representative on Freedom of the Media, 2003).

39   An overview of recent problems encountered in the use of minority languages in the electronic media in Council of Europe states is provided in the Report on the Rights of National Minorities by B. Cilevics, on which the Recommendation is based. Problems are reported in Croatia, Estonia, Ukraine, Azerbaijan, Moldova and Latvia, while restrictions in The Netherlands and France are also pointed out. See Assembly doc. 9862, 9 July 2003, paras. 68-78. For a review of the situation concerning legislation on the use of minority languages in the electronic/broadcast media in OSCE States see the study commissioned by the OSCE HCNM in connection with the adoption of the Guidelines: T. McGonagle, B. Davis Noll and M. Price (eds.) *Minority-Language Related Broadcasting and Legislation in the OSCE* (Oxford/Amsterdam: PCMLP, Centre for Socio-Legal Studies, Wolfson College and IViR, University of Amsterdam, 2003). To illustrate restrictions on the use of minority languages in other areas of the public domain, see the comments on the Latvian Law on the State Language by the Latvian Human Rights Committee, Fédération Internationale des Ligues des Droits de l'Homme, Press Release 15 May 1999, p. 3. See also the comments on the decision of the Constitutional Court of Latvia to abolish the norm of the Law on Radio and Television stipulating language restrictions in private broadcasting, Diena Press Report 06/09/2003.

40   Para. 17 vi of the recommendation.

41   The Assembly also names once again the states which have not yet signed or ratified the Framework Convention, while calling on them to do so.

42   See further, Martín Estébanez (note 11). The Assembly also deals with other important procedural aspects of the functioning of the monitoring mechanism under the Framework Convention (para. 12 of the recommendation).

the Languages Charter and the Framework Convention.[43] The Assembly also requests member states to sign and ratify Protocol No. 12 to the ECHR[44] as soon as possible. This Protocol adds an autonomous prohibition of discrimination, including in the linguistic field, to the ECHR. The support by the Assembly of its previous proposal introduced in Recommendation 1492 (2001), demanding that the Committee of Ministers confer on the European Court of Human Rights the power to give advisory opinions on the interpretation of the Framework Convention, seems questionable, even if it is possibly considered as a strategic step towards the justiciability of its provisions.[45]

From a substantive perspective, little inspiration can be drawn from the European Court's jurisprudence thus far regarding the interpretation of Framework Convention provisions.[46] The general endorsement by the European Court of positive measures in order to guarantee effective equality,[47] a position which is stated less clearly by the Advisory Committee under the Framework Convention constitutes an exception. Further, the European Court has taken a negative stand towards the justiciability of the Framework Convention. The Court, taking up the arguments contained in Article 11 of the Explanatory Report on the Framework Convention, has recalled that 'unlike the Human Rights Convention which sets forth immediately binding obligations, the Framework Convention was intended to contain "mostly programme-type provisions setting out objectives which the parties undertake to pursue" and which are not "directly applicable"'.[48]

Even though the Framework Convention is formulated in terms of State obligations rather than subjective rights, this does not reduce its obligatory character and corresponding capacity to establish state duties. The obligatory content of the articles of the Framework Convention can be considered to be more precise than those of the ECHR. They establish state duties directly, whereas state duties have to be 'constructed' by the European Court in connection with the subjective rights enumeration contained in the ECHR. For example, Article 11 of the Framework Convention states that: 'the Parties undertake to recognise that every person belonging to a minority has the right to use his or her surname (patronym) and first names in the minority language and the right to official recognition of them'. The concrete duties derived from this provision even if not fully specified, are easily deduced.

Admittedly, some of the framework convention's provisions are flexibly worded: expressions such as 'promoting the conditions', 'as far as possible' etc... are frequently

---

43   Para. 7 of the recommendation.
44   Ibid. para. 12 vii.
45   Some remarks on this proposal are presented in Thornberry and Martín Estébanez (note 8) p. 429.
46   See Ibid. pp. 58-60.
47   In the *Belgian Linguistic Case* the ECHR further delimited the conditions for non-discriminatory, 'preferential' treatment. See Case Relating to Certain Aspects of the Laws on the Use of Languages in Education in Belgium, Application Nos. 1474/62; 1677/62; 1691/62; 1769/63; 1994/63; 2126/64; Judgement of 23 July 1968, (Merits), 1, B, para. 10.
48   Assembly doc. 9492, Annex 6, para. 4.

used. Nevertheless, establishing all possible 'duty scenarios' in concrete situations is not always the object of the law, and its justiciability is not generally questioned as a result. Thus the myth compelling 'a clear-cut divide between the non-justiciable (and always 'obscure') minority rights and the justiciable (and always 'precise') general rights',[49] does not seem applicable to the Framework Convention. The Advisory Committee's doctrine testifies to the ease of establishing state duties and instances of appropriate and inappropriate state behaviour in compliance with the Framework Convention provisions. The problem of justiciability of the Framework Convention thus seems to reside on enforcement possibilities. Concretely, on the absence of an international supervisory mechanism which persons belonging to minorities or minority groups can resort in order to obtain redress if states fail to implement the framework convention provisions. The aim would be to guarantee that state duties are implemented in practice.

The report of the Committee on Legal Affairs and Human Rights, on the basis of which Recommendation 1623 was adopted, places emphasis on 'strengthening the implementation mechanism of the Framework Convention'.[50] The report maintains that an "effective monitoring procedure, based itself on legal rather than political approach, but in the meantime, politically supported by the Committee of Ministers, will become the fastest way to arrive at universal interpretation of the Framework Convention provisions ...".[51] The request for a competence of the European Court to give advisory opinions concerning the interpretation of the Framework Convention is reiterated in this context. However, it is actually the perceived lack of political support for the implementation of the monitoring results of the Advisory Committee by the Committee of Ministers which is the underlying problem that this proposal seeks to address.

The question remains of whether the 'overview role' previewed for the European Court would actually provide the solution to the problem of the implementation of the Framework Convention. From a substantive perspective, the perception by the European Court of its proposed role first as fulfilling 'the need to avoid divergent interpretation of the concepts common to both instruments' and, second, as supplementary to its role in connection with the ECHR, could cast some doubts on the progress the European Court's role envisaged would imply. This is especially the case considering the restraint with which the European Court has approached minority questions under the ECHR.[52] Although positive steps can be identified, especially in recent jurisprudence, progress in this field has not been steady. In addition, from a procedural perspective, the

---

49   See G. Pentassuglia 'Linguistic Diversity in the Larger Setting: Discussing the Models of Minority Right Enforcement in Europe and their Role from the Perspective of Sovereignty' paper presented at the European University Institute (RSCAS-Law) conference: *'Linguistic Diversity and European Law'* (Florence, 12-13 November 2001), also in *'On the Models of Minority Rights Supervision in Europe and How They Affect a Changing Concept of Sovereignty'* 1 European Yearbook of Minority Issues (2001/2) p. 36.

50   Assembly doc. 9862, paras. 28-29.

51   Ibid. para. 32.

52   Thornberry and Martín Estébanez (note 8) pp. 39-73, especially pp. 68-73.

'advisory' role previewed for the European Court does not seem a sufficient guarantee of justiciability of the framework convention provisions which allow for individuals or groups to obtain redress to specific claims. Its results are likely to respond to punctual questions rather than resolving the implementation problem overall. The broad margin of appreciation of the states in implementing the Framework Convention provisions is likely to remain. The 'supervisory role' by the European Court in the light of the existing instruments, including the Framework Convention, in *Beard v. UK*,[53] did not yield positive results.

From the Framework Convention's side, the basic human rights logic applied by the Advisory Committee, and its awareness of jurisprudence under the ECHR, has allowed for its interpretation of Framework Convention provisions to cohere with the articles and jurisprudence under the ECHR, in accordance with Articles 19 and 23 of the Framework Convention. The Assembly's proposal in Recommendation 1623, for the Advisory Committee 'to consider thematic issues and to comment on them, so as to assist states and minorities in developing good practices',[54] seems a more advisable and more practicable avenue for consolidating existing doctrine in the substantive interpretation of this instrument. It is likely that the Advisory Committee's doctrine (as well as that of the Committee of Experts under the Languages Charter) will progressively permeate the European Court's thinking also without a direct involvement by the Court in the supervision of the Framework Convention, especially given the proven consideration by the European Court of parallel developments in the international law of minority protection which *Beard v. UK*[55] illustrates well. Although the latter judgement may have not met expectations, its content can be explained by the early stage of development of the doctrine in the interpretation of the Framework Convention at the time in which the judgement was delivered.

As to the justiciability concern, efforts in support of the adoption of an additional protocol to the ECHR guaranteeing positive protection of minority rights should not dissipate in the search for alternative means of European Court's involvement. While the idea of a broader 'Constitutional' role for the European Court takes shape,[56] in the current particularly difficult situation derived from massive and undemanding invitations for accession, it is under the ECHR that the European Court can more easily find a role in guaranteeing minority protection. Whilst inter-governmental acceptance for a fully fledged, judicial role for the European Court in the implementation of the Framework Convention provisions remains a political desideratum, the reliance of the Committee of Ministers on future jurisprudence from Additional Protocol 12 to the ECHR is clearly a delaying tactic.

---

53   Application 24882/94, Judgement of 18 January 2001, paras. 104-105. See comments Ibid. p. 71.

54   Para. 12 ix of the recommendation.

55   (note 53).

56   See further R. Harmsen 'The European Convention on Human Rights after Enlargement' 5 *The International Journal of Human Rights* (2001) p. 29.

From the perspective of the Framework Convention, the experience of the European Social Charter[57] provides a good model. Under the optional collective complaints procedure incorporated into the Revised European Social Charter[58] (Article C, Part IV) and delineated in the 'Additional Protocol to the European Social Charter Providing for a System of Collective Complaints'[59] non-governmental organisations can submit complaints alleging the unsatisfactory application of the Charter. Under this mechanism, the European Committee of Social Rights determines whether or not State parties have ensured the satisfactory application of the Charter.[60] A two-thirds majority is required before the Committee of Ministers addresses a recommendation to the state party when its application of the provision concerned has been considered as unsatisfactory by the Committee of Experts. Still, the publicity surrounding the Committee of Expert's conclusions (including via the Assembly's involvement) constitutes an important leverage towards satisfactory implementation. A similar mechanism could be put in place for facilitating redress of collective minority complaints of unsatisfactory implementation of the Framework Convention, delineated in an additional protocol to it. Such a mechanism would contribute to the implementation of the Framework Convention provisions which demand minority participation.[61] The same applies to the Languages Charter.

Minority Language 'Awareness'

The role of the Assembly in bringing linguistic minority protection issues into the political agenda of the Council of Europe cannot be overstated. Outside the context of the formalised 'monitoring procedures' already discussed, the Assembly has addressed outstanding 'situations' affecting the fate of linguistic minorities. The Assembly has also given attention to linguistic minority issues, when addressing Council of Europe concerns, even where these issues had previously been ignored. One example of this comes from the Assembly's consideration of transfrontier cultural exchanges and language teaching[62] five years after the adoption of the 'European Outline Convention on Transfrontier Co-operation'.[63] A more recent illustration is the Assembly's unsuccessful attempt to introduce 'language' among the grounds for discrimination previewed in Article 2 of the Protocol to the Convention on Cybercrime concerning the Criminalisa-

---

57 See M. Scheinin 'Economic and Social Rights as Legal Rights' and A. Rosas and M. Scheinin 'Implementation Mechanisms and Remedies' in A. Eide, C. Krause, and A. Rosas (eds.) *Economic, Social and Cultural Rights, a Textbook* (Dordrecht: Kluwer Law International, 2001) pp. 49-51 and p. 435 respectively. The present author is also grateful for the oral remarks by K. Drzewicki on the Charter's system.

58 Adopted on 3 May 1996. European Treaty Series No. 163.

59 Adopted on 9 November 1995, European Treaty Series No. 158.

60 Article 8 of the Additional Protocol.

61 See Article 15 of the Framework Convention.

62 Recommendation 1013 (1985).

63 European Treaty Series No. 159.

tion of Acts of a Racist and Xenophobic Nature Committed through Computer Systems opened for signature on 28th January 2003. [64] Article 2 contains the definition of 'racist or xenophobic material' under the protocol. [65]

Although aspects of foreign language learning have occasionally been addressed by the Assembly since the 1960s, [66] it was only in 1998 that the Assembly first dealt, in a joint and thorough manner, with 'foreign' and 'minority' language protection from a language learning perspective. [67] In Recommendation 1383 (1998), the Assembly expressed concern about the predominance of the English language to the detriment of other majority languages and emphasised the importance of learning regional languages. It supported linguistic diversification on the basis of international economic competition, and the preservation of cultural diversity. [68]

The Assembly has expounded on linguistic minority protection requirements in the field of education in Recommendation 1352 (1998) on access of minorities to higher education. The Assembly emphasises the need for governments to avoid prescribing the exclusive use of the official language of the state, and to provide access to suitable levels of public education in their mother tongue to persons belonging to a linguistic minority, in order to prepare them for higher education. [69] The Assembly qualifies the doctrine established by the Permanent Court of International Justice in its Advisory Opinion on the Greek Schools in Albania, [70] on the equal right to establish and manage private schools and other educational establishments which operate in minority languages, [71] by pointing to the need for governments 'to recognise the fundamental liberty to engage in higher education activities and to establish institutions for that purpose'. Similarly to the Permanent Court, the Hague Recommendations adopted under the auspices of the OSCE High Commissioner on National Minorities in 1996 indirectly refer to an equal right, pointing specifically at the need to avoid discrimination in the entitlement to seek

---

64   European Treaty Series No. 189. Some remarks on the Protocol are included in Thornberry and Martín Estébanez (note 8) pp. 214-215.

65   See Assembly's Opinion No 240 on a 'Draft Additional Protocol to the Convention on Cybercrime concerning the Criminalisation of Acts of a Racist and Xenophobic Nature Committed through Computer Systems', adopted on 27 September 2002. See further Ibid. pp. 430-431.

66   See for example Recommendation 535 (1968) and Resolution 379 (1968) on Promotion of Modern Language Teaching in Europe, and Recommendation 594 (1970) on the Development of Modern Language Teaching in Turkey.

67   See Recommendation 1383 (1998) paras. 3-4 in particular.

68   For a discussion on the reverse policy implications of economic competition on linguistic and cultural diversity see F. Grin 'Market Forces, Language Spread and Linguistic Diversity' and T. Skutnabb-Kangas 'Linguistic Diversity, Human Rights and the "Free" Market' in Kontra, Phillipson, Skutnabb-Kangas and Várady (note 8), pp. 169-186, and pp. 187-222, respectively.

69   Para. 6, i. and ii. of the recommendation.

70   Minority Schools in Albania, PCIJ Series A/B, No. 64.

71   Ibid. p. 5.

sources of funding, including from the State budget.[72] The Assembly chooses instead to understate that educational institutions should receive official support on a non-discriminatory basis once their satisfactory quality has been established and a genuine demand demonstrated.[73]

The Assembly does not request the provision of higher education in minority languages by the State. It emphasises, however, that all citizens should have the possibility to study their own language and culture, including at university level. It further previews other measures aimed at facilitating the access of linguistic minorities to education generally.[74] The Committee of Ministers' response to the Assembly recommendations could, at best, be described as lukewarm,[75] even though the Assembly's suggestions frequently fall short of the standards previewed in the Languages Charter.

The need to protect culture and cultural works in all European languages in the context of globalisation, and the protection of all languages against the risk of extinction, is further emphasised in Recommendation 1539 (2001) of the European Year of Languages.[76] Earlier on, however, the Assembly started to draw attention to specific country situations in which, in its opinion, linguistic diversity is under threat. Even though linguistic protection as such did not become a main objective of the work of the Assembly in dealing with specific minority situations until the mid-1990s,[77] instances where the survival of linguistic communities is at risk have since become a recurrent object of its attention.[78]

The Assembly's identity preservation concerns have also been linked to concern about rising tensions involving an important linguistic component. Besides the attention devoted by the Assembly to the Turco-Bulgarian crisis already mentioned, in Resolution 1172 (1998) on the situation of the French-speaking population living in the Brussels periphery, the Assembly addresses recommendations to the parties directly involved in the tensions as well as the central authorities of the state, calling for linguistic identity

---

72   See The Hague Recommendations Regarding the Education Rights of National Minorities and Explanatory Note available electronically on http:www.osce.org/hcnm/recommendations, paras. 8-10.

73   Para. 6 iv of the recommendation.

74   See also the Assembly report 'The access of minorities to higher education', Rapporteur: T. Isohookana-Asunmaa, doc. 7888, 18 July 1997.

75   Reply to Recommendation 1353 (1998) from the Committee of Ministers, adopted on 12 May 1998 at the 631st meeting of the Ministers' Deputies, Assembly doc. 8120.

76   See in particular paras. 6 and 7 of the recommendation.

77   The weight of linguistic aspects involved in the Turco-Bulgarian crisis during the 1980's can be considered as an exception in this context. See further Thornberry and Martín Estébanez (note 8) pp. 393-394.

78   This is illustrated by Recommendations 1291 (1996) on Yiddish culture, 1333 (1997) on the Aromanian culture and language; and 1521 (2001) on the Csango minority culture in Romania, as well as in Resolution 1171 (1998) on endangered Uralic minority cultures. Access to minority language education and media are highlighted throughout these recommendations as an important element of protection. See further, Ibid. pp. 418-419 and 433-434.

preservation and for integration, and an active role of the state in promoting intercul-turalism. The Assembly perceives Belgian accession to the Framework Convention as an important step for the protection of the French-speaking population.[79]

The modalities of this accession, however, subsequently raised the concern of the Assembly. In Resolution 1301 (2002), on the protection of minorities in Belgium, the Assembly endorses the opinion of the Venice Commission[80] and recognises, in view of the power sharing arrangements in the country, the French-speakers in the Dutch-language region and in the German-language region as well as the Dutch-speakers and German-speakers in the French-language region as minorities within the context of the Framework Convention.[81] The Assembly draws attention:

> to the problems that could arise if the Kingdom of Belgium makes a declaration upon ratification of the framework convention which might seek to exclude from the convention's scope of protection a group of persons that, although not belonging to a minority at the state level, would be in danger of losing its identity by the operation of democratic institutions at the regional level. Such a declaration would probably have to be understood as a reservation incompatible with the object and purpose of the framework convention itself.[82]

In Recommendation 1623 (2003) on the rights of national minorities, however, the Assembly acknowledges that its advice has been ignored, reiterating its regret about the reservation made upon signature of the Framework Convention by Belgium.[83]

The recognition by the Assembly of linguistic minority groups which qualify for minority protection seems to be in contradiction with the views of the Human Rights Committee as expressed in *J. Ballantyne, E. Davidson and G. Mcintyre v. Canada*[84] that minorities referred to in article 27 of the ICCPR: 'are minorities within ... a State, and not minorities within any province'.[85] While several members of the Human Rights Committee, including Europeans, contested this viewpoint, preferring to leave open

---

79   Ibid. pp. 421-422.
80   Opinion on possible groups of persons to which the Framework Convention for the Protec-tion of National Minorities could be applied in Belgium.
81   Para. 16 of the resolution.
82   Para. 12 of the resolution. In para. 4, the Assembly openly refers to the possibility that this reservation violates 'the Vienna Conventions on the Law of the Treaties'. This seems to refer to Articles 19 (c) and 2 (d) of the Vienna Convention on the Law of the Treaties adopted on 22 May 1969 by the United Nations Conference on the Law of the Treaties.
83   Para. 4 of the recommendation. For an analysis of the reservation practice in the Council of Europe cotext, see S. Spiliopoulou Åkermark 'Reservation Clauses in Treaties Concluded within the Council of Europe' 48.3 *International and Comparative Law Quarterly* (1999), pp. 479-514.
84   Report of the Human Rights Committee, Part II, UN Doc. A/48/40 (1 November 1993) 91. Also in GAOR, Forty-eight Session, Supplement no. 40 (A/48/40).
85   UN Doc. A/48/40, para. 11.2.

the possibility of protection of a minority group within an autonomous province which may not be in a minority position in the State,[86] the emphasis by the Assembly on the 'identity preservation' parameter seems to be the only qualification of its upholding a fully-fledged minority protection entitlement for minorities which are so only within an autonomous territorial subdivision.

Unqualified protection of 'the persons belonging to the majority in the whole of the state but who constitute a minority in one or several of its regions' had been previously incorporated by the Assembly in Article 13 of its proposal for an Additional Protocol to the ECHR contained in Recommendation 1201 (1993). The definition contained in Article 1 of the Languages Charter for its part seems rather to conform to the Human Rights Committee's majority views. It excludes from the scope of the Charter the protection of the official languages of the state, which normally comprise, and are often limited to, the language spoken by the overall majority of the state population. While the particular views of the European Court of Human Rights in this connection are discussed in detail in the last section, a doctrinal split on this territorial question can be identified. As the case law illustrates, this question particularly affects linguistic minorities and remains also highly controversial at the domestic level. The doctrinal split identified at the international level can also be perceived among the various Council of Europe organs.

2.2. The approach of the CLRAE

The ground-breaking initiatives of the CLRAE within its sphere of competence, namely territorial democracy, have consolidated its position as the Council of Europe organ where the linguistic as well as other aspects of minority protection can find most fertile ground to develop. This would remain the case even if 'minority protection' as such were to be relegated in the Council of Europe's political agenda. The CLRAE has frequently identified aspects of minority identity protection in the course of its involvement in treaty making and implementation, and also in tackling various aspects of its own activity and identifying prospective avenues for action.[87] The recent CLRAE Resolution 159 (2003)[88] on tackling terrorism, which requests local authorities to ensure respect for cultural diversity and the peaceful coexistence of different cultures, minorities and communities, serves as an illustration. Aspects of linguistic protection as such have also become object of specific concern for the CLRAE.

---

86   Individual opinion by E. Evatt, co-signed by N. Ando, T. Bruni Celli and V. Dimitrijevic (concurring and elaborating).

87   See further Thornberry and Martín Estébanez (note 8) pp. 513-570.

88   The CLRAE Recommendations, Resolutions and other adopted texts are available electronically on http://www.coe.int/T/E/Clrae/_5._Texts/2._Adopted_texts/default.asp#TopOfPage.

Standard-Setting

Besides being the organ responsible for the initiative leading to the adoption of the Languages Charter,[89] the CLRAE has also dealt with standard-setting relevant to minority protection in other instances. In Recommendation 43 (1998), the CLRAE supports the delegation of competencies to local communities in the linguistic field, including the regulation of the use of the minority languages in public administration.[90] The approach of the CLRAE underscores the content of the stipulations on administrative authorities and public services already included in Article 10 of the Languages Charter. Yet, the Committee of Experts under the Charter has not been in favour of an outright delegation of the decision-making power on minority language use to the local level.[91]

CLRAE Recommendation 43 further touches upon aspects which have not been addressed in the text of the Languages Charter, such as the financial one. The disposal of sufficient financial means would seem a pre-condition for territorial authorities to play an important role in the implementation of the Charter,[92] and for pursuing linguistic policies generally. The CLRAE also insists on the need to avoid gerrymandering against minorities, a grounding principle in the implementation of the Charter given the importance of territory in articulating protection under this instrument. The CLRAE's proposals for a European Charter of Regional Self-Government and for a European Charter of Mountain Regions[93] are also of relevance for territory as an element of linguistic protection. However, these initiatives have not yet been endorsed by the Committee of Ministers. Finally, and also in accordance with the Languages Charter, in Recommendation 119 (2002) 'on the state of regional print media in Europe – Pluralism, independence and freedom in regional press' and the homonym Resolution 145 (2002), the CLRAE supports the creation and operation of transfrontier bilingual newspapers and magazines containing information on the border regions.

State Monitoring

Linguistic minority protection aspects have not become the explicit object of thematic 'ex-officio monitoring' of the implementation of the European Charter of Local Self-government by the CLRAE.[94] This is the case despite the instrument's concern with the

---

89   Explanatory Report on the Languages Charter, para. 6.
90   The concrete content of this recommendation is discussed in more detail in Thornberry and Martín Estébanez (note 8) pp. 516-517.
91   This has been the case, for example, with regard to the area of education. See the initial Report on the Application of the Charter in Switzerland, doc. ECRML (2001) 7, para. 66.
92   See P. Blair 'Successful Application of the Charter/General Conclusion' and J-M. Woehrling 'The Pivotal Role of Regional and Local authorities in Relation to the Charter' 3 *Regional or Minority Languages* (2002) p. 93.
93   See Thornberry and Martín Estébanez (note 8) pp. 549-556.
94   European Treaty Series No. 122. See further Ibid. p. 521.

questions of the financial resources of local authorities (Article 9); their competencies (Article 4); as well as the conditions of service and recruitment of local government employees (Article 6). However, the CLRAE has occasionally touched on these aspects in the course of its monitoring local and regional democracy in individual member states. This has mostly concerned CLRAE demands for some monitored states to sign and ratify the Languages Charter (such as in the case of France).[95] In a few instances the CLRAE has also addressed linguistic problems directly, for example when dealing with the question of elected representatives using their mother tongue at local government council sessions in Estonia, particularly in those areas where Russian language speakers constitute a majority of the population.[96]

Non-discriminatory approaches to monitoring performance in states in Eastern and Western Europe have been a positive feature of the CLRAE's monitoring activity. Nevertheless, no consistent or continuous pattern of assessment by the CLRAE of state performance in the linguistic field can be identified.[97] Systematic awareness of identity and linguistic protection aspects still needs to permeate the CLRAE's approaches to its various areas of competence and activities for this organ to realise its potential in addressing minority concerns, and linguistic concerns more in particular. This is especially the case given CLRAE's increasing influence *vis-à-vis* the Committee of Ministers.

2.3. *The Committee of Ministers, Summits, inter-governmental co-operation and the Secretariat*

Activities of the Committee of Ministers in the field of linguistic minority protection have mainly originated from the initiatives taken by other Council of Europe organs. Although some of the international treaties adopted as a result of the Committee of Ministers activity have laid the ground for the protection of minority languages,[98] the poor performance of the Council of Europe concerning cultural rights until the first Council of Europe Summit in October 1993, has been acknowledged by the organisation itself. It was only in addressing the question of minority protection in that summit 'that cultural rights began gaining ground'.[99] The summit did not however devote attention

---

95   See CLRAE Recommendation 78 (2000) on Local and Regional Democracy in France.

96   CLRAE Recommendation 81 (2000), para. 36.

97   By way of an example, the CLRAE has not assessed the linguistic diversity problems in Latvia, Estonia's neighbor, where problems of linguistic minority protection are possibly more acute.

98   Besides the European Outline Convention on Transfrontier Co-operation already mentioned, also some of the cultural objectives of the European Convention on Transfrontier Television (European Treaty Series No. 132) and Amending Protocol (European Treaty Series No. 171) in particular can serve as an instrument for minority language protection. See for example, Article 10, para. 3 of the convention.

99   See Report 'Cultural Rights at the Council of Europe (1949-1996)' 97.5 doc. DECS/SE/ DHRM Strasbourg, 1997, p. 7.

to their linguistic dimension, as the resulting declaration illustrates. The same applies to the second summit held in Strasbourg in October 1997.[100] One section of Chapter IV of the Action Plan attached to it, on New Information Technologies, later received follow-up with particular consideration to linguistic aspects.

In the subsequent 1999 Declaration on a European Policy for New Information Technologies appended to the Budapest Declaration for a Greater Europe without Dividing Lines,[101] linguistic diversity protection receives a parallel, equal treatment to diversity of content, as a means to promote political pluralism, cultural diversity and sustainable development. The Declaration supports state engagement in minority access to the new information technologies, as well as in the availability of a diversity of technical products and services, viewed as an instrument of expression of regional cultural identity.[102]

Governments are given a direct responsibility to ensure that in the domain of their competencies, linguistic criteria which meet the specific needs of concerned minorities are met by the state authorities, in the field of information systems in particular.[103] Nevertheless, the follow-up of the Declaration by the Council for Cultural Co-operation (CDCC) does not focus on linguistic minority protection.[104]

Even if aspects of linguistic minority protection have occasionally popped into the agenda of the CDCC,[105] it was only with the initiation of the project 'Linguistic policies for a multilingual and multicultural Europe', organised by the education committee of the CDCC, that a serious attempt of the inter-governmental structures to deal with the question of linguistic minority protection was made. Ensuing work resulted in the 'Guide for the Development of Language Education Policies in Europe: From Linguistic Diversity to Plurilingual Education'[106] (formerly known as 'Guide for Language Education Policy in

---

100   Recommendations to member states on the media and the promotion of a culture of tolerance find a politically acceptable niche only outside the text of the summit declaration. See Recommendation No. R (97) 21.

101   Available electronically on http://www.cm.coe.int/ta/decl/1999/99dec1.htm

102   The text of the Declaration is available in the Report on the Activities of the Council of Europe 1999 (Strasbourg: Council of Europe, 2000) Appendix B.

103   As the Committee of Expert's opinions under the Languages Charter illustrate, shortcomings in state practice in this field can be identified even in the richest European countries, and in the second round of monitoring under this instrument. See 'Application of the Charter in Norway, 2nd monitoring cycle', 2 doc. ECRML (2003), Strasbourg, 3 September 2003, para. 130.

104   See Thornberry and Martín Estébanez (note 8) p. 344.

105   See for example the item on Languages in the paper by. F. Audigier 'Practising Cultural Diversity in Education' presented in the Final Conference of the Project 'Democracy, Human Rights, Minorities: Educational and Cultural Aspects' of the CDCC held in Strasbourg on 21-23 May 1997, where a description of the Council of Europe activities in this field until 1997 is provided. 97.1 Doc. DECS/SE/CHRM pp. 21-24.

106   http://www.coe.int/T/E/Cultural_Co-operation/education/Languages/Language_Policy/ Policy_development_activities/Guide/default.asp#TopOfPage

Europe'). The Guide is complemented with a series of Reference Studies. The 'Framework of Reference for Languages' and a 'European Language Portfolio' have also been created to deal with the more technical aspects of language teaching and learning.[107]

Although the reviews of cultural policies in individual states undertaken since 1985 by the cultural committee of the CDCC (and presently pursued by the Rapporteur Group on Education, Culture, Sport, Youth and the Environment: GR-C), have occasionally raised issues of linguistic diversity, these do not seem to have become the object of strategic assessment resulting in linguistic diversity policy development in the states concerned. Concern for linguistic minority protection situations seems to have been largely absent from the confidential Committee of Ministers' 'monitoring procedures'.[108] It has been mainly under the Council of Europe 'Language Education Policy Profiles' programme, consisting of Council of Europe assistance with self-evaluation of national and regional policies, that member states have been invited to participate in a process of dialogue and discussion on the development of their language education policies. It is with the assistance of a team of visiting policy experts, that state performance has been assessed. The final reports of these processes are to be made available on the internet upon completion of the activity in each participating country.[109] Assistance to states in the field of linguistic minority protection has been provided by the Secretariat in the context of the Joint Programmes of Co-operation between the European Commission and the Council of Europe to strengthen democratic stability in the North Caucasus and Moldova. It has consisted in the convening of four seminars in the Russian Federation and two in Chisinau. Another seminar was held in Latvia in 2002.[110] Also a report on Language Education Policy Options in Kosovo was prepared by the Council of Europe for UNMIK in 2001.[111]

---

107 These are available electronically on http://www.coe.int/T/E/Cultural_Co-operation/education/Languages/Language_Policy/Policy_development_activities/Guide/default.asp#TopOfPage

108 With the exception of requests for the endorsement of the Framework Convention or the Languages Charter in the context of individual state monitoring. The consideration of linguistic aspects in the report originating from the 'Secretariat Assistance and Information' mission to Ukraine on 27-29 August 2001 seems to have constituted the only concrete reference. See further (note 8) pp. 269-313, p. 308 in particular.

109 Hungary, Norway, Slovenia, Lithuania, Cyprus and the Slovak Republic are the states which have so far accepted to participate in the programme. None of the respective reports are available on the Internet so far.

110 With the exception of one of the seminars held in Chisanau, which dealt with language proficiency for public servants, and the seminar in Nalchik, which dealt with 'the languages of the peoples of North Caucasus: problems and perspectives of development' the remaining seminars have dealt with aspects of minority language use in education.

111 P. Thornberry and M.A. Martin Estébanez (note 8).

The decision to suspend work on an additional protocol to the ECHR in the cultural field[112] points to the Committee of Ministers' increasing disengagement. This additional protocol had been envisaged in the Vienna Summit, in order to guarantee individual rights particularly for persons belonging to national minorities, The Committee of Ministers is satisfied to rely on the current monitoring of the Framework Convention, and the future competence of the Court in monitoring the implementation of Protocol 12 to the ECHR, even if 'a revelation' of the need to consider further standard setting has not been excluded.[113]

Linguistic aspects have emerged as the main element of agreement in intergovernmental discussions on the possible content of an additional 'cultural' protocol to the ECHR.[114] Three out of four rights included in the 'draft protocol', drawn up by the intergovermental committee of experts (the CAHMIN) which was mandated to begin work on the protocol, are directly concerned with language. These comprise the right to one's name, the right to use the language of one's choice, and the right to learn the language of one's choice. Although they would imply a slight improvement of linguistic rights in view of existing jurisprudence, the draft seems far from satisfactory, and insufficient for addressing the broader cultural question which the CAHMIN's mandate was supposed to respond to. The draft protocol has already been discarded.[115] Protection under the ECHR, which goes beyond that provided under Protocol 12 on non-discrimination, would seem necessary for the grounding of an effective system of linguistic minority protection by the European Court. Such a protection would lead to jurisprudence that could set useful markers for state performance. For this to become a possibility however, it would be necessary to overcome the current Committee of Ministers, arguably unfounded, reluctance.

3.   The European Court of Human Rights[116]

Linguistic freedom for everyone derives from the European Courts' core interpretation of Article 10 of the ECHR on the right to freedom of expression. Jurisprudence on the

---

112   Committee of Ministers' Decision 656/4.1 adopted on 26 January 1996. See further, Thornberry and Martín Estébanez (note 8) pp. 204-206.

113   Grouped reply by the Committee of Ministers to Parliamentary Assembly Recommendations 1134 (1990); 1177 (1992); 1201 (1993); 1255 (1995); 1285 (1996); 1300 (1996) and 1345 (1997), Doc. 8306, section A.

114   See CDCC Report Cultural Rights at the Council of Europe (1949-1996), doc. DECS/SE/DHRM (97) p. 80.

115   Grouped reply by the Committee of Ministers to Parliamentary Assembly Recommendations 1134 (1990); 1177 (1992); 1201 (1993); 1255 (1995); 1285 (1996); 1300 (1996) and 1345 (1997), doc. 8306, section A.

116   As a wealth of literature discusses the jurisprudence of the European Court of Human Rights in connection with linguistic minority protection in detail, the analysis here focuses on an overall assessment of the approaches of the European Court to this issue, that is its 'policy' with regard to linguistic diversity. It also explores possibilities for future development under the ECHR.

applicability of the right to freedom of expression to information and ideas, even if they may shock or disturb, and its interlinkage with the principles of pluralism, tolerance and broadmindedness, were already introduced in the *Case of Handyside v. United Kingdom*,[117] and often restated, recently in the *Cases of Sürek v. Turkey Nos. 1, 2 and 3*.[118] The European Court's doctrine that Article 10 does not 'distinguish between the various forms of expression'[119] and 'affords the opportunity to take part in the public exchange of cultural, political and social information and ideas of all kinds'[120] grounds the right to impart and receive information and ideas in any language.[121] Permissible restrictions to the right to freedom of expression, in accordance with the Court's jurisprudence, have generally concerned the content of expression and not its form. A different matter has been the Court's consideration of appropriate state involvement in the protection of expression in specific languages in accordance with Article 10 and other articles of the ECHR. Broad state powers have been recognized to privilege the use of particular languages (normally the official ones) and to determine the level of protection granted to them. These have actually resulted in limits to linguistic choice for some individuals and groups in some spheres of state competence.

A broad margin of appreciation has been given to states in the implementation of the language-connected provisions of the ECHR and its protocols, resulting in the favouring of the official language(s) of the state in various fields of its activity. Relevant arguments behind the European Court's acceptance of legislation and practices resulting in a limitation of linguistic diversity have been linked to considerations regarding public order (such as in connection with official personal name registration and change of name),[122] and the normal functioning of state institutions (such as the determination of a national parliament's working language,[123] or the consequences of the language chosen

---

117 Application No. 5493/72, Judgement of 7 November 1976, para. 49.

118 See Application No. 26682/95, Judgement of 8 July 1999, para. 58; Application No. 24122/94, Judgement of 8 July 1999, para. 33; and Application No. 24735/04, Judgement of 8 July 1999, para. 36, respectively.

119 The General Comment 10 of the Human Rights Committee on Article 19 of the ICCPR for its part refers to the freedom to seek and receive information and ideas 'of all kinds' and 'in whatever medium'.

120 See for example the Case of *Müller and Others v. Switzerland*, Application No. 10737/84, Judgement of 28 April 1988, para. 27.

121 Article 8 of the Framework Convention and the provisions of the Languages Charter have been very explicit in this connection. Also provision 32, 4 OSCE 1990 Document of the Copenhagen Meeting of the Conference on the Human Dimension of the OSCE (1990 OSCE Copenhagen document) states the right of persons belonging to national minorities 'to disseminate, have access to and exchange information in their mother tongue'.

122 Case of *Stjerna v. Finland*, Application No. 18131/91, Judgement of 25 November 1994, para. 39 of the Judgement.

123 Case of *Podkolzina v. Latvia*, Application No. 46726/99, Judgement of 9 April 2002, para. 34.

by elected representatives when making their Parliamentary Oath of Office).[124] Cases concerning spheres of public life entailing an even more active state role and engagement in public service provision, such as in the area of subsidised education, have been prominent.

In the 'Belgian Linguistic Case', the European Court stated that Article 2 of Protocol 1 to the ECHR on the right to education, 'contains no linguistic requirement'.[125] The reading of Article 14 of the ECHR in conjunction with Article 2 of its First Protocol, led the European Court to conclude: 'that the right to education shall be secured by each contracting party to everyone within its jurisdiction without discrimination on the ground, for instance of language', meaning that the state should not discriminate among the members of the population in their access to educational services supported by the state. The Court also concluded that this does not imply a duty for the state to provide education responding to the independent will/need of each individual: it 'does not have the effect of guaranteeing to a child or to his parent the right to obtain instruction in a language of his choice'.[126] As B. de Witte has pointed out, 'this only rejects a duty of differentiation pushed to the extreme but does not exclude a duty to differentiate when this can be reasonably claimed'.[127] The question which remains, however, is that of determining the level of state duty in that connection.

In the case of those persons belonging to a linguistic minority who can only understand or communicate effectively through a minority language, it is clear that right enjoyment in that language is a precondition for right enjoyment generally. State action should aim to guarantee that their rights can be exercised through that medium, taking into account proportionality criteria in relation to the specific right considered or the aspect of its enjoyment being guaranteed. An analysis of the European Court's jurisprudence would warrant us to recognize a division between rights which could be qualified as having 'accessibility features' and rights which do not. Rights lacking 'accessibility features' would be those impossible for those persons to enjoy unless this involves the use of a language they can effectively communicate through, normally the mother tongue. This is the case for example, of freedom of expression. In the case of rights having 'accessibility features', it is understood that a certain level of enjoyment can be achieved if the exercise takes place through a language other than the mother tongue. This would be the case in the possibility to enjoy the right to education if teaching is provided in a language different from the mother tongue, given the 'inbuilt' capacity of education to give access to at least 'generic' right enjoyment (i.e. devoid of particular identity features).

---

124   Case of *Mathieu-Mohin and Clerfayt v. Belgium*, Application No. 9267/81, Judgement of 2 March 1987, para. 57.

125   (Merits) II, A, para. 7.

126   Ibid., I, B, para. 11.

127   B. de Witte 'Surviving in Babel: Language Rights and European Integration' in Y. Dinstein and M. Tabory (eds.) *The Protection of Minorities and Human Rights* (Dordrecht: Martinus Nijhoff, 1992) p. 287.

Underlying the European Court's reasoning in the Belgian Linguistic Case, would seem to be the possibility that the non-speakers of the official language (especially children) can enjoy a 'generic' right to education, devoid of its identity aspects if teaching is provided in the official language. It would seem that the exercise of the right to education itself provides for the tools to access this 'generic' enjoyment through the learning of the majority language opportunities it provides. An indication that the ECHR's doctrine could reach beyond minority language protection in the enjoyment of those rights lacking 'accessibility features' alone, was given by the European Commission of Human Rights in its irreceivability decision in the case *Verein Alternatives Lokalradio Bern and Verein Radio Dreyckland Basel v. Switzerland*.[128] The Commission considered that a refusal to award a broadcasting license might raise a problem under Articles 10 and 14 of the ECHR: 'where the refusal would result in a significant proportion of the population being deprived of transmission in their mother tongue'.[129] Thus, the European Commission indicated its readiness to protect human rights enjoyment in a minority language as such, provided proportionality criteria were met in the given circumstances, without entering into considerations of the level of majority language proficiency of the population concerned.

Another positive sign was given by the European Court in the Case of *Informationsverein Lentia and Others v. Austria*.[130] In the European Court's considerations as to whether a violation of Article 10 existed, the Court stated that 'technical aspects are undeniably important, but the grant or refusal of a broadcasting license may be made conditional on other considerations, including such matters as the nature and objectives of a proposed station, its potential audience at national, regional or local level, the rights and needs of a specific audience, and the obligations deriving from international legal instruments'.[131] Especially by introducing the broad concept of 'rights and needs of a specific audience', the European Court opens the door for the minority language of a specific audience becoming a parameter for appropriate licensing, and thus a signpost for appropriate state performance in connection with right enjoyment by its minority population.

In spite of this positive outlook, whether the European Court will uphold an obligation for the State to guarantee freedom of expression in a minority language, including through the broadcast media, even with regard to persons who can only communicate effectively through that medium, remains to be confirmed in concrete jurisprudence. The same applies to a broader obligation for a similar guarantee in respect of minority language protection regardless the level of the majority language proficiency of the minority population. A decision in the latter respect would imply a much awaited proof of the Court's compromise with identity/cultural protection. This engagement,

---

128   Decision of 16 October 1986.

129   Ibid. section on the Law, para. 2.

130   Applications Nos. 13914/88; 14041/89; 15717/89; 15779/89; 17207/90; Judgement of 24 November 1993.

131   Ibid. para. 32.

however, seems to be missing still with regard to those rights having 'right accessibility' features such as the right to education.

In the recent judgement of the European Court in the *Case of Cyprus v. Turkey*,[132] the European Court seems to have confirmed its 'right accessibility' yardstick.[133] The leading argument for the European Court to uphold the need for secondary education in the minority language seems to be the preceding assumption by the authorities of a responsibility to provide primary education using that medium, and the consequences derived from it for the effective enjoyment of the right to education. The Court's decision in favour of education in a minority language seems to derive more from the conviction that the enjoyment of the right to education is curtailed if a forced change in the language of instruction is introduced at a secondary level of education (that is: the 'generic' right enjoyment accessibility is diminished when a change of the language of instruction takes place at an intermediate level of education), than from the veiled support for identity protection some would like to perceive.[134] This is endorsed by the Court's insistence that the right to education enshrined in Article 2 of Protocol 1 does not contain any 'linguistic' obligation.

Thus, while the outlook for minority language protection under the ECHR for those rights lacking 'right accessibility' features is positive, and there are indications of the possibility that the European Court would take identity concerns on board for those rights with 'generic' enjoyment accessibility features, such possibility seems reduced to situations where 'generic' right enjoyment devoid of identity considerations is impossible or diminished.

Regardless of these shortcomings, it should be borne in mind that the European Court's jurisprudence endorses the favourable treatment of minority languages which are considered as official languages of the state.[135] This includes official languages within specific regions. In addition, the objective criteria identified by the European Court which have resulted in a favourable treatment of official languages, such as the wider spread use of a language (including minority languages) within specific regions (and the subsequent need to protect the linguistic identity of those regions)[136] or the linking of

---

132   Application No. 25781/94, Judgement of 10 May 2001.

133   In this judgement the European Court established that 'having assumed responsibility for the provision of Greek-language primary schooling, the failure of the "TRNC" authorities to make continuing provision for it must be considered in effect a denial of the substance of the right at issue. It cannot be maintained that the provision of secondary education in the south in keeping with the linguistic tradition of the enclaved Greek Cypriots suffices to fulfill the obligation laid down in Article 2 of Protocol No. 1, having regard to the impact of that option on family life ...'. Ibid. para. 278.

134   See in particular, F. de Varennes 'The Right to Education and Minority Language' *EUMAP* Feature of 6 February 2004, on http://www.eumap.org/articles/content/96/964.

135   The *Belgian Linguistic Case* illustrates this (note 47).

136   Ibid.

the bearers of a given name to a family,[137] actually support minority language use and protection.

Thus, the European Court's decisions favouring official languages seem to have responded more to a minimalistic perception of human rights fulfillment than to the favouring of monolingualism or the majority languages of the state. The question remains whether this minimalistic perception of right fulfillment and the broad margin of appreciation given to States by the European Court in the linguistic field, resulting in support for the use of the official language alone, is sufficiently grounded nowadays. For instance, the link between the use of a particular (often official) language and public order starts to be questionable in many spheres of life. This is due to the existence of well developed, widely spread and easily available means of language interpretation, translation, recording and portrayal in the context of new information technologies. The aforementioned examples concerning the official recognition of names in a minority language, or the ability of the state institutions to function well when allowing for the use of a minority language for example during parliamentary sessions, serve as illustrations.

Finally, two aspects of the recent jurisprudence should be highlighted. In the judgement on the Case of *Cyprus v. Turkey*[138] the European Court eluded to draw the full consequences of (linguistic) identity for right enjoyment by persons belonging to minorities. Most probably this resulted from its concern for the capacity of the state to provide an immediate response to particular minority needs in areas of competence where the state level of active engagement is strong. Yet, the Court started to acknowledge that the enjoyment of ECHR rights (no matter whether they possess right accessibility features) may require that identity aspects are taken on board in order to guarantee 'generic' enjoyment through mother tongue use. The second is the aforementioned reference in the *Lentia Case*[139] 'to the obligations deriving from international legal instruments'. Instruments such as the Framework Convention and the Languages Charter should not be kept as instruments running in parallel with the ECHR's jurisprudence, but an increasing interaction should be established between them. This connects with the previous discussion on the Assembly's proposals, and would seem to serve the 'Constitutional Court' role the European Court has been called upon to fulfil. Concepts inherent to the ECHR's jurisprudence, such as general public interest, cannot keep ignoring minority rights protection. The protection of minority rights, including linguistic minorities, has come to the top of the public interest and human rights agenda.

The level of state engagement in the 'positive' aspect of right fulfillment to be demanded by the European Court under a cultural protocol will likely aim to meet basic needs relating to the consideration of identity in the provision of state services. The Court will probably demand sensitivity from the State in the exercise of its responsibilities for service provision rather than support for extra-ordinary cultural or linguistic

---

137   As in the *Stjerna* Case (note 123).
138   *Cyprus v. Turkey*, Application No. 25781/94, Judgement of 10 May 2001.
139   (note 131).

activity. Ultimately, states lacking the capacity or will to abide by the provisions of an adopted protocol, will have no obligation to accede to it. At the same time this adoption would show the European commitment to treat minority protection as a genuine aspect of human rights protection in Europe.

4. Concluding Remarks

The streamlining of linguistic minority protection awareness in the policy approaches of the Assembly and the CLRAE and co-operation between these two organs would seem of essential importance in the present context, where the Committee of Ministers may be willing to stand back from proactive minority protection. In the willingness to demonstrate non-discrimination between 'old' and 'new' member states within the organisation, minority protection may well drop from the top of the intergovernmental co-operation agenda even at the declaratory level.[140] Following geo-strategic rearrangements in Europe after the 1990s, the Western European powers which have been pushing the international minority protection agenda forward over the last fifteen years to protect kin minorities, may turn towards alternative means to protect the interests of these groups. They may wish to pursue this in a manner which does not imply parallel obligations towards other groups within their own domestic sphere.

Against this background, the question of the 'justiciability' of minority rights acquires fundamental importance. International minority protection in Europe should finally stop to rely mainly on the role of kin states, an approach which has proven detrimental. The possibility that complaints procedures, including collective ones, be introduced in connection with the implementation of the Framework Convention or the Languages Charter is not far fledged in the light of existing experience with other treaties. This includes treaties adopted in the context of the Council of Europe, as well as in minority protection under the League of Nations system.[141] In addition, linguistic protection in particular has stood out as the core of an agreement on the judicial guarantee of cultural rights, especially for persons belonging to minorities, under the ECHR. The arguments put forward to explain the deadlock in the adoption of a suitable protocol to the ECHR by the Committee of Ministers' subsidiary bodies, demonstrate that what has been missing is actually political support. Concerns deriving from the possible assumption of additional state responsibilities in this field, and the possible overburdening this may imply, would seem largely unjustified. Any resulting state duties would be more likely to demand awareness and sensitivity in decision-making rather than additional resources.

---

140   This is discussed in Thornberry and Martín Estébanez (note 8) p. 445.

141   Among the wealth of literature, see P. Thornberry *International Law and the Rights of Minorities* (Oxford: Clarendon Press, 1991) pp. 38-52, which contains references to other works. For contemporary views among them see J. Stone *International Guarantees of Minority Rights* (London: Oxford University Press, 1932).

Thornberry's reading of the scope of state responsibility under Article 27 of the ICCPR is interesting to note. This related to the questioning of States by the Human Rights Committee in the early 1990s, when most Europeans remained largely unaware of the dramatic importance the minority question would acquire over the next fifteen years.

What is the situation of minority-language instruction in schools? Can the minorities publish and does the State assist in the publications of books and newspapers in that language? Is the minority language accepted as an official language? In what language are court proceedings conducted when members of minorities are parties to cases? Are the radio and television programmes in minority languages?[142]

According to Thornberry, 'the replies made by States have been sometimes brief and sometimes full, but no State, it appears, has doubted the legitimacy of such questions'.[143] Only if States can satisfactorily respond to these questions, a task which would be strongly facilitated by direct minority involvement, could the Council of Europe and Europe in general, meet the challenge of the linguistic richness of its inhabitants. It is for international law and for societies in Europe to respond to this challenge, which Professor Thornberry has helped us to visualise. The present author would like to take this opportunity to thank him for this and for the enriching experience of working with him.

---

142   Thornberry, Ibid. p. 200.
143   Ibid. p. 201.

Chapter 16

THE AFRICAN UNION AND THE PROSPECTS FOR MINORITY PROTECTION

Timothy Murithi[1]

Introduction

The history of minority protection in Africa is one of missed opportunities and betrayed communities. From the arbitrary randomness of colonial borders to artificial statehood and the over-centralisation of power within these fictitious nation-states, minorities continue to face conditions that undermine their well-being. The issue of minority protection, therefore, remains a major challenge for the social and political institutions of the continent. The Organization of African Unity (OAU) largely functioned as a club of states, or more precisely a club of Heads of States, and did not make genuine efforts to implement, for example, the Protocols enshrined in the African Charter on Peoples' and Human Rights.[2] The OAU did not actively promote an agenda for minority protection through advancing more inclusive, equitable and accommodating structures of governance.

Indeed, the OAU did not intervene as much as it should have in the affairs of Member States to prevent war crimes and crimes against humanity which bequeathed upon the present generation of Africans the legacy of human rights atrocities and the domination, exploitation and manipulation of minority groups within states. The challenge remains to begin to redress past wrongs and enhance institutional protections for minorities on the continent.[3] The question is whether the newly established African Union (AU), the successor organisation to the Organization of African Unity, will be able to adopt a more interventionist stance than the one adopted by its predecessor. This chapter assesses some of the institutions that the AU has adopted and the mandates that have been developed that may enhance the implementation of policies that will promote minority protection.

---

1   Programme Officer, Programme in Peacemaking and Preventive Diplomacy, United Nations Institute for Training and Research (UNITAR).
2   *African (Banjul) Charter on Human and Peoples' Rights*, adopted June 27, 1981, OAU Doc. CAB/LEG/67/3 rev. 5, 21 I.L.M. 58 (1982), entered into force 21 October 1986.
3   C.A. Odinkalu 'Back to the Future: The Imperative of Prioritizing for the Protection of Human Rights in Africa' 47 *Journal of African Law* (2003) pp. 1-37.

Nazila Ghanea & Alexandra Xanthaki (eds.), Minorities, Peoples and Self-Determination, pp. 299-313.
© *2005 Koninklijke Brill NV. Printed in The Netherlands. ISBN 90 04 14301 7.*

Minorities in Africa: The Legacy of the Organization of African Unity

National, ethnic, linguistic or religious minorities (henceforth minorities) have, according to established international legal instruments, the right to existence and the right to respect for and promotion of their own national, cultural, linguistic heritage in relation to the rest of the population. The perpetual challenge is how this translates from policy into practice. Africa is not immune to this challenge. Following the arbitrary colonial construction of nation-states on the continent, most groups within these states would essentially be considered either minorities or majorities depending on which state they are situated in. Thornberry in his seminal text International Law and the Rights of Minorities observes that 'the minorities question has never contained itself entirely within national boundaries. Minorities in some states were majorities in others'.[4]

The African Charter on Human and People's Rights (Banjul Charter),[5] which was inaugurated on 27 June 1981, in Banjul, Gambia, was a legal instrument established by the Organization of African Unity to promote and protect human and communal rights. This led to the creation of the African Commission on Human and Peoples' Rights as an institution of the OAU. The Banjul Charter noted that 'fundamental human rights stem from the attributes of human beings which justifies their national and international protection.'[6] It therefore set the foundation for a framework for promoting the protection of individuals and peoples or communal groups in Africa.

With specific reference to communal groups, under which minorities would fall, Article 19 of the Charter states that 'all peoples shall be equal; they shall enjoy the same respect and shall have the same rights'. Nothing shall justify the domination of a people by another.' Article 20 further notes that 'all peoples shall have the right to existence. They shall have the unquestionable and inalienable right to self-determination. They shall freely determine their political status and shall pursue their economic and social development according to the policy they have freely chosen'.

With reference to what we presently refer to as war crimes and crimes against humanity, Article 23 states that 'all peoples shall have the right to national and international peace and security'. Elsewhere, Article 12, states that 'the mass expulsion of non-nationals shall be prohibited. Mass expulsion shall be that which is aimed at national, racial, ethnic or religious groups'. In effect, any attempt by Member States to 'ethnically cleanse' communal groups within their borders was prohibited by the Banjul Charter. Therefore, the necessary instruments were in place during the era of the OAU to ensure the effective protection of minorities and the promotion of their social, economic, and political rights. As with many other regions of the world, the rhetoric was not upheld in reality. African governments, which had the monopoly over the means of coercion, did

---

4   P. Thornberry *International Law and the Rights of Minorities* (Oxford: Clarendon, 1991), p. 1; see also, S. W. Baron *Ethnic Minority Rights: Some Older and Newer Trends* (Oxford: Oxford University Press, 1985).
5   (note 2).
6   Ibid. preamble, para. 6

not always respect the provisions of the Banjul Charter to the letter. There were therefore major political hurdles and challenges when it came to the effective implementation of its Articles. A coherent continental response to the issue of minority protection was largely sidelined.

Throughout the Cold War, the US-Soviet geopolitical matrix of power politics, with its overt and covert interventions in African states, systematically undermined the stability of Africa. Minorities that were caught in a violent confrontation with states became pawns in this superpower rivalry. The OAU (as a club of Heads of States) was unable to take the issue of 'minority nations' against states and effectively address it. Under the shield of the principles of international relations (and law) states were able to prevent other states from interfering in their internal affairs. Specifically, Article 2 of the UN Charter[7] outlines 'the principle of the sovereign authority of all its members' and admonishes Member States to refrain from challenging the 'territorial integrity or political independence of any state'. The Charter also states that 'nothing contained in the present Charter shall authorize the United Nations to intervene in matters which are essentially within the domestic jurisdiction of any state'. Article 3 of the OAU Charter similarly notes that Member States will respect 'the sovereign equality of all Member States' and exercise the 'non-interference in the internal affairs of states'.[8] While these provisions were established primarily to protect countries from external interference they ended up providing a *carte blanche* for Member States of the OAU to do as they pleased within their borders. The OAU, in its incarnation as a club of Heads of State, was therefore reluctant to raise issues regarding the alienation, deprivation or exploitation of minorities within states because its leaders were unwilling to speak up or act against their peers.

African states, like states elsewhere around the world, have jealously guarded their sovereignty and were for the most part left to do their will within their borders. Given that during the Cold War many of the African governments did not have transparent systems of governance, and some were overtly dictatorships, the issue of minority rights was effectively sidelined or excluded entirely from the list of political priorities. Minorities that may have had any legitimate claims were left to the mercy of governments that did not take too kindly to efforts to challenge the authority of the state. It is the legacy of this reality that has laid the foundation for many of the problems that the continent faces today with regard to minorities within states.

In the post-Cold War world there was renewed hope that the issue of minority protection, as an issue related to the prevention of conflict and the promotion of peace,

---

7   *Charter of the United Nations* (1945), http://www.un.org/aboutun/charter (accessed 7 August 2004); and *Statute of the International Court of Justice* (1945), http://www.icj-cij.org/icjwww/ ibasicdocuments/Basetext/istatute.htm (accessed 7 August 2004).

8   *Charter of the Organization of African Unity* (1963), abrogated and replaced by the *Constitutive Act of the African Union* (2000), http://www.africa-union.org/Official_documents/ Treaties_%20Conventions_%20Protocols/Treaties_Conventions_&_Protocols.htm (accessed 7 August 2004).

would be finally addressed. These aspirations were short-lived as the tragedy of the genocide in Rwanda unfolded in 1994 which saw Hutus pitted against Tutsis, with moderate
and extremist elements on both sides. The OAU did not have the political will or means
to foresee or intervene in the crisis. During this post-Cold War era, issues relating to
minorities featured in most of the conflicts that were continuing to take place across
the continent. In Sudan, a country embroiled in a persistent conflict, a pre-dominantly
Arab-Muslim government in the north of the country engaged in a violent confrontation with a pre-dominantly Christian and Animist southern population. This conflict
was further complicated by grievances over the oil wealth contained in the southern
parts of the country, which the government claimed as state property and the minorities
in the south claimed as rightfully theirs. The minorities in the south had been agitating
for self-determination and the government in the north had its concerns about the territorial integrity of the state. The issue remains unresolved and has generated a significant
humanitarian crisis with several minority groups at risk.

With the onset of the twenty-first century the protection of minorities and indigenous peoples within states remains an issue to be addressed by the African continent
and its institutions. [9] The targeting of minority groups in conflict situations has been
witnessed in the Democratic Republic of the Congo with its multiplicity of ethnic
groups, in Burundi in tensions between Hutus and Tutsis, in Uganda the Acholi peoples
in the north of the country, in Cote D'Ivoire with minority Muslim groups in the north
of the country, in Senegal with the minority in the Cassamance region, in Morocco and
with the minorities in the Western Sahara region, and increasingly in parts of Nigeria
where communal groups are engaged in violent confrontation. The ongoing indiscriminate attacks on minority populations are the net effect of a culture of policy blindness on
the specific issue of minorities within states. While some of the ongoing conflicts on the
African continent do not stem strictly from the issue of minority claims against the state,
many stem from the grievances that minority groups have against their host states and
the inability, or unwillingness, of the state to adequately respond to these grievances.

Attaining sustainable peacebuilding on the continent is vital to the restoration of
the social and political well-being of both majority and minority groups on the continent. The issue is where to go from here and what can be done to enhance the effective
implementation of the provisions for the protection of minorities on the continent.

African Union Institutions and Protocols and the Prospects for Minority Protection

With the advent of the African Union (AU) there has been much ceremonial fanfare,
and a renewed sense of hope that the emergence of a new continental organisation with
more interventionist powers creates an opportunity to improve the situation on the
continent. The creation of the African Union is at the very least an acknowledgement

---

9   P. Thornberry *Indigenous Peoples and Human Rights* (Manchester: Manchester University
     Press, 2002).

that the situation with regards to the OAU was untenable. More of the same in terms of the 'politics of indifference' would have continued to perpetuate the conditions that undermined the prospects for peace on the continent, which of course would also have implications on the prospects for minority protection.

It is worth noting that in its interventions the AU will not always take the lead on specific challenges and will occasionally defer to the efforts of the Regional Economic Communities established around the continent, namely: the Economic Community of West African States (ECOWAS), the Southern African Development Community (SADC), the Inter-Governmental Authority on Development (IGAD), the Maghreb Union and the Economic Community of Central African States (ECCAS).

The Constitutive Act of the African Union[10] adopted by the Assembly of Heads of State on 11 July 2000, in Lome, Togo, replaced the Charter of the Organization of African Unity. The African Union was formally established in July 2002, in Durban, South Africa. It assumed and absorbed all the assets and liabilities of the OAU. So the legal instruments established by the OAU are still valid and part of the corpus of AU legislation.

The Prevention of Discrimination Towards Minorities: Needs and Opportunities

While the AU has not yet created a set of instruments specifically focusing on the issue of minority protection, which might be an initiative that can be developed as the organisation evolves, it has created an amalgamation of institutions and legal instruments which, taken as a totality, can lay the foundation for more effective minority protection. Indeed, significant interventionist powers that can be used to enhance the protection of minorities, among other issues, have been bestowed upon the African Union, but whether these will translate into concrete political action on the ground or turn out to be just another political 'sleight of hand' by the continent's leaders remains to be seen.

In terms of the issues relating to minorities in Africa the situation remains relatively unchanged since the era of decolonisation. As discussed above, the imposition of arbitrary rule sowed the seeds of some of the problems confronting minorities today. The needs of minorities in Africa are numerous, but for the purposes of this chapter, they can be categorised as follows:
- the need for closer trans-border co-operation on the African continent in general
- the need for minority groups to have their cultural and linguistic freedoms safeguarded, including the right to choose freely to belong to a minority
- the need for minorities to have the right to establish contact with members of the same group across the borders
- the need for freedom of movement

10   *Constitutive Act of the African Union* (2000), Assembly of Heads of State and Governments of the African Union, 36th Ordinary Session, http://www.africa-union.org/About_AU/Constitutive_Act.htm (accessed 7 August 2004).

- the need to associate freely and participate in public affairs
- the need to be represented within local and state organs
- the need for a degree of local autonomy in the governance of their own affairs

Much remains to be done on the continent in order to attain these needs. The inception of the AU provides the continent with a unique opportunity to bring about this objective. Prior to assessing some of the instruments that the AU has established for protection we can assess some of the opportunities, norms and mechanisms that will inform the work of the preventive organisation.

The AU is developing a set of norms that will commit Member States to respecting, protecting and fulfilling their human and minority rights obligations. The AU will not be implementing these norms but monitoring the compliance of Member States. The AU is in the process of developing mechanisms, some of which are political instruments while others are legally binding. In a document that was prepared by the Chairperson of the African Union Commission, Mr. Alpha Konare, entitled the Strategic Framework of the African Union Commission, the AU sets out an objective (number 5) to 'promote a society based on the rule of law and African citizenship'.[11] In particular this document notes that 'the lack of good governance and democracy, the violation of individual and collective rights' remain a key problem that the AU needs to address. As a strategy to respond to this issue, it proposes to reinforce and where necessary 'establish governance systems to promote peace, stability and human security, thereby minimizing the causes of conflicts on the continent.' In particular, it commits the AU to advocate for norms that 'popularize the duty to protect human kind'.[12] In this regard, the AU will strive to popularise norms and mechanisms that advance the recognition of the basic rights for all Africans to life, liberty non-discrimination and equality before the law as well as the equal enjoyment of civil and political rights.

Protection of Minorities: Monitoring and Enforcement Mechanisms

As noted earlier, the AU will need to further develop a specific set of monitoring and enforcement mechanisms to prevent discrimination or the targeting of minorities. This aims to allow individuals and communities to preserve their differences so as to avoid forced assimilation into a majority culture.

In the meantime several institutions and instruments have been established that can fulfil this role if there is the political will behind them. With regard to the range of prevention instruments, from diplomatic channels to military intervention, the AU has established a range of institutions that incorporate the following elements:
- Complaints procedures
- Fact finding missions

---

11   African Union *Strategic Framework of the African Union Commission 2004-2007* (Addis Ababa: African Union, 2004) p. 16.
12   Ibid p. 17.

– Dialogue and diplomacy
– Organs and offices of the African Union
– Technical co-operation between the different branches of the AU

Peace and Security Council

In December 2003 the African Union established its Peace and Security Council, following a provision in Article 5(2) of the Constitutive Act which authorises the Assembly of the African Union to establish organs as may be necessary to fulfil its objectives.[13] This led to the drafting of a Protocol on the Peace and Security Council[14] at the close of the inaugural summit in July 2002, in Durban, South Africa. The Peace and Security Council has 15 member countries (ten elected for a term of two years and five for a term of three years). The Chairperson of the African Union is assisted by a Commissioner in charge of Peace and Security who provides operational support to the Peace and Security Council as well as deploying efforts and taking the necessary steps to prevent, manage and resolve conflicts.

The Peace and Security Council was officially launched on 25 May 2004 in Addis Ababa, Ethiopia. It has the mandate to promote collective security and enhance an early-warning framework to facilitate the timely and efficient response to conflict and crisis situations that, for example, may put minorities at risk. The Peace and Security Council will assess potential crisis situations and be in a position to authorise and legitimise the AU's intervention in such situations. The right of the Union to intervene in a Member State with respect to crisis situations is stipulated in Article 4(h) of the Constitutive Act[15]. In particular, Article 7 item (e) of the Protocol on the Peace and Security Council, states that the Council can 'recommend to the Assembly (of Heads of State), intervention, on behalf of the Union, in a Member State in respect of grave circumstances, namely war crimes, genocide and crimes against humanity, as defined in relevant international conventions and instruments'.[16] This is a major qualitative difference between the Charter of the OAU and the legal instruments at the disposal of the AU. For the first time in the history of Africa, the continental organisation working through an appointed group of states has the authority to intervene in internal situations that might lead to atrocities being committed against minority groups within states. To reinforce this provision the AU is working for the establishment of an African Standby Force to cooperate where appropriate with the United Nations and sub-regional African organisations. In effect, the AU will continue to maintain a working relationship with the United Nations and

---

13   (note 10).
14   *Protocol relating to the establishment of the Peace and Security Council of the African Union* (2002), Assembly of the African Union, 1st Ordinary Session, http://www.africa-union.org/Official_documents/Treaties_%20Conventions_%20Protocols/Protocol_peace%20and%20security.pdf (accessed 7 August 2004).
15   (note 10).
16   (note 14).

other international organisations on issues to do with conflict prevention and peace-building, and, by implication, issues to do with minority protection.[17]

Article 7 item (g) also states that the Peace and Security Council can 'institute sanctions whenever an unconstitutional change of Government takes place in a Member State'.[18] This provision is also provided for in Article 30 of the Constitutive Act of the African Union. The AU is also in a position to institute sanctions whenever an unconstitutional change of Government occurs anywhere in the continent. This can have an indirect impact on the well-being of minorities since in most cases minorities turn out to be victims of unconstitutional changes of government. However, in some cases minorities can be the perpetrators involved in the over-throw of governments if their grievances are not addressed. The AU has still to qualify this Article and set out clearly whether instances of self-determination and 'liberation' movements that challenge oppressive governments fall within the same frame of reference. Despite this, the AU is demonstrating a commitment to good governance and a willingness to legally sanction any infractions against the legally established constitutional order of a Member State. Ultimately, the success of the Council's work depends essentially on the commitment of the AU Member States, sub-regional groupings, civil society, minority groups and individuals to enable the Council to conduct its work.

The work of the Peace and Security Council has already been initiated. For example, the AU Peace and Security Council met on 27 March 2004 to assess the situation in Côte D'Ivoire and resolved to support the initiatives of the Economic Community of West African States (ECOWAS). On 25 May 2004 the Peace and Security Council met, under the chairmanship of Nigerian President Olusegun Obasanjo, to analyse the security situation in Africa and particularly the African agenda for conflict prevention, management and resolution. This meeting assessed the situation in the Sudanese region of Darfur, where minorities are faced with tragic conditions following an ongoing conflict, as well as the situation in Somalia which remains precarious.

The Pan-African Parliament

Article 18 of the Protocol on the Peace and Security Council states that it will 'maintain close working relations with the Pan-African Parliament in furtherance of peace, security and stability in Africa'.[19] The Pan-African Parliament has a consultative and advisory function within the African Union. Article 11 of the Protocol Relating to the Pan-African Parliament states that the Parliament will be able to 'discuss or express an opinion on any matter, either on its own initiative or at the request of the Assembly or other policy organs and make any recommendations it may deem fit relating to, inter alia, matters pertaining to respect of human rights, the consolidation of democratic institutions and the culture of democracy, as well as the promotion of good governance

---

17   Ibid.
18   Ibid.
19   (note 14).

and the rule of law'.[20] This will be a useful alternative forum for raising issues relating to minority rights, which can function as a people-driven system of checks and balances to ensure that the 'politics of indifference' that plagued the OAU does not take root in the evolving African Union.

The African Court on Human and Peoples' Rights

The AU established a Protocol to the African Charter on Human Rights and People's Rights (the Banjul Charter discussed earlier), which was finally ratified on 25 January 2004. This Protocol led to the creation of an African Court on Human and Peoples' Rights.[21] The Court further reinforces the Pan-African systems for the protection of human and minority rights. The Court is empowered to act both in a judicatory and advisory capacity. Article 2 of the Protocol states that 'the Court shall, bearing in mind the provisions of this Protocol, complement the protective mandate of the African Commission on Human and Peoples' Rights conferred upon it by the African Charter'.[22] Article 3 further notes that 'the jurisdiction of the Court shall extend to all cases and disputes submitted to it concerning the interpretation and application of the Charter, this Protocol and any other relevant Human Rights instrument ratified by the States concerned'.[23] This means that AU Member States that have ratified the Protocol establishing the Court are subject to its jurisdiction. With regard to the Court's judicatory power, Article 5 paragraph 1 states that cases can be submitted by:
- the AU's African Commission on Human and Peoples' Rights;
- the State Party which has lodged a complaint to the Commission;
- the State Party against which the complaint has been lodged at the Commission;
- the State Party whose citizen is a victim of human rights violation;
- African Intergovernmental Organisations.

Paragraph 3 of Article 5 also states that 'the Court may entitle relevant Non Governmental Organizations (NGOs) with observer status before the Commission, and individuals to institute cases directly before it'.[24]

Given that the Court's mandate covers human and *peoples'* rights, it empowers minority communities by providing them with an avenue for highlighting any issues to do with the deprivation of their human rights, as recognised by the African Charter.

---

20   *Protocol to the Treaty Establishing the African Economic Community Relating to the Pan-African Parliament* (2001), http://www.africa-union.org/home/Welcome.htm (accessed on 7 August 2004).

21   *Protocol to the African Charter on Human and Peoples' Rights on the Establishment of an African Court on Human and Peoples' Rights* (2004), http://www.africa-union.org/home/Welcome.htm (accessed 7 August 2004).

22   Ibid.

23   Ibid.

24   Ibid.

NGOs and individuals can also institute cases with the Court, which provides additional opportunities for raising issues concerning victims of a violation of a right as outlined in the Banjul Charter.[25] The only caveat is that in order for the Court to be able to receive individual petitions the State against which the complaint has been lodged must first have recognised the competence of the Court to receive such communications. There are therefore ongoing campaigns to ensure that all African states ratify the Protocol.

While this system for the protection of human and peoples' rights has some limitations, the adoption of the Protocol is an important step forward for the continent. As with most institutions the effectiveness, credibility and success of the Court will depend on the will of the States to adhere to the rulings of the Court and to provide it with the necessary resources to carry out its mandate.

The New Partnership for Africa's Development (NEPAD)

The New Partnership for Africa's Development (NEPAD) is a policy and programme framework established by Member States of the African Union to orient and implement Africa's development agenda. It is not an autonomous organisation, and with an intergovernmental institution of its own, NEPAD can more appropriately be conceptualised as a blueprint or vehicle for the African Union to achieve its development objectives and increase its participation in international affairs on the basis of partnership, rather than through the docile compliance or exploitation that is a feature of the continent's history.[26]

The relatively rapid evolution of NEPAD from concept to creation has created critics and supporters of the initiative. Critics argue that, like previous revival programmes, NEPAD was flawed in its concept and design. They condemn the programme's heavily reliance on a neo-liberal market economic framework which some argue is what hampers Africa's development, thereby making NEPAD a part of the problem rather than a solution.[27] Heavy subsidisation of commodities by developed countries undermines Africa's ability to trade and to create wealth. In addition, programmes that compel African governments to repay their debts instead of investing in health care and education only reinforce dependency and underdevelopment. In contrast, supporters view NEPAD as a means to begin redressing the disadvantages that Africa faces in the global arena, by acting as a forum and framework where alternative strategies can be deliberated and where localized solutions can be designed and implemented.

---

25   R. Murray *The African Charter on Human and Peoples' Rights: The System at Work* (Cambridge University Press, 2002); see also, U.O. Umozurike *The African Charter on Human and Peoples' Rights* (The Hague: Martinus Nijhoff, 1997).

26   NEPAD *New Economic Partnership for Africa* (2001), for more details on NEPAD see http://www.nepad.org (accessed 9 August 2004).

27   P. Bond (ed.) *Fanon's Warning: A Civil Society Reader on the New Partnership for Africa's Development* (Trenton, NJ: AIDC, 2002).

The AU NEPAD programme offers a broad outline for the promotion of human and minority rights, but does not specifically outline how concrete initiatives will be implemented or supported. There is therefore scope to further elaborate on the provisions for rights protection within the AU, particularly with reference to minority and cultural rights, economic rights, social rights, women's rights, and environmental rights.

However, the AU NEPAD programme does recognise that poor political leadership characterised by human and minority rights violations, economic mismanagement and local and foreign corruption are root causes of Africa's current condition.[28] To remedy this, NEPAD further acknowledges that establishing and ensuring the rule of law is a key aspect of enhancing the African Union's capacity to monitor and promote human and minority rights. As we saw earlier, Article 30 of the Constitutive Act of the Union[29] (which states that 'governments which shall come to power through unconstitutional means shall not be allowed to participate in the activities of the Union') places an emphasis on constitutional government and the protection of democracy, minority and human rights.

When the Declaration on the Implementation of NEPAD was adopted at the African Union's Assembly held in Durban in 2002, it included a more specific Declaration on Democracy, Political, Economic and Corporate Governance that established the African Peer Review Mechanism. Member States are invited to voluntarily join the African Peer Review Mechanism for the purpose of participating in a self-monitoring programme with a clear time frame for achieving certain standards for promoting inclusive governance, participatory democracy and human/minority rights promotion through constitutional governments.

Due to entrenched patterns of political behaviour, Africa continues to be afflicted by bad leadership and economic mismanagement, which have resulted in the ongoing conflicts and failing development initiatives. Without a doubt, resources diverted from fighting these wars could be used to promote human and minority rights. There is a case for the dissemination of the programmes that the AU proposes to the African people, and civil society should have the role of documenting and monitoring the progress that governments are making.

The AU's success in the promotion of minority rights will be measured by some key indicators. In addition to the promotion of the rule of law, an indicator of AU impact on the promotion of minority rights will be its success in protecting Africa's war-affected regions from predatory global economic forces. In particular, some multinational organisations are fuelling violent conflicts leading to human rights atrocities by supporting the illicit trade in diamonds, oil and timber with governments whose legitimacy is being challenged by minority groups. This is witnessed in the Democratic Republic of the Congo, Sudan, and historically in Sierra Leone, Liberia and Angola. Linked to this issue

---

28   P. Chabal, 'The Quest for Good Governance and Development in Africa: Is NEPAD the Answer?', 78.3 *International Affairs* (2002) pp. 447-462.

29   (note 10).

of capital flight, the AU should mobilise international partners to ensure that the wealth generated by Africa's natural resources is not stored away in private banks for the benefit of the few but instead used to finance the development of viable health care, education and other economic projects in Africa. Such an approach would begin to address some of the concerns and needs of minority and majority communities within states. Related to this is the issue of debt cancellation. This would allow the diversion of funds from payment as interest to money which could instead be used for governance, human and minority rights and development projects.

An indicator of the AU's impact will also be the extent to which it can promote and enhance the labour rights of the African working population. Under the current political trends and economic neo-liberal doctrine, capital can flow freely across borders but labour cannot. This places African citizens at a distinct disadvantage as capital can be siphoned out of the continent by business enterprises after exploiting the local commodities and markets. However, highly restrictive immigration laws prohibit skilled Africans from travelling to other parts of the world for employment which would allow them to repatriate capital back to assist in the development of their continent.

The Role of Cultural Norms in Promoting the Protection of Minorities

One aspect of the African Union's overall strategy for promoting stable communities, building sustainable peace and creating conditions that can enhance minority protection that needs further elaboration, is the role of cultural norms and customary law.[30] African cultures have developed their own means of addressing issues to do with diversity and difference within communities. Cultural notions of rights and responsibilities that can contribute to establishing social cohesion need to be emphasised, revitalised and incorporated into the development of the corpus of African Union legislation and institutions.[31] Africa has a wealth of methods and principles for promoting coexistence and accommodation, found for example in the notion of *ubuntu*, which states that 'a person is a person through other people'. The *ubuntu* framework for resolving disputes exists today and it can complement and add another dimension to issues of minority protection. Like other African traditions, an *ubuntu* framework places more of an emphasis on forgiveness and restorative justice than on punitive justice. Restorative justice seeks to restore the human dignity of the violated party and rebuild social harmony by encouraging the perpetrators of crimes to confess and show genuine remorse, and where possible make a reparation which provides victims with the basis for granting forgiveness and embracing reconciliation. In cases where the rights of an individual or a minority group have been violated, using an *ubuntu* framework can strengthen societies

---

30   M. Mutua *Human Rights: A Political and Cultural Critique* (Philadelphia: University of Pennsylvania Press, 2002).

31   A. An-Na'im *Human Rights in Cross-Cultural Perspectives: A Quest for Consensus* (Philadelphia: University of Pennsylvania Press, 1992).

and promote the culture of shared responsibility for the well-being of all sectors of the community.

The colonial systems of justice were superimposed on top of African systems of justice and governance, and have been retained in most post-colonial state structures. Justice should not be meted out through predetermined and inflexible prescriptions by applying the same model to every local population or country. It needs to be context-specific and relevant to the local communities' concepts of justice, and sensitive to the social and cultural traditions. The African Court of Human and Peoples' Rights can therefore gain some insights from long-established African traditions and incorporate these norms into its future development.

Ultimately, to enable culture to begin to play a significant role in the reconstruction of the continent, through individuals, societies and states working in partnership with the African Union, the Union needs to further develop educational and training programmes for officials and civil society actors based on African cultural values. However, it should be kept in mind that not all traditions are empowering, particularly on issues to do with gender equality. Progressive cultural principles which promote human dignity and the well-being of the individual and of minority groups within society can provide valuable insights into how Africa can be reconstructed by using its own indigenous value-systems.[32] They can also provide the basis for ensuring that potential grievances that minorities may have such as access to political participation and the right to determine their own affairs, power sharing, inclusive governance and the equitable distribution of resources among all members of society are addressed more effectively from a cultural perspective.

Recommendations and the Way Forward

At the time of this publication, the programme of action for activating the legislation and institutions of the African Union is still evolving. There are additional issues that the AU needs to address to ensure that the rights of minorities are more effectively protected. All AU states are members of the United Nations, so continued referral to the existing and emerging instruments of the UN will be necessary. Ideally, the emerging institutions of the AU discussed above should complement and pool resources with the efforts of the UN. For example, the AU has to deepen its collaboration with civil society organisations as well as the United Nations Commission on Human Rights and its Working Group on Minorities. Collaborations could include the establishment of an African Union Special Representative on Minority Rights with a mandate to highlight minority rights violations within Member States in order to prevent potential conflict escalation situations. The task of such a Special Representative would also be to generally oversee the mainstreaming of minority rights promotion across the continent.

---

32   M. Mutua 'The Banjul Charter and the African Cultural Fingerprint: An Evaluation of the Language of Duties' 35 *Virginia Journal of International Law* (1995) pp. 339-80.

The recently established post of the UN Special Advisor on the Prevention of Genocide to the UN Secretary-General will also be a key partner that the AU needs to collaborate with to avoid the recurrence of events like the Rwanda crisis. The UN Special Advisor will work closely with the UN High Commissioner for Human Rights to examine existing and potential threats of genocide, which is the same mandate that the AU's Peace and Security Council has for the African continent. It therefore makes sense for these two organisations to pool resources and reinforce their joint authority with regards to situations that might lead to genocide.

Europe is also facing the challenge of closer integration and the implications that this has for minority groups. There are also tensions that still exist between minority groups and the states within which they reside. In this regard, the Council of Europe has developed a framework for minority protection that can also provide some insights into how institutions can further be strengthened and enhanced on the African continent. The Council of Europe is an organisation for cooperation between governments and parliaments in Europe. Its aim is 'to achieve greater unity between its Member States in order to facilitate their economic and social progress and to safeguard the principles of a pluralist democracy, respect for human rights and the rule of law.'[33] The Council seeks to compel its Member States to embrace these norms and principles and to ensure that all the people that live under their jurisdiction are able to enjoy human and minority rights as well as fundamental freedoms. In order to ensure this, it has created a range of instruments including The Framework Convention for the Protection of National Minorities.[34] In 1985 the Council established a European Charter on Local-Self Government; in 1992 it established a Charter for Regional and Minority Languages; and in 2000 a Race Equality Directive. Recently, in June 2004, European leaders finally adopted a Constitution for the European Union which has within it provisions for the protection of national minorities, including legislative frameworks on anti-discrimination laws. The AU can gain some insights into protecting and promoting minority rights in Africa from this range of instruments.

In addition, the Organization for Security and Cooperation in Europe (OSCE) has established a High Commissioner for National Minorities whose task is to supervise the implementation of commitments that the participating States have undertaken in the field of human and minority rights as well as in the promotion of democracy.[35] The High Commissioner undertakes silent missions to countries to assess the degree to which the rights of minorities are being respected. The Commissioner has the ability to provide

---

33   C. Barnes and M. Olsthoorn *The Framework Convention for the Protection of National Minorities: A Guide for Non-Governmental Organizations* (London: Minority Rights Group International, 1999) p. 2.

34   *Framework Convention for the Protection of National Minorities* (1994), Doc. H(94) 10, Council of Europe, http://assembly.coe.int/Documents/AdoptedText/TA01/EREC1492.htm (accessed 8 August 2004).

35   Organization for Security and Cooperation in Europe (OSCE), *The OSCE Handbook*, Vienna: OSCE, 2000, http://osce.org (accessed 8 August 2004).

the Chairman-in-Office, who reports to the Permanent and Ministerial Councils, with information and recommendations concerning the potential escalation of a dispute as a result of individual or minority discrimination in participating states. This preventive diplomacy dimension has succeeded in offsetting potentially tense dispute situations and can also provide a useful model for the African Union Commission to adopt for its Member States.

Conclusion

This chapter assesses the African Union's capacity to ensure the protection of minorities within African states through the array of Pan-African instruments and institutions, sanctions, legal instruments and strategies that minorities may appeal to in case of the violation of their rights. Africa continues to be afflicted by violent conflict, and the history of recent wars, notably the Rwandan genocide, shows that much remains to be done. The challenge facing the African Union will be to find a way to ensure a more effective means of implementing the existing instruments of international law and promote the emerging instruments of Pan-African law. Given the recent creation of the African Union, continental policy transformation on the issue of minorities is bound to be gradual rather than immediate. The mainstreaming of the idea of minority rights and minority protection within international law and international relations discourse still remains a challenge. One can expect, however, that the institutions that the African Union has adopted will provide the continent with a more robust system of monitoring and implementing minority protection. The extent to which African countries and peoples, under the auspices of the AU, can actively and effectively intervene in situations that negatively impact on the rights of minorities will ultimately depend on the respect given to the emerging institutions, and the provision of adequate resources to enable them to conduct their affairs effectively.

Chapter 17

THE KURDISH QUESTION IN TURKEY: HISTORICAL ROOTS, DOMESTIC CONCERNS AND INTERNATIONAL LAW

Bülent Gökay[1]

Overview

On 25 May, 2000, Professor Thornberry and I organised a workshop at Keele University on 'Turkey's Kurdish question – an international perspective' where Patrick presented a very lively debate on 'National Minorities and the European Convention on Human Rights' with particular reference to the situation of Kurds in Turkey. This workshop was the beginning of an intense and productive process of discussions, exchanges of information and discovery for me. This chapter is the result of this still on-going learning process.

The Kurdish issue in Turkey is one of the most painful ethnic problems of recent years. In the last two decades more than 30,000 people have been killed and more than a million displaced.

In a way, Turkey's Kurdish problem is a typical ethnic conflict of the late industrial age. Such international contextualisation of this conflict can be used to examine the ways in which the broader changes of the 1990s have affected the unique development of the political process in Turkey. There may be some resistance in Turkey to the drawing of such analogies with other ethnic conflicts. Nationalism, with its investment in particularism, would have it no other way, and all nationalisms have a perennial aspiration or conceit, which is a belief in their uniqueness. Turkey, with its nationalisms, is no exception to this rule. There seems to be great benefit, however, in trying to reduce that appearance of singularity and uniqueness, to which all inter-ethnic and nationalist conflicts are easily prone, to a broader international pattern.

The Kurdish problem in an International Context

Turkey's Kurdish problem, while being unique in some aspects, shares many common characteristics with other similar conflicts. From the former Yugoslavia to Chechnia,

---

[1]   Senior Lecturer, School of Philosophy, Politics, International Relations and the Environment, University of Keele, UK.

Nazila Ghanea & Alexandra Xanthaki (eds.), Minorities, Peoples and Self-Determination, *pp. 315-335.*
© *2005 Koninklijke Brill NV. Printed in The Netherlands. ISBN 90 04 14301 7.*

from the Middle East to Africa, the conflicting hopes and fears of diverse ethnic communities capture the international attention during a period of rapid and often violent change.

Today at the beginning of a new millennium, the issue of accommodating national identity within the existing constitutional structure presents a serious global challenge. This proves particularly demanding given the often conflicting political goals of minority and majority groups within one state. Disenfranchised minorities seek a realignment of state borders, either through secession or irredentism, while majority groups become the target of nationalist politicians who urge consolidation of the state and the prioritisation of the dominant ethnic group. This prioritisation often is at the expense of minorities and this exclusivist dynamic often results in 'romantic' nationalism of the most crudely chauvinistic type. The internecine wars in the former Yugoslavia and the Russian conflict in Chechnia represent this phenomenon to differing degrees.

Crises of national identity come to the fore in many contemporary disputes, and in a number of instances attempts to assert or reinforce ideals of national identity have not only resulted in the breakdown of constitutional order, but have also led to serious violations of individual and collective rights. There are tragic cases such as those of Rwanda, Bosnia-Herzegovina, and more recently Kosovo and Chechnia, where the question of identity has been resolved through genocide, or ethnic cleansing of minority groups. This proliferation of conflicts surrounding issues of national identity and the difficulties in installing effective mechanisms for dispute resolution has highlighted the necessity for reconsideration of existing practices and procedures.

Why Study Inter-communal Tensions?

There is little doubt that many of those working in this field as teachers, academics and researchers do so out of a belief that by understanding the processes of violent conflicts, something positive and practical can be done to improve the situation. But having such motivations and beliefs does not mean that the results of our academic work are effective in bringing about change. It does not follow, however, that even if there are no practical applications, that the academic work is not 'useful'. Most historians who have studied war and conflict situations have not felt the need to relate their findings to practical applications, although a few have. We might, therefore, without any feelings of deficiency, regard the results of our work as being of civilisational value, acting as another 'voice' in the study of humankind. Hence the study of inter-ethnic conflicts, such as Turkey's Kurdish problem, can be justified without reference to its practical applications.

However, we are emerging from the long darkness of the Cold War, where so much political thinking was dominated by ideological simplifications, oppression of the weak and the selfish policy of containment, into an era where there is more hope but a lot of confusion. It is not just the writings of academics that are of importance, but also their ability to interact, and to seed society with new ways of viewing international political problems. Much of this perspective-seeking will come from the students we teach and train, some of whom will become political actors, or work in NGOs, or become teachers themselves. Maybe, in the years to come, peaceful alternatives to international and inter-communal conflicts will become the conventional way of dealing with at least some disputes and develop into another "settled norm".

It seems that in a fast changing world in which internal conflicts are becoming more and more internationalised more emphasis should be placed on the effects of external factors. Outside powers, international organisations, the media, diaspora communities and shared experiences around the world, as well as the international environment as a whole, have all played their part in the origins, escalation and continuation of internal conflicts in the 1990s. The key to a more effective international response to inter-ethnic and nationalist conflicts clearly lies in a better understanding of the interaction between external factors and the specific features, historical roots and dynamics of the local conflict.

Nationalism, Identity and the Kurdish Problem in Turkey

Jonathan Glover writes that there are two histories of nationalism.[2] One history is of peoples rightly struggling to be free. They eventually break away from their colonial power to attain the dignity of self-governing nationhood. This is the story of most European nations and of their quarrels that culminated in war in 1914. The other history is of nationalism as tribal conflict. Which one is the history of the Kurds in Turkey?

The origins of nationalism are often traced to the revolutionary upheavals of the 18th century. There is a kind of general agreement that the star of nationalism rose 'bright and clear' in 18th century France and America. Since the French Revolution nationalist forces in different parts of the world have repeatedly challenged the assumptions, practices and institutions of the traditional world. Many explanations of nationalism seek its roots in the transition from agricultural to industrial society. It may be that, historically, the rise of nationalist doctrine closely followed the break up of traditional forms of society.

Nationality is often thought of as something 'natural' or pre-social. So, one may consider that Turks are different from Kurds in the way that the fish of the Mediterranean are different from those of the Black Sea. This sense of naturalness is reinforced by stories nations often have about their own past. According to Olafson:

> The relation of my past experience to the one I am now having is not that the former causes the latter, but that the former has meaning for me now. Its function is not to cause recent consciousness but to be for present consciousness. An effect is not aware of its various causes, but a consciousness is aware of and thus accumulates its past experiences and proceeds in light of them.[3]

---

2   J. Glover 'Nations, Identity, and Conflict' in R. McKim and J. McMahan (eds) *The Morality of Nationalism* (Oxford: Oxford University Press, 1997) p.11.

3   F. Olafson, cited by D. Carr *Time, Narrative and History* (Bloomington: Indiana University Press, 1986).

Nationalists often think of their nation in ways influenced by a traditional model of a pure or ideal case. This ideal version is of people inhabiting a single, unified territory. According to this view, the people are a tribe. They are a single ethnic group. They have a common language. They have a shared history, and a common culture. This culture may include shared religious beliefs.

Many of us care about what sort of people we are, and many of the characteristics we want to have are long-term. And this may involve a long-term process of self-creation. The process of self-creation is partly that of a novelist telling a coherent story about a character. The mixture of freedom and constraint is similar. What the character can do depends partly on circumstances and partly on other people in the story. There are also limits on how far acting out of character is possible. This story we create about ourselves, partly by what we do and partly by how we edit and narrate the story of our past, is central to the sense of our own identity. But the story is bound up with the context in which it takes place. This is partly physical context, such as being forced into exile, or being excluded from the places where the earlier parts of the story took place. It is partly the context of other people. What I did was done with them or done in response to what they did or said. The values that guided how I acted, and that colour the tone of the narrative, were inevitably shaped partly by them. In the case of nations these make up a particular historical context.

Historical context provides a political and social space in which the identity of a nation is constituted. The past helps to construct the narratives that shape identity through notions of authenticity and continuity. While doing so, the past itself is given a new meaning. It is important to understand this context in order to explain the particular way a 'nationalism' is constructed.

In the light of this, let us now look at the Kurds in Turkey. The Kurdish sense of national community developed in the late 19th and early 20th centuries, more or less at the same time that Turks and Arabs also began to embrace an ethnic sense of identity in place of the idea of the Ottoman religious community (the *millet*). The Ottoman Empire was anything but a nation-state.

The European concept of the nation was foreign to the Middle East until the 19th century. It was from Europe that the concept was welcomed. Europeans actively incited first Greek and then Slavic nationalism. Tsarist Russia took a keen interest in the Armenians. Basically, as a reaction to these movements, a number of new ideologies took root in leading intellectual circles of the Ottoman Empire during the last decades of the 19th century.

Ottomanism stressed the common interests of all Ottoman citizens. Pan-Islamism found its strongest champion in Sultan Abdulhamid (1876-1909). It had a definite anti-colonialist nuance. Abdulhamid promoted Pan-Islamism as a counter-balance to emerging nationalisms, hoping to gain support among Muslims outside, as well as inside, the Empire. Following the overthrow of Abdulhamid, the Committee of Union and Progress promoted Pan-Turkism. Pan-Turkism, the romantic idea of uniting all Turkic peoples in a single political unity, may originally have been a reaction to the tsar's Pan-Slavism. It seems that the nationalisms of the other Muslim elements emerged largely as a response and reaction to the increasing prominence of Turkish nationalism and Pan-Turkish aspirations.

A general awareness of Kurdish national identity emerged mainly in this period. The specific conditions of the 19th century Ottoman Empire are significant in identifying the main aspects of this emerging Kurdish national identity.

History of the Kurds and Kurdish Leadership

There is no doubt that a Kurdish people had existed as an identifiable group for at least two thousand years. But it was only in the late 19th century that they acquired a sense of ethnic community as Kurds.

The majority of Kurds are probably descended from waves of Indo-European tribes mainly moving westwards across Iran, probably in the middle of the second millennium BC.

By the time of the Islamic conquests, in the 8th century AD, the term 'Kurd' had a socio-economic rather than an ethnic meaning. At this time, 'Kurd' meant nomad and from the 11th century onwards many travellers treated the term 'Kurd' as synonymous with 'bandit'.

The term 'Kurdistan' was first used in the 12th century as a geographical term by the Selchuks. Kurdistan was considered a peripheral region, lying along the geopolitical fault line between the main power centres of the Middle East.

Historically, the Kurdish tribes were organised under emirates (principalities). These emirates enjoyed 'de facto independence' until the 16th century when the continuing struggle for regional ascendancy between the Ottoman and Iranian Empires ended their independent status.

Sunni Kurdish emirates were persuaded to act on behalf of the Sunni Ottoman Empire. 'Kurdistan' became part of the Ottoman Empire. The Ottoman administration granted the Kurdish fiefdoms and emirates a certain degree of autonomy. The continuing tension between the Ottoman and Persian empires required the former to tolerate the special autonomy of the Kurdish emirates in return for the support of the Kurds against the Persian Empire.

The leading Kurdish families, who were granted posts in the Ottoman civil and military bureaucracy, governed the Kurdish provinces. As a consequence, there emerged considerable differences between the governmental structures of Kurdish and non-Kurdish provinces. The autonomous status of Kurdish tribes continued to be recognised by the Ottoman Empire until the mid-1800s. A relative calm descended upon Kurdistan and its autonomous principalities.

As autonomous entities, the Kurdish emirates functioned as built individual 'sub-systems' within the general system of the Ottoman Empire. Indeed, the constitutive logic of the Ottoman Empire was the articulation of these sub-systems within a broader system. The autonomy enjoyed by these sub-systems was a necessary condition of their continuing existence, and of the general system of the Empire. The emirates, with their autonomous existence, constituted and defined the politico-social space in which the 19th century 'Kurdishness' was defined.

By the 19th century, the Ottoman Empire was faced with a series of deep problems. Diplomatic and international pressures from other powers, accompanied by the separatist tendencies of numerous ethnic groups, forced the Ottoman rulers to restructure the administrative and political structures of the Empire. The Empire was beginning to crumble on the fringes. Once nationalism raised its head in the Balkans and then elsewhere within the Empire, pressure increased. The conventional administrative, political and economic structures of the Empire started to erode under this multi-level pressure.

In Kurdistan this was reflected in the erosion of the conventional consensus between the Kurdish emirates and the Ottoman palace. Administrative reforms in the first half of the 19th century aimed to destroy the autonomy of the periphery through the centralisation of the economy, politics, and administration. Finally the emirates were abolished.

The removal of the emirates destroyed the dominant political organisation in Kurdistan and led to the individualisation of Kurdish tribes. This resulted in tribal confrontations. The local governors appointed by the central authority could not fulfil the role of the emir in the prevention of tribal conflicts. By the beginning of the 19th century, banditry had become a growing problem throughout much of Kurdistan.

The failure of the central government to restore law and order in Kurdistan resulted in the emergence of new actors in Kurdish politics: the sheikhs. The palace-appointed governors had neither power nor legitimacy. The sheikhs had both. They were the only figures in Kurdistan whose authority and influence exceeded the limits of the tribes. Gradually the sheikhs became the new political leaders of the Kurds.

From the late 19th century onwards, Kurdish sheikhs led most Kurdish rebellions. Two rebellions were of particular importance. The revolt of Sheikh Ubeydulah in the 1870s aimed to establish a state for the Kurds on the territories occupied by the Ottoman and Persian Empires. Fifty years later in 1925, the Sheikh Said rebellion seriously shook the young Turkish Republic.

Most influential Kurdish leaders in the late 19th and early 20th centuries were sheikhs. Most leading figures of modern Kurdish nationalism in Istanbul have also been from sheikh families. The sheikhs fulfilled the role of mediator between the religion of Islam and Kurdish nationalism. In this way, nationalism and religion became intertwined for the Kurds. The nationalist ideas found their way into the *tarikats* (religious sects) and *tekiyyes* (dervish lodges) in Kurdistan. In this way, sheikhs, *tarikats* and *tekiyyes* became the components of the social space in which 'Kurdish national identity' was constructed.

In this process the institution of the Caliphate was of particular significance. During all the destructive confrontations between the emerging nations and the multi-national empire in the late 19th and early 20th centuries, the Caliphate maintained its status. It could not prevent the emergence of independent nations – Arabs gained their independence when the Caliphate was still in power. But the Caliphate was still important in maintaining the unity of the remaining Muslim elements.

This was important, especially for those Muslim elements living on the edge of the state's politics. The Caliphate, as an institution, had for centuries guaranteed the vital bond between the Ottoman political centre and the Muslim elements of the periphery, which tolerated the ethnic plurality.

This was particularly significant for the Kurds, who for centuries enjoyed an autonomous administration. The removal of the Caliphate in 1924 replaced this bond between the centre and Kurdish periphery with the tyranny of the centre imposed on the Kurds. In this way, the removal of the Caliphate became another important factor affecting the social and political space in which Kurdish national identity was created. The idea of a separate Kurdish identity clashed with the state ideology in Turkey.[4]

To sum up, Kurdish nationalism in the late 19th and early 20th centuries was not modernist. It was not a manifestation of a will to overcome traditional modes of organisation. It did not emerge as a reaction to the Ottoman state system either. It did not propose a state organised around rational and universal models of identity and practice. Neither was it an angry reversion to the fundamental principles of pre-modern practices.

Kurdish nationalism emerged as a mobilisation of identities occurring in the wake of the great transformations brought about by three central tensions within the late Ottoman society. The political and social space in which Kurdish national identity was created was conditioned by three interconnected tensions: tension between the periphery and the centre; tension between traditions and modernisation; and tension between Islam and secularism.

Turkey: From Empire to Republic

The first Prime Minister of the Turkish Republic, Ismet Inönu, presented the country to the League of Nations as the 'land of Turks and Kurds'. Following the Treaty of Lausanne (signed on 24 July, 1924), the territory of the Republic of Turkey covered, to a large extent, the territory of Kurdistan as it was defined under the Treaty of Sevres. The Turkish representative declared at the Lausanne negotiations, 'the Kurds and the Turks are essential components of the Republic of Turkey…. the government in Ankara is the government of the Turks as well as Kurds'. But the Treaty made no mention of Kurds.[5]

On 29 October 1924, the Grand National Assembly accepted a new constitution and declared Turkey a republic. The constitution forbade the use of Kurdish in public places. Law number 1505 made it possible for the land of large landowners to be expropriated and given to the new Turkish settlers in Kurdistan. The word 'Kurdistan' was omitted from all educational books and Turkish geographical names were gradually

---

4   R. Olson 'The Emergence of Kurdish Nationalism and the Sheikh Said Rebellion, 1880-1925', http://www.xs4all.nl/~tank/kurdish/htdocs/his/said.html (accessed 10 May 2004).

5   Gajendra Singh 'The Kurdish Equation. Turkey: Once bitten, twice shy', http://www.atimes.com/atimes/Middle_East/EA24Ak03.html (accessed 10 May 2004); Gul Demir and Niki Gamm, 'The Lausanne Treaty at 80', http://www.turkishdailynews.com/old_editions/07_25_03/feature.htm (accessed 10 May 2004).

substituted for the Kurdish equivalent throughout the country. All of these events contributed to the already dissatisfaction that already existed among the Kurdish population with the new secular regime.[6]

The first Kurdish uprising since the proclamation of the republic, that of Sheikh Said, occurred in February 1925. Due to their traditional position and the high esteem in which the Kurdish population held them, it was largely the Nakshbandi order and its sheikhs who led this uprising, aiming at Kurdish national goals. While the Sheikh Said rebellion was basically nationalist in nature, its mobilisation, propaganda and symbols were those of a religious rebellion. It took a full-scale military operation to put it down. Tens of thousands of people were killed and driven into exile.[7]

More Kurdish uprisings happened in the following years. The major ones took place in Agri Dagi (Mount Ararat) in 1930 and in Dersim in 1938. Both the 1925 and 1930 uprisings involved ethnic demands for autonomy. Since Alevi Kurds populated the city of Dersim, the character of the Dersim uprising was both ethnic and religious[8].

At the outset of the 1950s, the official view echoed constantly as the following: 'In Turkey no Kurdish minority ever existed either nomadic or settled, with national consciousness or without it'. In 1961 president Gursel stated: 'Kurds were in fact of Turkish origin and that there was no such thing as the Kurdish nation … no nation exists with a personality of its own, calling itself Kurdish, Kurds were not only compatriots, but also racial brothers of the Turks'.[9] In 1973, President Demirel repeated the position of the state in abundantly clear, 'anybody who does not feel Turkish, or who feels unhappy in Turkey, is free to go elsewhere". He said, "For over 1,000 years, the Kurds have lived in what is now Turkey. There was no Kurdish state in that whole time, but there were Kurds.' Therefore, 'no one should expect an independent Kurdish state.'[10]

---

6   Hence one extreme nationalism raised similar feelings on the other side. Nothing feeds a group's nationalism more than the nationalism of another group. The nation-building process always involves the systematic over-evaluation of the self and the systematic devaluation of others. This practice makes mutual respect impossible. Respect involves an appreciation of others for their own sake; it sees other groups as worthy of preservation and exploration. In the case of the Kurds in Turkey, the extreme policies adopted by the founders of the Turkish Republic from the 1920s onwards left no other way for the Kurds but violent rebellion whenever possible. "Nationalism is negativity; nationalism is a negative spiritual category because it thrives on denial by denial", writes. D. Kis 'On Nationalism', in R. Ali and L. Lifschultz (eds) *Why Bosnia? Writings on the Balkan War* (Stony Creek, Conn.: Pamphleter's Press, 1993) p.127.

7   P. White 'Ethnic Differentiation among the Kurds: Kurmancî, Kàzàlba§ and Zaza', http://www.mafhoum.com/press2/65S23.htm (accessed 10 May 2004).

8   N. Watts 'Relocating Dersim: Turkish State Building and Kurdish Resistance, 1931-1938' 23 *New Perspectives on Turkey* (Istanbul: Economic and Social History Foundation of Turkey, Fall 2000) pp. 7-17.

9   D. McDowall *A Modern History of the Kurds* (New York: I.B. Tauris, 1996) p. 395.

10   Cornell Chronicle, 'Former Turkish leader discussed U.S. alliance and mission in Iraq', http://www.news.cornell.edu/Chronicle/03/10.16.03/Demirel_cover.html (accessed 10 May 2004).

The summer of 1980 was a chaotic time in Turkey. Political violence and sectarian unrest mounted in the cities and spread through the countryside. The work of parliament had come almost to a standstill, and the country was left without an elected president. On September 5, Ecevit aligned the Cumhuriyetci Halk Partisi (CHP) with Erbakan and his National Salvation Party (NSP) to force the resignation of Demirel's Foreign Minister, Hayrettin Erkman, whose strongly pro-Western views had won him the approval of General Staff officers. The next day, the NSP sponsored a massive rally at Konya, where Islamists (also seen as fundamentalists) demonstrated to demand the reinstatement of Islamic law in Turkey, reportedly showing disrespect for the flag and the national anthem. These acts were regarded as an open renunciation of Kemalism and a direct challenge to the military. On 7 September 1980, General Evren met secretly with armed forces and police commanders to set in motion plans for another coup. In the early hours of 12 September 1980, the armed forces seized control of the country.[11] The military regime lasted until the end of 1983. Even though the target of the military regime was the leftist movements, it was also very oppressive to ethnic and religious communities. The Chief General Kenan Evren's description of Kurds is still remembered, 'the term Kurd does not have any meaning; when the mountain people walk on the snow their boots release sound like "Kard", "Kurd", this is the origin of the word Kurd'.

In 1982, the Minister of Education informed all provincial governors that folk songs in east and south-east Anatolia could be used for ethnic or separatist purposes; therefore, they must only be sung in Turkish[12]. In October 1983, the generals introduced Law No. 2932 prohibiting the use of the Kurdish language.

The 1980s passed with the denial of the existence of the Kurds in Turkey both by the state and intellectual circles. In March 1987, a senior government minister asked, 'is there such a thing as a Kurd? … The only people prepared to call themselves Kurds are militants, tools of foreign ideologies'.[13]

For a brief period in the wake of the 1991 Persian Gulf War, President Turgut Ozal spoke in measured terms of a more liberal policy towards the Kurds, and laws prohibiting the use of the Kurdish language were repealed.[14] But following Ozal's death in April 1994, it has become clearer than ever that when it comes to the Kurdish question, it is not the civilian elected government which determines policy but the army-dominated National Security Council.[15]

11   US Library of Congress, Federal Research Division, Country Studies, http://countrystudies.us/turkey/17.htm (accessed 10 May 2004).
12   McDowall (note 9) p. 424.
13   Ibid. p. 431.
14   C. Kutschera 'Mad Dreams Of Independence, The Kurds of Turkey and the PKK', http://www.xs4all.nl/~tank/kurdish/htdocs/lib/dream.html (accessed 10 May 2004).
15   A.B. Celik 'Kurds and Nationalism' 18 *New Perspectives on Turkey* (1998) p. 149.

Turkey, Europe and a New Beginning in Relation to the Kurds?

On 3 November 2002, Turkey broke sensationally with its political old guard. The former governing parties all recorded less than 10 percent of the national threshold and are no longer represented in the National Assembly. Turkey's voters turned in vast numbers to a new political party with firm Islamic roots. The Justice and Development Party (AK Party) was formed in August 2001, by moderate members of Turkey's outlawed pro-Islamic Virtue Party. Recep Tayyip Erdogan, once mayor of Istanbul, led the AK Party. Its roots lie in two former Islamic parties, Welfare and Virtue, both banned by Turkey's secular establishment.

The elections threw up a number of fundamental questions. Would Turkey become a more Islamic country? What was behind the election victory? Why did the traditional parties fail? How would the election results affect Turkey's relations with Europe? But more significant than the above questions is the fact that the recent election results revived a deep-rooted perception in the Western world that liberal democracy cannot exist in an Islamic country!

The AK Party, which grew out of popular Islamist support, won despite an intense campaign presenting it as a threat to the secular regime. The AK Party is described by its founders not as a religious party, but as a party in which religious people feel at home. One way of looking at this is to attribute this result to the fact that the people were very angry with the failure and arrogance of the established parties and say that the election result was an expression of the growing discontent with the country's corrupt political elite. Certainly there is an element of truth in this. Turkey has experienced a worsening economic crisis since 2001. Two million workers have lost their jobs and the value of the Turkish currency has halved again against the US dollar. Still, it would be wrong to reduce the AK Party's success to just an expression of the people's anger and disappointment with the centre parties.[16]

The AK Party is consistent on the position that it respects traditional moral values, but does not want Turkey to shut itself out the Western world, but rather to join the European Union. It represents not a militant religious response to secularism in general but rather the European human rights reaction against the authoritarian aspects of the secular system in Turkey. It does not want to establish a religious regime based on Shari'a law, but they wish to establish basic human rights to allow people to freely express their beliefs – religious, political or ethnic. This is what most of Turkey's population has wanted for decades: to exercise their faith freely and quietly.

At the end of April 2002, Turkey ratified the International Convention on the Elimination of All Forms of Racial Discrimination, 30 years after having signed it.[17]

---

16   N. Narli 'AKP Victory Was Foreseeable in 2001' *Turkish Daily News*, 04/11/2002, http://www.bianet.org/2003/03/21_eng/news14337.htm (accessed 10 May 2004).

17   For further information see: http://insanhaklarimerkezi.bilgi.edu.tr/calisma_grup/uluslararasi_belgeler_eng.asp (accessed 10 May 2004).

And a 15-year state of emergency, which once covered 11 war-torn provinces in mainly Kurdish south east Turkey, was lifted as part of recent EU-backed moves by Ankara to improve the status of the Kurdish minority. More than 50,000 people have returned to villages from which they were evacuated during the conflict with the Kurdish Workers Party ('Partiya Karkaren Kurdistan'or PKK).

The new government regards the continuation of the economic stabilisation process and EU accession as major goals. There has been some criticism of the tactics of Prime Minister Abdullah Gül and party leader Recep Tayyip Erdogan, but their claim to have pushed forward Turkey's accession to the EU is credible. The government's decision to implement the reforms needed to obtain a certificate of good conduct from the EU in December 2004 will determine the political agenda for the coming years. The government's positive attitude to the reforms enjoys widespread support.

The Kurdish Minority in Turkey and International Law

International law maintains that the existence of minorities is a question of fact, not law.[18] What this means is that the state does not have the last word in deciding if minorities exist on its territory – this is to be decided on the basis of the factual situation. Little guidance can be found on the meaning of 'national minority' in Article 14 of the European Convention on Human Rights. The European Court of Human Right's jurisprudence (discussed below) is described by one author as 'evasive',[19] although 'undeveloped' is a better term. On the other hand, the European Commission (henceforth 'Commission') and European Court of Human Rights (henceforth 'ECtHR') have frequently spoken of and dealt with minorities. The Kurds of Turkey appear in a stream of cases emanating from the continuing conflict in Turkey – cases in which questions of minority identity are central.

General norms of minority rights insist on the fundamental principle of self-identification as a member of a minority or otherwise. In the privileged sphere of privacy, self-identification must be regarded as an absolute right; in other cases the notion of minority existence may be predicated on a combination of objective and subjective characteristics.[20] The acceptance of minority existence by state authorities results in a certain 'pluralism of communities' and thus perhaps to a 're-imagining' of the national community.[21]

As noted, freedom of expression may be restricted on the grounds, *inter alia*, of 'territorial integrity'. The issue has been cautiously mentioned by the Commission and ECtHR on the basis of a rough distinction between argument and advocacy on the one

---

18   For a statement of principle, see General Comment 23 of the Human Rights Committee under the ICCPR – UN Doc. A/49/40, pp. 107-10.

19   P. Thornberry 'National Minorities and the European Convention on Human Rights', in B. Gokay (ed.) Kurdish Question in Turkey – Looking Ahead, and Back, *Special Issue of the TASG-News*, p. 5.

20   Ibid.

21   B. Anderson *Imagined Communities* (London: Verso, 1991).

hand, and incitement to violence on the other.[22] In the case of the *United Communist Party of Turkey and Others v Turkey*,[23] the applicant Party [the United Communist Party of Turkey or TBKP] contested the party's dissolution by the Turkish Constitutional Court. The state's application to the Turkish Constitutional Court claimed that the TBKP sought to establish the domination of one social class over the others, had included the word 'communist' in its name, and had carried on activities likely to undermine the territorial integrity of the state and the unity of the nation. The Constitutional Court rejected the State Prosecutor's submissions on the first issue, but upheld the others on the grounds that Turkey was unitary, indivisible and there was only one nation. The Constitutional Court averred that by asserting the existence of 'two nations' in Turkey – Turks and Kurds – the TBKP's programme – 'was intended to create minorities, to the detriment of the unity of the Turkish nation'; 'nationals of Kurdish origin' were precluded from forming a nation or a minority distinct from the Turkish nation. The Commission decided unanimously that there had been a violation of Article 11 of the European Convention on Human Rights. The ECtHR unanimously upheld the claim under Article 11, agreeing with the Commission that political parties were within its protection even if their activities 'are regarded by the national authorities as undermining the constitutional structures of the State'.[24] The ECtHR was impressed by the TBKP's commitment to peaceful and democratic debate on the 'national' question, as expressed through its documentation. One of the 'principal characteristics' of democracy is 'the possibility it offers of resolving a country's problems through dialogue'.[25]

In other cases, the ECtHR finds regular violations by the state of rights to life, liberty and property of Kurds, without identifying the *reason* for violations as the Kurdish ethnicity of victims.[26] In *Tanrikulu v. Turkey*, the ECtHR discussed the claim of the applicant who alleged that her husband had been killed because of his Kurdish origins under Article

---

22   See the Turkish cases infra, especially *Surek and Ozdemir v. Turkey*, Application Nos. 23927/94 and 24277/94, 3 March, 8 July 1999, especially para. 60 and the dissent by Wildhaber *et al.* Inflammatory remarks can legitimately be subject to restrictions 'where such remarks incite to violence against an individual, a public official or a sector of the population...[in such cases] the national authorities enjoy a wider margin of appreciation' – *Ozturk v Turkey*, Application No. 22479/93, Judgment of 28 September 1999, para. 66. Cf. *Zana v Turkey*, 69/1996/688/880, Judgment of 25 November 1997, paras. 58-60, in Thornberry (note 19) p.7.

23   *United Communist Party of Turkey and Others v. Turkey*, Application No. 19392/92, Judgement of 30 January 1998, can be found on http://sim.law.uu.nl/SIM/CaseLaw/hof.nsf/o/34e0674b5f3434c6c1256640004c3741?OpenDocument (accessed 10 May 2004).

24   Press Agency Ozgurluk, 'European court condemns Turkish ban on Communist Party', http://www.blythe.org/nytransfer-subs/98rad/European_court_condemns_Turkish_ban_on_Communist_Party_ (accessed 10 May 2004).

25   *United Communist Party of Turkey and Others v. Turkey* (note 23).

26   F. Hampson 'Recent Turkish Cases: Their Contribution to the Case Law of the European Court of Human Rights' 4.3 *Human Rights Law Review* (1999) pp. 9-16.

14 of the European Convention on Human Rights.[27] The case was dismissed for want of evidence.[28] An Article 14 point is often not pursued because it is covered by another article. However in *Ozgur Gundem v. Turkey*,[29] where the applicants had argued that 'any expression of Kurdish identity was treated by the authorities as advocacy of separatism and PKK propaganda',[30] a phenomenon which 'could only be explained by prohibited discrimination',[31] the ECtHR decided affirmatively that there had been no discrimination.[32]

On 30 April 2002, the Committee of Ministers of the Council of Europe adopted an Interim Resolution[33] urging the Turkish authorities to respond to the Committee's repeated demands that the situation of former Members of Parliament Sadak, Zana, Dicle and Dogan be remedied. The Committee called on Turkey to reopen the proceedings, or undertake other *ad hoc* measures, so that all consequences of the violation of the right to a fair trial should be erased.

Recent Positive Reforms in Turkey

In the National Program of Turkey for Adoption of the *Acquis Communautaire*, it is stated that the reform process towards accession to the EU is the second biggest transformation of the state since the Ottoman Empire; the first was the establishment of Turkey in the 1920s.[34] Whatever reforms have been carried out in Turkey have appeared as a requirement of integration with Europe. In return the EU has supported the democratisation process and projects concerning human rights and minority rights in Turkey.[35]

Considerable political pressure is building up in support of granting Turkey a definite and imminent date to begin EU accession talks. US President George Bush has openly and frequently lobbied Danish Prime Minister Anders Fogh Rasmussen, at that time holder of the EU presidency (the latter half of 2002), and both German Chancellor Gerhard Schröder and British Foreign Secretary Jack Straw have come out in support of giving Turkey a specific time to begin negotiations.

A major constitutional reform was adopted in October 2001 which aimed to strengthen guarantees in the field of human rights and fundamental freedoms and limit capital punishment. A new Civil Code was adopted in November 2001. Three sets of

---

27   Thornberry (note 19) p. 9.
28   Ibid.
29   Ibid. p. 12.
30   Ibid.
31   Ibid.
32   Ibid.
33   IntResDH(2002)59 concerning the judgement of the European Court of Human Rights of 17 July 2001 in the case of *Sadak, Zana, Dicle, Dogan v. Turkey* in Thornberry (note 19) p. 12.
34   For National Programme see www.mfa.gov.tr (accessed 10 May 2004).
35   See Å. Lundgren 'The European Union as a Democracy-promoter' in *Civil Society, Democracy and the Muslim World*, Transactions Vol. 7 (Istanbul: Swedish Research Institute in Istanbul, 2002) pp. 93-101.

reform packages were adopted in February, March and August 2002. The adoption of these reforms demonstrates the determination of the majority of Turkey's political leaders to move towards further alignment with the values and standards of the European Union. These reforms were adopted under difficult political and economic circumstances, and represent a major shift in the Turkish context. The building of political consensus around these changes was prepared by an intensive public debate concerning EU accession, which took place in Turkey during 2003 with the participation of political parties, civil society, business and academic circles.

In June 2002, the European Council of Seville in June 2002 welcomed the reforms adopted in Turkey. It encouraged and fully supported the efforts made by Turkey to fulfil the priorities defined in its Accession Partnership. The implementation of the required political and economic reforms will bring forward Turkey's prospects of accession in accordance with the same principles and criteria as are applied to the other candidate countries. New decisions could be taken in Copenhagen on the next stage of Turkey's candidature in the light of developments in the situation between the Seville and Copenhagen European Councils, on the basis of the regular report submitted by the Commission in October 2002 and in accordance with the Helsinki and Laeken conclusions.[36]

The reform package adopted by Parliament in August 2002 was particularly far-reaching. Among the amendments adopted were the lifting of the death penalty in peacetime, the possibility of radio and TV broadcasting in Kurdish, the widening of freedom of expression and greater freedom for non-Muslim religious minorities.

The National Security Council recommended on 30 May 2002 that the state of emergency in two provinces of south east Turkey be lifted. The Turkish Parliament endorsed this recommendation and this measure came into force on 30 July 2002. The National Security Council also recommended the lifting of the state of emergency in the two remaining provinces by the end of 2002.

Part of the impetus behind this developing consensus comes from the significant legislative changes Turkey has made, particularly in the course of the last two years. Turkey passed several reform packages since 2002, notably the Harmonisation Laws of 2002-2003, aimed at increasing its compliance with the Copenhagen criteria for EU accession. If implemented, these reforms, taken together with other changes such as the lifting of the state of emergency (known as the OHAL) in the south east and improvement of the conduct of elections, will significantly ameliorate the situation facing Kurdish people in the south east, and improve Turkey's general human rights, political and social situation immensely.

The reforms related to economic, social and cultural rights contain a number of positive elements. Provisions forbidding the use of languages other than Turkish prohibited by law in Articles 26 and 28 have now been abolished, which is a positive develop-

---

36   See Conclusions of the European Council on Turkey since Luxembourg, http://europa. eu.int/comm/enlargement/turkey/pdf/european_councils_.pdf (accessed 10 May 2004).

ment. Existing restrictive legislation and practices will need to be modified in order to implement this constitutional reform, as the Turkish authorities have recognised. There has been no improvement in the real enjoyment of cultural rights for all Turks, irrespective of their ethnic origin.

A number of substantial prison reforms have been adopted and Turkey has been encouraged to ensure that these reforms are fully implemented. The disproportionate use of force in breaking up prison protests is to be regretted. The continuing loss of life as a result of hunger strikes is unacceptable from a humanitarian point of view. Irrespective of the political motives of those involved, efforts should be stepped up to prevent further deaths. Free debate on these issues should be allowed.

Reform of the judicial system has begun. The independence of the judiciary, the powers of State Security Courts and military courts and compliance with rulings of the European Court of Human Rights remain matters of concern.

Outstanding Legal Concerns

As the European Union pointed out in the conclusion of its 2002 Regular Report that Turkey 'does not meet the political criteria' required to enter into EU accession talks. One of the country's most significant failures is the continuing high number of cases filed against it in the ECtHR. The report details that between 1 October 2001 and 30 June 2002, no fewer than 1,874 applications against Turkey were made to the ECtHR. Of these, the majority, 1,125, came under Article 6 (the right to a fair trial), casting fundamental and profound doubt on the legitimacy of Turkish domestic justice. A further 304 cases came under Article 5 (the right to liberty and security); 246 under Article 3 (the prohibition of torture); 104 under Article 11 (freedom of assembly and association); and 95 under Article 10 (freedom of expression). Moreover, when eventually heard, judgements in these cases went overwhelmingly against Turkey; as of August 2002, Turkey had lost 260 ECtHR cases and won a mere 11.[37]

Even more seriously, the report also noted that, 'Turkey's failure to execute judgments of the European Court of Human Rights remains a serious problem.' It cited 90 cases in which Turkey failed to carry out the ECtHR's orders, and a further 18 freedom of expression cases in which the state failed to rectify the consequences of domestic criminal convictions which violated the European Convention on Human Rights. This concurs with the conclusion of the Committee on Legal Affairs and Human Rights of the Council of Europe Parliamentary Assembly, which has argued that Turkey consistently fails to implement adverse ECtHR judgements. Most human rights organisations in Turkey estimate that less than 5 per cent of people detained, some for an extended period of time, are ever formally arrested.[38]

---

37   Commission of the European Communities, *2002 Regular Report on Turkey's Progress towards Accession*, 9 October 2002. Also *Hurriyet*, 10 October, 2002.

38   In its 1998 report, the Turkish human rights organisation Mazlum-Der reported that out of 35,914 people who it was aware had been detained the number of people actually arrested

Many elected officials in the Kurdish regions, particularly those from the pro-Kurdish parties, report that the state undermines their abilities to act in several ways.[39] The most common is simply to cut their operating budgets drastically. The Mayor of Hakkari, a member of the pro-Kurdish party DEHAP, told a recent mission that the central government had cut his budget by 80%, leaving him unable to make any investments to develop the local economy. Public officials in Hakkari had been unpaid for 15 months, a far from unusual state of affairs in Turkey.

Similarly, the Mayor of Tunceli, although a member of the CHP, now the official opposition in parliament, claimed that the state had reduced his budget from 160 million lira per month to around 3 or 4 million lira, around 3 euros a month. Often he received nothing at all. To pay his officials, the mayor was forced to sell off public land piecemeal. Furthermore, the mayor claimed that when he mentioned the problem to the Minister for Social Security, the minister sequestered the mayor's own personal assets and forced him to pay state workers with his own money.[40]

The effects of these budgetary cuts are multifarious. They encourage corruption, as officials need to extract rents to make up for their shortfalls in income. They delegitimise elected representatives, who are unable to enact policy changes, and thus undermine the process and the credibility of democracy in Turkey. They also progressively impoverish the regions, predominantly Kurdish, in which the cuts take place.

---

was only 1,279, approximately 3.5 per cent of detainees. For the same period, the Istanbul branch of another human rights organisation, Insan Haklari Derneği (IHD), reported it was aware of 23,312 people detained in Istanbul, of whom 560 had been formally arrested, approximately 2.4 per cent of those detained. The Human Rights Foundation of Turkey, Türkiye Insan Haklari Vakfı (TIHV) reported that it was aware of 48,095 persons detained by the police during the first eleven months of 1999. Of these, 2,056 were arrested, some 4.3 per cent of those detained. These statistics indicate that over 95 per cent of those detained by the police were released without charge.

IHD's annual balance sheet has a slightly different criterion (see Human Rights in Turkey Summary Tables linked from http://www.ihd.org.tr/eindex.html (accessed 1 August 2004), but this again demonstrates the fact that approximately ten times as many people are detained as are ever jailed:

1996	20,434 detained	2,071 jailed
1997	27,308	1,273
1998	42,991	3,659
1999	50,318	2,105
2000	35,007	1,937
2001	35,389	2,634 (NB figures for Jan-Sept only)

39   The group Reporters Without Borders has protested after police beat nine journalists who were covering the crushing of a demonstration against electoral fraud in south east Turkish city of Diyarbakir. Three journalists needed hospital treatment. *BIA News Centre, 3/0/04,* http://www.bianet.org/2004/03/01_eng/index_eng.htm (accessed 30 March 2004).

40   Ibid.

The Turkish state also frequently removes elected officials from office directly. The Kurdish mayor of the city of Van was ousted from his position in September by the Administrative Court, despite the fact that Article 312 of the Turkish Penal Code, under which he was convicted of 'sedition', has been changed as part of Turkey's reform package.[41]

On 15 April, 2004, the International Secretariat of OMCT (Organisation Mondiale Contre la Torture) was informed that there were serious risks to the personal integrity of torture victims Mr Selahattin Öge and Mr Sidik Özen, who had been forced into hiding in Bingöl, Turkey.[42] According to the information presented by the OMCT, 7-8 people raided the house of Mr Selahattin Öge on April 12, 2004 at about 11.30 pm in the Yorgançayir (Karahamza) village of Karliova, Bingöl. When Mr Selahattin Öge's family asked the people who they were, they replied that they were members of an illegal organisation. However, family members recognised some of them as village guards.

It is important to note that on 19 February 2001, Mr Selahattin Öge had been arrested, detained and tortured by members of the security forces wearing ski masks, following which he was left for dead in the grounds of the Karliova Boarding School, in a rural area of Karliovaas. A fact-finding mission was reportedly conducted into these events and a report was produced. Following this, Bingöl Heavy Penal Court acquitted the alleged perpetrators and the case was taken to the Supreme Court.

As a result of this past incident, during the raid on April 12, 2004, Mr Öge's son reacted out of fear for his and his family's lives and shot towards the people who were raiding their home. A fight reportedly ensued, during which Mr Selahattin Öge and his neighbour, Mr Sidik Özen, escaped and went into hiding outside the village, as they feared that they would be killed if the authorities take them into custody.

In the early morning of 13 April 2004, police officers conducted an operation in and around the village, ostensibly looking for the two men. Family members and the other villagers, who have since been prevented from entering the village by the security forces, have contacted local NGOs, who have attempted to call several officials concerning the case. The Governor of Bingöl has reportedly refused to meet with NGOs in order to discuss the case of Mr Selahattin Öge and Mr Sidik Özen, despite serious concerns for their lives.

The International Secretariat of OMCT is gravely concerned for the physical and psychological wellbeing of Mr Selahattin Öge and Mr Sidik Özen and urges the Turkish authorities to take all measures necessary to guarantee their personal integrity and to allow them to return home. OMCT also calls on the authorities to ensure that the victims and their families are no longer subjected to harassment of any kind. OMCT is concerned that this latest raid on the house of Mr Selahattin Öge was related to the case that was before the Supreme Court, and OMCT called on the authorities to ensure

---

41   *Anatolia News Agency*, 19 September 2002.
42   Greek Helsinki Monitor (part of the OMCT network), *Turkey: Case TUR 150404 – serious risks to the personal integrity of torture victim Mr Selahattin Öge and of Mr Sidkin Özen*, 15/4/ 04, http://www.greekhelsinki.gr/bhr/english/index_more.html (accessed 1 August 2004).

that no further pressure of this type is brought to bear on the Mr Selahattin Öge and Mr Sidik Özen in this context.[43]

The human rights organisation IHD requested that the UN International Convention on the Elimination of All Forms of Racial Discrimination be signed by Turkey on March 21, which is Newroz but also the International day for the Elimination of Racial Discrimination. IHD published a communiqué for Newroz[44] and referred to the fact that in 1966 the United Nations General Board called on countries to lift all kinds of racial discrimination and proclaimed March 21 as the International Day for the Elimination of Racial Discrimination.[45]

On 1 April 2004, the European Parliament, on 1 April 2004, presented a highly critical evaluation of Turkey's progress towards EU entry conditions. The report praised the EU-oriented reforms already enacted in Turkey – including some taboo-breaking constitutional amendments – but said implementation on the ground was lagging behind. The European Parliament castigated Turkey for 'the continuing influence of the army in politics, business, culture and education, continuing torture practices and mistreatment, the intimidation of human rights defenders, the discrimination of religious minorities and the fact that trade union freedom is not fully guaranteed'. It singled out the detention of four activists and pro-Kurdish former MPs,, Leyla Zana, Hatip Dide, Orhan Dogan and Selim Sadak, who were sentenced to 15 years in jail in a much-criticised verdict in 1994 for collaborating with armed Kurdish rebels. Zana has become something of a *cause célèbre* for the European Parliament, which awarded her its Sakharov prize for human rights in 1995.[46]

On 9 June 2004, Leyla Zana was released from prison after spending 10 years in a Turkish jail. A Turkish court ordered the release of Zana, along with the three other Kurdish legislators after a state prosecutor called for their sentences to be quashed. Their release came amid repeated warnings from European institutions that the continued imprisonment of the four legislators would affect Turkey's efforts to join the European Union. After their release, Turkish Justice Minister Cemil Cicek said, '[t]his is the last bargaining chip in the hands of those who were seeking excuses in Turkey's EU bid.'[47] The four pro-Kurdish former MPs arrived at the Turkish Foreign Ministry in Ankara on the afternoon of Friday 11 June 2004 where they had a 45-minute meeting with the Turkish Foreign Minister Abdullah Gül. Since Recep Tayyip Erdoğan was in the US to

43   Ibid.

44   A new year festival celebrated by the Kurds, which also become a symbol of political struggle. See for example the Kurdish Democratic Party of Iraq, http://www.kdp.pp.se/newroz.html, (accessed 1 August 2004).

45   *BIA News Centre, 24/3/04*, http://www.bianet.org/2004/03/01_eng/index_eng.htm (accessed 10 May 2004).

46   EU Business, *EU parliament gives frosty review of Turkey's entry bid, 1/4/04*, http://www.eubusiness.com/afp/040401153702.66xsvdgl (accessed 10 May 2004).

47   Democracy Now, *Kurdish Political Prisoner Leyla Zana Released After a Decade in Jail, 10/6/04*, http://www.democracynow.org/article.pl?sid=04/06/10/1425202 (accessed 1 August 2004).

attend the G-8 Summit, Deputy Prime Minister and Foreign Minister Abdullah Gül received the ex-deputies of the defunct Democracy Party (DEP) on behalf of the Turkish Prime Minister. Leyla Zana said at the meeting, 'While we were in prison, Turkey has changed a lot and the world has changed too, and so have we.'[48]

Turkey's state TV and radio aired its first ever Kurdish language broadcasts on the same day, Wednesday 9 June 2004, transmitting short programmes in the once-taboo tongue under reforms passed as part of the country's push to join the European Union.

Until 1991, speaking Kurdish was outlawed in Turkey. On 9 June 2004, the country's state-run broadcaster, TRT, aired 30-minute programmes in the most commonly used Kurdish dialect, Kirmanji. Broadcasts in another Kurdish dialect, Zaza, will began on 9 June and will be aired every Friday until further notice. The move was intended to improve the country's much-criticised human rights record and boost Turkey's chances of joining the EU. Private language institutes started Kurdish classes in April 2004 but state schools are still not allowed to teach the language.

The move was no small step for Turkey, which fought a 15-year war with separatist Kurdish guerrillas that killed 37,000 people, mostly Kurds. Turkish authorities had long said that allowing Kurdish education or broadcasts would promote separatism and reward the rebels. Kurdish rebels declared a unilateral ceasefire in 1999 after the capture of guerrilla leader Abdullah Ocalan, but announced in early June 2004 that they were ending the truce.

Apart from the two Kurdish language dialects, Turkey also started broadcasting in three other ethnic languages in the second week of June 2004: Bosnian, Arabic and Circassian. Turkey's parliament legalised limited programmes in Kurdish and other ethnic languages in 2002 to meet EU membership requirements but bureaucratic wrangling within the state-owned broadcaster, TRT, delayed the broadcasts. The delay drew criticism from the EU, which said that Turkey must do more to apply laws after they are passed.

The Kirmanji dialect broadcast on TRT television on 9 June 2004 featured a news programme with Turkish language subtitles and a music clip in Kurdish without subtitles. Earlier the same day, TRT radio aired a similar 30-minute programme, starting at 6.10 am (03.10 GMT), followed by a 30-minute Turkish translation. The same news programme was aired in different languages in the same week and featured a piece on the EU's representative in Ankara, Hansjoerg Kretschmer, praising Turkey's EU reforms, but criticising their slow implementation. As part of Turkey's bid to join the EU, the Turkish parliament also legalised education in Kurdish and other ethnic languages in 2002.

Turkey lifted a ban on speaking Kurdish in 1991 – a law that also freed up Kurdish-language music on the radio. Kurds are not recognised as a minority in Turkey and many Turkish nationalists fear that allowing Kurdish in public settings could encourage

---

48   TurkishPress.Com, *Leyla Zana: Turkey Has Changed A Lot And The World Has Changed Too, And So Have We, 12/6/04,* http://www.turkishpress.com/turkishpress/news.asp?ID=21012 (accessed 1 August 2004).

separatist sentiments. Turkey hopes that the language reforms will prompt EU leaders to set a timetable to negotiate Turkey's membership into the 25-nation European bloc.[49]

Despite significant recent rights reforms, Human Rights Watch said in June 2004 that the Turkish government should further improve its record in four key areas. They said that freedom of expression, torture and ill-treatment, freedom of assembly and internal displacement are all areas where important initial progress has been achieved but where significant additional efforts are needed to demonstrate lasting positive change. Human Rights Watch outlined specific outstanding reforms, and emphasised the importance of close government oversight in achieving adequate implementation.

'The government and the judiciary deserve real credit for these achievements,' said Jonathan Sugden, Human Rights Watch's researcher for Turkey. 'If Turkey can maintain this momentum and take further bold action, June 2004 may well turn out to be the critical turning point for human rights in Turkey.' In June 2004, Human Rights Watch, together with other international and domestic human rights organisations (International Federation for Human Rights, Amnesty International, the Human Rights Foundation of Turkey, the Human Rights Association and Mazlum-Der) met with the ministers of human rights, justice, and the interior at the government's invitation, and pressed for urgent progress in the four key areas.

Human Rights Watch said Turkish officials needed to understand the extremely urgent nature of the outstanding tasks. 'The remaining human rights problems are serious,' said Sugden. 'With the EU calendar so tight, the ministries will have to move decisively this summer if they want to guarantee success.'

In September 2004 the European Commission is scheduled to publish its regular report on Turkey's progress towards meeting the political criteria for EU membership, which concern human rights, the rule of law and respect for minorities. In December 2004, on the basis of this report, the European Council will decide whether Turkey should proceed to the next stage of its candidacy for EU membership.

'Receding political violence and the growth of civil society have helped to bring about recent reforms, but the EU accession process has clearly been an important engine for positive change,' said Sugden. 'Most Turkish and international human rights organizations are keen to see this process continue and deepen. If the Turkish government ensures the necessary progress on the ground, then human rights organizations will be very keen to report it.'[50]

Conclusion

There is no doubt that Turkey has exerted considerable energy towards reforming the legal framework of its institutional and political practices over the past two years, and

---

49   EU Business, *Turkish state TV set to begin Kurdish-language broadcasts next week*, 4/6/04, http://www.eubusiness.com/afp/040604125044.mxw9t3id (accessed 1 August 2004).

50   Greek Helsinki Monitor, *Turkey: EU Bid Hinges on Further Rights Reforms*, 15/6/04, http://www.greekhelsinki.gr/bhr/english/index_more.html (accessed 1 August 2004).

deserves a portion of the acclaim it has received for its efforts. Turkey has made some progress with regard to the various international conventions on human rights. In April 2002 the Turkish Parliament ratified the 1969 UN Convention on the Elimination of All Forms of Racial Discrimination. Turkey introduced a reservation to Article 22 of the Convention, to the effect that cases involving Turkey can only be referred to the International Court of Justice with its consent. In July 2002, Turkey signed the European Agreement Relating to Persons Participating in Proceedings of the European Court of Human Rights. No progress has been made in acceding to other major international human rights instruments such as the Statute of the International Criminal Court, the UN International Covenant on Civil and Political Rights, and the UN International Covenant on Economic, Social and Cultural Rights.

It is critical, however, to remember just how far Turkey had to come to even enter the frame for credible consideration as a modern functioning democratic state with appropriate respect for human rights. It has truly been a long road, and although Turkey has taken many strides along it, many more remain.

It is equally crucial to recall that genuine reform of the sort needed to meet the Copenhagen criteria in both form and spirit, particularly the requisite of 'stability of institutions guaranteeing democracy, the rule of law, human rights and respect for and protection of minorities,' needs more than merely formal legal change. It also requires a demonstrable commitment on the part of authorities at all levels to enforce and ensure the new frameworks in practice. That in turn necessitates both a firm ideological commitment to deep and genuine reform on the part of major power holders, and a period of transition, often extended, during which new modes of institutional and administrative behaviour are established and learned and cadres of officials entrenched in old modes of thinking and action are replaced.

Bibliography

Aceves, W.J., 'Actio Popularis: The Class Action in International Law' [2003] *University of Chicago Legal Forum*

Afshari, R., *Human Rights in Iran, The abuse of cultural relativism* (Philadelphia: University of Pennsylvania Press, 2001)

Aikio, P. and M. Scheinin (eds.), *Operationalizing the right of indigenous peoples to self-determination* (Turku/Abo: Abo Akademi University, 2000)

Alfredsson, G. and M. Stavropoulou (eds), *Justice Pending: Indigenous Peoples and Other Good Causes* (The Hague: Nijhoff, 2002)

Alfredsson, G. and R. Ring (eds.), *The Inspection Panel of the World Bank: A Different Complaints Procedure* (The Hague: Martinus Nijhoff Publishers, 2001)

Al-Haj, M., 'Multiculturalism in Deeply Divided Societies: the Israeli Case' 26 *Journal of Intercultural Relations* (2002)

Ali, R. and L. Lifschultz (eds.), *Why Bosnia? Writings on the Balkan War* (Stony Creek, Conn.: Pamphleterís Press, 1993)

Ali, T., *The Clash of Fundamentalisms ñ Crusades, Jihads and Modernity* (London: Verso: 2002)

Alston, P. (ed.), *The United Nations and Human Rights, A Critical Appraisal* (Oxford: Oxford University Press, 1992)

Alston, P. (ed.), *Peoples' Rights* (Oxford: Oxford University Press, 2001)

Alvarez, A, 'Latin America and International Law' 3.2 *American Journal of International Law* (1909)

Anaya, S.J., 'A Contemporary Definition of the International Norm of Self-Determination' 3 *Transnational Law and Contemporary Problems* (1993)

Anaya, S.J., 'The Capacity of International Law to Advance Ethnic or Nationality Rights Claims' 75 *Iowa Law Review* (1990)

Anaya, S.J., *Indigenous Peoples in International Law* (Oxford: Oxford University Press, 1996)

Anderson, B., *Imagined Communities* (London: Verso, 1991)

Anderson, B., *Imagined Communities: Reflections On The Origin And Spread Of Nationalism* (London: Verso, 1991, Rev. ed.)

Andreopoulos, G.J., (ed.) *Genocide: Conceptual and Historical Dimensions* (University of Pennsylvania Press, 1994)

An-Naíim, A. (ed.), *Human Rights in Cross-Cultural Perspectives: A Quest for Consensus* (Philadelphia: University of Pennsylvania Press, 1992)

Annan, K.A., *The Question of Intervention: Statements by the Secretary-General*, (New York, 1999)

Baderin, M., 'A Macroscopic Analysis of the Practice of Muslim State Parties to International Human Rights Treaties: Conflict or Congruence' 1.2 *Nottingham Human Rights Law Journal* (2001)

Baderin, M., *International Human Rights and Islamic Law* (Oxford: Oxford University Press, 2003)

Baker, R.S. and W.E. Dodds, *The Public Papers of Woodrow Wilson* (New York: Harper, 1925-1927)

Ball, M.S., 'Constitution, courts, Indian tribes' 12 *American Bar-Foundation Research Journal* (1987)

Banton, M., 'Racial discrimination at work: Bristol cases, 1980-89' 17.1 *New Community* (1990)

Banton, M., *International Action Against Racial Discrimination* (Oxford: Clarendon Press, 1996)

Banton, M., *The International Politics of Race* (Oxford: Polity, 2002)

Barkan, E., *The Guilt of Nations: Restitution and Negotiating Historical Injustices* (Baltimore: John Hopkins University Press, 2001)

Barnes, C. and M. Olsthoorn, *The Framework Convention for the Protection of National Minorities: A Guide for Non-Governmental Organizations* (London: Minority Rights Group International, 1999)

Baron, S.W., *Ethnic Minority Rights: Some Older and Newer Trends* (Oxford: Oxford University Press, 1985)

Barros, J., *The Aaland Islands Question* (New Haven: Yale University Press, 1968)

Barry, B., *Culture and Equality: An Egalitarian Critique of Multiculturalism* (Cambridge, Mass: Harvard University Press, 2002)

Barsh, R.L., 'Indian claims policy in the United States' 58 *North Dakota Law Review* (1982)

Barsh, R.L., 'Indigenous Peoples and the UN Commission on Human Rights: A case of Immovable Object and Irresistible Force' 18 *Human Rights Quarterly* (1996)

Bartkus, V.O., *The Dynamic of Secession* (Cambridge: Cambridge University Press, 1999)

Bayevsky, A. (ed.), *Self-determination in International law: Quebec and Lessons Learned* (The Hague: Kluwer Law International, 2000)

Beckett, C. and M. Macey, 'Race, Gender and Sexuality: The Oppression of Multiculturalism' 24.3/4 *Women's Studies International Forum* (2001)

Bentwich, N. and A. Martin, *Commentary on the Charter of the UN* (London: Routledge and Paul, 1950)

Berger, T. R, *Long and Terrible Shadow, White Values, Native Rights in the Americas 1492-1992* (Vancouver: Douglas & McIntyre, 1991)

Berman, P, *Terror and Liberalism* (London: Norton, 2003)

Berting, J. *et al.* (eds.), *Human Rights in a Pluralist World* (Westport CT: Meckler 1990)

Bilanakis, N., E. Pappas and M. Dinou, 'The impact of political suppression and torture on the second generation, A comparative study' 8. 1 *Torture* (1998)

Binder, G., 'The Case for Self-determination' 29 *Stanford Journal of International Law* (1993)

Bloed, A. (ed.), *The Challenges of Change; The Helsinki Summit of the CSCE and Its Aftermath* (Dordrecht: Martinus Nijhoff Publishers, 1994)

Bloed A. and P. van Dijk (eds.), *Protection of Minority Rights Through Bilateral Treaties* (Dordrecht: Martinus Nijhoff Publishers, 2000)

Bond, P. (ed.), *Fanon's Warning: A Civil Society Reader on the New Partnership for Africa's Development* (Trenton, NJ: AIDC, 2002)

Boraine, A., *A Country Unmasked: Inside South Africa's Truth and Reconciliation Commission* (Cape Town: Oxford University Press, 2000)

Borrows, J., 'Domesticating Doctrines: Aboriginal Peoples after the Royal Commission' 46 *McGill Law Journal* (2001)

Boyle, K., 'Human Rights, Religion and Democracy: The Refah Party Case' 1 *Essex Human Rights Review* (2004)

Bradford, W., 'With a Very Great Blame on Our Hearts: Reparations, Reconciliation, and an American Indian Plea for Peace with Justice' 27 *American Indian Law Review* (2003)

Brady, J.E., 'The Huaorani Tribe of Ecuador: A Study in Self-determination for Indigenous Peoples' 10 *Harvard Human Rights Journal* (1997)

Brierly, J.L., *The Law of Nations*, (Oxford: Oxford University Press, 1960)

Brilmayer, L., 'Secession and Self-Determination: A Territorial Interpretation' 16 *Yale Journal of International Law* (1991)

Brölmann, C., R. Lefeber and M. Zieck (eds.), *Peoples and Minorities in International Law* (Dordrecht, London: Martinus Nijhoff, 1993)

Buchheit, L.C., *Secession: The Legitimacy of Self-determination* (New Haven, Yale University Press, 1978)

Buergenthal, T., 'A new public order for Europe' 11 *HRLJ* (1990)

Bull, H. (ed.), *Intervention in World Politics* (Oxford: Oxford University Press, 1984)

Caney, S. and P. Jones (eds.), *Human Rights and Global Diversity* (Ilford: Cass, 2001)

Carr, D., *Time, Narrative and History* (Bloomington: Indiana University Press, 1986)

Cassese, A., *International Law in a Divided World* (Oxford: Clarendon Press, 1994)

Cassese, A., *Self-Determination of Peoples, A Legal Reappraisal* (Cambridge University Press, 1995)

Castellino, J., and P. Walsh (eds.) *Indigenous Peoples in International Law* (Kluwer: Raoul Wallenberg Institute, 2004)

Castellino, J., 'Order and Justice: National Minorities and the right to secession, 6 *International Journal on Minorities and Group Rights* (1999)

Castellino, J. and S. Allen, *Title to Territory in International Law: A Temporal Analysis* (Dartmouth: Ashgate, 2003)

Celik, B., 'Kurds and Nationalism' 18 *New Perspectives on Turkey* (1998)

Chabal, P., 'The Quest for Good Governance and Development in Africa: Is NEPAD the Answer?' 78.3 *International Affairs* (2002)

Chapman, M., 'Indigenous Peoples and International Human Rights: Towards a Guarantee for the Territorial Connection' 26 *The Anglo-American Law Review* (1997)

Charney, J., 'Self-Determination: Chechnya, Kosovo and East Timor' 34 *Vanderbilt Journal of Transnational Law,* 2001

Choudhury, B.K., *Genesis of the Chakma Movement (1772-1989): Historic Background* (Agartala: Tripura Darpan Prakashani)

Christiansen, F. and U. Hedetoft, *The Politics of Multiple Belonging, Ethnicity and Nationalism in Europe and Asia* (Aldershot: Ashgate, 2004)

CHT Commission, *'Life is not oursi: Land and Human Rights in the Chittagong Hill Tracts, Bangladesh* (Copenhagen: IWGIA and Netherlands: Organizing Committee CHT Campaign, 1991)

Clark, D and R. Williamson (eds.), *Self-determination: International Perspectives* (London: Macmillan Press, 1996)

Claude, I., *National Minorities* (Cambridge: Cambridge University Press, 1955)

Cleveland, S.H., 'Powers Inherent in Sovereignty: Indians, Aliens, Territories and the Nineteenth Century Origins of Plenary power over Foreign Affairs' 81 *Texas Law Review* (2002)

Cobban, A., *The Nation-State and National Self-Determination* (London: Apollo Editions, 1969)

Cohen, J., *Conflict Prevention in the OSCE; An Assessment of Capacities* (The Hague: Netherlands Institute of International Relations, Clingendael, 1999)

Cohen, S., *States of Denial, Knowing about Atrocities and Suffering* (Cambridge: Polity, 2001)

Commission on British Muslims and Islamophobia, *Islamophobia: Issues Challenges And Action* (Stoke: Trentham Books, 2004)

Committee for the Protection of Forests and Land Rights, *Mobilise Support to Stop the Eviction of Indigenous Peoples from Ancestral Lands in the Chittagong Hill Tracts, Bangladesh in the name of Afforestation and Protection of the Environment* (Chittagong Hill Tracts: CPFLR, 2001)

Coomans, F. and F. Grünfeld, I. Westendorp and J. Willems (eds.), *Rendering Justice to the Vulnerable: Liber Amicorum in Honour of Theo van Boven* (The Hague: Kluwer, 2000)

Cowan, J. et al, *Culture and Rights: Anthropological Perspectives* (Cambridge: Cambridge University Press, 2001)

Craig, E., 'Accommodation of Diversity in Education ñ A Human Rights Agenda?' 15 *Child and Family Law Quarterly* (2003)

Crawford, J., *Creation of States in International Law* (Oxford: Oxford University Press, 1979)

Crawford, J. (ed.), *The Rights of Peoples* (Oxford: Clarendon Press, 1988)

Crawford, J., 'State Practice and International Law in Relation to Secession' 85 *BYIL* (1998)

Daes, E-I., 'Some Considerations on the Right of Indigenous Peoples to Self-determination' 3 *Transnational Law and Contemporary Problems* (1993)

Daes, E-I., 'Equality of Indigenous Peoples under the Auspices of the United nations Draft Declaration on the Rights of Indigenous Peoples' 7 *St. Thomas Law Review* (1995)

De Groof, J. and G. Lauwers, 'Education Policy and Law: The Politics of Multiculturalism in Education' 14 *Education and the Law* (2002)

de Varennes, F., *Language, Minorities and Human Rights* (The Hague: Martinus Nijhoff Publishers, 1996)

Delanty, G., *Community* (London: Routledge, 2003)

Dickey, A., 'The Race Formula of the Race Relations Acts' *The Juridical Review* (1974)

Dinstein, Y. and M. Tabory (eds.), *The Protection of Minorities and Human Rights* (Dordrecht/Boston/London: Martinus Nijhoff, 1992)

Dinstein, Y., (ed.) *International World in an Evolving World, In Tribute to Professor Eduardo Jimenez de Arechaga* (Montevideo: Fondacion de cultura Universitaria, 1994)

Donders, Y.N., *Towards a Right to Cultural Identity?* (Antwerp: Intersentia, 2002).

Donnelly, J., 'In Search of a Unicorn: The Jurisprudence of the Right to Development' 12 *California International Law Review* (1985)

Doswald-Beck, L., 'The Legal Validity of Military Intervention by Invitation of the Government' 56 *BYIL* (1985)

Draper, M., 'The Activities of the OSCE High Commissioner on National Minorities:

June 2002-June 2003' 2 *European Yearbook of Minority Issues* (2002/03)

Duncan Hall, H., *Mandates, Dependencies and Trusteeships* (Washington: Carnegie Endowment, 1948)

Dunne, T., and N.J. Wheeler (eds), *Human Rights in Global Politics* (Cambridge: CUP, 1999)

Eide, A., *A Review and Analysis of Constructive Approaches to Group Accommodation in Divided or Multicultural Societies,* Forum for Peace and Reconciliation in Ireland, Consultancy Studies 3 (Dublin: Stationery Office 1996)

Eide, A., C. Krause and A. Rosas (eds.), *Economic, Social and Cultural Rights, a Textbook* (Dordrecht: Kluwer Law International, 2001)

Elias, T.O., 'The Doctrine of Intertemporal Law, 74.2 *American Journal of International Law* (1980)

Falk, R.A. (ed.), *The International Law of Civil Wars* (Baltimore: Johns Hopkins Press, 1971)

Falk, R., *Human Rights Horizons, The pursuit of justice in a Globalising World* (New York: Routledge 2000)

Farer, T., 'The Regulation of Foreign Armed Intervention in Civil Armed Conflict' 142 *HR* (1974)

Fawcett, J.E.S., 'Intervention in International Law' 103 *HR* (1961)

Ferencz, B., *Defining International Aggression,* (Dobbs Ferry: Oceana, 1975)

Fottrell, D. and W. Bowring (eds.), *Minority and Group Rights In the New Millennium* (The Hague: Kluwer Law International, 1999)

Franck, T.M., *The Power of Legitimacy Among Nations* (Oxford: Oxford University Press, 1990)

Franck, T.M., 'The Emerging Right to Democratic Governance' 86 *AJIL* (1992)

Franck, T.M., *Recourse to Force* (Cambridge: Cambridge University Press, 2002)

Freeman, M., 'The Problem of Secularism in Human Rights Theory' 26 *Human Rights Quarterly* (2004)

Freeman, M., 'Are there Collective Human Rights?' 43 *Political Studies* Special Issue (1995)

Freeman, M., 'Past Wrongs and Liberal Justice' 5 *Ethical Theory and Practice* (2002)

Gain, P. (ed.), *The Forest (Amendment) Act 2000 and the (draft) Social Forestry Rules 2000: A Critique* (Dhaka: Society for Environment and Human Development, 2001)

Gál, K., *Bilateral Agreements in Central and Eastern Europe: A New Inter-State Framework for Minority Protection?* ECMI Working Paper No. 4 (Flensburg: European Centre for Minority Issues, 1999)

Gayim, E., *The Principle of Self-Determination: A Study of its Historical and Contemporary Legal Evolution.* (Oslo: Norwegian Institute of Human Rights, 1990)

Gearty, C. and A. Tomkins, *Understanding Rights* (London: Mansell, 1996)

Ghanea, N., *Human Rights, the UN and the Baháís in Iran* (The Hague: Kluwer Law, 2002)

Ghanea, N., (ed.) *The Challenge of Religious Discrimination at the Dawn of the New Millennium* (Leiden: Martinus Nijhoff, 2003)

Gilbert, G., 'Autonomy and Minority Groups - A Right in International Law?' 35.2 *Cornell Int'l LJ* 307 (2002)

Gilbert, G, 'Autonomy and Minority Groups: A Right in International Law?í, 35 *Cornell International Law Journal* (2002)

Goodland, R., *Tribal Peoples and Economic Development: Human Ecologic Considerations* (Washington: World Bank, May 1982)

Graham, L., 'Indigenous Peoples: Reparations and the Indian Child Welfare Act' 25 *Legal Studies Forum* (2001)

Gray, C., *International Law and the Use of Force* (Oxford: Oxford University Press, 2000)

Habermas, J., 'Intolerance and Discrimination' 1.1(2) *International Journal of Constitutional Law* (2003)

Hadden, T., 'The Pendulum Theory of Individual, Communal and Minority Rights' 3 *Critical Review of International Social and Political Philosophy* (2000)

Hadden, T. and E. Craig, *Integration and Separation: Rights in Divided Societies* (Belfast: Centre for International and Comparative Human Rights Law, 2000)

Hampson, F., 'Recent Turkish Cases: Their Contribution to the Case Law of the European Court of Human Rights' 4.3 *Human Rights Law Review* (1999)

Hannum, H., 'Rethinking self-determination' 34 *Virginia Journal of International Law* (1993)

Hannum, H., *Autonomy, Sovereignty and Self-determination: The Accommodation of Conflicting Rights* (Philadelphia: University of Pennsylvania Press, 1996)

Hannum, H., 'Sovereignty and its Relevance to Native Americans in the 21st Century' 23 *American Indian Law Review* (1999)

Harmsen, R., 'The European Convention on Human Rights after Enlargement' 5 *The International Journal of Human Rights* (2001)

Harris-Short, S., 'International Human Rights Law: Imperialist, Inept and Ineffective? Cultural Relativism and the UN Convention on the Rights of the Child' 25 *Human Rights Quarterly* (2003)

Hastrup, K. (ed.), *Legal Cultures and Human Rights: The Challenge of Diversity* (The Hague: Kluwer, 2001)

Henderson, J.S., 'Mikmaq tenure in Atlantic Canada' 18.2 *Dalhousie Law Journal* (1995)

Heraclides, A., 'Secession, self-determination and Non-Intervention: In Quest of a Normative Symbiosis' 45 *Journal of International Affairs* (1992)

Hervey, T. and J. Kenner (eds.), *Economic and Social Rights under the EU Charter of Fundamental Rights - A Legal Perspective* (Oxford: Hart, 2003)

Higgins, R., *Problems and Process: International Law and How We Use It* (Oxford: Oxford University Press, 1994)

Hilpod, P., 'Humanitarian Intervention: Is There a Need for a Legal Reappraisal?' 12 *European Journal of International Law* (2001)

Hoffman, R., 'A presentation of the Framework Convention for the Protection of National Minorities and its contribution to the protection of minority languages' 2 *Regional or Minority Languages* (1999)

Hogan-Brun, G. and S. Wolff (eds.), *Minority Languages in Europe; Frameworks, Status, Prospects* (London: Palgrave, 2003)

Holley, M., 'Recognizing the Rights of Indigenous People to their Traditional Lands: A Case Study of an Internally-Displaced Community in Guatemala' 15 *Berkeley Journal of International Law* (1997)

Holt, S., 'The Activities of the OSCE High Commissioner on National Minorities: January 2001-May 2002' 1 *European Yearbook of Minority Issues* (2001/02)

Holt, S. and J. Packer, 'OSCE Developments and Linguistic Minorities' 3.2 *UNESCO MOST Journal on Multicultural Societies* (2002)

Horowicz, D., *Ethnic Groups in Conflict* (Berkeley: University of California Press 1985)

Howard, D, *Coloring the Nation. Race and Ethnicity in the Dominican Republic* (Oxford: Signal Books; Boulder: Lynne Rienner, 2001)

Howland, C.W., 'The Challenge of Religious Fundamentalism to the Liberty and Equality of Women: An Analysis under the United Nations Charter' 35.2 *Columbia Journal of Transnational Law* (1997)

Huntingdon, S.P., *The Clash of Civilisations and the Remaking of World Order* (New York: Simon and Schuster, 1996)

Iorns, C., 'Indigenous Peoples and Self-Determination: Challenging State Sovereignty' 24 *Case Western Reserve Journal of International Law* (1992)

IWGIA, *The Indigenous World 1999-2000* (Copenhagen: IWGIA, 2000)

Jackson, I.C., *The refugee concept in group situations* (The Hague: Martinus Nijhoff, 1999)

Jackson, R., 'Juridical Statehood in Sub-Saharan Africa' 46 *Journal of International Affairs* (1992)

Jennings, I., *The Approach to Self-Governance* (Cambridge: Cambridge University Press, 1956)

Joseph S., J. Schultz and M. Castan, *The International Covenant on Civil and Political Rights: Cases, Materials, and Commentary* (Oxford: Oxford University Press, 2000)

Joseph, S., J. Schultz and M. Castan (eds.), *The ICCPR ñ Cases, Materials and Commentary*, 2nd edn., (Oxford: Oxford University Press, 2004)

Joyner, C.C. and B. Grimaldi, 'The United States and Nicaragua: Reflections on the Lawfulness of Contemporary Intervention' 25 *Virginia Journal of International Law* (1985)

Kapur, D. *et al.* (eds.), *The World Bank: Its First Half Century*, (Washington: The Brookings Institution, 1997)

Karlsreiter, A., (ed.) *Media in Multilingual Societies, Freedom and Responsibility* (Vienna: OSCE Office of the Representative on Freedom of the Media, 2003)

Kelly, P. (ed.), *Multiculturalism Reconsidered* (Cambridge: Polity, 2002)

Kelsen, H., *Law of the United Nations* (New York: F.A. Praeger, 1951)

Kemp, W. (ed.), *Quiet Diplomacy in Action: The OSCE High Commissioner on National Minorities* (The Hague: Kluwer Law International, 2001)

Kingsbury, B., 'ìIndigenous Peoplesî in International Law: A Constructivist Approach to the Asian Controversy' 92 *American Journal of International Law* (1998)

Kingsbury, B., 'Reconciling Five Competing Conceptual Structures of Indigenous Peoples' Claims in International and Comparative Law' 34 *New York University Journal of International Law* (2002)

Kingsbury, B., 'Self-determination and ìIndigenous Peoplesî' 86 *Proceedings of the American Society of International Law* (1992)

Kirgis, F., 'The degrees of Self-Determination in the United Nations Era' 88 *American Journal of International Law* (1994)

Kivisto, P., *Multiculturalism in a Global Society* (Oxford: Blackwell, 2002)

Klebes, H., 'The Council of Europeís Framework Convention for the Protection of National Minoritiesí, 16 *HRLJ* (1995)

Knop, K., *Diversity and Self-Determination in International Law* (Cambridge: Cambridge University Press, 2002)

Koenig, M., 'Democratic Governance in Multicultural Societies: Social Conditions for the Implementation of International Human Rights Through Multicultural Policies' 11.2 *Management of Social Transformations* (2003)

Kontra, M. and R. Phillipson, T. Skutnabb-Kangas and T. Várady (eds.), *Language: a Right and a Resource, Approaching Linguistic Human Rights* (Budapest: Central European University Press, 1999)

Koskenniemi, M., 'National Self-Determination today: Problems of Legal Theory and Practice' 43 *International and Comparative Law Quarterly* (1994)

Kretzmer, D., *The Occupation of Justice* (Albany, NY: State University of New York Press, 2002)

Kristiansen, T. (ed.), *And the Winner Might BeÖDemocratic Elections and Independent Journalism* (Kristiansand: International Reporter, 2004)

Kritsiotis, D., 'The Kosovo Crisis and NATOs Application of Armed Force Against the Federal Republic of Yugoslavia' 49 *International and Comparative Law Quarterly* (2000)

Kukathas, C., 'Are There Any Cultural Rights' 20 *Political Theory* (1992)

Kymlica, W., *Multicultural Citizenship: a Liberal Theory of Minority Rights* (Oxford: Clarendon Press, 1995)

Kymlicka, W., 'Theorizing Indigenous Rights' 49 *University of Toronto Law Journal* (1999)

Kymlicka, W., *Liberalism, Community and Culture* (Oxford: OUP, 1989)

Kymlicka, W., *Multicultural Citizenship* (Oxford: Oxford University Press, 1995)

Kymlicka, W. and W. Norman (eds.), *Citizenship in Diverse Societies* (Oxford: Oxford University Press, 2000)

Kymlicka, W., *The Rights of Minority Cultures* (Oxford: Oxford University Press, 1995)

Lador-Lederer, J., *International Group Protection* (Leiden: A.W. Sijthoff, 1968)

Lauterpacht, H., *International Law and Human Rights* (London: Stevens and Sons, 1950)

Lauterpacht, H, *Recognition in International Law* (Cambridge: Cambridge University Press, 1947)

Leiser, B.M. and T.D. Campbell (eds.), *Human Rights in Philosophy and Practice* (Aldershot: Ashgate, 2001)

Lemkin, R., *Axis Rule in Occupied Europe (Carnegie Endowment for International Peace, 1944)*

Leuprecht, P., 'Le Conseil de líEurope et les droits des minorités: les droits des minorités linguistiques' 27 *Cahiers de Droit* (1986)

Lewis, B., *What Went Wrong? ñ Western Impact and the Middle East Response* (London: Weidenfeld and Nicolson, 2002)

Lijphart, A., *Democracy in Plural Societies* (New Haven: Yale University Press, 1977)

Lokan, A., 'From Recognition to Reconciliation: The Functions of Aboriginal Rights Lawí, 23 *Melbourne University Law Review* (1999)

Lowe, V.A. and C. Warbrick (eds.), *The United Nations and the Principles of International Law, Essays in memory of Michael Akehurst* (London: Routledge, 1995)

Lowe, A.V. and M. Fitzmaurice (eds.), *Fifty Years of the International Court of Justice* (Cambridge: Cambridge University Press, 1996)

Luard, E. (ed.), *The International Regulation of Civil Wars* (Oxford: Oxford University Press, 1972)

Lundgren, Å., 'The European Union as a Democracy-promoter', 7 *Civil Society, Democracy and the Muslim World* (Istanbul: Swedish Research Institute in Istanbul, 2002)

MacKay, F., 'Universal Rights or a Universe unto Itself? Indigenous Peoples' Human Rights and the World Bank's Draft Operational Policy 4.10 on Indigenous Peoples' 17 *American University International Law Review* (2002)

MacLaughlin, J., 'Racism, Ethnicity and Multiculturalism in Contemporary Europe: A Review Essay' 17.8 *Political Geography* (1998)

Maivan-Clech, L., *At the Edge of the State: Indigenous Peoples and Self-Determination* (Ardsley, NY: Transnational, 2000)

Makkonen, T., *Identity, Difference and Otherness: The Concepts of 'Peopleí, 'Indigenous People' and 'Minority' in International Law* (Helsinki: Helsinki University Press, 2000)

Martiniello, M., 'Wievorkaís View on Multiculturalism: A Critique' 21.5 *Ethnic and Racial Studies* (1998)

Mayo, M., *Cultures, Communities, Identities* (Basingstoke: Palgrave, 2000)

McColgan, A., 'Principles of Equality and Protection From Discrimination in International Human Rights Law' 7 *EHRLR* [2002]

McCorquodale, R., 'Self-Determination: A Human Rights Approach' 43 *ICLQ* (1994)

McDowall, D., *A Modern History of the Kurds* (New York: I.B. Tauris, 1996)

McGarry, J. and B. OíLeary (eds.) *The Politics of Ethnic Conflict Regulation* (Oxford: Oxford University Press 1993)

McGoldrick, D., 'The Development of the Conference on Security and Co-operation in Europe after the 1992 Conference' 42 *ICLQ* (1993)

McGoldrick, D, *The Human Rights Committee, its Role in the Development of the ICCPR* (Oxford: Clarendon Press, 1991)

McGonagle, T., B. Davis Noll and M. Price (eds.), *Minority-Language Related Broadcasting and Legislation in the OSCE* (Oxford/Amsterdam: PCMLP, Centre for Socio-Legal Studies, Wolfson College and IViR, University of Amsterdam, 2003)

McKim, R. and J. McMahan (eds.), *The Morality of Nationalism* (Oxford: Oxford University Press, 1997)

Medda-Windischer, R., 'The European Court of Human Rights and Minority Rights' 25.3 *Journal of European Integration* (2003)

Mitchell, K., 'Educating the National Citizen in Neoliberal Times: from the Multicultural Self to the Strategic Cosmopolitan' *Trans. Inst. British Geography* (2003)

Moffat, C. (ed.), *Education Together for a Change: Integrated Education and Community Relations in Northern Ireland* (Belfast: Fortnight Educational Trust, 1993)

Mohsin, A., *The Chittagong Hill Tracts, Bangladesh: On the Difficult Road to Peace* International Peace Academy Occasional Paper Series (Boulder: Lynne Rienners Publishers, 2003)

Moore J.N., *Law and the Grenada Mission* (Charlottesville: Virginia University Press, 1984)

Moore, J.N. (ed.), *Law and Civil War in the Modern World* (Baltimore: Johns Hopkins University Press, 1974)

Morsink, J., 'Cultural Genocide, the Universal Declaration, and Minority Rights' 21.4 *Human Rights Quarterly* (1999)

Mowbray, A.R., 'The Role of the European Court of Human Rights in the Promotion of Democracy' [1999] *Public Law*

Mullaly, S., 'Feminism and Multicultural Dilemmas in India: Revisiting the Shah Bano Case' 24 *OJLS* (2004)

Murray, R., *The African Charter on Human and Peoples' Rights: The System at Work* (Cambridge: Cambridge University Press, 2002)

Musgrave, T.D., *Self-determination and National Minorities* (Oxford: Oxford University Press, 2000)

Mutua, M., 'The Banjul Charter and the African Cultural Fingerprint: An Evaluation of the Language of Duties' 35 *Virginia Journal of International Law* (1995)

Mutua, M., *Human Rights: A Political and Cultural Critique* (Philadelphia: University of Pennsylvania Press, 2002)

Myntti, K., *A Commentary to the Lund Recommendations on the Effective Participation of National Minorities in Public Life* (Turku/Åbo: Åbo Akademi University Institute for Human Rights, 2001)

Newton, N.J., 'Enforcing the Federal-Indian Trust relationship after Michel' 31 *Catholic University Law Review* (1982)

Newton, N.J., 'Indian claims in the courts of the conqueror' 41 *American University Law Review* (1992)

Nincic, D., *The Problem of Sovereignty in the Charter and the Practice of States* (The Hague: Martinus Nijhoff, 1970)

Nowak, M., 'Is Bosnia and Herzegovina ready for membership of the Council of Europe? The Responsibility of the Committee of Ministers and the Parliamentary Assembly' 20 *Human Rights Law Journal* (1999)

Odinkalu, C.A. , 'Back to the Future: The Imperative of Prioritizing for the Protection of Human Rights in Africa' 47 *Journal of African Law* (2003)

Okin, S.K., (ed.) *Is Multiculturalism Bad For Women?* (Princeton NJ: Princeton Univ. Press, 1999)

Orlando L., 'Aboriginal title claims in the Indian Claims Commission: United States v Dann and its due process implications' 13 *Boston College Environmental Affairs Law Review* (1986)

Orlin, T.S., A. Rosas and M. Scheinin, *The Jurisprudence of Human Rights Law: A Comparative Interpretive Approach* (Institute for Human Rights: Åbo Akademi University, 2000)

Osherenko, G., 'Indigenous Rights in Russia: Is Title to Land Essential for Cultural Survival?' 13 *Georgetown International Environmental Law Review* (2001)

Packer, J. and K. Myntti (eds.), *The Protection of Ethnic and Linguistic Minorities in Europe* (Åbo/ Turku: Institute for Human Rights, 1993)

Packer, J., 'The Role of the OSCE High Commissioner on National Minorities in the Former Yugoslavia' 12.2 *Cambridge Review of International Affairs* (1999)

Packer, J., 'The origin and nature of the Lund Recommendations on the Effective Participation of National Minorities in Public Life' 11.4 *Helsinki Monitor* (2000)

Parekh, B., *Rethinking Multiculturalism: Cultural Diversity And Political Theory* (Basingstoke: Macmillan, 2000)

Park, B., 'Comfort Women During World War II: Are US Courts a Final Resort for Justice?' 17 *American University International Law Review* (2002)

Pentassuglia, G., 'On the Models of Minority Rights Supervision in Europe and How They Affect a Changing Concept of Sovereignty' 1 *European Yearbook of Minority Issues* (2001/2)

Pentassuglia, G., 'State sovereignty, minorities and self-determination: A comprehensive legal view' 9 *International Journal on Minorities and Group Rights* (2001)

Phillips, A. and A. Rosas (eds.), *The UN Minority Rights Declaration* (Turku/Åbo, London: Åbo Akademi University Institute for Human Rights/Minority Rights Group International, 1993)

Poignant, B., 'Prospects for ratification of the charter by France' 2 *Regional or Minority Languages*

Pomerance, M., *Self-Determination in Law and Practice* (Leiden: Martinus Nijhoff, 1982)

Povinelli, E.A., *The Cunning of Recognition: Indigenous Alterities and the Making of Australian Multiculturalism* (Durham: Duke University Press, 2002)

Prémont, D., (ed.) *Non-Derogable Rights and States of Emergency* (Brussels, Émile Bruylant, 1996)

Pritchard, S. (ed.), *Indigenous Peoples, the United Nations and Human Rights* (Annandale, Australia: Federation Press, 1998)

Quane, H., 'The UN and the Evolving Right to Self-Determination' 47 *ICLQ* (1998)

Raday, F., 'Culture, Religion, and Gender' 1.4 *International Journal of Constitutional Law* (2003)

Räikkä, J. (ed.), *Do We Need Minority Rights? Conceptual Issues* (The Hague: Kluwer International, 1996)

Ramaga, P., 'The Bases of Minority Identity' 14 *Human Rights Quarterly* (1992)

Ratner, S., 'Does International Law Matter in Preventing Ethnic Conflict?' 32.3 *New York University Journal of International Law and Politics* (2000)

Rawls, J., *The Rights of Peoples, with, The Idea Of Public Reason Revisited* (Cambridge, Mass: Harvard University Press, 1999)

Renteln, A.D., *International Human Rights: Universalism Versus Relativism* (Newbury Park (Calif.): Sage, 1990)

Rigo-Sureda, A., *The Evolution of the Right of Self-Determination* (Leiden: A.W. Sijthoff, 1973)

Rosenstock, R., 'The Declaration on Principles of International Law' 65 *AJIL* 1971)

Roy R.D. and S. Halim, 'Valuing Village Commons in Forestry' 5.2 *Indigenous Perspectives* (2002)

Roy, C. (ed.), *Defending Diversity: Case Studies* (Utsjoki: The Saami Council, Swedish Section, 2004)

Roy, R.C.K., *Land Rights of the Indigenous Peoples of the Chittagong Hill Tracts, Bangladesh* Document No. 99 (Copenhagen: IWGIA, 2000)

Salomon, M. and A. Sengupta, *The Right to Development: Obligations of States and the Rights of Minorities and Indigenous Peoples* (London: Minority Rights Group International, 2003)

Sapiro, M., 'Changing the CSCE into the OSCE: Legal Aspects of a Political Transformation' 89.3 *American Journal of International Law* (1995)

Sargent, L., 'The Indigenous Peoples of Bolivia's Amazon Basin Region and ILO Convention 169: Real Rights or Rhetoric?' 29 *University of Miami Inter-American Law Review* (1998)

Schabas, W., *Genocide in International Law: The Crime of Crimes* (Cambridge: Cambridge University Press, 2000)

Schachar, A., *Multicultural Jurisdiction: Cultural Differences and Women's Rights* (Cambridge: CUP, 2001)

Schachter, O. and C. Joyner (eds.), *United Nations Legal Order* (Cambridge: Cambridge University Press, 1995)

Scheinin, M. and R. Toivanen (eds.), *Rethinking Non-Discrimination and Minority Rights* (Turku/Abo: Institute for Human Rights, 2004)

Schiek, D., 'Just a Piece of Cloth? ñ German Courts and Employees with Headscarves' 33.1 *Industrial Law Journal* (2004) pp. 68-73.

Shaw, M.N., *Title to Territory in Africa: International Legal Issues* (Oxford: Oxford University Press, 1986)

Shaw, M.N., *International Law* (Cambridge: Cambridge University Press, 5th edition, 2003)

Shihata, I., *The World Bank Inspection Panel* (Oxford: Oxford University Press, 1994)

Shuibhne, N.N., *EC Law and Minority Language Policy: Culture, Citizenship and Fundamental Rights* (The Hague: Kluwer, 2002)

Shukri, M., *The Concept of Self-Determination in the United Nations* (Leiden: A.W. Sijthoff, 1967)

Sicilianos, L-A. and M. Gavouneli (eds.), *Scientific and Technological Developments and Human Rights* (Athens: Ant. N. Sakoulas Publishers, 1999)

Sieder, R. (ed.), *Multiculturalism in Latin America* (Basingstoke: Macmillan, 2002)

Simma, B., 'NATO, the UN and the Use of Force: Legal Aspects' 10 *EJIL* (1999)

Simpson, G., 'The Diffusion of Sovereignty: Self-Determination in the Post-Colonial Age' 32 *Stanford Journal of International Law* (1996)

Sogal, Y., *The Limits of Citizenship* (Chicago: Chicago University Press, 1994)

Sørensen, M (ed.), *Manual of Public International Law* (London: Macmillan, 1968)

Spiliopoulou Åkermark, A., *Justifications of Minority Protection in International Law* (Dordrecht: Kluwer Law International, 1997)

Spiliopoulou Åkermark, A., 'Reservation Clauses in Treaties Concluded within the Council of Europe' 48.3 *International and Comparative Law Quarterly* (1999)

Spiry, E., 'From 'Self-Determination to a Right to 'Self-Development' for Indigenous Groups' 38 *German Yearbook of International Law* (1995)

Stone, J., *Conflict Through Consensus* (Baltimore: John Hopkins University Press, 1977)

Stone, J., *International Guarantees of Minority Rights* (London: Oxford University Press, 1932)

Taylor, C., *Multiculturalism and the Politics of Recognition* (Princeton: Princeton University Press, 1992)

The World Bank, *Accountability at the World Bank. The Inspection Panel 10 years on.* (Washington: The World Bank, 2003)

Thornberry, P., 'Self-Determination, Minorities, Human Rights: A Review of International Instruments' 38 *ICLQ* (1989)

Thornberry, P., *International Law and the Rights of Minorities* (Oxford: Oxford University Press, 1991)

Thornberry, P., *Indigenous Peoples and Human Rights* (Manchester: Manchester University Press, 2002)

Thornberry, P. and M. Amor Estebanez, *Minority Rights in Europe* (Strasbourg: Council of Europe, 2004)

Tomuschat, C. (ed.), *Modern Law Of Self-Determination* (Dordrecht: Nijhoff, 1993)

Trifunoska, S. and F. de Varennes (eds.), *Minority Rights in Europe, European Minorities and Languages* (The Hague: TMC Asser Press 2001)

Trifunovska, S., 'One theme in two variations- Self-determination for minorities and indigenous peoples' 5 *International Journal on Minority and Group Rights* (1997)

Triggs, G., 'Australiaís Indigenous Peoples and International Law: Validity of the Native Title Amendment Act 1998 (Cth)' 23 *Melbourne University Law Review* (1999)

Umozurike, U.O., *Self-Determination in International Law* (Hamden CT: Archon Books, 1972)

Umozurike, U.O., *The African Charter on Human and Peoples' Rights (The Hague: Martinus Nijhoff, 1997)*

Valenta, L., 'Disconnect: the 1988 Brazilian Constitution, Customary International Law and Indigenous Land Rights in Northern Brazil' 38 *Texas International Law Journal* (2003)

van den Berghe, P.L. and P. Frost, 'Skin Colour Preference, Sexual Dimorphism and Sexual Selection: a case of gene culture co-evolution?' 9 *Ethnic and Racial Studies*, (1986)

Van Den Burghe, F., 'The EU and the Protection of Minorities: How Real is the Alleged Double Standard' 22 *Yearbook of European Law* (2003)

Volp, L., 'Feminism Versus Multiculturalismí, 101 *Columbia Law Review* (2001)

Watson, C.W., *Multiculturalism* (Buckingham: Open University Press, 2000)

Watts, N., 'Relocating Dersim: Turkish State Building and Kurdish Resistance, 1931-1938' 23 *New Perspectives on Turkey* (2000)

Welhengama, G., *Minorities' Claims: From Autonomy to Secession* (Aldershot: Ashgate, 2000)

Wheatley, S., 'Deliberative Democracy and Minorities' 14.3 *EJIL* (2003)

Whelan, A., 'Wilsonian Self-Determination and the Versailles Settlement' 43 *International and Comparative Law Quarterly* (1994)

Wiessner, S., 'Rights and Status of Indigenous Peoples: A Global Comparative and International Legal Analysis' 12 *Harvard Human Rights Law Journal* (1999)

Wieviorka, M., 'Is Multiculturalism the Solution?' 21.5 *Ethnic and Racial Studies* (1998)

Williams, R.A, 'Encounters on the frontiers of international human rights law: redefining the terms of indigenous peoples' survival in the world' 39 *Duke Law Journal* (1990)

Williams, R.A., *The American Indian in Western Thought: The Discourses of Conquest* (Oxford: Oxford University Press, 1990)

Wilson, R.J. and J. Perlin, 'The Inter-American Human Rights System: Activities from Late 2000 Through October 2002' *18 American University International Law Review* (2002)

Woehrling, J-M., 'La Charte européenne des langues régionales ou minoritaires' 95-96 *Terminograme* (2001)

World Commission on Culture and Development ñ Our Creative Diversity (Paris: World Commission on Culture and Diversity, 1995)

Wright, Q., 'The Goa Incident' 56 *AJIL* (1962)

Wright, Q., *Mandates under the League of Nations* (New York: Greenwood Press, 1930)

Yutak Arai-Takahashi, Y., *The Margin of Appreciation and the Principle of Proportionality in the Jurisprudence of the ECHR* (Antwerp: Intersentia, 2002).